CONFRONTING THE COSTS OF WAR

CONFRONTING
THE COSTS OF WAR

MILITARY POWER, STATE, AND SOCIETY IN EGYPT AND ISRAEL

Michael N. Barnett

PRINCETON UNIVERSITY PRESS   PRINCETON, NEW JERSEY

Copyright © 1992 by Princeton University Press
Published by Princeton University Press, 41 William Street,
Princeton, New Jersey 08540
In the United Kingdom: Princeton University Press,
Chichester, West Sussex
All Rights Reserved

Library of Congress Cataloging-in-Publication Data
Barnett, Michael N., 1960–
Confronting the costs of war : military power, state, and society
in Egypt and Israel / Michael N. Barnett.
p. cm.
Includes bibliographic references and index.
ISBN 0-691-07883-1
ISBN 0-691-00095-6 (pbk.)
1. Egypt—Military policy.   2. Israel—Military policy.
3. Civil-military relations—Egypt—History—20th century.
4. Civil-military relations—Israel—History—20th century.
5. Egypt—Politics and government—1952–
6. Israel—Politics and government.
7. Civil-military relations.   I. Title.
UA865.B37 1992
322′.5′0962—dc20 91-32121 CIP

This book has been composed in Linotron Caledonia

First Princeton Paperback printing, 1993

Princeton University Press books are printed
on acid-free paper and meet the guidelines
for permanence and durability of the Committee
on Production Guidelines for Book Longevity
of the Council on Library Resources

Printed in the United States of America

3 5 7 9 10 8 6 4 2

Contents

Tables

Preface

ALTHOUGH warfare and the state have marched in tandem throughout history, they marched separately in the social science literature. Indeed, although war is credited with producing such major events as the rise of capitalism, the emergence of representative institutions, and the establishment of the modern administrative state, most sustained investigations of state power overlook the important role of international conflict. There is a discrepancy between the demonstrated effects of war on state-society relations and the theoretical attention it has received.

This study attempts to redress that disparity; it offers a theoretical framework for examining the relationship between war preparation (the government's mobilization of men, money, and material resources for external security) and state power, and then applies that framework to the cases of Israel and Egypt. Two questions are asked here. First, what are the determinants of the government's war preparation strategies? To address this question, the state must be situated in its domestic and international context. For some time now the field of international political economy has moved in this direction; most studies now acknowledge that the state's foreign economic policy depends on both its position in the international system and its relationship to societal forces. Security studies, however, seem wedded to a conception of the state that responds exclusively to systemic demands and is absolved from domestic constraints and imperatives. Yet it is not true that the moment a foreign threat surfaces societal constraints vanish, and the only challenge the government faces is foreign. Quite often state officials confront greater threats to their political survival from those very societal actors it expects to contribute to the war effort than it does from the foreign threat itself. This, I will show, was true for Israeli and Egyptian officials during periods of intense interstate conflict, officials routinely viewed as situated in a so-called strong state and theoretically resilient to societal pressures. Government officials must mobilize domestic resources to consolidate their international position and do so with care that these policies do not simultaneously weaken their political standing and undercut other highly valued domestic objectives. One of this book's principal objectives is to show how the government's security policy, particularly the basis of its military power—its access to the means of war, is shaped by its goals in and constraints from the domestic and international systems.

Although you can take the state out of war you cannot take war out of the state. The second question then remains, what links the government's war preparation strategies for mobilizing the means of war to changes in state power? All too often conflict processes are relegated to a residual category, dusted off and considered only when more commonly accepted explanations are exhausted or discarded. Yet, as often as crises of capital accumulation have shaped the nature of state power, so too have crises of national security caused state officials to mobilize resources for war and, in the process, transform the state's relationship to society and economy. I argue that the government's strategy for mobilizing its security-related resources and the terms under which it gains access to these resources that are often controlled by societal actors, are the principal factors linking war preparation and state power. In this way I leave open the possibility that war preparation can either enhance or diminish state power. Here I attempt to make explicit the relationship between war preparation and state power and to theorize about the conditions under which we can expect the former to shape the latter. Because the state is embedded in both international and domestic structures, an approach to state power needs to pay equal tribute to and integrate both realms.

If the first part of the book offers one way to think theoretically about the relationship between the government's mobilization of resources for war and the transformation of state power, then the second part demonstrates how contemporary Israeli and Egyptian politics are better understood once the role of international conflict has been more fully incorporated. Sadly, warfare has been all too common to both these countries (and the states of the Middle East in general), and, when Egyptian and Israeli officials were not actually involved in warfare, they were actively involved in preparing for the next round. Israeli and Egyptian officials, like their counterparts most places, rarely had the luxury to ignore how their security policies might affect their domestic objectives and, conversely, how their domestic policies might affect their standing vis-à-vis military rivals.

It is surprising, indeed, that the effects of such never-ending war preparation efforts on the state's relationship to society have been scarcely examined in Middle Eastern scholarship. But I find the relationship immediate and direct. Consider the following narrative. By all accounts both the Israeli and Egyptian states had a strong standing in their societies from the early 1950s through the mid-1960s. Israel, for instance, was founded by a cohesive and well-organized elite that: (1) articulated an ideology of socialist-Zionism, an ideology that foresaw a strong state presence; (2) dominated the Jewish community's prestatehood organizations and institutions and used organizational resources to diffuse its power and control over society; and (3) benefited from a high amount of unilateral transfers that enabled it to guide society in a manner that served its various interests. The Israeli state's domestic presence contrasted decidedly with its international standing, as Israel's sovereignty was publicly questioned and its borders militarily assaulted. This characterization has steadily reversed itself since 1967. Israel's sovereignty, though still publicly challenged by regional actors, can be defended militarily with a high degree of certainty. At the same time, even a cursory glance at the Israeli political scene reveals a politically paralyzed and financially dependent state—its once hegemonic status now in steady decline.

Much the same can be said of Egypt. Gamal Abdel Nasser constructed a highly powerful state apparatus that presided over a rather large public sector, was relatively autonomous from private economic elites, and had marshaled substantial ideological support for his socialism with an Arab face. This characterization quickly disappeared beginning in the mid-1960s and accelerated rapidly after the 1967 War. In 1973, Egypt reversed the military misfortunes of the 1967 War and went on to build a formidable military establishment. Every forward step taken by the Egyptian army seemed matched by a step backward for the Egyptian economy and polity. The state became more heavily indebted to foreign backers, presided over an economic policy that strengthened the role of a previously marginalized private economic elite, and increased subsidies on basic commodities to a more politically confrontational public.

War preparation has altered the contours of Egyptian and Israeli state-society relations. It contributed to the rise of Egyptian and Israeli state power before 1967, and more significant, it was arguably *the* principal factor behind the decline of state power in both countries after 1967. Israeli and Egyptian officials, sometimes intentionally and sometimes unintentionally, ventured on a path that bolstered the state's military preparedness, but at the cost of its control over society and economy. This represents an interesting twist on the common belief that war generally increases the state's control over society. At the height of security pressures, Israeli and Egyptian officials adopted a series of measures designed to increase the state's military power and maintain political support while simultaneously limiting the potential economic damage and, where possible, initiating a more market-oriented economy. Notably, after 1967 both Israeli and Egyptian governments attempted to promote the fortunes of the domestic capitalist class to increase its contribution to the war effort, governmental stability, and the economy's fortunes.

My hope is that this study will be of interest to scholars of international relations, comparative politics, and Middle Eastern studies.

Those in international relations might find of interest the theoretical integration of systemic-, state-, and societal-level variables for explaining an important area of national security policy. This study explores both the domestic political economy of foreign policy behavior and "the second image reversed" thesis; that is, it examines the effects of domestic forces on the strategic calculation of state actors and the effects of the international system on the development of state-society relations, respectively. Therefore, it continues a line of research that willfully blurs the distinction between international relations and comparative politics. Those in comparative politics might be interested in the reexamination of the conceptualization and measurement of state power, the changing fortunes of the capitalist class in Third World societies, and more generally the effects of war on state-society relations. Beyond these theoretical contributions, this study is relevant to Middle East scholars; it contributes to the relatively limited but growing body of literature that approaches contemporary Middle East politics from a broader set of theoretical concerns and concepts, oftentimes derived from outside the Middle East setting. By approaching Egyptian and Israeli politics from a macrohistorical view, I attempt to show explicitly that the framework is relevant to what might be considered widely divergent cases and implicitly that Egyptian, and particularly Israeli, history is not as unique as it might initially appear. Finally, although this is not a book about the Arab-Israeli conflict per se, it does survey a number of related issues that have escaped those who have already written on this well-worn theme.

I have incurred many debts in writing this book, and one of the real pleasures is to now acknowledge those who supported and assisted me over the last number of years. First and foremost, my advisers at the University of Minnesota, Raymond Duvall and Brian Job, contributed equally to the crystallization of many key ideas contained within. They were models of patience and concern, and I only hope that I can learn from their examples. Alexander Wendt has read more versions of certain chapters than either he or I care to imagine. Gehad Auda, Ellis Goldberg, Raymond Hinnebusch, Baruch Kimmerling, Baruch Mevorach, Michael Shalev, and Gabriel Sheffer were particularly helpful when it came to providing a more accurate reading of the Egyptian and Israeli cases. Ronald Aminzade, Ethan Kapstein, Joel Krieger, Jack Levy, Joel Migdal, Eric Mlyn, Mark Pitt, Martin Sampson, Gerald Steinberg, Michael Sullivan, David Sylvan, Charles Tilly, John Waterbury, and Jutta Weldes commented on various parts of the manuscript and strengthened my final product. The opportunity to give seminars at the Leonard Davis Institute at the Hebrew University of Jerusalem, at the Al-Ahram Centre for Strategic and Political Studies and the National Centre for Middle East Studies in Cairo, and at the Center for International Affairs at Harvard University permitted me to discuss my observations in front of critical, yet receptive, audiences. Finally, I want to thank Margaret Case at Princeton University Press, who guided the manuscript from its initial submission to its final form.

As often as field research is intellectually and personally rewarding, it is as often difficult and frustrating. Many people, some of whom have already been mentioned, made it a more positive experience, opened their doors and eased my stay, and kept me from disparaging the field research experience and reconsidering the benefits of doing theoretical work cloistered away in my office. I give them a collective thanks. I also want to recognize the many Israeli and Egyptian officials who graciously and generously gave of their time, returned my phone calls, and provided me with the opportunity to ask them about their recollections, understandings, and roles in the events that I am about to describe. Finally, my field research was supported financially by a MacArthur Field Research Award, a Dunn Peace Research Fellowship and a Mac-Millan Grant from the University of Minnesota, student loans, and logistically by the Department of Political Science at the University of Tel-Aviv.

Parts of chapters 2 and 5 appeared earlier in "High Politics is Low Politics: The Domestic and Systemic Sources of Israeli Security Policy, 1967–1977," *World Politics* 42, no. 4 (1990): 529–62. Reprinted with permission from Princeton University Press. Part of chapter 5 originally appeared in "The Domestic Sources of Alliances and Alignments: The Case of Egypt, 1962–1973," *International Organization* 45, no. 3 (1991): 369–95. Adapted with permission by MIT Press.

I dedicate this book to my parents. When at the age of five I announced that I wanted to be an archeologist, on my bed the next day was a book on the ancient Egyptian temples. When five years later I exclaimed that I wanted to prepare for a life in baseball and the foreign service, I received soon thereafter a Johnny Bench–autographed catcher's mitt and Morgenthau's *Politics among Nations*. They always supported and encouraged a healthy curiosity and inquisitiveness about the world around me. Thanks.

CONFRONTING THE COSTS OF WAR

CHAPTER ONE

War Preparation and State Power

THE STATE'S attempt to mobilize the instruments of coercion to defend its territorial integrity has been closely associated with the development of the state and changes in state-society relations. Two themes dominate this discussion. The first is the "ratchet effect," whereby the state, because of its pivotal role as defender of the country's external security, must mobilize the necessary resources and take extraordinary domestic measures, both economically and politically, to meet these foreign challenges. Once war ends, these war-associated changes rarely return to prewar levels, nor do many of the state's newly won powers return entirely to civil society.[1] Policies initially declared as temporary may become part of any decision maker's repertoire after war termination. For instance, historically the state's war-making capacities hinged, in part, on its ability to extract financial resources, which in turn, contributed to the further expansion of the state apparatus and its ability to monitor and access society. As such, a conventional characterization is that war hastens the development of an ever-expanding state apparatus with increasing control over society. If there is a winner during war, it appears to be the state over domestic forces.[2]

Although the ratchet effect is observed in numerous historical instances, the second theme notes those contrary episodes when international conflict has eroded the state's control over society. For instance, mobilizing resources for war was a major factor contributing to the German and Russian revolutions.[3] Although social revolutions are the most dramatic effect of war on the state's disintegrating control over society, more subtle tendencies are also evident. The government bargains with societal actors to contribute to and undertake those activities that enhance national security. One possible consequence of this bargain is that these societal actors may find themselves wielding greater power vis-à-vis the state after the war than they had beforehand. Tilly comments, "The process of bargaining with ordinary people for their acquiescence and their surrender of resources—money, goods, labour power—engaged the civilian managers of the state in establishing limits to state control, perimeters to state violence, and mechanisms for eliciting the consent of the subject population."[4] This feature is particularly visible in the government's policy for securing its required fiscal, material, and manpower needs. Douglass North, for instance, argues that the British Crown introduced more efficient, capitalist-oriented property rights as a way of mobilizing more revenue for war, yet these revenue-generating policies created a new set of societal constraints on future government actions.[5] In capitalist societies the state controls political power while private actors control production; therefore, a dominant government policy among advanced capitalist countries in the present era encourages and relies on private-sector activities for producing the instruments of warfare.[6] This policy has often reinforced the privileged position of the capitalist class in society. Indeed, that military activity strengthens and serves the capitalist class has become an article of faith in the Marxist literature.[7] The capitalist class is not the only societal actor to benefit from the state's policies. The introduction of mass conscription in Western Europe is closely associated with the rise of parliamentary institutions, forums later used by these newly enfranchised groups to influence and control state policy. This second theme, then, directs our attention to those processes most closely associated with national security that contribute to the state's diminished control over society.

This discussion points to a puzzle: although warfare and the state march in tandem in history, they march separately in the social science literature. That is, most sustained investigations of state power overlook the important role of international conflict. For instance, Charles Tilly recently constructed a fourfold classification of dominant explanations of state formation that depends on the emphasis each places on the roles of domestic or international forces and economic or noneconomic variables.[8] First, according to mode of production, "the state and its changes [derive] almost entirely from that logic, as it operates within the state's territory."[9] Second, the statist explanation "treats political changes as proceeding in partial independence of economic change, and presents it chiefly as a consequence of events within particular states."[10] Third, the world system identifies the logic of the world economy as generating diverse paths of state formation. And, fourth, a geopolitical outlook focuses on the role of interstate forces for producing variations in state power. As Tilly acknowledges, even those few studies that have studied the role of interstate forces in shaping state formation have done so unsatisfactorily.

Although Tilly is primarily concerned with state formation in Western Europe, the same argument and characterization is as, if not more, appropriate when extended to earlier studies of Third World state power and state formation. Students of Third World politics generally focus on the international political economy, predatory state actors, and developmentalism.[11] Almost completely ignored is how international conflict has shaped the nature of the Third World state. For instance, Huntington's classic work on political development recognizes the importance of war in shaping the development of the European state:

> War reached an intensity in the seventeenth century which it never had previously and which was exceeded later only in the twentieth century. The prevalence of war directly promoted political modernization. Competition forced the monarchs to build their military strength. The creation of military strength required national unity, the suppression of regional and religious dissidents, the expansion of armies and bureaucracies, and a major increase in state revenues. . . . War was the great stimulus to state-building.[12]

And although Huntington details and examines the role of the military in the Third World in general and the process of state formation in particular, he unfortunately fails to incorporate how interstate conflict might also have important consequences for patterns of Third World state building. More recently, Joel Migdal has forwarded a provocative and highly illuminating theory of variation in state capabilities in the Third World. Although Migdal goes farther than most by arguing that a central motivation for the state's attempt to control its society is because of interstate threats, his model brackets "the influence of war and the threat of war on state and society."[13]

The neglect of interstate conflict in shaping the nature of the Third World state is both puzzling and unfortunate. It is puzzling because most wars in the contemporary era have involved not advanced industrialized countries but rather Third World countries. It is unfortunate because most postcolonial states are in the simultaneous and vigilant task of defending borders created by outside forces and are, therefore, often under challenge, while engaged in the process of state and nation building that was made doubly difficult by the legacies of colonialism. In other words, because most Third World states are in the process of becoming in both the domestic and the international systems, the state formation process and state power will likely reflect this very fact.

In general, no matter the geographic locale, few studies have made explicit the theoretical linkages between war and the transformation of state power. Too often studies present an almost accidental characterization of the relationship between international conflict and state-society relations and leave the impression that this connection is historically specific and derivative of, or of secondary importance when compared to, other causal forces. In short, most accounts fail to provide an adequate theorization concerning the structural and decision-making factors associated with war that produce macrohistorical change.

This study represents one attempt to resolve this theoretical silence by proposing a strategy for investigating the relationship between war preparation and the transformation of state power in capitalist societies. I assert that the locus of this transformation can be found in both the government's strategies for mobilizing its security-related resources and the terms under which it gains access to these resources that are often controlled by societal actors. Only when the government places certain demands on and expects society to contribute directly to its military activities does one witness the transformation of state power. Two questions are asked here. First, what are the determinants of the government's war preparation strategies? Second, what are the effects of these adopted strategies on state power? I explore the first question by constructing a framework for investigating the government's war preparation strategies, the second by evaluating the causal relationship between these policies and changes in state power.[14] Although the proposed theoretical framework is designed for states in capitalist societies, I assume that with some modification and adjustment this model might prove instructive for noncapitalist contexts as well.

Three broad issues are involved. First, government officials pursue simultaneously their objective of war preparation as well as other valued domestic objectives such as economic development and political stability. "War preparation" is the process by which the state mobilizes these resources, or, as Charles Tilly argues, acquires the "means of carrying out . . . warmaking."[15] The government usually undertakes three war preparation activities, each of which can be expected to affect state power: (1) it must generate revenue, for without it the state would be unable to pay for its increased consumption of resources; (2) it must guarantee the provision of war material—from supplies to clothing, food, and the actual instruments of warfare; and (3) it must mobilize manpower. As Huntington argues, the "currency here is men, money, and material."[16]

The focus on the government's attempt to mobilize the means of war extends the analysis from the overly narrow focus on periods of actual warfare to the more enduring governmental activities associated with preparing for war and the daily need to protect the state's borders in an anarchic interstate system. Too often past studies of the relationship between war and state power have limited their focus to the outbreak of hostilities and failed to recognize how the transformative possibilities reside in the government's manner of mobilizing security-related resources. This is particularly important when examining events in the Middle East. For example, even though each Arab-Israeli war has been relatively brief, constant preparation for war since 1948 meant that both public and private life were geared toward interstate conflict. This extended period of heightened security awareness can be expected to have had a greater impact on state-society relations than could, for instance, six days of warfare in early June 1967. In short, the activities associated with preparing for war—and not the outbreak of hostilities per se—largely account for the changes in state power.

Yet war preparation is not the government's only goal. Realists generally assume that external security is the most important governmental objective, and this may be true in the sense that territorial integrity is a prerequisite for achieving all other goals. This does not mean, however, that external threats to the very existence of the state are either frequent in occurrence or immediate in their expected impact. In fact, as the solidification of the state system has made threats of territorial eradication fairly remote for most states, the relative threat deriving from domestic sources—particularly so for Third World states—has gained in prominence. In short, I hesitate to assume a priori that external security goals are always given priority in the foreign policy calculations of states; instead, I assume that state officials pursue both foreign policy goals, such as security, and domestic goals, such as economic development and political stability. It is an empirical question whether and when state officials opt for one set of preferences over another.

Therefore, the government's security policy is itself two-faced: it is concerned with both the construction of strategies vis-à-vis foreign threats and with those for mobilizing societal resources.[17] The government responds to external threats by attempting to mobilize societal resources. This study, then, situates the state in its domestic and international context and recognizes that its activities in one area affect its activities in the other.[18] Too often earlier studies have unnecessarily and inappropriately characterized state managers as responding to one logic, be it domestic or international, economic or political. Yet government officials must mobilize domestic resources to consolidate their international position and do so with care that these policies do not at the same time weaken the government's position domestically. States are interested in accumulating capital, coercion, and political control. Because the state is embedded in both the international and domestic realms our approaches to state power—indeed, our explanations of governmental behavior—must pay equal tribute to and integrate both realms.

A second issue notes that because the government operates in both domestic and international spheres, its war preparation strategies must be seen as a function of its objectives in the international and domestic arena and the constraints on its actions. Therefore, its mobilization policies are not determined solely from a technical calculation of the government's strategic requirements but are the products of competing social, political, and economic pressures. Lawrence Freedman writes:

> Neglecting the domestic dimension of security policy leads to a forgetfulness of the extent to which the people taking critical decisions also spend much of their time worrying about the levels of taxation, competing demands on public expenditure, promoting their personal and party images, getting re-elected, and so on. As a result, policy options which might be perfectly reasonable within some narrow security framework turn out to be wholly unrealistic in terms of the actual freedom of manoeuvre available to those responsible for taking the decisions.[19]

Even if there is widespread societal sympathy with the government's decision to go to war, such agreement in principle does not automatically include which segments of society should bear the burden of the costs of war. The government's alternatives about how it shall fund its military requirements and its decisions are likely to attempt to reconcile its domestic and foreign policy objectives and the constraints on its actions.

These sought-after security inputs are often controlled by societal actors, and government officials generally cannot compel these actors to comply; instead the government must negotiate with, cajole, and compensate them. Because the government is primarily concerned with mobilizing men, money, and material, I isolate the features of the state and society that condition the government's efforts. I assume that the government's actions will always be conditioned by its autonomy from dominant economic elites. In addition, its mobilization of financial resources is constrained by the state's capacity; military hardware is limited by the country's economic structure; manpower is shaped by the state's legitimacy. In other words, those states that are relatively autonomous from dominant societal actors, have high capacity, have access to a highly developed economic and industrial base, and are viewed as legitimate by their societies are better positioned to mobilize their required resources domestically. In this way, then, we are better able to evaluate the government's ability to rely on its own wherewithal for security needs or its requirement to seek external sources of military assistance. The government's internally or externally directed disposition depends on its domestic and foreign policy objectives and the constraints on its actions.

This approach improves on past efforts in the theoretical international relations literature. Although most international relations scholars acknowledge that the state's military potential is heavily conditioned by its ability to extract resources from society, rarely is this observation made explicit and central in their models.[20] This omission is common:

most security studies tend to posit either a state that is completely autonomous from society or a state that is wholly captured by dominant economic actors; they miss the political dimension of the government's mobilization of national security resources.[21]

Compare, for instance, the neorealist Kenneth Waltz with the neo-Marxist Ernest Mandel. Waltz is representative of neorealist and economic nationalist approaches to security policy by focusing on how the state's pursuit of military power and war-fighting potential is shaped by systemic forces. He implicitly assumes that "high politics," a state's security relationship with other states in the international system, is autonomous from "low politics," societal pressures and the domestic political economy.[22] Although he both recognizes that domestic resources and a diversified economy are important determinants of military power and distinguishes between actual and realized power, he makes the problematic assumption, particularly so when discussing capitalist countries in which control over economic resources is institutionally divorced from political power, that these societal resources can be mobilized without friction. Not all mobilization strategies are equally possible; moreover, neorealism and economic nationalism cannot tell us which strategies are more likely.

Waltz can be criticized for creating an autonomous state, but Mandel can be charged with the opposite—he grants the state little if any autonomy from domestic society.[23] Although he provides a nice discussion of "war potential," which roughly translates into the state's ability to manufacture the means of warfare, he slights the potential constraints on the state's access to societally controlled production. Mandel, like many Marxist-inspired writers, has adopted Clausweitz's dictum that war is a continuation of politics (economics) by military means and implicitly argues that war, a logical extension of capitalism, is fought to ease tensions in domestic and international capitalism and defend capitalist objectives.[24] As a result, the state, whose primary function is to reproduce capitalist class hegemony, is implicated as a willing partner in this fight for capitalist objectives; after all, it engages in those activities that benefit the capitalist class (the implication is that war is one of them). Adopting an instrumentalist view of the state levels any tension between the capitalist class and the state because, for all practical purposes, they are the same. The working class, when mentioned at all, is seen as an unwitting dupe and sacrificial lamb for capitalist class objectives.[25]

In sum, scholarship concerning international relations is generally inattentive to the constraints on the state's ability to mobilize societal resources for national security, the tensions between the government's objectives and those of societal actors. In this volume I demonstrate that these select properties of the state and social structure shape the government's ability to mobilize domestic resources and, hence, its war preparation strategies. In this way, this general framework for investigation identifies the relevant concepts and variables that both enable and constrain, and produces certain tendencies in, the government's war preparation strategies. This general framework is my window into history.[26]

The third issue concerns the effect of these adopted war preparation strategies on state power. Simply put, state power is most visibly transformed when the government attempts to restructure its relationship to society to increase the societal contribution to national security. The government cannot alter state-society relations without conflict; undoubtedly it will confront some degree of societal opposition. The more the government is constrained by society the more it will be forced to bargain on "equal" terms with societal groups for access to the means of war. Accordingly, while the government gains access to its desired means, it must often "return the favor," which might entail granting societal groups either new rights and benefits or some determination over the decision-making process. Three factors—the government's attempt to restructure the state-society compact, societal opposition to the government's movements, and the concessions the government makes in return for access to the means of war—are central to understanding how the government's war preparation strategies transform state power.

Because government officials are attempting to reconcile their competing foreign and domestic policy objectives, changes in state power are never produced by war preparation alone. Past approaches to changes in state power have erred in assuming that one factor could be isolated across time and space as the dominant causal force, and I have no intention of replicating past biases. I understand war preparation and these other influences as complementary, not competing, explanations. As Charles Ragin argues, "Whenever social scientists examine large-scale historical change . . . they find that it is usually a *combination* of conditions that produce change.[27] Chapter 2 identifies three types of war preparation strategies—accommodational, international, and restructural—and argues that state power is most visibly transformed when the government adopts the latter one and reworks the state-society compact to generate more resources for war.

Although this theoretical framework goes some distance in examining the conditions under which war preparation expands or erodes state power, greater attention must also be paid to the concept of state power. For example, the German Revolution of 1919, while replacing the Kaiser Wilhelm with the Weimar Republic, left intact a state apparatus that had expanded the state's reach into society following four years of warfare. Therefore, under current approaches to state power one could conceivably speak of both an expansion and a disintegration of the German state as a result of World War One. These two themes are discussing separate, yet complementary, aspects of the state's control over society. The state might conceivably extend its extractive capacities while either societal actors are strengthened or the state falls victim to a social revolution. Those that focus on the ratchet effect are discussing the state's infrastructural abilities and capacity to monitor, govern, and extract from society. Alternatively, those scholars that examine how war has acted to instigate social revolutions or strengthen societal agents are directing their analyses less to the state's institutional qualities and more to issues of societal legitimation, the ability of societal actors given their role in economic production to constrain the actions of state managers, and state-society relations broadly defined. For instance, Skocpol argues that during a crisis the state may force "concessions . . . at the expense of the interests of the dominant class, but not contrary to the state's own interests in controlling the population and collecting taxes and military recruits."[28] Crises, whether economic or security, are viewed as system-threatening events that require the state's intervention and implementation of system-saving policies, some of which may challenge the long-term interests of the dominant class and, in the process, increase the state's autonomy from economic elites.

I argue that both the state's infrastructural features and its relationship to society are necessary components for understanding the nature of state power. State power refers to the resources available to state managers in their governance of society in relation to societal actors. State power, then, speaks less to the ability of state managers to get societal actors to do what they would otherwise not do and more to the enduring resources contained within the state apparatus in relationship to societal constraints that condition governmental behavior. This concept of state power includes aspects and features of both the state and society and, therefore, provides for a better understanding of the relationship between war and state power.

In summary, this study examines the connection between war preparation, the sustained mobilization and consumption of resources by the government, and state power. I do not intend to establish regular patterns across history, for history is not spun deterministically from the researcher's framework; rather, I attempt to identify both some likely tendencies in the government's war preparation strategies, given its objectives and the relevant constraints, and the likely effects of these strategies on state power. My goal has four main components: to ascertain whether the framework is useful for explaining the government's war preparation strategies, to propose modifications in that theory based on the careful analysis of a particular historical setting(s), to examine closely the importance of historical factors for tracing causal processes, and to explore how and under what conditions one can expect changes in state power as a result of the government's preparations for interstate threats.

Egypt and Israel

The theoretical framework is extended to the cases of Egypt between 1952 and 1977 and Israel between 1948 and 1977. This study is comparative in two ways. First and most simply, it situates the Israeli and Egyptian experiences in the same theoretical framework. Some scholars commonly claim that Israel's so-called uniqueness entails its exclusion as an appropriate case (more on this later). Yet this study sets out to show that this theoretical framework can accommodate not only the Israeli experience but also the Egyptian, two countries widely assumed to differ in many important respects. Second, each country participated in a series of wars and partook in extensive war preparation activities of various lengths and intensities; these provide a good opportunity to examine the variety of conditions under which international conflict might affect state power. Moreover, because in both cases there were moments in which war preparation was intense and all-consuming and others in which it was still important but less salient, we can survey how war preparation strategies at one period produced important changes in state-society relations, which, in turn, set up new operating parameters for the government's war preparation strategies at later dates. In this way the present shape of state power in both Israel and Egypt is not the end of a predetermined path; rather, state power is significantly affected by the sequence of events and the choices and consequences of previous decisions. I shall now discuss each country in more detail.

Egypt. There has been relatively little analytical discussion about the determinants of the Egyptian government's war preparation strategies. Although there is some attention to the fact that as a Third World country Egypt is resource poor and therefore must seek foreign support for its military activities, these discussions are primarily descriptive.[29] Because the implicit assumption is that the primary reason behind the Egyptian government's reliance on foreign actors is its lack of resources, such an outlook fails to recognize that the mere presence of such resources does not guarantee the government's ability to extract these societally controlled resources either with ease or without undercutting its other objectives.

In contrast to those studies that stress Egypt's resource-scarce nature as a primary reason behind its strategic and alliance behavior, recent neorealist analyses of Egypt's alliance behavior have focused on its position and changes in the international system.[30] Although Egyptian officials were sensitive to change in the international distribution of military power, this approach overplays its importance and fails to recognize that Egyptian officials formed their alliance patterns because of not only systemic changes but also domestic political and economic constraints and concerns.[31] In other words, the assumption that Egyptian leaders were driven strictly by power politics does not adequately integrate how its alliance behavior in general and war preparation strategies in particular were driven by their domestic objectives as well. Chapter 4 demonstrates that Egyptian war preparation strategies were intended to reconcile the government's desire to increase its military power in the interstate system while protecting its other highly valued goals.

These war preparation strategies had important consequences for Egyptian state power. In less than twenty years Egypt participated in the Suez War, the Yemen War, the 1967 War, the War of Attrition, and the Yom Kippur War, but rarely are the effects of international conflict treated as central to the ebbs and flows of Egyptian state power. To the contrary, most interpretations of state power in modern Egypt focus on either the political, self-serving actions of government officials or the political economy of a late industrializing country.[32]

Yet Egyptian war preparation strategies had tremendous effects on state power. It is not coincidental that the 1956 Sinai War, the 1967 War, and the 1973 War of Ramadan are all seen as watersheds in Egyptian history. The 1956 War marked the beginning of state-led industrialization and Arab socialism, when Nasser nationalized Egypt's foreign-owned enterprises and paved the road for state capitalism. The Six-Day War signaled the end to Arab socialism and increasing societal pressures on the state. And the 1973 War paved the way for "al-infitah" (the economic opening) and provoked a shift in Egypt's superpower allegiance from the Soviet Union to the United States. Scholars of Egyptian history, however, by viewing international conflict as an intervening variable in more primary economic and political processes, have failed to recognize how the very preparation for war generated certain tendencies in its own right. The conventional characterization of the impact of war on Egyptian society is to treat it as a system-shifting occurrence. However, six days in early June or three weeks in October alone do not transform Egyptian history; rather, the political, economic, and security processes associated with and resulting from the 1967 and the 1973 wars, respectively, set the stage for the immense changes in Egyptian state-society relations after 1967. War was a major factor in the growth of Egyptian state power during its early years and its subsequent decline during the 1970s. The prevailing treatment of Egyptian state power—that it can be traced primarily to endogenous forces—accurately reflects most theoretical approaches to state power.[33]

Alongside an inadequate accounting for interstate conflict in producing change in Egyptian state power, has been state power's inadequate conceptualization. The widely conflicting accounts and interpretations of Egyptian state-society relations range from those who argue that the Egyptian state is all powerful to those who understand it as all ineffectual. For instance, while some scholars point to the state's authoritarian nature or its autonomy from private economic elites and implicitly argue that it is a "strong" state, more economically oriented and state structural analyses find that the state is "soft" or "weak," unable to impose its will on or to steer society.[34] The Egyptian state is all powerful yet unable to do anything. There is a partial explanation for these various interpretations: some scholars treat state power as derivative of the political system's openness, others understand it as its autonomy from dominant societal actors, and still others view it as tantamount to the state's capacity and ability to extract from society. One objective here is to demonstrate how prior theorization and conceptualization of state power can contribute to a better understanding of Egyptian politics.

Israel. Israel's selection as an appropriate case study requires some justification because many scholars argue that its distinctiveness demands its exclusion from social scientific theorizing. Its historical peculiarity is evidenced by its ideological hybrid of Zionism and socialism, the tremendous flows of Jewish immigration into Palestine and Israel, the prevalence and importance of international conflict in daily life, and the role of capital transfers in its economic development. Given these and other factors, Israel, so the argument proceeds, escaped the pains of development that engulfed other postcolonial states. At the same time, this postcolonial state achieved rapid economic development through a variety of "unique" circumstances. Israel is not a developing, Third World, or developed country. Because Israel is unique in many dimensions, it slips through the cracks of social science inquiry into historical peculiarity.

Israel is an appropriate case for the following reasons. First, Israel's "developed" status does not reflect its position for the vast majority of its history. Per capita income, levels of industrialization, and other economic indicators were not always worthy of "developed" status.[35] Only recently has Israel's per capita income rivaled that of the peripheral European countries. Second, the state-building process was undertaken by a highly motivated, ideologically driven elite, who attempted to transform themselves from a sociopolitical movement with a revolutionary vision into an institutionalized state apparatus.[36] Although Zionism was unique, it was similar to the liberating ideologies adopted by other African nationalists in their calls for national redemption, anticolonialism, and socialism. Third, the state had to be established, its authority recognized, and its political institutions developed. This state-building process occurred while absorbing both a relatively large immigrant population unfamiliar with the obligations demanded by the modern state and a hostile minority. Fourth, Israel's borders were imposed by British and French colonial interests in the Middle East. That its borders were artificially created, a product of battles against British colonial authority and hostile neighbors, and thereafter always contested and under challenge, places Israel's history alongside other Third World (notably African) countries.

Finally, as a postcolonial country Israel was confronted by many of those economic difficulties associated with other late industrializing countries. The Israeli political elite was both nationalist and socialist-leaning, which implemented a public policy designed to limit private capital accumulation. In a related manner, the state, according to Prime Minister Ben-Gurion, was essentially "etatist" and viewed as the engine of economic development. Accordingly, the state both sponsored a growing public sector and favored the Histadrut, the country's largest trade union and a principal owner of the means of production. Moreover, Israel's exports and foreign exchange earnings depended on two products, citrus and diamonds, and manufacturing and industrial goods dominated its import structure. Thus, its economic structure was beset and characterized by those features common to most other Third World countries.[37]

In general, Israel represents a good example of a postcolonial state attempting to mobilize scarce, if nonexistent, resources for national security while pursuing its other economic and political objectives. That it does not resemble all Third World countries does not deny Israel's appropriateness as a case study, but it does caution us against sweeping generalizations of any kind. Israel, like all countries (including Egypt), is the product of historical circumstances. I show, however, that many important features of its political economy and security policy can best be analyzed and understood from a broader theoretical perspective.[38]

Most dimensions of Israeli security policy, battle plans, crisis behavior, and military strategies have been the subject of investigation; but few studies have concerned themselves with the constraints on the Israeli government's mobilization of those resources required for national security. For instance, Avner Yaniv's interesting and exhaustive account of Israeli strategic behavior does at times note where domestic politics influenced its deterrence posture, yet such domestic factors are tangential to his other concerns.[39] When Mandelbaum speaks of the relationship between Israeli strategic behavior and domestic forces, his manner resurrects the economic nationalist state, as he argues that the Israeli leadership's deterrence posture was premised on its ability to rapidly expand its military power, and, therefore, "the economy was organized to promote as much independence as possible in the manufacture of defense equipment."[40] The Israeli government's ability to organize the economy is noted in passing, treated as an unexceptional talent even though a feat rare among most states. This feat is not explained by a reading of the Israeli political economy but presumably from the implicit assumption that the Israeli state, similar to all states in the interstate system, was able to subordinate the economy to the task of state building and military power. Although the Israeli government was able to organize the economy that was intended to further its military power, its ability to do so and its policies' correspondence to its domestic objectives are unexplored and overlooked.

In contrast to Mandelbaum who notes Israel's concern for self-reliance, Stephen Walt recognizes, as do many, that one dominant theme in Israeli strategic thinking has been to locate a secure and reliable Great Power patron.[41] Therefore, the emergence of the U.S.-Israeli strategic relationship after 1967 should come as little surprise and might be easily explained by systemic factors. Yet there is an important difference between the presence of a Great Power protector and the tremendous financial dependence that emerged between Israel and the United States after 1970, something that would have caused dread among many of Israel's first leaders who believed that financial independence was an important definitional component of national security. This financial dependence did not emerge simply because of systemic changes; rather, changes in the Israeli political economy were as, if not more, important in bringing about this result. And how is it that the Israeli government structured the economy in a way that furthered its arms independence, but simultaneously created a set of policies that eroded its financial autonomy? Former approaches are unable to explain these oppositional movements.

All too often the Israeli state is considered nearly autonomous, strictly responsive to systemic demands and absolved from societal pressures; therefore, the state can mobilize its required security-related resources with relatively little friction, if necessary. In short, the literature on Israeli security policy reflects what has taken place elsewhere in the discipline, particularly as it posits an economic nationalist state. Chapter 5 demonstrates that Israeli leaders' mobilization strategies—far from resembling the policies that might be associated with an omniscient state—were both constrained by domestic political and economic forces and shaped by foreign and domestic objectives.

Not only have the determinants of the government's war preparation strategies been ignored, but so too have their effects on state power. Most explanations for the Israeli state's preeminence in Israel's political economy point to a combination of the Jewish community's prestatehood organizations and institutions, Zionist ideology, and the political economy.[42] War, however, was neither tangential nor subservient to these factors; rather, it was intimately involved in shaping the direction of Israeli state power in its early years.[43] For example, the threat of war initially enabled the state to crystallize its control over the population and continued to demand society's cooperation and willing sacrifice. By the mid-1970s, however, many noted that the Israeli state seemed overwhelmed by social forces. There were both political challenges to Mapai, Israel's dominant party since the state's inception, from its closest political threat, Menachem Begin's Herut party, and a tremendous growth in the role of the private sector, which represented a change from the Zionist vision of a state-led socialist community. I argue that war preparation bore a primary responsibility for both the initial strengthening of the state and its subsequent weakening.

In summary, the treatment of Israeli and Egyptian war preparation strategies and their effects on state power demonstrate remarkable similarity. First, the general tendency has been to view both as strong, a characterization even more visible when examining the government's security policies, strategic behavior, and the mobilization of resources for national security. There is an implicit, often unstated, contention: if the government is forced to search elsewhere for its required means of war, then it is because these resources are not contained domestically, not because the government's access to these resources is significantly, politically, and economically constrained. Although these were resource-scarce countries, there were also substantial constraints on the government's ability to mobilize existing resources. Moreover, government officials in both countries responded to systemic and domestic pressures, and did not have the luxury of focusing on security pressures to the exclusion of domestic ones. Even when security pressures were their greatest, Israeli and Egyptian leaders attempted to ensure that their security policies did not undercut their domestic political and economic objectives.

Second, scholars of Israel and Egypt have argued that each country represents something of a paradox because the state is large and powerful, while society is only now passing through its embryonic stage, developing those instruments that would allow it to confront, challenge, and circumscribe the state's authority. There was only a state in Israel in 1948, only a state in Egypt in 1952. In Israel the cause is Zionism; in Egypt the cause is the five-thousand-year uninterrupted presence of a state and its centrality in controlling the rhythm of the Nile. In characterizing these countries as possessing "heads without bodies," scholars of Israel and Egypt are only partially correct in asserting that his or her country is unique because of the nature of the state: the Israeli and Egyptian states, for various reasons outlined in chapter 3, are distinct.

Be that as it may, these states' prominence and centrality situates them beside other Third World states. Whether because of, for instance, the state's "overdeveloped" nature or the politics of late industrialization, it has been a common refrain that most Third World states stand rather large when compared to the states of the advanced industrial setting. The Israeli and Egyptian cases, though unique for different reasons, are no different in this respect.

Third, earlier scholarship has failed to locate interstate conflict and its related processes as central to the rise and decline of state power in both Egypt and Israel. The general tendency is to view war as reinforcing the state's already central presence. Although this was generally true of the pre-1967 environment, why this is so has never been fully explored. After the June 1967 War, however, war preparation was central, not secondary, for bringing about tremendous changes in Israeli and Egyptian state power. And, rather than leading to the state's aggrandizement, war preparation led to its very decline. This study presents the counterintuitive conclusion that Israeli and Egyptian officials, rather than centralizing their control over the economy during a decade of intense international hostility and violence, moved in the opposite direction and purposefully decentralized their control and promoted the growth of domestic capital because they sought war preparation, political stability, and economic growth. Therefore, in contrast to Western European formation in which war was central in promoting the state's domestic presence, in Israel and Egypt we are confronted with the opposite case in which a once prominent and central state contributed intentionally and unintentionally to its own decline. War preparation contributed to both the growth and the diminution of state power in Israel and Egypt. The intellectual challenge is to explain the outcomes with the same theoretical framework.

Therefore, these case studies make two contributions. First, they demonstrate that we can approach, analyze, and understand the development of both Israeli and Egyptian state-society relations with macrohistorical tools and concepts. My immediate intention, then, is to view these seemingly distinctive and unique countries within a comparative framework. Second, it is important to recognize and incorporate the importance of conflict processes for interpreting the course of Egyptian and Israeli state power. I am about to tell a story concerning the development of the Israeli and Egyptian states until 1977. In some respects, then, my aim is modest: to reinterpret well-known outcomes from a different theoretical approach. In other respects, however, my goal is ambitious: to provide an alternative but necessary way of examining the growth and development of state power.

CHAPTER TWO.

The Framework

THE RELATIONSHIP between the state and society has been summarily altered and shaped by the vigilant pursuit of national security and the participation in conflicts both latent and manifest. In chapter 1 I argued that war has been partnered with both the expansion and diminution of the state and that both are viewed as a direct outcome of the government's mobilization of societal resources to confront external challenges. The intellectual puzzle is to construct an explanation that offers an understanding of how war-related processes can provoke within state power alternate periods of expansion or decline. Accordingly, I present a theoretical framework that can establish the connection between war preparation and the fortunes of state power. This requires two sorts of tasks. The first, more involved, duty is demonstrating the logic that conditions the government's war preparation strategies; the second is demonstrating the microfoundations for macrohistorical change—that is, how these implemented policies can contribute to either the expansion or the decline of state power. In Charles Tilly's now famous phrase, "states made wars and wars made states." The purpose of this chapter is to delineate how this twofold process occurs.

The framework for investigating the relationship between war preparation and state power consists of four elements. The framework begins by positing a limited set of governmental objectives during war preparation. We should not interpret these assumed preferences of the government as my assertion that all governments hold to these imputed objectives; instead, I argue that *if* the government were to operate with these goals and given an identified decision context, then the government's war preparation strategies would tend in certain directions.

The second aspect of the framework is the government's decision context—those state and societal constraints that limit its ability to mobilize domestic resources for national security. The third element in the framework is the government's war preparation strategies. The government's adopted war preparation strategies are products of its objectives and decision context. These policies are assumed to be strategic *choices*, designed to reconcile possibly conflicting objectives under a specific decision context. I identify three broad types of state strategies: (1) an accommodational strategy that utilizes already existing policies; (2) a restructural strategy that deviates substantially from past policies and attempts to restructure the state-society relationship to increase the societal contribution toward the war effort; and (3) an international strategy that relies on foreign sources of strategic support.

Here I am interested in both what enables the government to select from a wide range of policy options and the factors that might dispose it toward one set of options over another. I examine the state's objectives and various features of the state and social structure in order to delineate the possible and the probable. In general, prewar state-society relations structure, but do not necessarily determine, the government's war preparation strategies. The degree to which war preparation—indeed war itself—restructures state-society relations depends on the social structure prior to and the decisions made by government officials concerning fiscal, production, and conscription matters during war preparation. Throughout the theoretical discussion and the empirical chapters I incorporate the motivations, intentions, and casual forces behind the government's decisions, for this enables us to better understand why it chose one option rather than another. These two aspects—how the social structure and international system condition, but do not determine, the government's decisions—play an important role in my analysis of war preparation strategies, both theoretical and empirical.

The final issue refers to how these strategic choices affect state power. The functional needs of the government for successful war preparation—that is, the tendency to extract greater resources from society—translates clearly into the state's expansion and increased control over society. Again, this has been a common characterization of war and state power in much of the theoretical and historical literature. In contrary instances, however, the government's attempt to simultaneously maintain political support and facilitate war preparation has divested the state's control over certain spheres of activity. I suggest that an accommodational or an international strategy tends to reinforce past tendencies in state-society relations, but a restructural policy (i.e., one that deviates from the institutionalized state-society compact) alters state power.

This argument requires some unpacking. Specifically, part of the difficulty encountered when attempting to discern the relationship between war and state power derives in large part from conceptual imprecision concerning state power and how it might be operationalized. After all, in chapter 1 I argued that much scholarship has treated war as, alternatively, increasing state power through an expansion of its infrastructural capacity, which is largely measured through tax data, or decreasing state power, as when the state confer new rights and powers on previously marginalized societal groups in exchange for their assistance in furthering the state's geostrategic goals. To overcome former difficulties, I present a conceptualization and measurement of state power that furthers the temporal and spatial examination and analysis of state power.

PREFERENCES AND CONSTRAINTS

In this section I begin by positing a set of state preferences. These assumed preferences of the state should not be interpreted as my assertion that all states conform to these imputed objectives; this is obviously an empirical issue that cannot be settled here. Instead, I argue that if the state were to operate with these goals, then under a particular environmental context certain war preparation strategies would likely follow. I examine the environmental constraints, heretofore referred to as the decision context, that limit the government's ability to pursue its preferences unconditionally. The government's preferences and its decision context form the first part of the theoretical framework.

State Preferences

Because the state is situated in both domestic and international structures, its objectives and policies reflect this dual orientation. At the most fundamental level, then, the state must be attentive to its reproductive conditions, its security, in both the domestic and the international realms. This Janus-faced "security dilemma," which becomes more tense during moments of international hostility, significantly challenges state managers; too determined an effort to protect their security in one sphere could undercut their security in the other. In such a scenario the government might have the following two objectives.

The first is war preparation, the government's intensified mobilization of resources with the intent of being prepared to undertake interstate war. Three features of this definition are worth highlighting. First, I am concerned with how the government mobilizes the material and human resources required for interstate defense. Mobilizing three types of resources is of principal concern: financial resources (in the absence of sufficient funds the government is unable to pay for its increased consumption of resources); the actual instruments of warfare; and personnel.

Although most states are involved in both an unceasing process of territorial defense and some level of security mobilization, I focus on those periods when the aforementioned mobilization activities undergo a significant increase as a result of an external threat. Therefore, one possible indicator of periods of war preparation is the increased percentage of the budget channeled to defense spending.[1]

Most readers, however, quickly recognize that an increase in the defense budget cannot be attributed automatically to an immediate or potential foreign challenge. It is quite possible that defense expenditures were motivated by such goals as prestige, the military bureaucracy, employment, or internal security—of which some or all characterize defense establishments of most, and particularly Third World, states. Rather than presume that the government's security expenditures are externally directed, I reconstruct the government's understanding of its situation and what motivates and gives meaning to its actions, as a method of corroborating the exact nature of its security concerns. In the empirical chapters on Israel and Egypt this entails recreating as accurately as possible how Israeli and Egyptian state managers understood the foreign challenges to the state's viability in the interstate system.[2] This method is not fail-safe because leaders often will attribute their behavior to one set of causes while others will ascribe it to another. After all, although few leaders are willing to concede that they engaged in a massive military build-up to diffuse societal tensions, history is replete with those instances in which governments apparently exaggerated the foreign threat as a way of furthering their own domestic causes.[3] In part I selected the Israeli and Egyptian cases because observers generally accept the fact that both governments confronted, and believed themselves under, very real foreign threats. And even if at times leaders of both countries exaggerated the external threat, each government's war mobilization activities had very real consequences. In summary, I isolate moments of war preparation by examining the government's understanding of its situation and the behavior generated by this interpretation.[4]

Although war preparation may be one important, if not the most important, critical objective of the government, it is not the only goal, for leaders are not so myopic. A second objective is political stability, insulating the government from would-be domestic challengers. For the government in the capitalist context this political concern is twofold: it must encourage business confidence by both introducing those policies that benefit the private sector and abstaining from those actions that run counter to capital's fundamental interests,[5] and it must remain mindful of its coalitional basis, which extends beyond the immediate concerns of the capitalist class to include other societal groups that, through formal or informal mechanisms, are either integral to the governing coalition or potentially injurious to its rule.

The government's constant and vigilant watch over its political life has two important implications. First, societal dissatisfaction can be registered in a number of ways, at the workplace, in the streets, in the voting booth, in capital markets, and so on. Governments, be they democratic or authoritarian, monitor the societal mood through means other than voting behavior or public opinion polls. The primary difference between democratic and nondemocratic governments has more to do with the degree of responsiveness they are likely to exhibit and the principal mechanisms used for expressing and incorporating societal preferences than with whether societal will is responsed to, expressed, or incorporated at all. Second, governments of all varieties have demonstrated a willingness to avoid certain policies because of the *predicted* societal response. Because leaders would like to avoid trouble where possible, they intentionally abstain from a host of policies given their anticipated effects. This reading exists in the analyses of both advanced capitalist and postpopulist societies, where governments refrain from a class of policies that might generate tremendous business or popular antipathy, respectively.[6] In general, the theoretical framework applies to all governments in capitalist societies, for no matter how insulated institutionally they might be, they must demonstrate some concern for their domestic basis of support and cannot run roughshod over societal interests.

Because the government is attempting to mobilize *material* resources for war preparation, a corollary of the above objectives is that it promotes an environment conducive to economic growth. Such growth provides an important basis for creating societal wealth, which may then be available to the government for its primary objectives of war preparation and political stability. Historically the doctrine of economic nationalism has been most closely associated with state's twin objectives of economic growth and national security. Economic nationalism at its broadest level asserts that government officials believe that the state's power in the interstate system is both built on a strong economic foundation and will implement those policies that create greater economic growth in general and develop key military-related sectors in particular.[7] Economic nationalism is associated with a host of diverse policies, from maintaining a balance of payments surplus and protecting certain strategic industries to the actual state control of leading military-related economic sectors.

Economic nationalism, then, says more about the *ends* of the state than it does its *means*. Although the goal of the state is left unquestioned, more elastic are the means adopted for this unchanging objective. After all, economic nationalism allows for both limited and heavy state intervention in the domestic economy, and it is conceivable that government officials might evaluate possible policies along efficiency grounds at some moments (as in desiring to run a balance-of-payments surplus) more than at others (as in protecting certain strategic industries even at substantial economic cost).

In this interpretation the means are understood as part of "technical rationality,"[8] for governments have held different ideas about what types of economic policies best further their goal of economic security. Governments' ideas concerning which economic policies best promote their primary objectives of political stability and war preparation have important consequences for preparation strategies. But because the governments' adopted means depend ultimately on both the economic ideas they currently advocate and the societal constraints on their actions, it is virtually impossible to include this objective of economic development into the theoretical framework in a parsimonious manner. I therefore bracket this corollary objective of economic development in attempting to derive the government's war preparation strategies but include it in the empirical studies.

What will the government do when its goals of war preparation and political stability conflict? First, war mobilization activity will not automatically challenge the government's political viability. In fact, substantial political costs can be generated if society perceives the government as lax toward national security. For example, both the Egyptian regime after the 1967 War and the Israeli government after the Yom Kippur War were confronted by a society under the impression that the government had shirked its duty as guardian of the national interest. That government leaders might be vulnerable to the charge of being careless with the state's security has operated in clockwork-like fashion every four years during U.S. presidential contests since World War Two. Therefore, let us assume that while initially modest levels of war preparation activities have a negligible impact on the government's political fortunes, more intensified activities can carry substantially higher political costs.

At some level possible costs are associated with the pursuit of each goal. At issue, then, are the government's preferences when forced to choose between its desired goals of war preparation and domestic stability. There are empirical and theoretical reasons to argue that the government will opt for external security over domestic tranquility. For instance, Theda Skocpol among others notes that during times of war the state may move against domestic class interests to mobilize its required resources.[9] Jürgen Kocka observes,

> the assumption seems to be justified that, in times of war, when aggression is directed externally and self-preservation is a prime concern, policies derived from considerations of system stabilization may to some extent contradict the ruling socio-economic interests. . . . The civil and military authorities will, if necessary, injure particularistic class interests; this may even include the interests of the privileged, if this is seen as unavoidable for the effective management of the war.[10]

This observation is consistent with the theoretical claims of realism and neorealism that argue that the state's primary objective is external security.

Alternatively, there are good reasons to consider the alternative hypothesis: the government will chose domestic stability over war preparation, even if this choice subverts its ability to prepare adequately for war. For instance, Chubin and Tripp note that in the beginning of the Iran-Iraq War Iranian leaders privileged domestic politics over the prosecution of the war, "epitomized by the slogan 'Revolution before victory.' Indeed the war became an extension of the domestic power rivalry, to which arming, structure, strategy, and the conduct of the military was subordinated."[11] Moreover, Khomeini's decision to accept a negotiated settlement in principle is largely attributed to the possibility for domestic turbulence because of the political and economic costs associated with the eight-year conflict. And even during World War One German leaders were reluctant to undertake security mobilization past a certain point because of the potential risk to political order:

> The continuing class character of the State . . . may well be at the root of . . . the government's insufficient willingness to deal effectively with the social tensions or to establish any internal control over particular interests for the sake of the war effort. . . . The dependence of the holders of civil and military power on the most important groups in socio-economically dominant class turned out to be so close as to make impossible the fundamental reforms which would have been necessary for an improved military capability and strength.[12]

Finally, an argument could be made that in the contemporary era where wars of annihilation are rare if not nonexistent, few state managers would prefer to prosecute a war at the risk of exposing themselves to societal insurrection. As I suggested earlier the principle of sovereignty in the modern era has virtually guaranteed the continued existence of most states in the interstate system, but less certain is the longevity of state managers. In short, the international system has secured the state's survival, but the domestic system has not done the same for government officials.

The question is whether the government would continue to increase societal extraction for war even at risking its own political survival. This empirical issue cannot be settled definitively here. As I suggested earlier, I hesitate to assume a priori that external security goals are always given priority in the foreign policy calculations of states; instead, I assume that state officials pursue both foreign policy goals such as security and domestic goals such as economic development and political stability. Although I assert that governments strive to avoid trading off between these two goals, both strong theoretical arguments and historical evidence support the claim that the government prefers one over the other.

I see a Janus-faced state, one concerned with challengers in both the domestic and the international arenas. This vision implies that the government is motivated by multiple and, hence, potentially conflicting objectives. The attempt to embed more fully state actors in both domestic and international systems stands in contrast to other state-as-rational actor treatments. For instance, many Marxist and realist approaches tend to see the government's activities as the rational outcome of a single dominant objective, whether the reproductive requirements of capitalism or the state's power in the international system, respectively. Therefore, in contrast to the assumption that a policy represents the logical result of a single-minded government, I am interested in how its potentially contradictory objectives are both reconciled and affected during moments of heightened security concerns.

Decision Context

> The restrictive conditions, rooted as they were in the
> organization of production relations and the distribution of
> social and political power . . . limited the State's room for
> maneuver to mobilize the economy and society for War.
> (*Jürgen Kocka*, Facing Total War)

The decision context structures the range of political and economic costs associated with governmental policies available for extracting revenue, directing production, and raising armies for war; it thereby shapes the actual strategies adopted by state managers. Although any number of environmental factors can impinge on governmental actions, the relevant decision context is dependent on whether it is attempting to mobilize financial, productive, or human resources; that is, the government's capabilities are policy dependent. Four elements of the relationship between the state and society are particularly relevant. First, because I am discussing the government's war preparation strategies in capitalist societies, the state's relationship to the capitalist class is an important constraining feature, regardless of the type of material resource the government is attempting to mobilize; the investment decisions of this class shape its material base.[13] Second, the state's capacity incorporates the institutional "capacity to actually penetrate civil society, and to implement logically political decisions through that realm."[14] This is most important when examining the government's ability to mobilize financial resources. Third, the economic structure identifies the possibility of domestic military production. Finally, the state's legitimacy affects its conscription policy. Below I elaborate how these four dimensions of the decision context structure the financial, production, and conscription policies available to government officials.

Financial Policy. The government's financial policy is shaped by both the underlying distribution of societal power and the state's institutional capacities that enable it to penetrate, extract from, and monitor society. Because the state is institutionally separated from organized production, it does not produce its own source of revenue.[15] Therefore, all state managers are attentive to and constrained by the flow of resources upon which the deployment of the state's means depends, and the ability either to develop alternative sources of financial means or to loosen its dependence on the capitalist class substantially increases its autonomy. This independence may come from either the acquisition of foreign loans, which might give the state an additional instrument of control over society, or a fiscal crisis of the state, which might compel the government to devise new fiscal strategies.[16]

Those states with high capacity have an array of policy instruments, including both indirect and direct methods, that enable the government to extract domestic revenue with a greater degree of dexterity than do those states lacking such characteristics. Therefore, those states with little institutional capacity tend to utilize indirect methods.[17] For instance, in early capitalist Europe this meant increasing the taxes on foreign trade because the costs of measurement and collection of taxes was relatively low and even lower where trade occurred almost exclusively by water and few ports existed.[18] This dependence on trade for generating the state's revenue is as true for much of the contemporary Third World as it was for eighteenth-century England; therefore, most Third World states obtain the bulk of their revenue here and utilize such tools as tariffs, quotas, and the like. Indirect methods add a secondary advantage: not only are they hidden and easier to collect, but because they are regressive and the tax is passed on to the consumer, they also serve the interests of the capitalist class and possibly the government's political basis as well. For example, taxation was extended in England owing to a series of wars that occurred in the latter part of the seventeenth century, and "the bulk of the increased taxation necessitated by war seems to have been borne by consumers rather than producers, and the new direct taxes touched the mercantile and manufacturing classes relatively lightly."[19]

Production Policy. The government's mobilization of war material is constrained by the country's economic structure and the private control over production. The economic structure is commonly understood to incorporate the "profile" of the country's production of goods and services. This is particularly important for determining the possibility of domestic production of the instruments of warfare because there is an intimate connection between the size and sophistication of the economy and the possibility of large-scale arms production.[20] As Herbert Wulf puts it, "modern arms production requires a capacity for high technology in several branches of industry. The production process is highly complex and requires inputs from a diversified industrial base."[21] It is not coincidental, then, that those countries self-sufficient in most major weapons systems—notably West Germany, France, Britain, the Soviet Union, and the United States and to a lesser extent Brazil and India— are the same countries that also have a large GNP, expansive industrial base, and numerous high-technology industries. In a related manner, many Third World leaders have professed a desire to achieve independent arms production and thereby decrease their dependence on and susceptibility to Great Power manipulation, but their efforts have been frustrated by a lack of appropriate technology, an insufficient industrial base, and an inability to achieve the desired economies of scale.[22] In general, those countries that have an expansive and sophisticated industrial base are better suited to the requirements of modern arms production.[23]

The existence of an industrial base is no guarantee that the government can secure its required war material from domestic sources because the means of production are controlled by private actors. This societal constraint on the government's access to military production is an important but often overlooked feature of many Marxist and non-Marxist explanations of its war production policy.[24] Again, in capitalist societies the government is institutionally divorced from the economy; therefore, it must not only remain sensitive to how its policies affect business interests but also negotiate with and encourage private actors to act in a manner that serves the government's aims.[25]

Therefore, the existence of an expansive and sophisticated economic base that can potentially produce the instruments of warfare implies the government's initial policy will be to rely on the efforts of the private sector. Domestic arms production might be encouraged through such noninterventionist policies as increased demand, investment incentives, and/or protectionist policies.[26] Even states with substantial autonomy prefer to depend on the efforts of the private sector, for this not only averts any potential political costs associated with a restructural policy but the bureaucracy may also lack the managerial expertise to direct war production. The case of the United States during World War Two is interesting in this respect. President Roosevelt found himself in the uncomfortable position of having to rely on the efforts of many of those industrial capitalists that had opposed his New Deal policies. He was forced into this position because the bureaucracy lacked the managerial expertise to mobilize war production without significant assistance from these very individuals. Even so, the government created the Defense

Plants Corporation, which spent approximately "five billion dollars erecting new factories, mills, and shipyards, then leased the new plants to private industry."[27]

Conscription Policy. Governments' final requisite for war preparation is raising an army. The government's conscription policy is shaped by its legitimacy and its autonomy. The state's control over the means of coercion is one of its defining features; the existence of rival domestic military organizations is the surest evidence of the government's inability to establish its influence throughout society and can thus be interpreted as an expression of its lack of capacity and legitimacy.[28] In general, the government's conscription policy is a useful indicator of broader state-society issues.

There tends to be a direct relationship between the state's legitimacy and its ability to conscript widely. The state's legitimacy in the modern era is founded on the principle that the state's decisions and exercise of authority are derived, in spirit if not in practice, from societal participation. Therefore, the state and its political institutions must have a strong societal basis to garner societal compliance with its policies. For instance, in feudal Europe the military was manned by the elite and the aristocracy, in large part because of the lord's inability to secure the control over the population or the willingness to permit his citizenry to handle the instruments of rebellion. When war erupted the remainder of the necessary troop requirements were met with mercenary forces. As Perry Anderson notes: "The most obvious social reason for the mercenary phenomenon was, of course, the natural refusal of the noble class to arm its peasants wholesale. 'It is virtually impossible to train all subjects of a commonwealth in the arts of war, and at the same time, keep them obedient to the laws of the magistrates.' "[29] Anthony Giddens similarly argues that centralized military power played a large role in traditional states, and that for rulers to "build up the armed forces meant gathering together recruits and preparing them for military duties. Since it was impossible in most circumstances for such recruits to be welded into a 'bureaucratic army,' the military preparation of such soldiery could easily rebound upon those who instigated it, by creating potentially independent rival sources of power within the state."[30]

The emergence of the modern nation-state in Europe altered not only the relationship between state and society but also the government's conscription possibilities. As the nation-state's rule was premised on its adherence to constitutional principles informed by societal interests, the citizenry also was seen as having certain responsibilities and obligations to the state. One of the first areas where this principle of mutual obligation was recognized was military service.[31] "The nation-state and the mass army appear together, the twin tokens of citizenship within terri-

torially bounded political communities. . . . Military service emerged
as a hallmark of citizenship and citizenship as the hallmark of a political democracy."[32] Conversely, the same Third World states marked by
scant legitimacy are also characterized by an avoidance of mass conscription and a reliance on an army derived from those individuals who have
demonstrated their loyalty to the state either through kinship ties or
patron-client relations.[33] Only when the state is firmly entrenched in
society and its authority widely recognized is the government best able
to conscript widely; then the nondominant classes are permitted access
to the instruments of coercion and rebellion.[34] Universal conscription,
then, a fairly recent phenomenon, itself reflects the changing relationship between the state and society.

Even those states with universal conscription typically exempt certain
elements of the population. For instance, while under feudalism the military was generally serviced by those who had demonstrated their loyalty
to the state. Thus, within this domain of the nobility, the expansion of
wealth associated with capitalist development (also a product of warfare)
created a simultaneous explosion of revenue for the state, which enabled
it to expand permanently the size of the military.[35] Because the state
depended on the emerging dominant classes for its revenue, however, it
was possible and desirable for the bourgeoisie to escape military service,
something they capitalized upon with vigor. For example, the impressive army developed by King Frederick William I (1713–1740) "was
organized with infinite care to impose the least possible strain on the
fragile economy of his lands. The bourgeoisie, good fruitful taxpayers,
did not serve at all. The ranks were recruited so far as possible from
foreigners and peasants."[36] (The officers corps, however, continued to be
derived from the aristocracy and nobility). The rise of capitalism, therefore, instigated a trend in many countries where members of the capitalist class were either automatically exempt from or had certain avenues
available (e.g., tax, duty, or educational status) that allowed them to
avoid military obligation.[37]

In summary, the concept of the decision context—the range of policies available to the government—serves two functions in this analysis.
It both identifies the relevant constraints on the government's ability to
mobilize domestic resources for national security and outlines the various factors that might propel state officials in particular directions. For
instance, in the area of fiscal policy those state managers situated in a
decision context of little state autonomy and high state capacity have a
significantly greater number of policy options available to them; they are
better able to extract resources from society than are those state managers situated in a decision context of little relative autonomy and little
state capacity. It is now possible to suggest some specific tendencies in
the government's war preparation strategies.

STATE STRATEGIES FOR WAR PREPARATION

As the government adjusts to and copes with the increasing demands of national security, it is confronted by not only this motivating threat but also the prospect that those policies designed to successfully confront the external challenge may undercut its domestic basis. Consequently, the government attempts to mobilize the required resources at a minimal level of political cost.[38] As the government attempts to perform this balancing act, it can choose among three broad types of mobilizing strategies: accommodational, restructural, and international. These broadly defined strategies identify not only the location of the resource (domestic or international) but also some potential political costs involved with each undertaking. Regardless of the decision context, the government commences with an accommodational strategy. Once this avenue is exhausted, its choice of a restructural or an international strategy depends on the decision context and some additional features of the international system, the state, and society. In this way we are able to present some hypotheses concerning the possible direction of Israeli and Egyptian war preparation strategies.

Types of Strategies

In this discussion I assume that the accommodational, restructural, and international strategies are noncomplementary; however, it is immediately apparent that the state's mobilization strategies usually evidence a mix of these strategies. This is as true for the state's war preparation strategies as it is for its strategies of domestic shocks from the international economy. Although this typology obviously distorts what actually occurs, it is useful for analytical simplification and hypothesis generation.

An accommodational strategy is defined as the reliance on and modest changes in already existing policy instruments. The heart of an accommodational strategy is that the state restricts its policy selection to those instruments presently contained in the state apparatus and thus adjusts its behavior to accommodate the present societal condition. Because an accommodational strategy preserves the routine and effectively honors the status quo, relatively few, if any, political costs accrue to doing what has already been done, something that is highly valued by the state. Therefore, the state invariably begins with this type of strategy. However, during periods of increased security demands it is highly unlikely that the state's security needs will be satiated through accommodational measures. Consequently, the government must consider either a restructural or an international strategy.

A restructural strategy is observed whenever state managers attempt to restructure the present state-society compact in order to increase the total amount of financial, productive, and manpower resources available to state officials for war preparation. Consequently, a restructural strategy includes a wide range of policies and actions: introducing everything from the income tax during World War One in the United States and mass conscription by European rulers to new property rights to increase the state's revenue base. This continuum, then, incorporates variations in the change in the institutional structure: from the administrative and regulatory rules and procedures that might include new policy instruments available to decision makers to the normative order that defines state-society relations.[39] The concern here is with the state's attempt to expand the means at its disposal, and/or alter the institutional relationship that defines state-society relations to increase the societal contribution for war preparation.

Because the state's intention is to rearrange the state-society compact to impose the costs of war on society, there is an increased likelihood that certain societal groups may disagree with the government's movements. In this way the state's ability to increase the societal burden is related to the domestic constraints that limit its choices.[40] Ikenberry's general observation concerning the state's adjustment strategy to domestic shocks from the international economy is also relevant to the state's war preparation strategy:

> The more constrained the state is by its relations with its economy and society, the more it will emphasize international strategies of adjustment. States that find it difficult to impose costs on their domestic societies will be more inclined to seek international solutions. Conversely, states that have the capabilities to redeploy domestic resources and impose the costs of change on society will emphasize domestic offensive strategies.[41]

A restructural strategy follows one of two forms. First, in a "centralization" scenario the state intervenes and increases its direct control over societal resources. This approach is most evident when the state, for instance, has inaugurated direct taxation, moved from a reliance on mercenary troops to a standing army, or nationalized key economic sectors.[42] Second, more germane to the state's material and financial needs is a "liberalization" scenario, in which the state disengages from or withdraws its control over society and economy to increase the societal contribution to the war effort.[43] Here the state attempts to withdraw from part of the economy to (it hopes) unleash "market forces" and thus expand the country's material base. In general, the centralization variant observes the state's increased control over the economy and society; in the decentralization scenario the state divests its authority over the economy and society and relies more fully on market mechanisms to fulfill the state's security needs. Recognize that the state might adopt simultaneously a centralization posture in one area (for example, the move toward mass conscription) while embracing a liberalization posture in another (for instance, the decision to rely on the efforts of private economic elites to produce its needed war material). The state's ability to adopt either a liberalization or a centralization posture, however, assumes that it is relatively unconstrained by its domestic context. In general, the more powerful a state is domestically the greater the emphasis it will give to a restructural solution.[44]

Finally, a state that is highly constrained by its domestic context is more favorably disposed toward an international strategy, which attempts to distribute the costs of war onto foreign actors. An international solution may emerge through either a formal or an informal alliance with another state in which security cooperation exists between two or more states, or possibly through the assistance of private actors, as in the role played by many great banking houses during early European warfare.[45] In general, there is an incentive for the state to adopt an international strategy when it perceives the increasing costs to mobilizing additional societal resources for war preparation.[46] For instance, during World War Two the Iraqi royal family, fearful of unfaithful societal elements and assured of the availability of British and Indian troops for its needs, proceeded to decimate and demoralize an Iraqi army upon which it could not depend. Its strategy was both to force the retirement of many personnel and to deliberately neglect those that remained so that they would "voluntarily" resign from military service.[47] And this international disposition might be more likely where leaders, unwilling to discount their own personal future, pass the costs of an alliance onto future governments. This need not imply that the state is either unwilling or unable to impose some national security costs on society; but it does imply, where possible, the state has an incentive to export the mounting costs of security.[48]

The obvious implication of this argument is that the government would seem automatically predisposed toward an international solution and avoid a restructural one altogether to supplement its pool of available resources. Two considerations, however, temper this conclusion. First, are such external arrangements available? And, even if they are, can they satisfy the state's security requirements? Rarely, if ever, is foreign assistance available in such quantities as to relieve the state from any domestic measures. The availability of foreign assistance depends on the state's power position, ideological legitimacy, and status in the international system.[49] For instance, Great Powers have a greater ability to impose the costs of war on foreign actors, while middle powers might be able to use their position in the interstate system to generate certain benefits from Great Power actors.

Moreover, the government's ability to rely on foreign actors depends on the type of resource being mobilized. For instance, in early European warfare, rulers that feared the domestic repercussions associated with military service could turn to mercenaries; however, in the modern era foreign troops are rarely attainable, and reliance on domestic manpower is necessary.[50] Alternatively, because in the contemporary era there are an increasing number of arms producers the state may more easily depend on foreign suppliers for its immediate needs and not be as compelled to intervene in the domestic economy to secure its weapons needs.

The second, more important, issue concerns the costs attached to such foreign arrangements. Almost invariably conditions and stipulations accompany foreign assistance that restricts the recipient's employment of these borrowed resources. This may be particularly troublesome in the context of war preparation because the donor may require the recipient avoid those security-related policies that the former views as contrary to its own foreign policy interests. In other words, there is a paradox: while the recruitment of a foreign benefactor can increase the amount of resources available for war preparation, these resources may be accompanied by restrictive conditions that undermine the very reason for which these resources are requested. This was evident in Sadat's constant struggle with the Soviets over how and when he could use the imported Soviet equipment during the early 1970s; the Soviets were fearful that Sadat's actions toward the Israelis might undermine the Soviets' policy of détente with the United States. Moreover, the perception by society that the state has sacrificed its national autonomy to foreign actors—for example, through the presence of foreign troops, naval bases, and restrictive policies—can also generate substantial domestic opposition. This was evident in the concern that introducing U.S. ground forces in Saudi Arabia after the Iraqi invasion of Kuwait in August 1990 might destabilize and delegitimize the Saudi regime. Finally, foreign aid often just delays, rather than eliminates, the costs of war; thereby, it simply increases the state's future obligation to foreign actors. Therefore, although the state has compelling reasons to opt for an international position, the aforementioned problems associated with such a strategy provide a strong rationale for those practices, such as military industrialization and neomercantilist economic policies, that increase the state's national autonomy and decrease its dependence on foreign actors.

In general, two sets of factors shape the government's decision to pursue an international strategy. First, the state's domestic movements are generally constrained. A state that is unable to mobilize domestic resources because of its lack of autonomy, legitimacy, capacity, and industrial base, is more likely to rely on the efforts of foreign actors. Second, if foreign aid is either unavailable or obtainable only with unacceptable conditions, the state will be more favorably disposed toward a restructural policy.

Thus far I have argued that the decision context establishes the possibility for, as well as the potential costs attached to, domestic intervention. The decision context alone, however, does not determine the direction of the government's energies, for it is precisely during periods of international conflict that it has deviated from established procedures and implemented (what were once considered) controversial policies. Many state officials used the pretext of war to restructure the state's relationship to society, which implies that the decision context is not the sole influence on the state's movements. Perhaps most important is the state's legitimacy and the societal cohesion that flows from that legitimacy during war. Azar and Moon argue that the "national will" is intimately tied to the state's legitimacy, "whether citizens are loyal and willingly support state policies—whether they accept the authority of the state and believe existing institutions are functionally competent, legally right, and morally proper."[51] A state with a high degree of legitimacy is better able both to mobilize societal resources and to undertake a restructural strategy. This argument is closely associated with the vast literature on societal cohesion and the general proposition that the threat of war produces a "rally around the flag" effect that increases the state's ability to adopt normally contested policies.[52] For example, during the Iran-Iraq War Sadaam Hussein expended considerable energy at myth making; he attempted to convince the population that they were contributing to a war to serve the interests of the nation, not Hussein himself. This was even more important once Khomeini declared that his principal war aim was the defeat of Hussein, and not necessarily Iraq.[53] In general, the existence of both high state legitimacy and societal cohesion increases the state's ability to implement a restructural strategy at a reduced political cost.

Because I have focused thus far on the government's initial war preparation strategy, the framework seems static. Yet state leaders are likely to adopt new policies as war proceeds, and the effects and effectiveness of the government's initial war preparation strategies are better understood. Specifically, state managers modify their initial war preparation strategy when confronted with the fact they either potentially jeopardized their goal of domestic tranquility or failed to generate the required security resources. In short, learning takes place as leaders absorb new information concerning the costs associated with and failures of their past war preparation strategies. Two factors are most important for forcing the government to re-evaluate its policies. First, the current strategy is unable to fulfill the state's immediate security needs. For instance, I already suggested that the government turns from an accommodational to consider either a restructural or international strategy because this strategy alone is unable to satiate its increased security requirements. Illustrative here is the experience of the United States during the Vietnam War. Initially the government relied on a "lower-class" army as it allowed exemptions based on education groups; however, the government, unable to maintain this policy once the troop deployments surpassed a certain level, moved to widen the conscription net and deny with greater frequency exemptions based on educational criteria. Second, the government may fear domestic instability as a result of its present policies.[54] In general, the failure of the government's initial war preparation strategies to meet its domestic and security-related objectives causes it either to target previously excluded societal groups in its mobilization efforts or to strengthen its reliance on foreign actors to generate its required security resources and maintain domestic stability.

In summary, the framework is based on a limited set of government objectives and the state and societal features that affect its ability to pursue its objectives without friction and, therefore, shape its probable war preparation strategies. Regardless of the decision context the state initially moves toward an accommodational strategy. Unfulfilled security needs or societal protests propel the state to consider either a restructural or an international policy. Those states relatively less constrained by their societies are better able to pursue a restructural policy and thus rely on their own societies for their security-related inputs; those states highly constrained in their access to societal resources find an international strategy more to their liking. However, even those states that might initially be presumed highly constrained by their societies might undertake a restructural policy during wartime, given a high degree of societal cohesion.

This conceptualization of the relationship between the decision context and the government's war preparation strategies assumes that it is *enabled* to undertake certain sorts of actions and disposed to act in certain directions, not that it necessarily will do so. Various reasons, including the anticipated objections of societal actors and the objectives of state managers, might potentially dissuade state actors from undertaking a policy that appears within its range of opportunities. For instance, even though the United States during the Vietnam War had a significant amount of institutional capacity and the ability to extract widely from society, President Johnson avoided the potential political costs associated with increased taxation and instead relied on large budget deficits financed by U.S. allies. Consequently, the government's preference for a restructural or an international solution cannot be decisively predicted ahistorically. My principal intention for this framework is to identify the important features of the domestic and international environment that make certain state actions either possible or prohibitive and to outline the various factors that might propel state officials in particular directions.

THE CONSERVATION AND TRANSFORMATION OF STATE POWER

The history of Western Europe is replete with examples of how state participation in war wrought tremendous changes in state-society relations. The European experience is taken as representative of the general assertion that wars and war preparation have generally led to the state's aggrandizement. This focus on the state's expansion, however, distracts us from the Polands,[55] the Israels, and the Egypts—states that experienced periods of growth and reversals as a consequence of war and its activities. For example, Tilly argues that in seventeenth-century England the state's inability to raise revenue from other means led it to rely more "heavily on capitalists as sources and instruments for the mobilization of the necessary funds and acquired commitments to the capitalists in the process."[56] As a consequence of this reliance, the capitalist class found itself with greater influence after war termination. In general, once states no longer seized nor directly produced the means of coercion but instead bought them from others, they often had to confer new rights and benefits to these lenders or sellers.[57] The common thread that links these various movements in state power is the condition under which state rulers gained access to the means of war. Governments generally cannot command but must bargain and negotiate with those who control the means of war. Consequently, the government's adoption of an accommodational, a restructural, or an international strategy carries important implications for the trajectory of state power.[58]

State power is most visibly transformed when the government adopts a restructural strategy to increase the societal contribution to war preparation. The exact relationship between the government's restructural strategy and state power is highly complex and indeterminate, but it might be simplified by rendering the progression in a diagram.

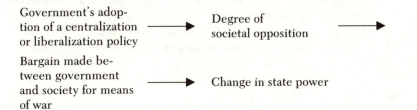

Four features are central to the relationship: (1) the government's ideas about the "efficiency" of various policies for increasing the societal contribution; (2) the strength and demands of societal actors that oppose the government's attempt to alter the state-society compact; (3) the bargain struck between state and society for access to the means of war;[59] and (4) the outcome of these constraint-shaped decisions for the trajectory of state power. Let me say more about each aspect and their relationships to each other.

The first issue concerns the ideas that leaders hold about what type of restructural policy would best increase their access to the means of war while maintaining their other principal objectives of political stability and economic development. The government can attempt either to centralize or liberalize its control over society and economy as a way of increasing the total societal contribution,[60] and its attempt to do so in the targeted financial, production, and manpower areas indicates which groups will be most effected by the government's attempt to change the state-society compact. Yet important factors are the governmental agents' initial beliefs and ideas of the most efficient economic organizing principles for mobilizing more resources for war. For instance, although economic nationalism holds that the economy should be subordinate to the goal of the state's power in the international system, it says little about whether a market-oriented or statist policy would best serve this end. Economic nationalists agree that an expansive industrial base is necessary for the state's military power, but this base could be built principally by state actors, as in the case of late-industrializing economies, or by private economic elites, as in the case of Great Britain. Which avenue is most desirable greatly depends on the ideas held by governmental officials.

The government cannot alter state-society relations in a frictionless manner, but it undoubtedly confronts some degree of societal opposition. This leads to the third aspect, the bargain struck between government and societal actors for access to the means of war. Specifically, the more the government is constrained by society the more it is forced to bargain on "equal" terms with societal groups for access to its desired resources. Accordingly, while the government gains access to its desired means, it must often "return the favor," which might entail that it grant societal groups either new rights and benefits, or some determination over the decision-making process.[61] These three factors—the government's attempt to restructure the state-society compact in a particular direction, the societal opposition to the government's movements, and the concessions the government makes in return for access to the means of war—are the keys to understanding the relationship between war preparation and state power.

What does this process and interaction say about the long-term effects on state power? At face value a centralization policy, one that witnesses the government's attempt to intervene in society and directly control societal resources, would seem to translate into an expansion of state power. This, the heart of the ratchet effect argument, has garnered most of the scholarly attention when discussing the effects of war on state power. In contrast, a liberalization policy should have the opposite effect, as the government's withdrawal of its control over society and economy should shift the state-society balance in favor of the latter. This is observed when the government moves to privilege the capitalist class because of the latter's role in providing for the material requirements of war.[62]

Yet the example of early British history demonstrates just how complex the relationship between war preparation and state power truly is. Douglass North argues that the British Crown introduced new property rights as a way of increasing society's material base, and these resources provided the material basis for not only the state's power in the interstate system but also the further expansion of the state's administrative means and penetration of society.[63] Yet the government increased its material base by handing more economic power to a small but increasingly important private sector. In other words, the government was able to widen its revenue base by narrowing the scope of its authority over a growing and more influential capitalist class. The same process is also observed when European rulers introduced mass conscription, for alongside the introduction of conscription went the construction of institutional linkages that incorporated new societal actors into the decision-making process, which, in turn, reduced the state's decisional autonomy.

In short, the war preparation process might invest simultaneously both the state with greater resources and societal actors with greater power and/or determination over the state's policies. In this way the state's increased control over societal resources can be seen as a "dialectic," for the state's increased control in some areas comes at the expense of a loss of control in others; new groups emerge that act as future constraints on the state's actions.

What might an accommodational and an international strategy hold for state power? Although both tend to reinforce established state-societal patterns, each also offers the possibility of structural change. Specifically, it is quite plausible that the government's decision to adopt a path intended to relieve it of challenging the status quo, may, in fact, heighten the contradictions and dilemmas already present in the system. For instance, Weiss argues that the Italian government's decision to rely on the efforts of industrialists for war mobilization created the tendency toward the concentration and centralization of capital, which led to the further erosion of the state's power vis-à-vis the capitalist class.[64] Rational calculations may bring about wholly unintended consequences.

The same general argument holds for an international strategy. If we understand a crucial element of state power to be the state's control over its revenue production (I argue this is indeed crucial), then a government that exports the costs of war essentially places its material well-being in the hands of foreign actors. In this way an international strategy poses real costs for state power because it leaves the state possibly weak and vulnerable to outside forces. This very possibility was not lost on economic nationalists.

In general, although an accommodational and international strategy can affect state power, a restructural strategy most profoundly contains the seeds of its transformation. A restructural strategy, one that attempts to redesign the institutional compact and essentially challenges and alters the previous state-society relationship, holds the greatest possibility for transforming state power. For this reason many scholars point to the role of war and international crises in promoting institutional change.[65] Although the exact impact of this restructural strategy depends primarily on government leaders' ideas about what is "efficient" and the societal constraints that they confront, it also depends on other factors not limited to the forums of negotiations, societal cohesion, state legitimacy, and so on. Be that as it may, this approach does provide a sensible way of thinking about the relationship between war preparation and state power.

AN EXCURSION ON STATE POWER

As North tells it, once the British Crown established new property rights to increase the revenue available for war it also increased the power of the capitalist class.[66] Was state power strengthened as a result? It depends on which theorist is consulted. After all, the state increased its extractive capacity, a commonly used measure of state power. In other words, the British experience is consistent with the ratchet effect, as the state increased its penetrative and extractive skills, which directly aided both the war effort and the state's authority over society. Yet the British Crown also conceded some control, as new institutions were developed that granted the capitalist class greater economic and political rights. In short, one version concludes convincingly that state power had expanded, while the other argues that it had been eroded at the hands of an emerging capitalist class.

This episode in British history aptly demonstrates a central issue: war can lead to the simultaneous strengthening of both certain societal actors and the state. Accordingly, an appraisal of the effect of the government's war preparation strategies on state power depends ultimately on the adopted conceptualization of state power. If state power is evaluated according to the means available to state actors, then war increased Brit-

ish state power because the Crown now had previously unavailable extraction tools. But if state power is evaluated relative to the constraints
imposed by societal actors and the ability of the state to act authoritatively, then war eroded British state power. In other words, the state's
"infrastructural" power, its ability to implement its policies, increased,
while its "despotic" power, the "range of actions which the elite is empowered to undertake without routine, institutionalized negotiation
with civil society groups," decreased.[67] In sum, a major problem with
past attempts to provide the causal linkage between war preparation and
state power has been the tendency to pack rather fluid and centrifugal
historical developments into ill-fitting concepts.

Throughout this discussion of conceptualizing and measuring state
power I borrow heavily from two alternative, yet complementary, litera-
tures: state autonomy and state capacity. Each approach contributes important conceptual and measurement insights; the former attends to the
societal properties that effectively constrain state action, whereas the
latter focuses on the means available to state managers in their daily
governance of society.

Defining State Power

State power refers to the resources available to state managers in their
governance of society in relation to societal actors. I am concerned with
both the intrinsic qualities of the state apparatus and its external societal
constraints. This is an important distinction, for state power speaks less
to the ability of state managers to get societal actors to do what they
would otherwise not do, but more to the enduring resources contained
within the state apparatus in relationship to society. I am interested in
"power to" rather than "power over."[68] In other words, that the government refrains from demonstrating and using its full-range of capabilities,
that it abstains from employing all available resources, does not mean
that they are nonexistent. Power may be understood as a resource that
exists regardless of whether actors decide to call on that power. As Giddens argues, "forms of domination cannot be reduced to acts of decisions
taken, or policies forged, by individual agents. . . . 'Decisions' and 'contested policies' represent only one aspect of domination."[69] I am less
concerned with behavioral regularities and more with the enduring
properties of the state and society that empower state actors in their
governance of society.

State power, then, has two contributing properties. The first are the
intrinsic qualities of the state, the enduring resources, the instruments,
tools, and the means extant in the state apparatus and available to state
managers in their daily administration and governance of society.[70]

Briefly, these resources are its control over the instruments of coercion, access to finances, control over production, and the bureaucratic and organizational instruments it has with which to implement its desired objectives. This understanding, then, excludes ideational resources such as legitimacy and status. Although I do not deny their importance, these resources are both difficult to specify in a precise manner and are, "more often than not, a consequence of other resources."[71]

The second determining property of state power is the societal constraint that conditions governmental behavior. I assume that the day-to-day control and management of the economy by private actors is the most powerful constraint on the state.[72] The argument is that "under capitalism all governments must respect and protect the essential claims of those who own the productive wealth of society. Capitalists are endowed with public power, power which no formal institution can overcome."[73] This is so because the economic decisions of capitalists shape the possibilities for continued economic growth, society's consumption opportunities, and the state's fiscal basis; too determined a challenge by the state might upset the economic sensitivities of the capitalist class, thereby jeopardizing these fundamental objectives of state policy. Although the state must be sensitive to other societal interests, the assumption here is that the private control over economic decisions is primary. This is, of course, a core assumption of the relative autonomy of the state literature,[74] which examines the situational conditions that increase (or constrain) the ability of state agents to formulate policies independent of dominant groups and subsequently implement those policies, if needed, in opposition to the interests of dominant classes in society.[75]

In summary, state power refers to the enduring resources contained in the state apparatus that are available to state managers in their daily governance of society and the societal constraints that effectively constrain and limit the actions of those very state managers. As Rueschemeyer and Evans argue, "obstacles to deeply penetrating state interventions . . . may lie as much in greater bureaucratic and political capacities as in the opposition of dominant classes."[76] It is, therefore, imperative that state power be evaluated and measured along both the means available to state managers and the societal constraints on their actions.

Evaluating State Power

State power is best reflected by certain features of the state's fiscal basis—the source and method of extraction of the state's income.[77] One feature common to all states, indeed of all theoretical approaches to the state, is the need to support the services that they provide. The need for revenue is the "great equalizer."

Although the state's fiscal basis is shaped by a number of factors, perhaps most important is the underlying societal distribution of power, and the state's institutional development and administrative competence.[78] The government's ability to increase taxation from the working class or corporate profits, or its need to resort to capital markets, is shaped by both the societal constraints on the state's actions and the means available to state managers. In general, state strategies used in revenue collection and its source of revenue reflect and reveal much of the underlying relationship between state and society.

I evaluate state power along two dimensions, corresponding to the means available to state managers and the societal constraints on their actions. As Radian argues, two distinct issues concern the state's tax policy: its construction and its implementation. Any measure of state power must incorporate both facets.

The Means.

> A state's means of raising and deploying financial resources
> tell us more than could any other single factor about its
> existing (and immediately potential) capacities to create or
> strengthen state organizations, to employ personnel, to coopt
> political support, to subsidize economic enterprises,
> and to fund social programs.
> (*Theda Skocpol, "Bringing the State Back In"*)

The state's extractive capacity has been a highly popular measure of state power. The ability to extract resources from the population, something that individuals of all socioeconomic classes resist, demonstrates and confers some degree of legitimacy and power onto the state.[79] As Organski, Kugler, Johnson, and Cohen argue:

> Taxes can indeed be used as a first step in measuring the extractive capacity of the political system; and since the government's share of national resources ought to increase as political development proceeds, extractive capacity ought to provide an accurate indication of political growth. . . . Given a state's almost limitless demand for revenues, charting the course of taxation is a plausible way of tracing at least in outline the development of the state and the rise of central power.[80]

For many scholars state power and extractive capacity are nearly equivalent concepts.

To gauge the scope and intensity of the means available to state managers I adopt two different measures of resource extraction. The first measure concerns the scope of the state's instruments and examines the *types* of extraction tools available to state managers. Key here is the distinction between direct and indirect methods. Briefly, a direct tax is one "collected directly (or via withholding) from the persons expected to bear the burden of the tax, in the sense of a reduction of real income."[81] In this respect, income taxes, taxes on wealth and property, and corporate taxes (although they do not fit neatly) are all viewed as direct taxes. Conversely, indirect taxes are those "collected from persons other than those expected to bear the burden."[82] Therefore, all customs duties, excise taxes, sales taxes, and stamp taxes can be shifted forward from the original point of collection to consumers of the product that is taxed. In general, indirect taxes are viewed as consumption-related, while direct taxes are seen as income-related.[83]

The general presumption, then, is that there is a positive relationship between a state's capacity and the types of extraction tools it has available.[84] Briefly, "direct taxes are much more difficult to collect than indirect taxes because they require more effective infrastructural power. Taxes on international trade and transactions are the easiest to levy because relatively little infrastructural power is needed to collect them."[85] For instance, most Third World governments depend heavily on indirect methods for extracting resources. Not only do these countries generally capture a larger proportion of their revenue from foreign trade because of their "openness," but they also lack feasible policy alternatives.[86] In general, there is a positive relationship between the directness and openness of the extraction technique and the state's capacity.[87] I follow Snider' suggestion that a crude but instructive indicator of the state's administrative prowess is the origin of the state's revenue; therefore, I adopt the measure of the ratio of direct taxes as a percentage of total revenue as one indicator of state power.[88] A state that derives a larger percentage of its revenue from direct methods has greater infrastructural capacity.[89]

I am interested in not only the range of policy tools but also their intensity. Specifically, I am concerned with the probability that the individual will comply with the state's policies and the effectiveness of the state's instruments for detecting those who fail to do so. Margaret Levi nicely encapsulates this argument with the notion of "quasi-voluntary" compliance, for "it is *voluntary* because taxpayers choose to pay, . . . [and] *quasi* because the noncompliant are subject to coercion—if they are caught." Consequently, compliance occurs "when taxpayers have confidence that (1) rulers will keep their bargains, and (2) the other constituents will keep theirs."[90]

Tax evasion, "the probability of the tax authorities to locate the tax evader,"[91] is a good measure of both the degree of willingness of individuals to adhere to the state's decrees and the probability that they will be caught should they fail to do so. In short, the extent of tax evasion is a good indicator of the state's monitoring and surveillance capacities and its overall legitimacy because states that are able to convince their occupants that their actions are both legitimate and unavoidable are better able to penetrate and control their territorial space in a more concentrated and heightened fashion.[92] Let me say a little more about each.

First, the state's possession of certain technologies and instruments that promote the enforcement of its laws and the monitoring of its environment enable it to catch those individuals who attempt to escape the state's reach.[93] In fact, the very ability of the state to present reasonable approximations of tax evasion represents considerable bureaucratic competence.[94] This surveillance aspect is a primary function of the state bureaucracy because it features an "exercise of control on the basis of knowledge. . . . For they [holders of office] acquire through the conduct of office a special knowledge of facts and have available a store of documentary material peculiar to themselves."[95] The state apparatus's ability to enforce its laws is enhanced by its possession of the "technologies of power," which is enhanced through such mundane activities as constructing an infrastructure, expanding literacy, adopting standard coinage and weights, and developing modern technologies (e.g., the computer and the photocopy machine); all these permit state officials to enforce and monitor society more effectively.[96] As Giddens astutely observes, one need possess no further evidence of the state's tremendous surveillance capabilities in core capitalist countries than the plethora of statistics and information concerning every aspect of human behavior.[97] This is in contrast to the "not available" figures in the Third World, which partially reflect the state's inability to monitor its society. In general, those states that have a well-developed surveillance and monitoring capacity are better able to minimize the extent of tax evasion. Not only is the state able to locate and punish the noncompliant, but the prospective dissenter is also dissuaded from attempting to circumvent the state's dictates because of the perception that doing so exposes her or him to state punishment.

Individuals have a motivation to evade tax authorities not only when they believe that the state is unable to detect and punish defectors, but also when they perceive that the tax is unjust and unfair and/or the requesting state has little legitimacy.[98] Levi argues that taxpayers have an ideological motivation for adhering to the tax bargain "as long as they are confident that others are contributing and only as long as they are relatively certain that the good will be provided once paid for."[99] The state must be viewed as credible deliverers of the promised services and just enforcers of the revenue bargain. Should it fail in either of these activities individuals are less likely to cooperate with tax authorities.[100]

Institutional linkages, the forums of negotiation between state and society, are critical for shaping the citizenry's evaluation of the state's legitimacy. In the contemporary era nearly all states claim to adhere to legal forms of domination, in which the state's laws are seen as deriving their authority from its citizenry.[101] These institutions of representation, then, are often important as both legitimating and penetrating devices for the state's policies.[102] Stated simply, individuals are more willing to contribute to the state's activities when they confer some measure of legitimacy upon the state, agree with the state's agenda, and believe they have some determination over it. This provides, then, one reason why authorities are better able to increase taxes during periods of war.

There are compelling reasons, then, to focus on the scope and intensity of the state's extractive capacities as an accurate indicator of the state's capacity and means to govern society. Much can be learned through examining the percentage of the revenue that derives from direct sources and the extent of tax evasion, for these measures indicate the development of the state apparatus, the ability of the state to survey and monitor its environment, and the legitimacy conferred upon the state by society.

The reliance on resource extraction as the *sole* indicator of state power, however, involves two problematic assumptions. First, resource extraction is typically evaluated with respect to some absolute amount that the state, under "ideal" conditions, should be able to extract. In other words, the government is judged according to the proportion of the absolute amount of the anticipated extraction it collects. The underlying assumption is of a state that maximizes its potential resource extraction; that is, the state wants as much as possible. Hence, any uncollected revenue indicates a state weakness in the face of external political and economic constraints. The conclusion is, then, that those states that extract more are more powerful. But governments may institute different extraction policies in the context of different objectives and may choose not to maximize resource extraction. Are we to assume, for instance, that the U.S. state is less powerful because it cuts taxes over a two-year period? This conclusion rightfully appears dubious, yet it follows logically from this measure of state power. As Afxentiou argues, such "tax effort indices are squarely based on the premise that the only criterion of tax policy is the success by which resources are transferred from the private to the public sector and mobilized for government-guided economic development."[103] A measure of state power of the kind employed by these scholars does not take into account the government's intentions.

There is a second, related, problem with this measure. Because power is equated with resource extraction—that is, the act of extracting—power is acknowledged only when one observes its use. This is most evident from the proposition that the citizenry resist all tax efforts by the state, thus implicitly adopting a definition of power that is the ability of the state to get its citizenry to do what it would not do otherwise. Alternatively, a state may have the power to extract more (as in the example of the United States) but may forgo such opportunities for various reasons. Thus, this perspective only considers what the government chooses to do, not what it potentially could have done; in this way it ignores the fact that power exists outside its empirical demonstration. It is important that any adopted measure(s) incorporates both the societal constraints that limit the state's fiscal strategy, and the state's administrative muscle and abilities that shape the state's fiscal policy. Therefore, although the state's extractive capacity does reveal some important features of state power, it is highly limited in some key respects.

The Constraints. The principal constraint on the state derives from the fact that it is institutionally separated from organized production and, therefore, does not produce its own source of revenue.[104] State managers must be attentive to and are constrained by the flow of resources upon which the deployment of the state's means depend. Accordingly, many scholars are quick to identify the state's relationship to financial resources as an important determinant of its autonomy.[105] As Stallings forcefully argues, "the sufficient condition [for relative state autonomy] is resources."[106] The concern, then, is how patterns of economic ownership shape and constrain the range of "acceptable" state financial policies. In general, one virtue of examining the underlying distribution of economic power for the constraints on state action is that we are able to isolate theoretically a critical aspect of power that does not rely on behavioral properties, which was a major downfall of resource extraction measures. Although it may be impossible to derive an exhaustive set of counterfactuals—that is, "the could have beens"—the ability to capture some logical features of power without resorting solely to observed actions may still exist.[107]

I propose to examine the state's fiscal basis and observe whether significant changes in the types of financial resources are available to the state, and the implicit and explicit conditions attached to them. In general, the constraints on the state lessen if it can secure a source of revenue not derived from the capitalist class's investment decisions. Consequently, the state's ability either to develop alternative sources of financial means or to loosen its dependence on the capitalist class substantially increases its autonomy.[108]

There are two possible sources of financial autonomy. First, acquiring foreign loans might give the state an additional instrument of control.[109] Specifically, international finance capital and foreign governments can provide considerable resources at the state's behest with relatively few strings. The state can then use these resources to oppose the interests of the dominant class; conditions that may enhance the position of dominant classes in society are often attached to loans from public sources.[110]

Second, other societally independent funds originate in the productive capabilities controlled by the state itself. Because societal power derives from the control over productive facilities, the state's control over production—particularly evident in the Third World—may limit the power of these private economic elites. The use of the state's ownership patterns as a measure of its autonomy, however, should be approached cautiously, for it is bound up with important conceptual issues that revolve around the function of the public sector in the capital accumulation process. For instance, how do we characterize those instances when the state undertakes those nonprofitable economic activities that serve the long-term interests of domestic and foreign capital, or when the public sector becomes another avenue for private actors to infiltrate and influence the state and its policies?[111] One can generalize E. V. K. Fitzgerald's argument concerning Latin America:

> The relationship [between the state and capital] is complicated by the fact that ever since the formation of nation states in Latin America the securing of profit within their oligopolized economies has depended upon privileges and concessions obtained by access to government, so that a "propertied" rather than an "entrepreneurial" business ethos obtains based on control over a limited market and exclusive licenses instead of mass sales and price competition. *This has reduced the ideological antagonism between "public" and "private" sectors observed in developed economies.*[112]

The public/private distinction is hazy in most of the Third World as well as in many advanced industrialized countries.

These issues do not necessarily vitiate the validity of state ownership as an indicator of autonomy, but it does caution us against sweeping generalizations. Specifically, great care must be paid to the composition of the state apparatus and whether it is staffed by those sympathetic to the interests of dominant class interests.[113] Simply put, if everything else is equal, a state personnel distinct from the capitalist classes is less likely to commit itself to this class's agenda. In general, the size of the public sector is a potentially useful indicator of the state's autonomy, but its validity is highly dependent upon a careful reading of the particular case.[114]

These indicators derived from the state's fiscal basis are intended as a guide to both the principal constraints on state's actions in general and the Israeli and Egyptian cases in specific. Whereas measures of extractive capacity are attractive given their crossnational and acontextual properties, indicators of the source of the state's revenue and the obligations they entail are appealing precisely because while they point to some important theoretical concerns, a precise evaluation requires greater attention to the dynamics of the state-society relationship under investigation.

In sum, state power is understood as the means available to state managers in relation to societal actors. This conception, then, is concerned with both the enduring resources that enable the state to penetrate, govern, and monitor society and the behavioral regularities associated with state actions. By carefully examining the fiscal relationship between the state and society, we may be able to generate a more accurate understanding of state power. Most important, this conception of state power provides for the more sensitive evaluation of the relationship between war preparation and state power, for it allows the distinct possibility that war might simultaneously expand the state's means while increasing the societal constraints on implementing and using those very means.

This chapter has attempted to instill greater precision in the causal linkages between war preparation and state power by examining three issues. First, I specified the determinants of the government's war preparation strategies. I argued that given the government's objectives and the preexisting environmental constraints, it would construct a strategy that attempts to prepare for war while shielding itself from domestic instability. Accordingly, regardless of the decision context, the government initially moves toward an accommodational strategy, one that tailors and restricts its policy considerations to the preexisting set of policy instruments, deviates little from past practices, and therefore carries few political risks. Either unfulfilled security needs or societal protests propel the government to consider a restructural or an international policy, which depends on the decision context, availability of and conditions attached to foreign assistance, the state's legitimacy, and societal cohesion. Its secondary choice may be further modified, given the existence of either societal resistance or an inadequate material base.

Second, I provided the causal linkage between the government's war preparation strategies and state power. The transformation or conservation of state power depends on the type of war preparation strategy adopted by the government and how the government "compensates" society for access to these societally controlled resources. My final endeavor was to present a conceptualization and measurement of state power that was both more in keeping with how we understand the nature of the state and power and more useful for evaluating the relationship between war preparation and state power.

This chapter has constructed the theoretical framework for investigating the state's war preparation strategies and their important transformative qualities for state power. The succeeding chapters, to which I now turn, extend this theoretical argument to the empirical cases of Egypt and Israel between the years 1952–1977 and 1948–1977, respectively. Here I attempt to entertain a dialogue between theory and data,[115] to employ the theoretical framework for both reinterpreting the course of Israeli and Egyptian history and subsequently using these cases to reevaluate the theoretical argument.

CHAPTER THREE.

Egypt and Israel in Historical Perspective

BY SITUATING the Israeli and Egyptian cases in their historical contexts, I thereby provide an understanding of both the initial enabling and constraining conditions on each government's war preparation strategies and the nature of state power in each country. This chapter focuses on those features of the social and economic structure identified as important determinants of the government's war preparation strategies and contributing factors to state power. This historical exposition and documentation of Egypt's and Israel's economic and political development isolates those features of each country that are important to the present study.

EGYPT

My discussion has two main points. First, I cosider the broad sweep of Egypt's economic development until 1952, concentrating on the development of the economic structure and ownership patterns as a result of its colonial past. I also examine the political structure from the time of Egyptian independence in 1922 until 1952. Second, I outline Egyptian state power at midcentury, with particular attention to the state's fiscal capacity and relationship to economic resources.

Colonial History

As a Third World country, Egypt's political and economic life has been colored and transformed by centuries of foreign rule and domination, most recently by the Ottoman Empire and Great Britain. Although Egypt had established some autonomy from the ruling Ottoman Empire under Muhammad Ali during the early 1800s, outside influence from both foreign governments and metropolitan capital increased throughout the nineteenth century, culminating in Britain's status as its colonial protector in February 1881. Although Egypt achieved formal independence from Britain in 1922, its sovereignty was stunted, as the government's policies were constantly monitored to ensure that British interests in the region were protected. Specifically, under the terms of the 1922 treaty Britain reserved several rights: to imperial communication;

to defend Egypt in the case of any foreign aggression or interference, direct or indirect; to protect the interests of minorities and foreign residents in Egypt; and to supervise the Sudan. Although the 1936 Anglo-Egyptian Treaty was a step toward greater Egyptian autonomy, the outbreak of World War Two caused Britain to invoke the "foreign aggression" clause and occupy the country militarily. Hereafter, the British objective was to maintain political and military influence in this strategic area while the Egyptian goal was to remove the most visible aspect of colonialism from its soil. After World War Two Egyptian officials regained some of their lost independence, but Britain retained a protectorate status over the Suez Canal. Egyptian actions were cautious and predicated on the assumption, corroborated by past and future events, that direct British military intervention was possible if British regional interests were threatened. Only after Nasser's overthrow of King Farouk in 1952 did Egypt have a political leader not instrumentally connected with either the dominant classes or foreign interests. In general, foreign domination and recent colonial penetration had an important impact on the development of the economy, and profoundly influenced and shaped all future attempts by the state to mobilize resources for national security.

Political Economy. Although Britain's military presence on Egyptian soil was the most visible display of the former's influence and control over Egyptian affairs, arguably in the economic sphere British policy was most evident, pervasive, and lasting. British colonial practices reinforced and exacerbated, though by no means determined, certain emerging patterns in the local economy and cemented Egypt's underdeveloped status and susceptibility to the world economy.

Although Egypt is commonly understood as an agricultural economy, this was not always the case. Egypt had achieved some moderate success at state-led industrialization during the reign of Muhammad Ali (1801–1832), but this early effort was halted by both domestic inefficiencies and foreign factors.[1] By the 1830s Egypt's industrialization program had come upon hard times, and the 1838 Treaty of London—which limited the size of the military (representing a large part of domestic demand), ended state monopolies, and established the principle of free trade—concluded Egypt's industrialization efforts and left it vulnerable to foreign influence.[2] Moreover, the capitulations, which granted foreign residents in Egypt special economic and political privileges, invited greater foreign leverage over Egypt's future. Issawi succinctly captures this chapter of Egyptian history: "The attempted leap from a subsistence to a complex economy had failed, and instead the country had landed on the road to an export-oriented economy. Egypt could now be integrated, as an agricultural unit, in the world-wide economic system."[3]

Its integration into the world economy was advanced by both Egyptian Khedives and British administrators. By the 1850s the agricultural sector, and cotton in particular, had become central to the country's economic well-being. To fund large-scale irrigation and public works projects for cotton expansion, a series of Egyptian rulers borrowed substantial funds from European banking houses in the mid to late 1800s. Although the economy expanded, so too did Egypt's foreign indebtedness.[4] This established a cycle: Egyptian rulers borrowed more funds to turn over current debts; this allowed foreign creditors to gain more control over Egypt's financial affairs. Egypt's financial status rapidly deteriorated during this period and climaxed in its official declaration of bankruptcy in 1876 and the imposition of foreign financial control on the Egyptian government. Hereafter British and French authorities and financiers established control over all aspects of Egypt's fiscal life. To fulfill Egypt's debt payments, greater tax hardships were placed on most of the working classes and peasantry. This development led to the anticolonialist Arabi rebellion in 1881, which gave Britain the provocation to take formal control of Egypt's military and economic activities. Although Gladstone's professed objective in Egypt was to defend the Canal, in fact it was nothing more than a thinly veiled plan to restore a measure of fiscal sanity to Egypt's treasury and ensure that Egypt's outstanding foreign debt of nearly LE 100 million would be honored.[5]

Cotton's dominance was cemented by British colonial and "free trade" policy; it dictated that because Egypt was a "natural" producer of agricultural products, the country should be limited to this particular economic activity.[6] British colonial policy furthered this along with the extension of capitalist property relations and irrigation, and they hoped this plan would also increase the state's income, which could then be used to repay foreign creditors.[7] The nurturance of agricultural and cotton production produced a powerful landed class. Although 12,000 landowners held at least fifty feddans each and 2,000 families maintained greater holdings, a few owners controlled most land (see table 3.1). These same

TABLE 3.1
Distribution of Land Ownership, 1894–1952

	Small Holdings (0–5 feddans)		Medium Holdings (5–50 feddans)		Large Holdings (50 + feddans)	
	% of owners	% of land	% of owners	% of land	% of owners	% of land
1894	83.3	21.7	15.4	34.3	1.3	44.0
1914	91.3	26.7	8.5	30.4	0.8	43.9
1930	93.1	31.6	6.3	29.7	0.6	38.7
1952	94.3	35.4	5.2	30.4	0.5	34.2

Source: Abdel-Malek, *Egypt: Military Society*, 57.

TABLE 3.2
Composition of Egyptian Imports and Exports, 1885–1929

	Imports (total value and percentage)				
	1885–89	*1900–04*	*1910–14*	*1920–24*	*1925–29*
Food, drink, tobacco	2,444	4,402	7,702	17,088	15,222
Percentage	30.8	27.0	30.5	27.5	27.1
Other consumer goods	3,210	6,419	9,497	26,253	21,849
Textiles	2,586	4,898	6,838	19,326	15,417
Percentage	40.4	39.4	37.6	42.3	38.9
Producer goods	2,291	5,478	8,054	18,727	19,155
Percentage	28.8	33.6	31.9	30.2	34.0
Total Imports	10,498	21,503	33,933	63,141	57,267

	Exports (total value and percentage)				
	1885–89	*1900–04*	*1910–14*	*1920–24*	*1925–29*
Agricultural produce	2,316	2,560	4,044	5,262	5,396
Cotton seed	1,352	1,766	2,299	3,210	2,610
Percentage	17.0	12.0	11.0	8.0	10.0
Cotton	7,548	14,228	23,788	49,851	42,306
Percentage	56.0	68.0	63.0	81.0	80.0
Other	3,609	4,084	10,165	6,789	5,027
Percentage	27.0	20.0	26.0	11.0	10.0
Total Exports	13,473	20,872	37,997	61,902	52,729

Source: Donald Mead (1967).

large landowners, dominating the political process, held most positions in the state.[8] Indicative of their access to political power was the fact that the king was one of the largest landowners in Egypt. Cotton's importance in the Egyptian economy grew under British tutelage.

Under Britain's counsel Egypt's pattern of foreign trade became typical of many Third World countries: export cheap agricultural and primary products to, and import finished, manufactured goods from, Western Europe (see table 3.2). Cotton soon became the dominant export crop, accounting for more than 80 percent of all exports by the early 1900s, and Egypt exchanged it for finished textiles from British factories. British free trade policy and the capitulations assured a continued dominance of both agricultural production and foreign control over the economy.

Britain's laissez-faire economic attitude in the rural sector was not extended to urban sector activity. While the land was largely under the control of an Egyptian agrarian bourgeoisie, credit, foreign trade, and shipping were nearly monopolized by non-Egyptians.[9] Here British policy, which included Egypt's inability to raise any sort of protective barriers, purposefully obstructed any Egyptian manufacturing development that might compete with British firms.[10] This policy, in combination with the relative profitability of agricultural and cotton production, meant that little manufacturing development ensued.[11] The manufacturing activity that did emerge, a result of activities associated with processing and distributing agricultural products, depended on foreign capitalist activity (due in part to their privileges from the capitulations). For instance, whereas before 1882 most investment decisions were in the hands of local officials and investors, the following decades record a rise in the paid-up capital operating in Egypt from LE 7,326,000 in 1892, to LE 26,280,000 in 1902, to LE 87,176,000 in 1907, nearly all of which was raised from foreign investors, and most investment went to areas other than manufacturing.[12] Although some industrial and manufacturing projects were initiated by domestic sources, these almost always ended in failure.[13] In general, the period before World War One witnessed Egypt's integration into the world economy, establishment of a mono-economy oriented toward the world market, and malnourishment of a manufacturing and industrial base that could further development.

Such was the case until the 1920s when Egypt's fledgling national bourgeoisie and the prominent Bank Misr group embarked upon a campaign to promote industrial and commercial enterprises owned and operated by Egyptians.[14] The Bank Misr group was largely derived from that fraction of the landed class that wanted to diversify Egypt's economic base and its control over industrial development.[15] The group soon shed its antiforeign stance, however, and encouraged foreign capital's participation because of the latter's resources and privileges.[16] Four developments stimulated this renewed concern for industrialization and its qualified success. First, the worldwide economic downturn in the 1930s alerted the agrarian classes of the dangers of relying on cotton alone for its economic well-being. As a result, some landed classes began to diversify their economic interests and to invest in the urban sector. Second, the government's attitude toward industry changed, as some officials now believed industrialization to be a necessary component of a vibrant economy and integral to their future revenue base. Third, in 1930 the government successfully negotiated with Britain some measure of fiscal autonomy and the right to raise protective tariffs. Finally, both world wars and the stationing of foreign troops on Egyptian soil stimulated a demand for consumer nondurables.[17] Such changes were even more dramatic when added to the fortunes of a growing domestic capitalist class and the beginnings of a small but expanding factory system and set of commercial enterprises.[18] Indeed, from 1930 to 1945 industrial investment rose dramatically and agricultural dropped off considerably. Despite such developments, however, the Egyptian economy was still dominated by agricultural production, as the proportion of the GDP that originated from the agricultural sector declined from 49 percent in 1937 to 44 percent in 1945, while manufacturing increased over the same period from 8 to 11 percent. Moreover, the pattern of foreign trade changed little from established patterns.

In summary, Egypt was characterized by the following pronounced patterns of economic activity. Agriculture and cotton dominated economic production. Although there were some strides toward greater manufacturing capacity, those patterns established by British colonial practices changed little. Moreover, a domestic bourgeoisie was stirring, but they were relatively weak when compared to the strength of the landed and foreign capitalist classes. Finally, the economy's dependence on both agricultural exports for its revenue and direct foreign investment for most investment capital meant that the entire economy was subject to the fluctuations and rhythms of the international economy.

Political Structure. Egypt's formal but nominal independence in 1922 established a monarchical form of government, with power shared between the king and the parliament. Egypt's largest political party, the Wafd, credited with obtaining Egypt's independence from Britain, won the vast majority of seats in the first parliamentary elections. King Fuad resigned himself to the electoral outcome and the Wafd's parliamentary supremacy. A cycle soon developed, however. King Fuad (and later Farouk) found a pretext in which to dismiss the parliament. The king succeeded in ruling alone for a short time, but then he realized that governing without the Wafd was nearly impossible because it ostensibly represented society's nationalist aspirations; moreover, Britain demanded the Wafd's reinstatement because of its desire to maintain political stability. The Wafd, though stridently anticolonialist, tempered its political demands for fear of British intervention if it went too far. This delicate balance between Britain's interests, the palace's desire for autocratic rule, and the Wafd's nationalism produced a highly unstable political situation that continued unabated from 1922 until 1952.[19]

Part of the political instability was a result of the division within the economy and the interests it generated. The agrarian capitalist class's interests were well-represented by the palace; the king himself was the largest landowner. The Wafd represented an amalgam of nationalist and anti-British interests, which included large landowners (indeed, ten of the fourteen original members of the Wafd's high command were large landowners), middle-sized landowners, merchants, government employees, some intellectuals, and the urban middle class.[20] The Wafd is best described as a "bourgeois nationalist party" whose leadership lent a conservative air, including a commitment to strengthening market forces based on Egyptian interests, while its more populist rank and file played a more radicalizing role.[21]

After World War Two this division between the landed and industrial classes created a political stalemate, which was aggravated by a continuing economic recession.[22] Egypt was experiencing "growth without development." Despite modest growth rates, any economic advance was limited to the capitalist classes, while the rest of society marched backward.[23] The key factor inhibiting development was land reform. The landed elite suppressed all attempts at land reform, which further impoverished the peasantry and created an exodus to the cities. The pace of industrial activity, however, was too slow to absorb the influx of peasants in search of jobs.[24] Because of such economic failings some members of the domestic capitalist class and intellectual circles supported the proposition that Egypt had to make the transition from an agricultural to a modern, industrial society if development was to proceed and revolution and social conflict were to be averted. There was little agreement, however, concerning which societal class should pay the price and subsidize the effort. Illustrative of this elite conflict was the policy debate concerning the overhaul of the taxation system in the late 1940s.[25] Because the masses clearly could not be taxed without their further radicalization and possible societal revolt, the controversy centered on which fraction of the capitalist class would bear primary responsibility. Industrial and rural elites each believed that they already bore an unfair share of the tax burden and demanded that the other provide the needed funds. The result was little change in the tax structure, dwindling revenues, and increasing societal conflict.

In general, the country appeared stalled in an economic and political crisis. The landed classes blocked any progressive change,[26] while the palace was too wedded to both British and landed interests to provide the needed political muscle and leadership. Finally, the expanding resource gap and internal class conflict stymied any chance of expanding the state's development efforts. The continuing domestic crisis provided the conditions for the Free Officers' entry into politics in July 1952.

State Power

British colonial policies were vital in transforming Egypt's economy and polity. That Great Power forces shaped the character of Egyptian state power situates the Egyptian experiences with that of most Third World countries. In explaining Egyptian state power at the time of the Revolution in 1952, however, it is important to recognize Egypt's unique historical development and how it differs from the typical Third World experience. Egyptian state power can be accurately gauged by examining the state's relationship to the economy and its fiscal capacities.

Two features characterize most Third World states that were affected by colonialism. First, the colonial power typically invests the state with a relatively impressive array of administrative and political resources, thus enabling it to control and maintain order in society. Hence, these bureaucratic powers are imposed by foreign powers; because they do not provide a direct expression of domestic forces, they leave the state both "powerful and fragile."[27] Although the state has a high degree of autonomy from societal interests because it is a creature of colonialism and not directly tied to domestic interests, it is fragile because of the corresponding difficulty of maintaining legitimacy from a society to whom it is alien. A second feature of the Third World state is its peripherality, which is a consequence of its economic role as a supplier of raw materials and agricultural goods to, and an importer of manufactured and processed materials from, core capitalist countries. This economic pattern establishes a set of domestic interests closely associated with those of foreign capital and a domestic economy heavily dependent on the international economy for its economic development. Thus, the state is constrained by both an international economy on which it was wholly and nakedly dependent for its resources and by a society with whom it lacks legitimacy.

This analysis does partial justice to the Egyptian state. Although it aptly captures Egypt's peripherality and dependence on and susceptibility to the international economy, it does not accurately characterize the Egyptian state's development and legitimacy. On the one hand, the idea of a central, organizing authority is not new, for Egypt has had a centralized political authority with an impressive array of administrative powers for approximately five thousand years. This centralizing tendency originated in Egypt's development as a hydraulic society and the need to control the Nile's rhythms and movements for successful irrigation and agricultural production. On the other hand, British colonialism was responsible for creating a more efficient and extensive state apparatus in two areas critical to Egypt's control over society—irrigation and taxation.[28] The state's administrative development was neither produced by nor solely imposed by foreign forces; it evolved through both internal and external factors. Egypt differs from its Third World brethren in a number of respects. First, while the state apparatus may have grown under Britain's guidance, the idea of a centralized political authority that demands obedience and allegiance is not alien to Egyptian society, but, as some claim, it is integral to Egyptian culture.[29] Second, although many Third World countries in the throes of state building are challenged by a lack of legitimacy, the issue facing Egyptian society had

more to do with the type of political authority than with its very existence. Third, unlike the rest of Africa, Egypt's borders were not the
creation of European forces, but a result of its own rich and long history.[30] Moreover, its borders contained a relatively homogeneous population that had a national identity, people who had an Egyptian identity.
Separate minority and ethnic identities were the exception, not the rule,
and posed little challenge to the state's legitimacy.

Because of such historical legacies the Egyptian state is often characterized as "powerful" or "strong." As opposed to these appraisals,
however, I see the Egyptian state as relatively weak in a number of respects, which is reflected in the state's autonomy and capacity. With
respect to the state's autonomy, although the state was not a creature of
foreign forces, colonialism created the socioeconomic conditions that
would limit the state's future actions and options. A dominant agrarian
capitalist class that had direct ties to the palace had prospered under
British aegis, both of whom had some interest in perpetuating the link
to foreign capital.[31] Although the relatively free elections indicated that
the Egyptian state had to consider the interests of the industrial classes
and masses, albeit in a much more limited fashion, the state evidenced
little autonomy from dominant societal interests. Consequently, the
state was stymied from initiating any reforms that might damage the
interests of the landed classes because of its dependence on agricultural
products for its revenue and its lack of financial resources with which to
launch such reforming measures. This, in part, caused the palace's atro-
phy and inability to promote those policies that may have averted the
1952 takeover.

The state also had little capacity. Despite the long history of centralized political authority and the presence of superficial administrative
powers, the state did not have the ability to implement its policies, even
if it had the autonomy, in most areas of public life. Many areas of the
state's authority were circumscribed because of the interests of foreigners. The principle of extraterritoriality, that Europeans in Ottoman
lands should be governed by European laws, which descends from the
capitulations of Suleiman the Magnificent (1535), was pushed farther in
Egypt because of the advantage Westerners enjoyed by virtue of their
home countries' military superiority and the political weakness of the
Egyptian regime during the 1800s. Britain's aptitude at circumscribing
Egyptian authority and the development of the means of the apparatus
are also evidenced in the mixed court system, which ensured that European interests in Egypt were protected by European law because supposedly "Islamic law" was unsuited to such a task.[32]

Moreover, the capacities that were developed were largely owing to
the efforts of colonial authorities. The Treaty of London that disbanded
the army created by Muhammad Ali, in combination with the growing

economic power of the local landed elite, both circumscribed the means available to the state and shifted political power to the agrarian classes. The British landing in 1881 restored some balance toward the state, but the bureaucratic administration became the creature of and controlled by British authorities and troops. For instance, Goldberg argues that "Egypt did not have a centralized and powerful state based on control of an irrigation system reaching back to the Pharonic era. It was the British who perfected and centralized the irrigation system so that it could become the basis for greater state control of the countryside."[33]

The Egyptian state's limited capacity due to external interventions is further demonstrated in its control over the instruments of coercion. From 200 B.C.E. until the reign of Muhammad Ali no native Egyptian was required to perform military service, "no matter how low his social status, Egyptians considered this exemption as one of their few precious rights."[34] Muhammad Ali intended to pursue his dreams of regional power through the use of Mamlukes, foreign officers, and slave labor from neighboring African countries; he preferred to use the fellahin (Egyptian peasantry) in agricultural rather than military service.[35] The Greek war of independence disrupted Ali's manpower plans, as he was now forced to recruit fellahin into a foreign-led army. "They resented their new role, especially because foreign rulers did not allow them to rise to positions of command."[36] Although compulsory military service was an unwelcome policy of Ali, those who could afford to buy their way out did so with zeal, which proved an important contribution to the state's purse.[37] The peasants, too poor to buy their way out of military service, served in greater numbers and provided the bulk of the enlisted.

Although this social stratification of the military, with the officers' corps trained and manned by foreigners and the ranks filled by the peasantry, was introduced by Muhammad Ali, it was solidified by foreign intervention. The Treaty of London forced Ali to permanently reduce the size of the military to no more than 18,000 men, less than one-tenth its prior maximum size,[38] and to maintain the privileged status of foreigners in the Egyptian army. In fact, the Arabi Revolt of 1881, which directly challenged European privileges in and control over Egyptian affairs and provided the pretext for formal British control over Egypt, was initiated by Colonel Arabi, who was moved to act because of the stratification of the Egyptian military and that native Egyptians were forbidden from rising above the rank of colonel.[39]

The indirect European control over the Egyptian military was formalized after the British occupation in 1881. If the army represents the ultimate means available to state managers in their governance of society, it is noteworthy that this instrument was now ruled by and reflected British interests, as the non-British foreign officers (mainly French and

German) under Egyptian employ were dismissed and replaced with British officers.[40] According to Tignor:

> The military was far more under the control of the British and its development much more carefully regulated. . . . The top positions within the army were held by the British, and every effort was made to ferret out discontent and deal with it firmly. The military crisis of 1894 only intensified these tendencies with the British administration. Egyptian officers could hardly expect promotions unless they had demonstrated loyalty to British rule. The military, then, did not develop in as autonomous a fashion as the bureaucracy.[41]

This, as can be expected, generated a fair bit of resent among the military in general and the officers' corps in particular. Perlmutter nicely captures the scenario:

> As the army declined under the British, so did professionalism, and the officer class gradually became alienated, lost all prestige, and eventually expressed nationalistic and even radical sentiments. The problem was not merely one of the professional soldier being loyal to the state: it was a question of what type of authority deserved his loyalty. . . . A crucial point was reached when the monarchy, in the estimation of the nationalist officers, became a pawn of internal and external imperialism.[42]

This scenario vividly describes what galvanized Nasser and his fellow Free Officers to "Egyptianize" the state apparatus and liberate Egypt from its colonial shackles.

Financial History. The Egyptian state's limited autonomy and capacity is reflected by its lack of control over its own finances. This financial profile is attributed to colonialism and the extraterritorial status given Europeans residing and doing business in Egypt. Because of the capitulations the Egyptian treasury became a tempting target for Europeans who claimed compensation because of wrongs committed by the Egyptian state. As Landes tells it:

> The result was a spoiler's field day. Nothing was too far-fetched to serve as an excuse for a raid on the viceroy's purse. If a man was robbed because of his own negligence, the government was at fault for not maintaining law and order. Indemnity. If a man sailed his boat poorly and caused it to founder, the government was at fault for leaving the sandbar there. Indemnity. One litigant, an Austrian noble named Castellani, succeeded with the help of his government in extorting 700,000 francs on the grounds, manifestly falsified, that twenty-eight cases of silk cocoons had been ruined by exposure to the sun when a train from Suez to Cairo started late.[43]

Egyptian control over its treasury deteriorated even further once the British became the legal executors of Egyptian finances in 1881.

Not only did Egyptian rulers have few mechanisms to shield their revenues from being looted, but they had few opportunities to increase the amount of revenue available. The capitulations of 1837 forbade the Egyptian state from introducing any taxes that might affect foreign residents without the prior approval of their respective governments, a ruling that effectively precluded any but the most nominal changes in the tax code. Foreign control over Egypt's tax policies became more pronounced once Britain occupied Egypt in 1881. Only two types of taxes were allowed during this period—building and land—both of which were minimal and whose costs could easily be transferred to nonpropertied classes. In fact, in the 1880s Lord Cromer, consular general of Egypt, revised an original land tax program to meet the interests of the landed class because "an alien government . . . has to be much more circumspect than any native government."[44] Consequently, direct taxes weighed heaviest on the agricultural population and the peasants,[45] while most revenue derived from customs duties. In general, the state was prevented from any kind of interventionist role in most areas of economic activity, and this included the ability both to raise tariffs to promote domestic industries and to impose new taxes to increase its revenues.[46]

This tax structure remained unchanged until 1930, when the British permitted the Egyptian government some measure of fiscal autonomy. The government promptly imposed its first tariffs on imports with Customs Duties Law No. 2, thereby dramatically increasing its revenue. The Egyptian state gained further tax autonomy when the capitulations ended with the Montreux Convention in 1937, which gave the state the right to determine its own tax laws. The tax system was immediately overhauled for the first time. Although the tax structure had weighed the heaviest on the agricultural population and the lightest on industrialists and merchants, the latter claimed such tax measures were essential and justified for economic investment.[47] After a political struggle, Tax Law No. 14 in 1939 taxed three new sources of wealth: (1) dividends from stocks and bonds and interest on bank deposits; (2) industrial and commercial wages and salaries; and (3) inheritance earnings amounting to a modest 5.6 percent. Moreover, the land tax was revised downward to a fixed 16 percent.[48] Thus, the newly devised tax structure accurately reflected the underlying societal distribution of political power. The landed classes, disfavored because of British colonial policy, successfully reduced their burden, while that of the growing urban labor and industrial classes increased. According to the Central Bank of Egypt, "Further tax legislation maintained the financial control and expressed the interests of the ruling class and the rich landowners on whom no taxation was levied for agricultural exploitation."[49] Such reform, however, did not offset the chronic budget deficits.

World War Two delayed desperately needed tax reform. The budget had expanded dramatically owing to both expanding the military's commitment and entry into the Palestine War and subsidizing the masses' deteriorating living conditions. Further tax revision finally occurred in 1949, which included a progressive income tax to replace the now antiquated durtax, a temporary tax on industry (which was repealed the following year), and a further decrease in the land tax from 16 to 14 percent.[50] The Egyptian ministries, however, were able to shift some burden from the small to the large landowners.[51]

Despite such tax measures and reforms, the dominant classes never agreed on the nature of the tax system and means of funding economic development, social welfare, and the Palestine War:

> Tax squabbles were a harbinger of future ruling class discord. Even though the landed notables had begun to diversify their economic activities, as yet there was not a unity of interests between landowners and industrialists. The rulers had yet to determine which sector of the economy was to pay for increased military expenditure and new programs for social welfare.[52]

The state's tax policy accurately reflects the underlying distribution of political power and established the parameters for future tax reform in post-1952 Egypt.[53]

In addition to the societal determinants of the state's fiscal policy, the source of the state's revenue followed a pattern similar to most Third World countries—heavy dependence on foreign trade for its tax receipts. "It . . . expresses the government's dependence on specific types of taxation measures, the imposition of which does not necessarily require an administration of a high degree of efficiency."[54] The state could more easily monitor border transactions and had the policy tools necessary to extract revenue here.[55]

In summary, the state's fiscal policy reveals both the societal distribution of political power of the Egyptian classes and the state's limited capacities (see table 3.3). Although the state took on increased budgetary commitments, it could not raise the needed revenue because of class interests. Moreover, even if it had found the strength to increase its extraction efforts, it is unlikely that it would have been able to enforce such policies in the face of determined evaders because of the state's limited infrastructural capacities. This, in part, led to the state's propensity for indirect measures that were inherently easier to collect and, at the same time, weighed heavier on the lower classes.

Thus, by 1952 Egypt was a typical underdeveloped country. Years of colonial rule had cemented Egypt's dependence on agricultural production with a powerful landed class at its political center. There was little manufacturing and practically no industrial activity. Most of its revenues derived from agricultural activity and custom duties. Nasser came to

TABLE 3.3
Origin of Egyptian Taxation Revenue, 1945/46–1951/52

	Government Revenue Obtained from Individual Sources (in percentage)						
	1945/46	*1946/47*	*1947/48*	*1948/49*	*1949/50*	*1950/51*	*1951/52*
Land tax	4.3	3.8	3.8	2.2	3.4	3.0	6.2
House tax	1.1	1.0	1.2	0.8	0.9	1.3	0.4
Income tax	8.7	7.0	8.7	6.7	6.7	6.3	7.1
Surplus profits tax	5.0	4.7	2.8	3.1	2.3	1.6	0.4
Inheritance tax	0.3	0.4	0.3	0.5	0.4	0.3	0.3
Tax on sale of property	1.5	1.1	1.2	1.1	1.1	1.1	1.2
Stamp tax	1.7	1.6	1.6	1.3	1.4	0.7	2.4
Customs duties	35.0	43.0	46.6	35.3	42.7	48.4	40.1

Source: Robert Tignor, *State, Private Enterprise, and Economic Change*, 238–39.

power intent on ridding Egypt of its colonial past in all its manifestations. If Nasser's entry into politics was a response to such colonial maladies, then such maladies would also limit his ability to implement his economic desires and military activities.

ISRAEL

This discussion, like the previous one on Egypt, focuses on some important features of the development of the Israeli social and economic structure, along with some preliminary observations about Israeli state power. The emergence of a dominant socialist organization during the British mandate can be best understood as a product of three factors. First, the Zionist ideology and its strong organizational features led to a well-developed and class-conscious labor movement that controlled a substantial portion of the country's economic and political life. That the labor movement had such a profound impact on the Jewish community's political economy was facilitated by a second factor: Palestine's role in the world-economy and the absence of a (powerful) foreign or domestic capitalist class in Palestine. And third, the Yishuv capitalized on the opportunities presented by British mandatory authorities to crystallize their political presence and control over economic resources. In other words, it was the absence of those very colonial practices and manifestations that contributed to Egypt's underdeveloped status, and the presence of a unique historical legacy that help to account for the successful implantation of socialist-Zionist interests in Palestine.

Finally, I discuss the implications of this historical development for Israeli state power at independence. In general, the combination of those factors identified from pre-independence that enabled the emergence of a strong socialist presence under the direction of Mapai provided the foundation for a relatively strong state after 1948. The most notable feature of the Yishuv's development and legacy is its socialist-Zionist ideology, which had left a permanent mark on the current Israeli political economy, patterns of economic organization and ownership, and political representation and power. I not only focus on the state's initial relationship to the economy and capital investment, but I also downplay the state's infrastructural capacities; at independence its bureaucracy, extraction capacities, and enforcement abilities, though comparatively impressive for a postcolonial state, were rather limited.

The Political Economy of the Yishuv

Early Zionism. Zionism emerged in nineteenth-century Eastern Europe and Russia as a reaction to the maladies caused by capitalist development and the European Enlightenment, both of which had virulent anti-Semitic symptoms. A synthesis of socialism, nationalism, and Jewish redemption, early Zionism envisioned that a return to Palestine and the creation of a Jewish state would "normalize" Jewish existence because one important political distinction between Jews and Christians was that the Jews were a nation without a territory.[56] The Jewish state would be different than its (Christian) Western European brethren, however, because the Jewish state would reject capitalism and develop socialism on its biblical homeland.

The Ottoman Empire, which nominally controlled the area, was generally suspicious of Jewish immigration; they believed that the Jews would not only become instruments of foreign powers attempting to strengthen their presence in Palestine but also present a nationalist movement sending the wrong signals to local populations. Consequently, after the particularly large influx of Jews in 1881 and 1891, the Ottomans attempted to restrict Jewish immigration and land purchases.[57]

That these Zionists pioneers were able to establish socialist enclaves in Palestine despite Turkish animosity can be attributed to four factors. First, the Great Powers intervened through their consuls to relax the official attitude, moves that only confirmed Turkish suspicions.[58] Second, the bureaucratic apparatus of the Ottoman Empire was extremely inefficient and local administrators could easily be bribed to overlook Jewish skirting of confining regulations. Third, because of their familiarity in dealing with hostile public authorities, Jews had developed a talent for finding breaches in the hostile restrictions that surrounded them.[59] Finally, there were no significant domestic or foreign capitalist (economic) interests in the region, and the early Zionist settlers represented, in some part, the first sustained attempt at the development of the Palestinian economy.[60]

Although there had been a continuous Jewish presence in Palestine that was chiefly involved in religious activities and decidedly apolitical, the "first wave" of Jewish immigration in 1881 injected a Jewish element with an explicitly political/nationalist component. Although the Jewish population never surpassed more than 20 percent of the total population in Palestine before 1917, Jewish numbers quickly swelled from about 23,000 in 1881 to 85,000 in 1917.[61] Moreover, although nearly 100,000 Jews immigrated to Palestine during this period, approximately half left shortly after their arrival because of harsh social and economic conditions. Those that remained—including such luminaries as David Ben-Gurion, Golda Meir, and Levi Eshkol—formed the nucleus of a revolutionary, visionary, and determined socialist-Zionist community that established the foundations for the future Jewish state and provided the core of most Israeli governments through 1977.

That these pioneers aspired to create a socialist-Zionist state in an undeveloped economy and inhospitable political environment stimulated the need for political creativity and economic fortitude. These first socialist-Zionist pioneers formed a cohesive group of professional politicians, who quickly formed workers' parties whose primary mission was to organize Jewish labor and develop a Jewish state. From these efforts emerged the two major socialist parties, Poale Zion and Hapoel Hatzair. The primary debate among these political parties "was not abstract philosophies, but . . . strategies of how to settle the country, build a society, and organize political resources and power."[62] This combination of tactical flexibility and organizational skill was necessary for overcoming future adversity.

Socialist praxis and economic hardships, however, became the mother of innovation and led to the creation of two important Zionist economic institutions. The first was the kibbutz. Because early Zionist thinkers emphasized a "return to the land," the special metaphysical qualities and redemptive powers of agricultural development and toil thus became the focus of early socialist-Zionist economic activities. Although the original intent of these first Zionist settlers was to find employment as either laborers for private farmers or on farms administered by the Zionist movement for training purposes, neither transpired because opportunities were lacking and "often administrators and tutors failed in the human relations of management," respectively.[63] As a result, a group of agricultural workers formed the first cooperative settlement at Degania in 1911, which launched the kibbutz movement. Agriculture soon became a dominant economic sector with the kibbutz at its spiritual center.[64]

The lack of capital for development and infrastructure, the presence of chronic unemployment, and a desire to control work conditions led to the establishment of the Histadrut (General Federation of Workers) by the two principal labor parties, Poale Zion and Hapoel Hatzair in 1920. Although the Histadrut was originally designed to be labor's representative in Palestine, it became much more encompassing; this quasi-nationalist umbrella organization soon controlled a significant amount of investment resources flowing into the Yishuv, owned the Yishuv's largest banking and industrial concerns, and provided many social and community services, including medical care, to its members, which included most of the Jewish population. The Histadrut was the Jewish economy's public sector, provider of work programs, and quasi-governing body. By the 1930s the Histadrut was in the peculiar (and enviable) position of both representing labor and developing the Yishuv's economy.[65]

In summary, a strong socialist-Zionist presence was established before the formal introduction of British authorities. In the context of certain systemic and societal features that did not thwart their objectives, the revolutionary and determined character of these early Zionists facili-tated the socialist-Zionist presence. In general, the Zionist community demonstrated how organizational fortitude and skill produced both novel political and economic arrangements and established the founda-tions for a Zionist state.

British Mandatory Period, 1917–1948. With the disintegration of the Ottoman Empire as a result of World War One, Britain became the caretaker of Palestine, Iraq, and Transjordan through the League of Na-tions mandate system. Unlike the aim of colonial acquisition, Britain was technically charged with introducing to these communities the proprie-ties of interstate participation; thus they sought "ways to build forces that could secure their interest in the region without a permanent colonial presence."[66]

Britain's principal motivation for seeking the Palestine mandate was to project its security interests in the region. This impetus was consistent with its pre–World War One aspirations. In general, the Great Powers had been attracted to Palestine for its religious significance, its strategic value, and, only minimally, its economic potential. As the homeland of the West's three major religions, it had immediate stature for the power that protected and controlled its territory and particularly its jewel, Jerusalem. Indeed, as opposed to any political or economic rationale, a primary motive for Western powers' controlling Palestine had more to do with arresting it from Moslem influence than for intrinsic strategic reasons.[67] A second reason for controlling Palestine lay in its importance as the land bridge linking East, West, and Africa. Once the Suez Canal and other maritime routes were established, however, Palestine's strategic significance lessened. From then on its primary military value lay simply in its proximity to the Suez Canal and the Great Power's ability to control its territory and deny access to a rival power.

Moreover, that Great Power interest in Palestine lay in its strategic and religious, but not economic, importance reflects the absence of foreign capitalist penetration. Historically, metropolitan capital was unimpressed with Palestine's potential economic opportunities for a number of reasons. First and foremost, unlike its oil-rich neighbors, Palestine is not blessed with abundant natural resources, important for both economic or national security. Second, its thinly populated area and the harshness of the soil limited the country's potential exploitation for agricultural production. Moreover, although the British mandate after World War One had placed the territory under Great Power jurisdiction, the nascent Arab-Jewish conflict and occasional outbursts of violence were enough to discourage any potential foreign investor.[68]

In general, the British had two broad objectives in Palestine. They sought primarily to protect their strategic interests in the area at a minimal political and economic cost. Second, they wanted to implement the mandate, which stipulated that it should protect the rights of local Arab inhabitants while implementing the Balfour Declaration.[69] The British attempted to implement these contradictory pledges, however, without sacrificing their strategic objectives.

That these socialist-Zionist pioneers were able to establish a dominant socialist foundation under the auspices of British colonial authority seems something of an anomaly. After all, Britain had made great efforts to impose capitalist property relations in its other colonial possessions and to fully integrate these territories into the world-economy with Britain at its core. Moreover, although initially Jewish immigration consisted mainly of ideologically driven socialists, it later included more numerous members of the merchant and bourgeoisie classes, driven to Palestine by European anti-Semitism and U.S. (and others') closed immigration policy.[70] To understand what enabled the early socialist-Zionists to imprint their vision on the Yishuv, one must examine the nature of the world-economy, the particular features of labor-class organization in Palestine, and British mandatory policy. In general, the absence of a well-organized foreign and domestic capitalist class and the presence of a strong, well-organized labor party was mainly responsible for Mapai's successes.[71] I first examine British mandatory policy and strategic objectives in Palestine; then I discuss Zionist organization and strategy in Palestine.

Britain's primarily strategic, not economic, motivation for acquiring the mandate and its commitment to introducing some form of political autonomy that would encourage local independence while protecting British strategic interests had important implications for the two nationalist communities. Although both Zionists and Arabs shared the common goal of establishing a state under its control, their political strategies and reaction to the opportunities presented by the mandate differed substantially, with a profound impact on their relative successes in institutionalizing their presence. The Arab leadership refused to partake in any political process that might be interpreted as recognizing Zionist aspirations. This unwillingness to cooperate in even the most limited measure cast aside an important opportunity for establishing a political foothold. The local Zionist leadership, however, capitalized on this limited autonomy to solidify their political stature in Palestine. The Zionists used British passivity and British offers of resources and responsibility to undertake specific tasks to create a skeleton state in Palestine. According to J. C. Hurewitz, "the Palestine Jews, who by the mid-1930s administered their own community affairs . . . were receiving valuable experience in self-rule. The various departments of the quasi-government were staffed with residents of the Yishuv, so that a core of civil servants were also being trained."[72] In general, the Arabs missed "the opportunity to use British authority and resources to succor fledgling, countrywide Arab institutions. . . . British despair of creating a viable unified political framework for Palestine worked to the Zionists' advantage, allowing them to create a basis for autonomous Jewish community with relatively consolidated social control."[73] Somewhat outside British compliance, however, there developed one other critical component of the future Jewish state, the means of coercion. At the turn of the century, before the British mandate, Jewish agricultural settlements established self-defense units called HaShomer. This initial organization was supplanted by the labor-controlled Haganah in 1921, which emerged as a consequence of the Arab Riots of 1920–1921 and the inability of British troops to protect the Jewish residents. Although unable to monopolize the means of coercion in the entire territory, Ben-Gurion was intent on monopolizing the principal coercive unit of the Yishuv: "The potential of Arab violence was so great as to make control of defense, no matter what the costs he might have to pay in maintaining Jewish consensus, something labor simply could not give up if the Yishuv was to survive and labor was to maintain social control."[74] Rival military organizations did emerge that challenged Haganah's dominance and Ben-Gurion's authority. Irgun Zvi Leumi (IZL) and Lehi were the two most famous military units outside Ben-Gurion's control. The kibbutzim, although certainly sympathetic to Mapai, also formed their own relatively autonomous military arm called the Palmach. Be that as it may, Ben-Gurion established the unwavering principle that the Haganah fell under the Zionist executive's authority, "and he placed at its head a civilian board of representatives of all sectors of the Yishuv, except the Revisionists, casting the Yishuv in the mold of a democratic state whose military was responsible to elected authority. In this way he differentiated between the Haganah and the IZL (as well as Lehi . . .)."[75]

In general, under the British the Zionists were able to establish "a quasi-government without sovereignty" that proved instrumental in their drive for statehood.[76] Not only was a skeleton state established, but because of their ideological stature and superior organizing skills, the labor parties also dominated the political landscape in the Yishuv. Ben-Gurion, surrounded by fellow party activists, had little difficulty becoming the head of the Yishuv.

Once Ben-Gurion had established firm political control over the Yishuv he could turn his attention to controlling those institutions that were world Jewry's linkage to Palestine.[77] Although the ins and outs of this internal Zionist struggle are not directly relevant here, it is important that once Ben-Gurion established command of the Yishuv by the late 1920s, he then wrested control of the World Zionist Organization (WZO) away from its recognized patriarch, Chaim Weizmann. This political centralization was furthered by the fact that the Histadrut had already obtained a fair amount of resources from the WZO to undertake the former's social and economic tasks. The implications of Ben-Gurion's tightening grip on power were enormous:

> Formally the labor leaders depended on the Zionist Executive [of the WZO] for both revenues and access to the British. The fact that the Histadrut had created such effective social control in the Yishuv, however, actually made the Zionist Executive, and later the Jewish Agency itself, dependent on labor leaders.[78]

Although WZO leaders attempted to use their subsidies of the Histadrut enterprises as a way of controlling the Histadrut's (and, implicitly, Labor's) operations in Palestine, Ben-Gurion argued that, because the interests of labor expressed the true national interests, revenues and spending should remain under Mapai's discretion. Even though at this point Labor did not represent the numerical majority in the Yishuv, this argument won the day—a tribute to the organizational prowess of Labor and its ability to mobilize resources at its behest.[79] The important implication here is that Ben-Gurion and Mapai controlled a substantial amount of capital transfers from world Jewry by the early 1930s.

Although the socialist-Zionist pioneers had successfully captured the symbol of the Jewish return to Palestine, the development of a thriving economy was critical to maintaining their stature, creating a viable Jewish state, and attracting future Jewish immigration.[80] In general, three factors enabled Labor to control the Yishuv's economy. First, foreign capitalist interest in the Palestinian economy was lacking. In this context

TABLE 3.4

Source of Investment Capital to Palestine, 1918–1937

	In Millions of Palestinian Pounds	Percentage
National and public capital	20	21
Private capital	75	79
Total	95	100

Source: Baruch Kimmerling, *Zionism and Economy*, 30.

it is important to recognize that although there was a shortage of capital for investment and development, foreign capital could not "distort" the development process; that is, local production did not reflect core capitalist needs, thereby enabling local interests to influence the development process more fully and according to their priorities. Hence, the early socialist-Zionist settlers were not confronted by the economic priorities of foreign capitalist interests; rather they faced a lack of economic opportunities. This forced the Zionists to devise new solutions to their problems that would allow them to gain greater control over Palestine.

Similarly, the notable absence of foreign capital aided and necessitated the local economy's development from other resources. A major step in this direction was taken in 1930 when Ahdut Ha'avoda and Hapoel Hatzair merged to form Mapai and thereby established firm control over Histadrut. Thereafter Mapai not only had a powerful organization with which to promote its economic and nation-building objectives, but it also had a base from which to secure its present and future political power; it demonstrated an adept capacity to use Histadrut to expand its political power by distributing benefits to its members.[81] Histadrut and Mapai became the quasi-governmental body in the Yishuv, and both were inextricably associated with, and symbolic of, the Zionist project. Moreover, in the same year that Mapai was formed the British allowed Yishuv authorities to collect taxes.

A second reason for Mapai's success was that a good percentage of capital imports and unilateral transfers from world Jewry were handed over to a fairly autonomous and hierchically controlled Histadrut. The Mapai-controlled Histadrut was a principal conduit for capital transfers to Jewish Palestine.[82] This left Mapai with relatively unquestioned control over a significant amount of capital investment that Mapai could channel according to its objectives. In fact, after the 1920s private transfers represented nearly 80 percent of all Jewish investment in Palestine (see table 3.4).[83] Thus, for many observers the rapid development of the Jewish economy was undeniably influenced and enabled by tremendous capital inflows and unilateral transfers.[84]

Finally, domestic capital was not able to challenge the power of Histadrut. A number of factors led to the relative weakness of the private
sector.[85] Capitalist interests were introduced only after labor established
its economic and political dominance, and the socialist parties could
claim responsibility for the development and protection of the Jewish
community.[86] In addition, most capital transfers were used for land acquisition, urban building, and consumption, while Histadrut investment
was employed for expanding the economic infrastructure.[87] Thus, Histadrut developed and owned some of the largest enterprises in the country. If propertyless workers found it necessary to organize politically and
economically to reproduce the conditions of their own existence, no such
impetus emerged among the late-coming capitalist class. Finally, labor
was organized permanently through Histadrut, but the private sector
was not; this meant that in economically difficult times labor was in a
better position to provide economic relief.[88] By 1948 the Histadrut
owned most major industrial, manufacturing, and banking concerns
while the capitalist class was characterized by small, family-owned
enterprises.[89]

If the pattern of ownership in Palestine was unlike other British colonial possessions, the economic structure deviated somewhat from the
prevailing norm. This economic development reflected not only capital
inflow and immigration throughout the 1930s but also the tremendous
wartime demand and Palestine's virtual economic isolation from core
capitalist influences between 1939 and 1945. During this period, manufacturing and services quickly surpassed agriculture as the most important productive activity, as manufacturing's share of production rose
from 26 percent to 41 percent.[90] In general, although citrus products
continued to represent a significant percentage of the Yishuv's exports,
the economy diversified over this period. Moreover, England was the
Yishuv's most important trading partner, which meant that its trade pattern resembled that of other colonies; substantial autonomous capital
flows controlled by Histadrut meant that the economy could develop at
the dictates of local political authorities, not as a reflection of core capitalist interests.

In general, Mapai's symbolic status, economic power, and control
over materialistic rewards proved an unbeatable political combination.
The successful establishment of a socialist society was a function of the
presence of a highly-motivated, socialist-oriented, Jewish elite, the absence of a well-organized or economically important foreign and domestic capitalist class, and opportunities offered by British authorities. Although private capitalists were quite important for land acquisition and
accounted for approximately 60 percent of domestic output by 1948,
their political power never matched their economic standing. As Shalev

astutely points out, the privileged position of capital is owing to its control over investment, which is fundamental to "the prosperity of the society as a whole. . . . The prosperity of Palestine was dependent mainly on Jewish immigration and capital inflow and thus on factors exogenous to the Yishuv economy."[91] These capital flows, moreover, were at the relative behest of Histadrut and Mapai. Mapai's charismatic and ideologically driven leadership, with David Ben-Gurion as its driving force, was unarguably the pulse of the Yishuv and presented an unbeatable political force to any other societal challenge.

Israeli State Power

The transition from quasi-government to sovereign state raised two important concerns for the future state's initial control over society. The first issue was the capacity of the state to implement its policies and penetrate society, the state-society linkages, and the role of Mapai. The second issue concerns the state's relationship to the economy in general and its source of revenue and control over investment capital in particular. In general, ample evidence suggests that the Israeli state had significant control over society at independence.

State Capacity. An important consideration for the successful transition from quasi-government to sovereign state was the relative ease with which various societal groups recognized the Jewish state's legitimacy and authority.[92] The pluralistic power structures that existed during the mandate period rapidly disintegrated, and under the state's authority political power was unified and centralized. This process of centralization had three dimensions. The first was the new state's relationship to world Jewry. The functions of such extraterritorial institutions as the WZO and the Jewish Agency that had once played an important role during the Yishuv, particularly with respect to land acquisition and immigration, now seemingly duplicated official state activities. Although there was some tension and friction over what institutional function and role world Jewry would play in the development of the Jewish state, most authority quickly transferred to the Israeli state.[93]

The second dimension was located in the state's political system. Most important, those political parties and associations that operated during the prestate years had to recognize the new state's legitimacy and authority. In general, the political system that existed during the mandate was quickly transferred to the state.[94] Although Mapai was undoubtedly the dominant political actor in the Yishuv, one hallmark feature of this period was the inclusion of a multitude of political associations and organizations in the decision-making process. This was institutionalized into the framework of the state by establishing a parliamentary democracy with a proportional representation system. In the Israeli system political parties are awarded an equal percentage of seats in the Knesset as they record in the national election; thus, a political party need obtain a mere one percent of the national vote to be awarded representation. The rather lenient requirements for political representation create a propensity for coalition governments. In fact, although Mapai was the dominant political party and formed every government between 1948 and 1977, it never received an absolute majority and was thus forced into a series of coalition governments with smaller parties.[95] This gave these smaller, primarily religious, parties greater political power than would otherwise be expected.[96] The most important cabinet posts—for example, fiscal and defense posts—were always reserved for Labor, and "minor" ministries—that is, education and religion—were given to junior coalition partners.[97]

Although there is a tendency for a highly decentralized political process, in fact the system has strong centralizing tendencies. Citizens vote not for individuals per se but for party lists; who comprises that list, and in what position, is controlled by the party elite and not open to the party rank and file. The party's leaders dominate the Knesset delegation by closing the nominating process. Thus, although the Knesset is (formally) the supreme political authority, the winning coalition controls both the Knesset and the cabinet, and strict party control prevails; this combination undermines the Knesset's autonomy and independent decision-making authority. Therefore, the cabinet embodies most political authority, while the Knesset's most important activities revolve around monitoring, not determining, the state's financial and economic policies.[98]

If the decision-making process was centralized during these early years, then it was owing in part to Mapai's status as a dominant party.[99] Mapai's stature during these early years was based on five features. First, it was able to control effectively both the Histadrut and major regulatory and policy instruments of the state, which meant that its finger was on the pulse of the Israeli economy. Relatedly, the Yishuv's political parties lost their access to independent sources of financing and resources from organizations outside Palestine. Thus, groups that once had direct access to financing now depended on a Mapai-controlled state apparatus.[100] Second, Mapai was able to guarantee a continuous rise in the standard of living, which afforded it an economically unassailable position. Third, because Mapai guarded both the state apparatus and Histadrut, it could distribute material rewards and engage in clientalistic practices to bolster its political fortunes.[101] For example, all new immigrants were made automatic members of Histadrut's labor exchange and medical services. Fourth, its leadership was relatively cohesive, so that political decisions could be implemented and regulated in the face of opposition groups.[102] Finally, Mapai had successfully coopted and controlled all the major symbols of pre-1948 Israel (e.g., the Haganah), and its own history was bound up with the drive toward and establishment of the Jewish state. The ideology of Mapai soon came to be the ideology of all new immigrants.[103]

Mapai's control over the state's institutions and the Histadrut was further fused by the close network and association between the state managers and the dominant societal elite. Most of the state and societal elite had immigrated from Eastern Europe and Russia during the "second wave" of Jewish immigration between 1904 and 1917.[104] Many of the first state managers had helped establish the kibbutzim, risen through the ranks of the Histadrut, were party activists, and had attended Mapai party meetings that produced both broad state and Histadrut policy. A notable example was Prime Minister Ben-Gurion, who was the secretary-general of Histadrut before becoming Israel's first prime minister. Thus, if Histadrut was structurally favored because it both represented the work force and controlled a substantial proportion of the country's economic production, such partiality was reinforced by the fact that many early state managers were their close associates. The capitalist class and lower classes were much less likely to have access to the political elite.[105]

In general, the Israeli political system represents something of a paradox. On the one hand, there are diverse entry points for political parties and associations wishing to influence the direction and content of state policies. No political party has ever captured an electoral majority, producing a series of coalition governments. Moreover, political parties are not only an important state-societal linkage, but they also determine the political composition of the Histadrut, thereby providing a further point of control and influence over the economy. Mapai, no matter how apparently hegemonic, could not authoritatively determine the direction of the state's policies in all areas of activity.

On the other hand, political power was highly centralized. Despite the strong tradition of autonomous and diverse political parties, the influence of most is insignificant. This is particularly true during the period before 1977, and particularly true of security and economic policy. Although Mapai never captured an outright majority, it always held the most important posts of prime minister, treasury, and defense, where it had greater policy space, while strong party discipline situated most political authority in the cabinet and lessened the independence of the Knesset. Finally, the state elite and the societal elite were closely associated, embodied in the patterns of association between the Histadrut and the state.

Although policy formulation was fairly centralized, its implementation was more problematic. The state benefited from its early administrative experience under the British, but "it did not inherit . . . an adequate civil service and an organizational apparatus for formulating and carrying out fiscal, monetary, and foreign exchange policy required by a government ready to shoulder heavy economic responsibility."[106] Thus, a principal objective of Israeli state managers was to develop a state apparatus that would be responsive to their directives, institutionalize their dominant ideology, and maintain control over society.[107] In general, in the state's infant condition there were few mechanisms for monitoring and extracting resources from society other than tremendous societal dedication to the nationalist project.

The state apparatus, though scant, was highly centralized and ideologically cohesive. As previously mentioned, during the Yishuv there developed a set of clientalistic practices whereby the party's leaders effectively controlled major economic institutions and political authority with little challenge from non-Mapai sources.[108] These practices survived the transition to statehood, and Mapai continued to infuse the state apparatus with its political appointees. These clientalistic practices implied that the party controlling the state guarded and dispensed both financial resources and benefits.

The final dimension that contributed to the state's control over and ability to govern society was its monopoly of the instruments of coercion. Although there was an important challenge to the state's (and implicitly Ben-Gurion's) authority by the rival IZL and Stern Gangs during the War of Independence (this is discussed in greater detail in chapter 5), Ben-Gurion deftly depoliticized and professionalized the military by ensuring its subordination to political and civilian authorities.

Despite such centralizing features and the state's impressive command over society, the state's capacity was still rather limited and can be appreciated by examining its fiscal basis. The Israeli tax system evolved directly from the British taxation system established during the mandate period. The British dismantled the Ottoman system, which depended on the agricultural sector and customs duties for its revenues.[109] In its place the British established a tax policy that included the dominance of customs duties. The importance of customs duties for the state's revenue diminished once income tax collection began to rise in the later years of the mandate period. Excise taxes were another important source of income. Income taxes, however, had been successfully resisted by both Jews and Arabs alike until World War Two, when the isolation of

Palestine from the world-economy and the accompanying drop in customs duties, in combination with expanding economy, led to their acceptance in September 1941. Despite such policy victories, the weak administrative apparatus precluded any real enforcement or collection mechanisms.

Originally, all taxes were paid directly to the British colonial authorities; however, during the 1930s Yishuv leaders were hard pressed to raise enough revenue to cover the increasing costs of defense. In response, they openly requested that the Jewish population default on their official colonial taxes and redirect that sum to the Yishuv. This became more pronounced once the income tax was established. Such a strategy could not have been successful had it not been for the Yishuv's high degree of legitimacy.[110]

Once the state was established this legitimacy proved useful and necessary. In 1948 98.1 percent of the state's income was financed from internal sources. Of this figure, 25.5 percent derived from income taxes; 4.3 percent from property taxes; 62.5 percent from customs duties; and 7.7 percent from transaction fees.[111] Although this represented an unqualified success when compared to other Third World countries, the state's tax collection efforts evidenced future difficulties and frustrations owing, in part, to the state's limited infrastructural capacities.

Relationship to the Economy. Mapai maintained its control over the economy and investment capital by virtue of the fact that it controlled the state's regulatory instruments, oversaw most capital flows (which came principally in the form of unilateral transfers), and managed the Histadrut and its enterprises.

The Histadrut remained intact with its enterprises under its control. This was partly a function of the fact that, although the Histadrut was the Yishuv's quasi-governmental organ and owner of the most important economic concerns, it was not seen as a threat to the state's legitimacy because Mapai was in command of both the state and the Histadrut. Moreover, because of tight party hierarchy, the government believed that it could coordinate state and Histadrut policy without transferring Histadrut enterprises to the state's domain to regulate its concerns. Moreover, the Histadrut gave Mapai an additional power base, distinct from the state apparatus, with which it could continue its clientalistic and recruitment practices.

That Mapai was the manager of both the state and the Histadrut is open to two interpretations. First, one may view the Histadrut as a principal owner of the means of the production; because of its structural position within the economy, it constrains the state's actions. There is some truth to this proposition, for the Histadrut and the state generated considerable friction over economic policy in the following years. The relative decline of Mapai in the Histadrut in the 1960s signaled some important changes in Mapai's ability to monopolize the policy-making process and effectively maintain its control over society. Such friction, however, became more evident later once the Histadrut enterprises underwent an organizational restructuring that included greater autonomy and emphasis on capitalist, as opposed to political, rationality.

Second, one may view Histadrut as an instrument of the state in general and of Mapai in particular, particularly during these first years. In other words, unlike the institutional constraint on government's decision-making flexibility, Histadrut becomes an instrument that increased the state's maneuverability. Although Mapai was not a monolithic organization immune to intraparty struggles, the conventional interpretation is to subsume the Histadrut to its objectives and considerations.[112]

In addition to the state's control over the country's major economic enterprises, domestic capital was not an important political force or economic constraint on state actions and was limited to peripheral areas of the economy.[113] Moreover, there was little foreign ownership in Palestine; in fact, the challenge to future Israeli governments was to entice foreign direct investment. In neither the political nor the economic sphere did capitalist interests represent much of a challenge.

Moreover, as already noted, a significant percentage of investment capital came in the form of unilateral transfers controlled directly by the state. Thus, the state did not depend on capital to determine the direction and vibrance of economic growth. For example, in 1958 the private sector, which included the Histadrut, was responsible for a mere 47 percent of total investment funds—and this represented a steady increase since statehood.[114] In general, Mapai had considerable control over the reigns of the state and the economy during most of this period, and a substantial portion of its revenue base and investment capital was derived from external sources that came with few restrictions and conditions. The dynamic of capital accumulation, exogenous to the state in the form of capital transfers, was controlled by a Mapai-dominated state apparatus.

In summary, the Israeli state was relatively powerful in 1948. This stature was nurtured during the prestate years as a result of the peculiar features of the socialist-Zionist ideology and its organizational features: the absence of foreign capital, the relative weakness of domestic capital, and the opportunities presented by the British mandate. The successful establishment of a socialist-Zionist community must be understood by referring to the opportunities presented by the systemic and domestic context and the presence of certain historical forces.

At independence Mapai was in control of both the Histadrut and the state, with few immediate economic and political challengers. Despite its seemingly unchallenged presence, the Israeli state's implementation capacities were relatively undeveloped. This was so, despite British authorities' allowance for developing a skeleton state during the mandate period. Although Ben-Gurion would have both to protect the fruits of his Zionist crusade from threatening Arab foes and to promote the economic and social well-being of his newly created state, he could rest assured that his position was relatively unchallenged domestically; he was, in fact, situated in a state that effectively controlled society.

CHAPTER FOUR.

Explaining Egyptian War Preparation Strategies

THERE WAS no shortage of costly or difficult tasks confronting Egyptian governments from 1952 through 1977. These challenges arrived from all directions. From the international system Egyptian leaders had to confront both declining Great Powers and emerging regional powers, a dynamic that was duly reflected in the amount of scarce resources they channeled toward defense expenditures (see table 4.1). Between the years 1952 and 1956 Nasser confronted a decreasingly ominous relationship with Great Britain and an increasingly dangerous one with the Israelis that culminated in the 1956 Suez War. The second period between 1957 and 1967 demonstrates continuous concern with the Arab-Israeli conflict and greater regional activity, the latter climaxed in Egypt's entry into the Yemen War in 1962. After 1967 reclaiming the Sinai and restoring Egyptian pride became the most important concern of the Egyptian government. The 1973 War did not bring any relief from the defense burden because defense still commanded tremendous attention for various reasons, not the least of which were the need to rebuild an army depleted by the previous war and the uncertainty of the regional and international systems.

Significant demands and challenges also emanated from the domestic sphere. Initially Nasser and the Free Officers had to consolidate their power; later their domestic standing was cause for continual concern. This was never more true than after 1967 when the government had to contend with the aftershocks of the June War and Sadat began to shift the class basis of the government to the upper classes and away from the masses that Nasser had mobilized. Moreover, no matter the class basis of the regime, the Egyptian government's political standing was based on its ability to continue improving the standard of living in a resource-poor country that needed to confront the economic and political legacies of colonialism. In general, there was no shortage of overwhelming and rather costly objectives. As Amin Huwaidi, a former minister of war, commented, Egyptian leaders faced a "three-dimension dilemma": defense, investment for economic development, and expenditures intended to stabilize the regime. The difficulty is balancing the three and finding a way to limit their expenditures.[1] It would not be too surprising, then, if the government's war preparation strategies were determined

TABLE 4.1
Egyptian Defense Spending, 1950–1976

	Defense Outlays	Defense as Percentage of GNP
1950/51	108.9	3.9
1951/52	132.1	4.7
1952/53	126.6	4.9
1953/54	166.3	5.7
1955/56	258.2	8.4
1957/58	189.8	5.5
1959/60	220.5	6.1
1960/61	294.3	7.0
1961/62	315.3	7.1
1963/64	324.4	8.5
1965/66	475.5	11.0
1965	437.0	8.6
1966	494.0	11.1
1967	645.0	12.7
1968	690.0	12.5
1969	805.0	13.0
1970	1,262.0	19.0
1971	1,495.0	21.7
1972	1,510.0	—
1973	4,071.0	31.0
1974	6,103.0	22.8
1975	4,859.0	—
1976	4,365.0	37.0

Source: A. Dessouki and A. Al-Labban, "Arms Races, Defense Expenditures, and Development," 69–70.

not solely by strategic-rational calculations but also by the government's extrasecurity objectives and the constraints on its actions. This chapter examines the Egyptian government's war preparation strategies and various attempts to mobilize resources for national security while protecting and furthering its other domestic political and economic goals from 1952 to 1977.

CONSOLIDATION AND INTENT, 1952–1956

On July 23, 1952, the Free Officers overthrew King Farouk in a nonviolent takeover and established a military government. Much has been written on the Free Officers, and this study need not retrace well-worn ground.[2] The objectives behind the Free Officers Movement and the constraints on its actions, however, are of immediate relevance. The Free Officers movement—a response more to continued frustration and exasperation over Egypt's directionless drift than to a well-articulated set of goals and objectives—galvanized around a number of broad themes, including ending imperialism and feudalism, establishing a stronger and more powerful army, ridding the country of a corrupt king, and promoting economic and political reforms. This stance is illustrated by Nasser's public address in March 1955, in which he set forth the six main tenets of the revolution: ending imperialism, eradicating feudalism, breaking the political and economic domination of capital, establishing social justice, founding a truly democratic polity, and creating a powerful army.[3] At this initial point, then, radical social change was far from their minds; the Free Officers wanted to "Egyptianize" society, economically, politically, and culturally, to instill a sense of nationalism in all spheres of Egyptian life.[4] Although the Free Officers verbalized grandiose dreams of Egyptian greatness that seemingly contradicted its present condition, those dreams were shared by many citizens.

However desirous these broad goals, without political control and a stable domestic environment such greatness was unattainable. Thus, the Revolutionary Command Council's (RCC) initial overriding objective was political control and elimination of potential challengers, whether governmental, societal, or foreign.[5] Nasser took a number of steps at the cabinet level to solidify his personal power, including the elimination of his immediate rivals through a series of political intrigues and dealings that culminated in President Naguib's ouster in 1954.[6]

Nasser also moved to oust from the country any overt political opposition and challenge. One of the first governmental actions in September 1952 was the immediate suspension of the constitution and all party activities. On January 23, 1953, the government attempted to fill the political vacuum by creating the Liberation Rally. This party, like those that followed, was intended primarily to consolidate the regime's position; similar to the Parliament, the party was principally a legitimizing device for the ruling elite.[7]

Although initially there was little overt societal opposition to their takeover, in all likelihood because of the Free Officers' apparent moderation in their goals and the hope that the economic stalemate that had characterized the Egyptian economy since World War Two might now end,[8] the government's attempt to restrict the decision-making process to a small circle and to present itself as uniquely able to represent societal demands did not meet with enthusiastic applause from all societal groups.[9] The Wafd and the Moslem Brotherhood responded to the government's political suppressions by demanding increased political representation and autonomy from governmental control. The government, in turn, demonstrated a willingness to use force and repression against these and other domestic opposition groups. Nasser's quest for political supremacy led to the Moslem Brotherhood's failed assassination attempt on his life; Nasser responded by jailing many of its leaders and outlawing its activities.

As the government restricted political participation it claimed to be greater than the sum of the parts, able to protect society from the particularistic demands of societal interests and, at the same time, promote them. This characterization accurately reflected Nasser's ambivalence toward the masses: although he would aptly control and unleash a form of populism as a method for bolstering his political legitimacy, he had little trust for the masses' ability to function according to the needs and desires of the ruling elite.[10] If Nasser's political fortunes were partially dependent on mobilizing the masses at his behest, then they were not given any institutionalized forum for influencing those policies made in their name. As a result, any societal input depended on Nasser's sense of the mood of the people.[11]

A second objective was the promotion of economic development, which was equated with industrialization.[12] A nonideological, reform-minded group, the Free Officers believed that the road to industrialization could be paved by the efforts of domestic and foreign capital.[13] Consequently, they attempted to eliminate those perceived societal blockages to development and entice greater capitalist participation in Egypt's development efforts.[14] For instance, Nasser used those policies, such as reducing tax rates on profits for both domestic and foreign capitalist interests, that encouraged private sector investment.[15] Moreover, not insignificantly, many of these economic policies also secured the government's political power. For instance, one of the few reforms to which they were committed before they took power was land redistribution. Such land reforms both eliminated a barrier to development and the landed aristocracy, the most powerful societal actor in Egypt, and created a new "second stratum" of well-to-do agrarian interests loyal to Nasser's regime.[16] Only after 1956 did Nasser turn against the foreign capitalist class, and only after 1961 did he uproot the domestic capitalist class and move decidedly in the direction of Arab socialism. For the meantime, however, Nasser was more than willing to leave to private economic interests the herculean task of lifting Egypt from economic backwardness.

Nasser's final objective was to end foreign and colonial influence over Egypt's destiny and to project Egypt's importance in regional and global politics. The Free Officers had emerged, in part, as a response to two external threats: continued British control of Egyptian soil and the Palestine War. Its principal national security concern, however, was reserved for Great Britain, Egypt's colonial occupier and Suez Canal caretaker. There were tremendous nationalist pressures to rework England's Suez Canal lease when it expired in 1955; Britain, however, appeared equally determined to retain some control over the waterway. It was clear that the two countries—one hoping to promote a sense of stalled greatness, the other attempting to retain one remaining souvenir from its shrinking empire—would collide. Nasser's fears that Britain might use military force to defend its status and control was justified by history.

Israel was a secondary concern; this threat seemed distant and removed when compared to the British occupation of the Suez Canal. Nasser himself discounts the significance of the Palestinian cause in galvanizing the Free Officers to act and suggests that his experience in the 1948 war convinced him to fight the forces of imperialism closer to home.[17] In fact, "like most Egyptians, before 1955 Nasser exhibited a certain ambivalence toward Israel and the Arab-Israeli conflict."[18] After the Suez Treaty was negotiated in 1954 and British forces evacuated the Suez Canal in 1955, however, Israel's status as a threat to Egypt's security rose considerably. Such perceptions were not unfounded. In 1954, in what became known as the Lavon Affair, Israeli agents masquerading as Egyptian nationals planted a number of bombs that destroyed foreign property in Cairo, an inept attempt to embarrass the Nasserite regime and to distance it from the West. This botched operation increased Nasser's wariness of the Israelis and reinforced his belief that Israel was attempting to foster domestic instability to hasten his downfall.[19] Moreover, the issue of Palestine became the way in which Arab leaders were able to demonstrate their dedication to the Arab cause and to jockey for Arab leadership. Once Nasser committed himself to advancing pan-Arabism and sponsoring fedayeen raids into Israel as a way of facilitating his rise in the Arab world, his devotion to the Arab-Israeli conflict became more pronounced. His actions, encouraging an escalation in the number of clashes between the Egyptians and Israelis, promoted the ever present possibility that such clashes might erupt into a second Arab-Israeli War. As is well known, such hostilities did lead to war—Israel's Suez campaign of 1956. In general, Nasser was determined to rebuild Egypt's army, for a strong military would help demonstrate his resolve on the Arab-Israeli conflict and signal Egypt's greatness and might in regional affairs.

In sum, the Free Officers came to power with a commitment to end both feudalism and imperialism, to bring Egypt into the industrial age, and to establish its prominence in regional and global affairs. Before Nasser could promote his Egypt-first strategy, however, it was imperative that he firmly establish his political power. Nasser became the nucleus of a decision-making process that was barely institutionalized by assuring a tremendous concentration of power in the governmental elite's domain.

Nasser's pursuit of his various objectives were both facilitated and hindered by various features of the state and social structure. Perhaps the most important tool at the government's disposal would be the state apparatus. Initially the RCC relied on the already established administrative network, which was staffed primarily by the landed aristocracy and those who were sympathetic with its interests.[20] Very soon, however, the RCC began to weave its own military appointments and trusted followers into key locations in the state apparatus. By swelling the ranks of the bureaucracy with hand-picked officials, the RCC could assure that it would be of a like mind.[21] Vatikiotis writes:

> By December 1954 he [Nasser] was able to appoint trusted army officers in key bureaucratic offices to supervise the work of civilian departments. Despite the use of civilian, economic, and other experts in cabinet posts (Finance, Economy, Commerce, Industry, Foreign Affairs, and Agriculture), he was able, by the appointment of committees and commissions directly responsible to him, for the coordination of policy, to impose effective control over all activities of the state.[22]

In short, before the revolution the administrative apparatus was staffed by those connected with wealth and prestige, civil servants, and landowners. Afterward the upper reaches of the government were inundated with a military-technocratic elite.[23] The Free Officers infused the expanding bureaucracy with both military personnel and technocrats who were independent of and opposed to the dominant interests of society.[24] Thus, under Nasser there was an uninterrupted centralization and personalization of political power and the decision-making process, which was further enhanced by the relative cohesion and unity of the state apparatus. Not only were the government's objectives determined by a handful of officials, but the means were also increasingly controlled by a cohesive, hierarchically structured, and responsive bureaucracy and public sector. The combination of a centralized decision-making network and subservient state apparatus allowed Nasser to be rather proficient at formulating his desired policies.

Similar to most postcolonial settings, Nasser's ability to centralize decision-making power said little about his ability either to implement his decrees or the constraints on his actions. First, although Nasser might be able to swell the bureaucracy with hand-picked monitors, enhancing the state's infrastructural capacities was not so simple; in fact, translating words into effective action was an entirely different matter. The state's weakness was exemplified by its dependence on indirect taxes, for it had little hope of extracting funds from the population directly. Second, at the most basic level Nasser was severely limited by the simple fact that Egypt was a resource-poor country. The agricultural sector continued to dominate the economy, which meant that the government depended heavily on cotton for its foreign exchange earnings and imported most of its manufacturing and industrial goods. At the same time, Nasser was determined to overcome Egypt's agrarian and resource-poor characteristics through the efforts of domestic and foreign capital, which meant that he was heavily constrained by the sensitivities of the dominant classes. As Nasser attempted to push Egypt into the community of industrialized countries, he depended on the actions and decisions of the capitalist class.

The combination of such ambitious foreign and domestic goals and the significant material limitations meant that there was always the danger of running a severe resource gap. In one way Nasser might be able to overcome Egypt's resource scarcity: attracting foreign and Great Power interest in Egypt's future. A consistent theme of Egyptian policy is the promotion of Egypt's regional importance in order to supplement the country's economic and military capabilities.[25] Luckily both the Soviets and the Americans considered Egypt prime cold war real estate. Nasser, extremely sensitive to the external climate, discerned the opportunities that might accrue to a "neutral" strategic state in a heated cold war between the United States and the Soviet Union and attempted to exploit Egypt's bargaining leverage vis-à-vis both countries to Egypt's financial benefit. At this early juncture, there was no preordained reason—ideological, political, or "economic"—why Nasser should be either pro-Soviet or pro–United States. In fact, there were compelling reasons for leaning toward the West. Nasser, far from enamored with state-led industrialization, was content to rely on the efforts of the capitalist class, and many officers in the Egyptian army had trained in the United States. Be that as it may, Nasser was quite willing to play the two superpowers off one another in an attempt to receive the kinds of financial and strategic assistance he requested with relatively few strings or conditions. Perhaps the events that led up to the nationalization of the Suez Canal in July 1956 provide the best example of Nasser's maneuvering. Unable to finance the Aswan Dam project from Egyptian sources alone, Nasser, hoping to incite a bidding war between the two superpowers, went to the West while querying the Soviets at the same time. In general, foreign assistance was designed to allow him to shield both capital and labor from the pains of his rather expensive set of objectives.[26]

In summary, during this period Nasser's primary concern was securing power, silencing any manifest societal opposition, and ridding the country of the government's principal antagonist, the landed aristocracy. This Nasser did swiftly and effectively. Despite such successes, Nasser could not act without restraint. The state apparatus, although dutiful, had little institutional capacity; the economy was controlled by foreign and domestic capital, and Nasser could only cajole, not dictate, their investment decisions; and the country was resource-poor. These limitations led Nasser to promote Egypt's image as a cold war prize and seek out a foreign patron to facilitate his domestic and foreign policy objectives.

The government's objectives, the constraints on its actions, and Egypt's position in the international system had important consequences for its war preparation strategies. Nasser's nationalist rhetoric and attempt to nationalize all aspects of Egyptian life seemingly indicated a propensity toward a restructural policy; this might be particularly likely because his rise to power was relatively uncontested and the RCC had a fair degree of societal support. Rather than adopting a restructural policy, however, Nasser largely followed the mobilization practices of the Farouk regime because his objective of trying to court capital for his development strategy while promoting himself as a friend of masses, not to mention the state's rather limited infrastructural capacities, led him to shield capital and labor from a too excessive burden. This was most visible in the government's financial policy. Nasser turned first to an accommodational policy, using indirect methods where possible, but this was quickly succeeded by an international strategy, given the continuing resource gap. Egypts' relatively small industrial and manufacturing capacity left Nasser little choice but to rely on an international strategy for the military's war material. Finally, Nasser demonstrated a loyalty to the Farouk regime's conscription policies that disproportionally burdened the masses. I argue that Nasser's reliance on accommodational and international strategies was a product of the economic infrastructure, the state's capacities, Nasser's populist appeal, and the strength of the capitalist classes and their intended role in Egypt's development.

Financial Strategies

Defense spending climbed over this period as Nasser was intent on creating a modern military that could both confront Egypt's potential enemies and signal to regional and global actors that Egypt had reemerged on the scene and recovered from years of colonial tutelage. The neverending concern was how to fund such escalating military costs while furthering the regime's other objectives of political stability and capitalist development.[27]

Discovering a financial spring was no easy chore. As a self-proclaimed populist and friend of the masses in a desperately poor country, Nasser could hardly increase their financial contributions without either questioning his populist credentials or jeopardizing his political basis. More-over, given the meager living standards of the masses it was unlikely that any expended tax effort would satiate his budgetary needs; it was more likely to incur the citizens' resentment.

Nor was Nasser willing to further burden the domestic and foreign capitalist classes because this could potentially undercut his industrialization plan. In fact, the government lowered their tax burden during this period. For instance, Law No. 306 of 1952 exempted foreign companies from taxes on commercial, industrial profits, and movable properties within the free trade zones; Law No. 424 of 1953 exempted foreign experts from general income tax; Law No. 430 of 1953 exempted joint stock companies engaged in certain agricultural and industrial activities from paying taxes on profits; and other tax legislation designed to encourage domestic capital was introduced.[28] As a result, business income taxes as a percentage of total government receipts declined from 1952 until 1955. The principal method of augmenting national income was, accordingly, by borrowing from domestic and international lending agencies (see appendix 3).

This was the situation until 1955 when Egypt's defense spending rose by nearly 75 percent as a result of the border tensions with the Israelis and the delivery of the first Soviet-made weapons. The government's response to these budgetary pressures was to pass legislation designed both to raise funds for national security and encourage private sector investment. Defense Tax Law No. 277 of 1956 increased direct taxes and excluded taxes on commercial profits in selected industrial and manufacturing activities.[29] Such measures, modestly raising the domestic burden on the masses but only negligibly on the economic elites, accurately reflected the length to which the regime would go to pursue simultaneously its objectives of development, defense, and stability. These tax policies, carefully designed to further the government's foreign and domestic policy goals, could not satisfy its fiscal requirements.

Because it was politically and economically unreasonable to expect that warfare, investment, and welfare could be underwritten by domestic sources, Nasser quickly decided that attaining these various goals could only be made via the assistance of outside patrons. At this point Nasser capitalized on Egypt's status in the international system and attracted Great Power interest. In addition to a very liberal aid package, the Soviets began to subsidize Nasser's arms purchases in 1955. Egypt was charged half-price for all military equipment (and Soviet equipment already was approximately half the cost of Western arms), and the balance due on imported hardware was loaned at 2 percent per annum over a ten- to fifteen-year period.[30] All accounts were assessed in sterling; the exchange value was fixed according to the price of gold, and payments could be made in barter.[31] Thus began a policy where Egypt shipped tremendous quantities of cotton and agricultural products to Eastern Bloc countries for weapons.[32]

In general, Nasser's financing strategy reflected his objectives and situational constraints. Working within the parameters established by the pre-1952 governments and his own ideological posture and reformist economic objectives, he extended tax concessions to the capital classes to entice them toward greater investment and increased the burden on the masses only lightly because of his pronounced redistributive ethos. Unwilling to jeopardize his development program and only meekly able to burden the masses while retaining their political support, Nasser began to mortgage Egypt's financial future. He met the fiscal residual by public sector borrowing and foreign financing. In sum, Nasser's international financial policy, a direct result of domestic circumstances and objectives, convinced him to limit his domestic extractive efforts. Although the tendency toward deficit financing gave little cause for alarm at these modest rates, it established a pattern that would prove difficult to correct in the future. The present and future rule would be to borrow rather than to choose between governmental priorities.

Production Strategies

Egyptian arms production dates to the period of Muhammad Ali's rule in the 1820s. In fact, Muhammad Ali accomplished something that present-day Egypt and many other Third World countries only dreamed of: widespread and autonomous military industrialization. These arms industries, owned solely by the state, covered all aspects of military production, from warships to various types of ammunition. Egypt attained such manufacturing proficiency by combining French entrepreneurial skills and knowledge with Egyptian technology and financial backing. In other words, Ali built an arms industry, by some accounts comparable in quality with French arms production, without depending on imported technology or financial aid from the European states.[33] Egypt achieved an autonomy not since matched by most Third World countries.

This golden age of Egyptian arms production lasted a scant two decades. European interventions in Egypt's political and economic life, signaled by the Treaty of London of 1838, reduced the size of the Egypt's army from 200,000 to 20,000 troops. This reduction in domestic demand killed many of Egypt's military factories.[34] Subsequent efforts to revitalize Egypt's military industries did not take hold until the 1860s, but by this time Egypt, dependent on European financing and technology, was hopelessly behind more advanced and efficient arms manufacturers. Egypt could no longer competitively produce weapons, nor could it promote its development owing to Britain's control of Egypt's fiscal and economic policy. The British finalized the death of Egyptian arms production by forcefully disbanding the remaining arms industry in the late 1800s.[35]

Modern arms production was not revived until World War Two when there was greater demand from both foreign forces stationed in Egypt and Egypt's troops.[36] This, in combination with the arms shortage during the war, stimulated greater interest in rekindling military production and the role that foreign powers and private business could play in its development. Although these more recent efforts were undertaken by the private sector, following the war the state nationalized the country's military industries,[37] and they have remained so ever since.

When the Free Officers took power in 1952 arms production became a top concern for a number of reasons. First, after the experience of the Palestine War, many of the RCC, Nasser among them, who had served against the Israelis, had been frustrated by Egypt's lack of firepower and unreliable sources of supply. Broadly defined national security requirements were another driving force; military industrialization and weapons self-sufficiency were viewed as critical to maintaining Egypt's independence. This quest was altered after 1950 when Egypt was the target of an arms embargo by the Western powers, which demonstrated daily the importance of domestic production. Third, military production was seen as building the foundation for economic development because it provided civilian employment and created a highly skilled labor force. Finally, if Egypt was to fight frequent wars and to maintain an active and radical voice in foreign policy, then some domestic arms production was essential.[38] In general, arms production was a political act, intended to demonstrate autonomy and strength to the Arab World and points beyond.[39]

While Nasser's initial military industrialization program attempted to achieve self-sufficiency in all types of weapons, Egypt's lack of technology and scientific know-how forced him to rely on Western assistance. Although this strategy might lead to Egypt's dependence on the West, Nasser's policy was designed to minimize this effect by having all technology and equipment be transferred on a turn-key basis only.[40] By the early 1950s the Egyptian government established, among others, a small munitions plant and an aircraft factory at Helwan, near Cairo. Nasser set up all these companies with imported technology and foreign assistance.[41] It became evident later, however, that the wholesale transfer of technology alone did not by itself eliminate dependence, for Egypt's military industries were wholly dependent on foreign advisers and scientists for arms production.

The need to acquire arms became more critical after the rapid escalation of border clashes between Egypt and Israel in 1954 and the widespread fear that war was imminent. Because the domestic arms industry was incapable of supplying the military's needs, Nasser began actively searching for a willing foreign sponsor. Although the United States was Nasser's first choice, for many Egyptian officials had been trained on U.S. equipment and in U.S. military strategies and combat techniques,[42] his repeated overtures were repeatedly refused. Nasser made one final attempt to secure U.S. assistance after Israel's raid into Gaza in 1955, but Secretary of State Dulles, intent on propelling Egypt's entry into the U.S.-sponsored regional defense pact, informed Nasser that no arms would be forthcoming until he boarded U.S. containment policy. Soon thereafter Dulles had an apparent change of heart, for on June 30, 1955, he notified Nasser that Egypt would be allowed to purchase arms. Now Nasser played the rejector, as he informed the United States that he would hold out for a more favorable agreement, one that would allow him to acquire the arms through barter. Further inquiries of Britain, Belgium, and Sweden were similarly unsuccessful.[43]

The Soviet Union was the only other country that could adequately supply Egypt's diverse needs and provide acceptable financing terms.[44] Therefore, Nasser's decision to break the Western-constructed arms embargo and sign on with the Soviets was driven more by pragmatism than by ideology.[45] The Soviets, always searching for a foothold in the Middle East and a chance of grabbing a prize actively sought by the Americans, were more than happy to approve the Egyptian request. The Egyptian-Soviet arms deal of September 20, 1955, situated Egypt in the Eastern camp, broke the Western arms embargo, exacerbated regional tensions, inflamed Egypt's defense burden, shocked the Americans, and worried the Israelis.

Egypt's arms relationship with the Soviets was a mixed blessing. On the one hand, it now had an arms supplier and patron that would willingly sell it (within limits) its requested arms. On the other hand, the Soviets steadfastly refused to promote Egyptian military industrialization, and Egyptian factories were subsequently confined to the repair and maintenance of Soviet-bought equipment. The Soviets, ever jealous and guarded of their technology, were hopeful that this restrictive policy would promote an Egyptian arms dependency (thereby making the Egyptians susceptible to their wishes) and reluctant to provide Egypt with little more than the ability to repair their bought arms.[46]

Conscription Strategies

Egypt's pre-1952 conscription policy was inherently class-based and biased. Before 1952 military service was compulsory for all Egyptian males between the ages of eighteen and thirty. Although service was universal, its length varied according to the recruit's educational status. Those individuals who had attended up to nine years of school served for three years; secondary school graduates served for two and one-half years; and university graduates served for one year. Because there was a high correlation between educational status and class origins, this conscription method favored the upper class. The formula was uniformly applied except where health requirements were not satisfied. This health exemption incorporated a fairly large pool, for two-thirds of all potential conscripts did not serve because of either health or educational deficiencies. Thus, the army mobilized only 120,000 out of a potential pool of 350,000 eligible men.[47]

Once the Free Officers arrived in 1952 there were greater pressures to broaden the scope of military service owing to a fear of British and Israeli intentions and a desire to project Egypt's power. Although the army did expand slightly, it did so only by implementing modest changes in the conscription formula, one that maintained the class bias.[48] How does one explain the fact that the Free Officers—a reformist, nationalist-minded group intent on expanding Egypt's military power—deviated little from the pre-1952 formula inherited from a reactionary King Farouk? There are two related possibilities. First, the RCC depended on capital for its development needs. Those states that have followed a private capitalist accumulation path have historically excluded the upper classes from military service, as they are viewed as performing other, notably income-generating, functions. Second, the current conscription criteria generally met the military's immediate strategic requirements; therefore, there was little reason to risk societal resistance and possibly jeopardize the government's development goals by introducing a major change in current practices.

To a large extent Nasser's war preparation strategies belied his vocal nationalism and populism. When security requirements became more pronounced after 1955 clearly the upper classes, viewed as essential to Egypt's development future, were excused from sharing equally in the defense burden. This was reflected in all aspects of the government's war preparation strategies. Nasser's financial strategy evidenced both accommodational and international tendencies. Although the masses disproportionally shouldered the existing domestic burden, Nasser showed little stomach for imposing too great a hardship because the state's infrastructural capacity was limited, and he feared that further moves in this direction might jeopardize regime stability. Thus, Nasser adopted an international strategy and established a quasi-alliance with the Soviets to export the increasing costs of defense. Whereas Soviet financial assistance was sought because of socioeconomic constraints, Soviet material support was needed because of the economy's material limitations. There was little change in the government's conscription policy, largely because it relied on the capitalist class for its development plan and current practices adequately met the military's needs. Again, Nasser's vocalized nationalism and populism did not lead him toward a restructural policy; rather, for the time being he willingly relied on past domestic policies and international actors for his defense needs.

FROM THE SUEZ WAR TO THE 1967 WAR

The 1956 War was anything but a contest in which Egypt undertook extensive battle preparations. The Egyptian army, completely surprised by Israel's attack, was evicted from the Sinai in a few short days. Soon after Israel reached the banks of the Suez Canal, Britain and France launched a planned attack on the Suez, ostensibly for the purpose of separating the Egyptians and Israelis and protecting the waterway, but actually attempting to extract retribution for Nasser's nationalization of the Suez Canal Company a few months before. After tremendous pressures and threats from the United States and the Soviet Union, the British and French withdrew from the Canal. Israel departed from the Sinai a few months later after more threats from the United States and international guarantees concerning its right of passage through the Straits of Tiran and a demilitarized Egyptian-Israeli border.[49]

Nasser was able to turn a military defeat into a diplomatic victory: he was viewed by many as a victim of and a solitary fighter against a consortium of old and new imperialist forces. His anti-imperialist credentials firmly established, he began to project himself more forcefully in regional affairs. This had two immediate consequences. The first, a direct product of their invasion, was a more genuine antipathy toward the Israelis. Vatikiotis writes that Nasser "came to see Israel more and more as a serious threat to Egypt's perceived economic and political role in the region. He no longer exhibited the same ambivalence about it as he did before 1955. Rather his belief in the artificiality and non-organic intrusiveness of the Jewish state became firmer."[50] After 1956 Israel was viewed as the final testimony to imperialist forces in the region, planted in the middle of the Arab World and obstructing true Arab unity. It was important, however, that such animosity not result in an unintended conflict with Israel. Nasser maintained a policy of "no war/no peace," a strategy calculated to ensure that the next Arab-Israeli War would occur on Nasser's terms, for he was convinced that before Egypt could confront Israel militarily, the Egyptian society, army, and economy had to be transformed and modernized. This implied a rather cautious military posture toward Israel, careful not to push too far, too fast.[51] Although there were moments when the Arab-Israeli conflict heated up, notably in 1964 over Israel's plan to divert the Jordan River, not until May 1967 did it take on greater prominence.[52] Thus, the ten years of relative quiet on the Egyptian-Israeli border between 1956 and 1967 belied his embittered attitude toward Israel.

The second consequence of Nasser's new anti-imperialist credentials was a greater activism in Arab affairs. In fact, his cautiousness toward the Israelis stood in direct contrast to, and was a result of, the turbulence in intra-Arab politics. This period witnessed the union and dissolution of the United Arab Republic, the short-lived marriage between Syria and Egypt between 1958 and 1961, and the overthrow of the pro-U.S. government in Iraq with one more consistent with Nasser's ideology. And as Nasser attempted to export his vision of politics to other parts of the Arab World, he was confronted by conservative Arab states, notably Jordan and Saudi Arabia, who did not share his conception of Arab politics. The most violent manifestation of this clash of ideologies was the Yemen War from 1962 to 1967, with Nasser sponsoring the Royalists against the Saudi-backed Monarchists. Such intra-Arab struggles left Nasser with little time or energy to concentrate on the Israelis. In general, Nasser's greater involvement in the Arab-Israeli conflict and Arab affairs guaranteed that national security would occupy a top priority in the Egyptian cabinet and budget. This was particularly so after Egypt's entry into the Yemen War (see table 4.1).[53]

As important as were the systemic and regional effects from the Suez War, arguably more important were the domestic consequences. First, Nasser's new-found prestige and anti-imperialist credentials gave him the courage and motivation to nationalize most foreign-owned banks, insurance companies, and commercial agencies in 1957. These nationalizations, which were more ad hoc reactions to international conflicts than the result of any concerted economic plan, would have tremendous implications for the Egyptian political economy.[54] Whereas before 1956 his goal of Egyptian industrialization had been frustrated by the private sector's lack of enthusiasm, Nasser could now promote industrialization without their unbridled assistance. The state became a principal producer and owner of productive resources, and state-led industrialization now seemed foreordained. These economic actions, unimaginable before the Suez War, gave Nasser a firmer hold over political power.

Although the nationalizations of foreign capital did not translate into a greater level of hostility toward domestic capital, they seemed to give Nasser the confidence that the government could promote economic development without their assistance. The 1960 five-year plan, while listing domestic capital's participation, particularly so given its technical expertise and ability to help finance far-reaching economic projects with the public sector, also pointed to the government's increased impatience with domestic capital's perceived reluctance to partake fully in the development process.[55]

This increasingly strained relationship between Nasser and industrial capital ended abruptly with a series of sweeping land reforms and the nationalizations in 1961 of the largest banks in Egypt, National Bank of Egypt and Bank Misr. This silenced the landed aristocracy and domestic capital as important societal actors. Although these nationalizations were paraded by the government as a justifiable response to capital's continued reluctance at providing for the development needs of the Egyptian people, its decision appears to have been motivated by the general threat these two large financial institutions posed for the state's rule and control over the economy and polity.[56] "The new ideology of the regime was embodied in 'al-Mithaq' or the Socialist Charter," a document that decreed the government's intention of radicalizing the political economy and imposing a socialist solution with an Arab face.[57] Although the private sector continued to exist and in fact dominated some areas like agricultural production, the result was that the government had centralized its control over the economy, established its prominence in economic affairs, and undercut the private sector.[58]

The expanded public sector rewarded Nasser in two ways. First, it became an instrument of political and economic control,[59] and the government continued to infuse it with military men and technocrats loyal to its vision. Although in the mid-1960s the expanding state apparatus and declining economy fostered the beginning of a rivalry between the technobureaucratic elite and the military appointments, the latter continued to win owing to the former's lack of an independent power base.[60] Second, the state now controlled a vast amount of productive assets and economic surplus and became the dominant economic power.[61] The nationalizations and expansion of the public sector transferred power to a growing and ever-powerful state bureaucracy that was accountable primarily to Nasser.

Nasser's unreigned decision-making authority and control over the state apparatus did not mean that he could be cavalier about his domestic standing. He wielded three mechanisms for quelling societal discontent. The first was distributing and withholding economic rewards. This was evident in his ability, on the one hand, to nationalize the economic holdings of those who represented a domestic challenge and, on the other

TABLE 4.2
Private and Public Industrial Output in Egypt, 1963/64–1970/71

	Private Sector Output		Public Sector Output		
	Total[a]	Percentage Change	Total[a]	Percentage Change	Private Output as % of Total
1963/64	274,276	—	610,613	—	30.99
1964/65	264,268	–3.7	704,605	15.4	27.28
1965/66	280,618	6.2	852,681	21.0	24.76
1966/67	282,436	0.6	926,184	8.6	23.37
1967/68	292,132	3.5	886,680	–4.3	24.79
1968/69	313,673	7.3	—	—	—
1969/70	333,278	6.3	—	—	—
1970/71	359,446	7.8	1,078,338	—	25.00

Source: Girgis, *Industrialization and Trade Patterns in Egypt*, 49.
[a]Totals in Egyptian 1,000 pounds.

hand, to subsidize the standard of living of the urban masses. The second method was through controlled political mobilization. Nasser offered society another state-controlled institution, the Arab Socialist Union (ASU), for channeling societal preferences and giving these forces the pretense of sharing political power. This party, like previous attempts, was rarely viewed by the masses as a legitimate or adequate forum for channeling societal expression,[62] and it was therefore never totally effective at controlling society. This became more obvious throughout the mid-1960s with an increased number of societal protests. Although much of the resistance was attributed to the Moslem Brotherhood,[63] it was clear that the economic downturn during the mid-1960s was an important contributing factor. Consequently, when neither the pretense of shared authority nor economic rewards and sanctions could satisfactorily quell societal discontent, Nasser turned to repression. For instance, he responded to the societal disturbances of 1965 and 1966 by arresting a number of the Moslem Brotherhood.[64] Thus, although Nasser could depend on a high degree of support from the masses, his support was not unquestioned.

This radical restructuring between state and society erased some important constraints on the government's ability to mobilize resources for national defense. After all, the government's developmentalist economic policy and reliance on domestic capital had been an important constraint prior to 1960, but now Nasser's already tight control over the decision-making process was augmented by the state's tremendous relative autonomy. It would seem, therefore, that the government would be better able to implement a restructural policy if so desired. This did not happen, however. Specifically, once defense spending began to increase with the Yemen War in 1962 the government showed little desire to implement any major change in its mobilization practices. Nasser was the consummate politician, ever sensitive to his standing in the hearts of the Egyptian people and thus duly hesitant to place too great a burden on their shoulders. And given the Soviet Union's steadfast willingness to assist Nasser's domestic and regional dreams, he was more than willing to construct an international solution when required. Furthermore, although the state now controlled a significant degree of economic production, what production it controlled was not immediately suitable to meeting the military's weapons needs.[65] This meant that the Soviet Union was once again indispensable. The government's conscription policy seemed a more likely candidate to undergo a restructural strategy because there was evidence that the Yemen War had led to some manpower pressures and Nasser no longer relied on the upper classes for his development needs. Whether Nasser capitalized on such space was another matter.

Financial Strategies

It is useful to divide the government's financial strategy into two periods: one before Egypt's entry into the Yemen War in 1962 and one afterward. Budgetary pressures increased owing in large part to the costs of the Yemen War. Also at this point the economy declined while defense pressures increased; therefore, the government began to face graver dilemmas and greater challenges.

As already indicated there was a dramatic change in state-capital relations over this decade, and such radical events could not help but effect the government's fiscal basis. The most important changes in the government's financial strategy derived not necessarily from perceived budgetary pressures, but, as already noted, from the implication of international changes for Nasser's political base. The government's general response to moments of external pressure was to nationalize a segment of the economy, which essentially represented a 100 percent tax.[66] Although the official explanation was that "government control over Egypt's major economic resources was essential in order to forestall an attack on the revolution by the wealthy middle classes and to ensure the most efficient use of those resources for Egypt's development," these nationalizations were designed to thwart any potential opposition to the government.[67] Specifically, the 1956 Suez War brought about the nationalizations of foreign-owned enterprises; the Iraqi overthrow in 1958 triggered the nationalizations of some minor domestic holdings; and the Syrian secession from the UAR in 1961 provoked a wave of land reforms and the nationalization of the banking industry. These nationalizations, then, served the dual purpose of (potentially) servicing development and ridding Nasser of an oppositional force. Although these moves were not part of the government's war preparation strategies or (immediate) economic objectives, the nationalizations profoundly shaped the government's options for meeting future budgetary problems.

These nationalizations substantially alleviated the government's present fiscal problems, but they could not eradicate them from occurring in the future. This became particularly clear after 1961 when budgetary pressures and balance of payments difficulties increased as the costs of the Yemen War increased. The government did introduce some modest tax increases on inheritance, duty, and estate income, ostensibly to promote social welfare and egalitarian principles; however, no less an authoritative source than the Central Bank of Egypt writes that such moves had little effect on the tax burden because direct taxation to indirect taxation maintained a 1:3 ratio during this period and thus represented an implicit tax exemption for what remained of the upper-income groups.[68] Vatikiotis writes that Nasser "promised a welfare state more or less without a prayer of being able to finance it because, in a formally declared socialist Egypt, social welfare could not be financed by direction taxation."[69] Whether because of the country's low standard of living, political considerations, lack of state capacity to extract, or some combination thereof, the government would not consider financing its outlays through either forced savings or direct taxation. This left the government few options.

Indirect taxation was one option. The government relied on indirect methods because it lacked the administrative muscle to extract through more direct means, and political repercussions were attached to a more highly visible tax.[70] Although pursued through various instruments, indirect measures commonly weighed heaviest on the lower classes.[71] The agricultural sector became an important revenue source, as the government established its control over the peasantry mainly through building cooperatives and directing strategic inputs, which allowed it both to increase its revenue base by underpricing agricultural products before selling them at higher prices on the world market and bolster the regime's fortunes by subsidizing food for the urban population.[72] Additional revenue was raised in 1962 by increasing excise taxes on such commodities as sugar, cement, benzine and imposing new taxes on such items as wool, cotton, and heavy fuel products.[73] These tax policies were clearly biased in favor of certain workers, the expanding public sector, and the nonlanded classes and biased against the rural sector; that is, policies generally burdened the masses more than the upper classes.[74]

Because domestic measures could not satiate the government's budgetary dilemmas it turned to foreign assistance. By 1963 over half the budget was financed through public sector borrowing. Its annual debt, which increased fivefold between 1959 and 1963, was the government's principal method of supplementing its domestic revenue and financing its budget deficit.[75] Be that as it may, borrowing probably appeared economically affordable, for Arab socialism appeared to be going strong; the economy was experiencing rapid economic growth, high growth rates, and tremendous increases in industrial and manufacturing output.

This was the scene until 1964, when a balance of payments and foreign currency reserves crisis emerged. Until the early 1960s the Egyptian government had covered its foreign currency needs through a combination of sterling reserves left from the Farouk era, the economic nationalizations, and aid from both the East and the West; the former funded development, and the latter financed its wheat imports. By 1964, however, the government's reserves were depleted. The immediate causes of the crisis are found in the crop failure of 1961, the U.S. suspension of PL 480 in response to Nasser's involvement in the Yemen War (which meant that Egypt had to expend currency reserves for wheat), and the underestimated cost of both defense in general and the Yemen Civil War in particular.[76] The latter proved a particularly damaging exploit. Although the costs of the war were not considered excessive at the rate of approximately LE40 to 60 million a year, it was enough both to restrict the implementation of the second five-year plan and shove the economy further toward deterioration.[77] In fact, the government appeared somewhat uneasy about fully disclosing the costs of the Yemen War; the figures were underreported to forestall substantial societal resistance to the perceived economic hardships and assist Nasser's desire to maintain political control.[78]

The government made few moves to redress these economic imbalances with domestic measures. The masses were not expected to bear any greater burden because the economic downturn seemed to have contributed to increased societal opposition in 1965. And although Nasser successfully countered such outbursts with governmental force, he was left with little taste for raising the domestic burden.[79] In fact, even the upper classes escaped the government's reach. Nasser had demonstrated a strong propensity to use such external shocks to move economically against the upper classes, but at this point he opted to forego introducing any further radical measures against the surviving bourgeoisie for fear that this might provoke a revolutionary situation.[80]

Consequently, the government looked to foreign assistance to solve its balance of payments deficit.[81] Again, the principal Soviet role was alleviating a prime source of balance of payments difficulties—weapons imports. Earlier in 1962 the Soviets had increased the arms discount from 33 percent before 1962 to 40 percent between 1962 and 1966 and made all debts repayable after twenty years at low interest rates in the local currency.[82] The Soviets followed through on these earlier concessions; in

September 1965 Egyptian and Soviet leaders agreed to: (1) write off 50 percent of military debts (which totaled $460 million) as the Soviet contribution to the Yemen War; and (2) postpone all installments due over the 1966–1970 period.[83] Moreover, the Soviet-Egyptian Trade Agreement on December 30, 1966, which was intended to establish the terms of trade between the two countries for the next five years, had the Soviets shipping military equipment, oil, and other raw materials in exchange for Egyptian cotton, rice, vegetables, and fruit. Mohammed Heikal, commenting in Al-Ahram, wrote that Egypt paid only LE6.6 million every year, while the Soviets agreed to provide Egypt with a $275 million loan at 5 percent interest to provide for Egypt's five-year plan.[84] The Soviets were apparently willing to bankroll Nasser's security objectives.[85]

In summary, the most profound change in the government's revenue base occurred by whittling away the upper classes through a series of nationalizations. These measures, which provided a temporary reprieve from any resource gap, were not taken to forestall budgetary pressures (though it had this consequence), but rather to silence Nasser's domestic opponents. Once the economic crisis hit in 1964, the government avoided any overhaul of the its budgetary and extraction policies for fear of domestic resistance. Moreover, Nasser's reluctance to disclose fully the costs of the Yemen War to an already impatient public dramatized his unwillingness to reveal to society the full costs of his adventures, particularly if society believed it was being asked to forego its own economic welfare. Hinnebusch writes that "Nasserism was weakened by a mounting imbalance between commitments and resources which climaxed in the mid-sixties. The capacity of the regime to mobilize resources was constrained by Egypt's poverty and the inefficiency and corruption of its economic apparatus; yet its commitments—to an ambitious development program, a large army, salaries for a technocratic elite and a substantial welfare state—had enormously expanded."[86] The government showed no great resolve in the face of an expanding resource gap, for this would have undercut its ruling strategy.[87] As long as the Soviet Union and other international lending agencies were willing to subsidize the burden, Nasser would be reluctant either to alter his financial strategy or to decrease the scope of his objectives.

Production Strategies

Before 1956 Nasser had hoped to develop an autonomous arms industry that would be capable of producing most of the military's weapons needs. Because such dreams were just that, Nasser turned to the

Soviets in 1955. This did not terminate his desire or efforts toward his initial goal, but once he signed the arms pact he discovered that both East and West Bloc countries, though for different reasons, were unwilling to aid his cause. First, so long as Egypt demonstrated its willingness to climb into the Soviet bed, few Western countries would aid its domestic arms industry. Beginning in 1958, however, Nasser began assembling West European, and primarily West German, scientists who had participated in aeronautics and rocketry programs during World War Two. The task for these imported scientists was twofold: to develop jet fighters and ground-to-ground missiles. Its efforts ultimately failed because no West or East European government was willing to sell Egypt the required technology.[88] Second, the shift to Soviet equipment meant that Egypt's Western-style arms factories were mismatched to its current military imports and needs. Third, the Soviets, jealous and guarded of their own technology, were reluctant to aid Egypt's arms production. Fourth, there was chronic overproduction with no foreign markets able to absorb the excess supply. These problems led Egyptian arms industries to begin producing more and more for the civilian market, everything from margarine to twelve-cylinder engines and the ultimate "civilianization" of the arms industry.[89] Moreover, once the balance of payments crisis hit in 1964, military industries, which previously were not expected to turn a profit to justify their existence, were now required to do just that. Because of these and other problems, domestic arms production became dormant by the end of the 1960s, where it would remain until the next decade.[90]

The Soviet reluctance to aid Egypt's military industrialization program had exactly the intended effect: Egypt became more dependent on the Soviet Union for its military needs. In general, any move to deepen military industrialization was premised on not only having the appropriate economic structure but also on Soviet technical and scientific assistance. Without such assistance Egypt was forced to abandon what little arms production it had in favor of an international strategy.

Conscription Policy

The government also maintained its conscription policy of burdening the lower classes more than the upper classes. Although during the Yemen War the government experienced increased manpower pressures, particularly officers, its response was not to distribute more evenly the burdens of military service, but rather to conscript more university graduates on a limited basis.[91] This accommodational policy belied what appeared to have been within Nasser's reach because this was a period in which the state enjoyed tremendous legitimacy: it no longer relied on a now politically insignificant and economically weakened capitalist class for the country's development needs.

There are four reasons for this status quo orientation. First, expanding the conscription net to include more university graduates would potentially undermine the government's development objectives. Skilled professionals were in high demand in the expanding industrial, manufacturing, and service sectors; placing them in the army might come at the expense of economic development and the second five-year plan. At this point no one was willing to sacrifice development for defense. Second, although in hindsight it became clear that the army was performing less than adequately in Yemen, some within the military argued that this was not because of the demographic profile of the typical Egyptian soldier but rather because the army was fighting on an alien terrain. Third, at this point most weapons were labor-intensive; they did not really require the educated classes for their successful operation. Only after 1967, and particularly so after 1973, did military technology require a more highly educated Egyptian soldier.[92] Fourth, Nasser may have been reluctant to widen the conscription net, for he had already publicly declared that his regional adventures were not coming at tremendous additional costs; to drastically alter the government's conscription policy would therefore visibly contradict such statements.

The Suez War proved a milestone in Egyptian history. Nasser's nationalization of the foreign capitalist class presented him with the basis and motivation for state-led industrialization and a new solution to either external threats or dwindling resources: strip the most powerful societal actors of their economic resources. Such actions and augmentations of the state's treasury, however, could not sustain Nasser's growing commitment to investment, social welfare, and national security. Given his previous policies, political basis, and the state's limited capacities, Nasser was unwilling and unable to supplement his resource base with domestic measures; consequently he shunned any restructural measures in favor of, first, an accommodational policy, and, second, an international strategy.

Moreover, the country's crumbling military industries were rendered moribund as a result of Soviet policies. Here the costs of adopting an international strategy became painfully evident. The Soviets were more than willing to sponsor Egypt's grandiose objectives (particularly because they apparently annoyed the Americans), but they also wanted something in return, namely some control over Egyptian policies. More important for future events, the government's conscription policy maintained its class bias. Nasser's war preparation strategy remained unquestioned and undisturbed so long as the Soviets were willing and loyal sponsors and security pressures were not overwhelmingly viewed as having disastrous strategic consequences. A major external shock was necessary before the government rethought the wisdom of its present course.

DEFEAT, CONSOLIDATION, AND REDEMPTION, 1967–1973

The disastrous 1967 War proved Nasser correct in his estimation that a premature war with Israel would be unsuccessful for the Arabs. What began in late May as an attempt to maintain his leadership in the Arab World ended in early June with a transformed Middle East. Regardless of whether Nasser wanted to challenge militarily Israel at that moment, Egypt's dismal, half-hearted confrontation of the Israelis challenged the very basis of his regime and created tremendous distress and soul-searching for most in the Arab World. Both conservative (Jordan and Saudi Arabia) and radical (Syria and Egypt) regimes had failed either to promote a transformation to the good society or to challenge the Israelis militarily, economically, or politically. Egypt's defeat was the Arabs' defeat.[93]

Nasser's personal political standing emerged comparatively unscathed from the debacle. Immediately after the war Nasser announced his resignation and nominated Zakaria Muhi al-Din, former RCC officer rumored to be pro-Western, to take his place.[94] The masses responded to this news with a tremendous gathering and show of support on Nasser's behalf on June 9 and 10. It seemed as if society had to salvage something from this bitter defeat. Although the people could blame many in the state apparatus for leading Egypt down the path of utter defeat, they could not go the full distance and blame Nasser personally. Nasser embodied defiant nationalism, and to bring him down would seem to give the West the victory it ultimately sought.[95] Ajami observes that there was a popular need to believe in someone, as "the leader was dissociated from the defeat and invited to go beyond his political apparatus and to purge the elements that had supposedly captured and undermined his revolution."[96]

Therefore, Nasser escaped society's wrath, but the regime was not so fortunate. Societal dissatisfaction expanded dramatically after 1967 as the masses began to mobilize in a semiautonomous fashion. The principal complaints were registered at the military and its performance in the recent war, the state's nondemocratic character, and the general discrediting of its institutions.[97] The first large-scale demonstration after the June defeat came in March 1968, at the Helwan Steel plant, in opposition to the meager sentences given to military officers held responsible for the June War. Although the protests had initially been organized by the government in support of its policies (it was started by the Arab Socialist Union's Ali Sabri in defense of Nasser), it soon turned into an uncontrollable mass demonstration against the state's security apparatus. "A common popular complaint in those days was 'We accept the regime did not do much for us, but being a military one, it could at least have given account of itself in the war against Israel.' "[98] Alongside these demonstrations by the workers was the student protest movement, born after 1967 not so much as a criticism of socialism per se but rather against an economic system that seemed to reward those who were either part of the military or had military connections.[99] The student movement was particularly infuriated by the military's showing in the 1967 War; not only was the military accruing economic benefits through personal connections, but it had also given a poor accounting of its activities when called upon to confront the Israelis. Nasser took advantage of the opportunity by "cleansing" the Egyptian government of its impure elements, a move that both satisfied, in part, society's demand for accountability and justice and increased his control over the opposition.[100]

Accordingly, the events of June 1967 had an important effect on the composition of the state managers. Until 1967 the military and the technocratic elite ruled together in relative harmony.[101] Although there was some strain between military appointments, made through political connections, and technocrats, who saw themselves as having considerable professional skills,[102] these latent tensions visibly emerged after the June War. The technocratic elite contended not only that the military defeat was partly owing to the military's distraction from its original duty of defending the country, but that it also had led Egypt down the road of economic bankruptcy.[103] Nasser sympathized with this interpretation of events—it would also serve his political objectives—and began to strip the armed forces of those responsibilities not directly relevant to national security. These purges handed the technocrats a more visible and integral role in the decision-making process.[104] These moves, inaugurated by Nasser's March speech, marked the public emergence of a more "pragmatic" Nasser, one who was willing to suspend radicalism at home in favor of domestic stability and military power.

Accompanying this bureaucratic transformation was a changed orientation. Many technobureaucratic elite were Western-educated, skeptical of Arab socialism, and ambivalent toward the radicalization of Egyptian life. Although Arab socialism was never intended as the private sector's swan song, it clearly was an attempt to keep its activities under state guidance and control. During the 1960s, however, those government officials, who had once supported and benefited from the state-led plan and its distribution of rewards and privileges, began to change direction "once the initial etatist expansion ended and career and enrichment opportunities stagnated. . . . [These elite] lost whatever stake it had in Nasser's policies."[105] Nasser joined in this movement, as he began to purge the cabinet of military men and insert in their places many civilians and academics, such as Abdel-Aziz Higazi who left his position in the Department of Economics at Cairo University to become the treasury minister. Nasser did so because these new government officials were viewed as "professionals," willing to implement Nasser's economic policies; they placed greater controls over the public sector and asserted greater market discipline over its operations.[106] These changes in the composition and attitudes of state officials, in combination with the tremendous political and economic pressures, would have an important impact on the government's war preparation policies.[107]

Nasser staked his very survival and prestige on his ability to confront the Israelis.[108] The Arab-Israeli conflict had been personalized. Whereas before 1967 Nasser's anti-Israeli stance was motivated by Palestinian justice and pan-Arabism, with Israel's capture of the Sinai "the confrontation was transformed into one between Egypt the aggrieved party and Israel the aggressor state."[109] And, if the Israelis were not willing to voluntarily relinquish the land, which was unlikely, then it was incumbent upon Nasser to wrest away control with military force. As Nasser proclaimed, "What was captured by force will be retaken by force." Part of this strategy was to place continuous pressure on Israel's military positions on the Suez Canal, which led directly to the War of Attrition in 1969. Nasser hoped that by shelling Israeli positions on the East Bank he would both convince them that the costs of occupation were too high and demonstrate his own resolve to a watching and waiting public. He did not figure on the Israelis upping the ante, however, and they responded by bombing the Suez cities and engaging in deep penetration strikes. In addition to a death toll that exceeded that of the June War, the destruction of the Canal cities created a massive population exodus to Cairo, where many became homeless, destitute, and unemployed. This furthered the societal pressures on the regime and increased its financial straits. Nasser's launching of the War of Attrition clearly demonstrated how the costs of no action outweighed the costs of action.[110]

The costs of action were more than the toll registered along the Suez because these costs extended to the government's attempt to implement those policies that would mobilize societal resources for war.[111] As defense devoured an increasing percentage of the economy—it went from 11.1 percent of GNP in 1966 to nearly 33 percent in 1973—the question was how the government would afford this military inflammation without eroding its other principal objective of political stability.[112] Although there was widespread societal agreement concerning the need to confront the Israelis, there were two significant problems. First, society was ahead of the government in demanding a continuation of the Arab-Israeli conflict as soon as possible. The 1968 student movement argued for war at a timetable far ahead of what the government thought was militarily sound. There were significant pressures on the government to demonstrate its resolve in as timely a manner as possible. The student movement's demands, however, potentially undermined the government's political basis, for the administration feared imposing further economic hardships on the Egyptian population that would provoke antigovernment opposition. This was all the more true because the war would not begin for a number of years and the population could not be expected to tolerate indefinitely a stalled standard of living. This meant that private consumption had to be kept at sufficient levels so that a too rapid decline would not unleash antiregime disturbances.[113] These dynamics made the government's balancing act that much more difficult.[114]

Although the Arab-Israeli conflict would take on greater urgency after 1967, the extent to which the government would subsume its other objective of economic development to territorial recovery was an open question. From December 1967 through March 1968 there was an ongoing cabinet debate concerning this very issue: Would defense receive a greater share of societal resources, ostensibly suspending development? Those who argued for privileging development contended that an expanding economy would provide the financial and productive basis for a more effective war effort. Although the debate was settled in March 1968 with the dictum that "development should proceed side-by-side with the defense effort," such slogans belied the government's actions as it became evident that war preparation was its first priority and the economy's health would be sacrificed for this purpose.[115] It was readily understood that the economy was in desperate need of repair and that there already existed tremendous foreign exchange and balance of payments difficulties, but Nasser maintained a course designed to recover the Egypt's lost prestige and territory; this came at the direct expense of future economic growth. The June War signaled the end of an expanding state apparatus and the suspension of economic growth.[116]

In general, although Nasser had escaped the direct wrath of society, he was under greater political pressures after 1967 as a result of the growing societal dissatisfaction with the continued Israeli occupation of the Sinai, and the (lack of) progress toward economic development. The failures on both fronts called into question Nasser's personal legitimacy and his radical policies. The government's fortunes were now dependent on its ability to successfully confront the Israelis, yet those very activities that were needed to do so, if prolonged too long, might undercut both the government's future and the economy's well-being. Because of the economic and security crises the government was unwilling to impose many domestic solutions necessary to relieve the pressures on either one, for this inevitably implied imposing tremendous burdens on society, which could threaten the regime's survival. The Egyptian government had to walk a tightrope, with the Israelis in one hand and domestic oppositional forces in the other; either could potentially tip the government over the side.

In the midst of this balancing act came an additional political crisis. Nasser died of a heart attack in September 1970 soon after he accepted the Rogers Plan for ending the War of Attrition. This left the cabinet ministers vying for political supremacy. Vice-President Anwar Sadat, assumed to be a nonthreatening, temporary head-of-state, outwitted his closest rivals and consolidated power in 1971. Although the political intrigues that led to Sadat's "corrective movement" of May 1971 are a critical story of this period, it is important not to become obsessed with the "cult of personality." Ajami notes that because Egyptian politics were navigated by two men it is tempting to view the course of Egyptian history (war preparation strategies) as the result of their personalities and idiosyncracies. Both seemed to be master politicians and inaugurated important changes in Egyptian history: Nasser oversaw Egypt's entrance into the Soviet fold and Arab socialism, while Sadat is widely understood as presiding over economic liberalization and the turn to the West.[117]

Although there were important personality differences, more important for understanding the course of this period were the constraints that both men had to confront.[118] Consider the following two episodes that relate to the government's objectives and the domestic economic and political constraints on its actions. The first episode was at the opening of the Third Session of the National Assembly on November 19, 1970—one of Sadat's first public addresses following Nasser's death. Sadat followed both Nasser's pledge to do battle with the Israelis, and his lead by linking his personal prestige with territorial recovery. Sadat stated that: "The tasks of the coming stage—I think—can be defined as follows: *First*: the battle first, second, and last. By battle I do not mean just fighting. I mean the total liberation of all Arab lands occupied by the 1967 aggression. *Second*: Behind the battle-front we have economic and social work which should not cease for one second."[119] In fact, he possibly upped the stakes by declaring 1971 "the year of decision." The costs of no action continued to outweigh the costs of action.

Second, although Sadat is widely viewed as the engineer of Egypt's return to a market-oriented economy, Nasser himself provided the groundwork for this move as his post-1967 policies demonstrated a movement to the Right and a modest embracement of the bourgeoisie.

Notable here is the "Khamshish Affair."[120] Briefly, in the mid-1960s Nasser established the Higher Committee for the Liquidation of Feudalism (HCLF), an institution whose mission was to deepen the socialist experiment in the countryside. An agent of the HCLF was murdered in the village of Khamshish in April 1966, and local village notables, whose status was challenged by the socialist reforms, were charged with murder. Khamshish quickly became a symbol of the government's resolve to deepen the socialist experiment in the face of reactionary forces. Soon after the June War, however, Nasser terminated the HCLF, announced in a cabinet meeting that he viewed it as partially responsible for the June defeat, and that "the first task of the government was to rectify previous mistakes. The starting point was to lift the sequestration imposed on the properties of the rural elites."[121] The rural peasantry quickly identified this posture as a sign of things to come, the return of the old landed classes, and the general deradicalization of the regime. As Ajami comments, "the wind was blowing in all directions," and Nasser hoped to bid for the allegiance of the bourgeoisie. Sadat, then, was not the first to demonstrate a willingness to embrace the upper classes.[122] True, Sadat might have felt general sympathy and affection for the upper classes while Nasser might have tolerated their existence because of their potential contribution to the government's economic and political objectives. But even Sadat could not ignore the legacies of Nasserism and the populist policies that flowed from it.[123] Both leaders were not captured by social forces or swept away by environmental conditions, but they had similar objectives—challenging the Israelis while maintaining their political basis—and confronted similar constraints. This fundamental fact lent tremendous consistency to their war preparation strategies.

All that said, the post-1971 represented a break from the past in one important respect: it was then that the costs of four years of war preparation and lack of activity on the Arab-Israeli front on regime stability were becoming painfully clear.[124] In fact, it seemed that just as the foreign threat diminished, as the War of Attrition had ended in 1970 and Sadat had launched a diplomatic offensive in early 1971, that the domestic threat accelerated due to a rapidly deteriorating Egyptian economy and rising discontent among the Egyptian people. Briefly, domestic opposition forces registered three principal objections. The first was the nondemocratic character of Sadat's regime; this, however, was also raised by the student movement of Nasser's regime. Sadat could not match Nasser's legitimacy, and citizens viewed him as less able to incorporate societal demands.[125] Therefore, many groups challenged the government's authoritarian nature and called for greater societal representation and participation. Second, Sadat began to incorporate into his coalition those groups estranged from the Nasser regime. Specifically, Sadat's appeal to industrial capital and the landed elite caused the lower classes to worry that he would erase the gains they had made under Nasser.[126] The third complaint questioned the government's handling of the Arab-Israeli conflict. Society was being expected to make a never-ending sacrifice for no apparent reason. Sadat's 1971 "year of decision" had ended, and war with Israel was still no closer at hand.[127] The students, challenging the government's continued indecisiveness as a way of demonstrating the bankruptcy of the regime, were particularly confrontational; this left the government that much more wary of imposing any further hardships.[128] In general, Sadat was aware of the rising costs of inaction: the economy was not likely to recover from this stasis, and severe domestic disturbances were likely to follow as well.[129] If Sadat's assent to power did effect Egyptian war preparation strategies in any way, however, it was that his newcomer status made him more leery of increasing the domestic burden. He had to earn his own legitimacy through some bold action.

That bold action would not come initially at the expense of the Israelis but of the Soviets in July 1972. Sadat, in a bold and unexpected move, informed the Soviet leadership, his principal source of financial and material assistance, that their military advisers were no longer needed and should promptly leave Egyptian soil. There was little to indicate that Egyptian-Soviet relations had entered a particularly dangerous phase or that Sadat was about to embark on such a daring course of action. In fact, after Nasser's death both Sadat and the Soviets took care to ensure that the status quo prevailed for the time being; the Soviets wanted to make sure that they still had some leverage over the Egyptians, and the Egyptians wanted to make sure that they could still rely on Soviet assistance. And soon thereafter, prompted by Sadat's "corrective movement" in May 1971, which worried Soviet officials once Sadat purged the "pro-Soviet" Ali Sabri group from the cabinet, the parties formalized their relationship on May 27, 1971; the Soviets and the Egyptians signed "The Soviet-Egyptian Treaty of Friendship and Cooperation."[130] This was the first such treaty signed between the Soviets and a noncommunist country. The terms ensured that the Soviets would continue to have a hand in Egypt's economic path toward socialism, while the Egyptians received further guarantees of Soviet assistance. In this respect, then, the treaty represented a continuation of past practices or, as some East European officials described it, "window dressing."[131] Be that as it may, the treaty apparently hid a number of concerns Sadat had of the strategic relationship and how he might best receive the kind of material assistance he required for both his domestic goals and battle preparations.

The post-1971 period was indeed one of change in both Egyptian domestic politics and its strategic relationships. One objective here is to show how the two were connected.

The government followed a set of war preparation strategies that reflected its attempt to further its mobilization of resources for war while remaining attentive to societal sensitivities. The government capitalized on the tremendous societal agreement that Egyptian pride had to be restored by attempting to localize some of the burden. This would be most visible in the government's manpower policy stance as it implemented a restructural strategy. The government's ability to maintain a heavy military burden, however, was challenged by societal turmoil after 1971. At this point Sadat released some domestic pressure through a partial demobilization and an international strategy. But the bold restructuring that occurred in the government's conscription policy was not matched by similar endeavors in its financial or material strategies. Here government officials demonstrated a strong propensity toward accommodational and international strategies, handicapped as it was by an economic and fiscal crisis, societal tensions, and the need to maintain a coalition that would support the government's foreign and domestic policies.[132] Consequently, during this period the government implemented various domestic mobilization practices and an international strategy that reflected a common concern for the regime's stability. This meant that the Soviets, and other willing allies, would become critical to the government's ability to maneuver between societal and systemic forces.

Financial Strategies

If the government was determined to recapture the Sinai and right the wrongs of the Arab-Israeli conflict, it would have to do so under financial duress. There were two immediate problems. First, the pre-1967 fiscal, foreign currency, and balance of payments crisis was produced by the three major drains on Egypt's hard currency reserves: the costs of the Yemen War and the Arab-Israeli conflict, the need to purchase greater quantities of wheat on the international market, and the failure of ISI. According to Abdel Aziz Higazi, the treasury minister, the June War aggravated the already present inflationary pressures, the balance of payments deficit, and the foreign debt.[133] The government's immediate need to rebuild its army through massive weapons imports only added to its economic woes.

Not only did the government have to mobilize more resources for national security, but there were also fewer resources to mobilize. Egypt had just lost its three major sources of revenue in the 1967 War: a total of $400–$500 million annually from the Suez Canal ($230–$250), Sinai oil fields ($100), and tourism ($100).[134] The importance of these resources for Egypt's fiscal well-being is underscored by the fact that revenue estimates from the Suez Canal alone covered nearly two-thirds of the balance of payments deficit for 1966.[135] And because the government had decided to suspend all efforts toward economic development, it was unlikely that its resource base would experience a miraculous recovery.[136]

The combination of the lost revenue, the fiscal crisis, and immediate costs of defense produced a wildly underfinanced government budget. Deputy President Zakaria Moheiddin issued a statement upon introducing the new budget and tax increases to the National Assembly after the 1967 War: "It is the duty of every citizen to keep the targets of struggle always in sight and adapt his life to new circumstances."[137] Although the government's public posture was illustrated by Moheiddin, it became apparent that the government would protect both society—and thus itself—from the full costs of war.

As the government scoured the domestic landscape for possible sources of revenue, it was faced by a rather limited selection that was partly a result of its own doing and a consequence of its own ideology and past practices. The government could not increase direct taxation to any significant end. According to the Treasury Minister Abdel-Aziz Higazi, the nationalizations of 1961 had effectively rid the country of any corporate sector, a hypothetically important source of income. And the government refused to raise substantially the financial burden of the masses because they were already impoverished, and this would risk societal resistance.[138] Moreover, the regime's ideology was based on a redistributive ethic, one that promised to secure material gains for the lower classes. To deviate from this posture, even during a period of national emergency, could possibly unravel the state's ideological foundations. Finally, even if the government had decided to raise direct taxes, their possible effectiveness was highly questionable because past increases had always met with qualified success given the bureaucracy's limited oversight capacities. For instance, while the government imposed a national security tax on personal incomes (amounting to 25 percent of the defense tax), a 25 percent tax on cultivatable land, and a tax increase on the upper classes, their effectiveness was always suspect. Therefore, direct methods were eliminated as a solution to the government's fiscal woes.

Because the government did not have the facilities with which to survey domestic financial flows, it was highly sensitive to overburdening the masses. Its past practices had rid the country of a significant capitalist class, and it depended most heavily on those taxes most easily monitored and most easily shielded from the public eye.[139] Possibly even more important, indirect taxes were raised because "that is where the money is."[140] Although the government imposed a number of indirect taxes, including a stamp duty,[141] and increased the prices on government-subsidized commodities, its central target was the public sector, which consisted of approximately 400 enterprises. "The diversion of public funds to war costs, the ability of the government to extract resources more easily from the public sector than the private sector, all placed the public sector under severe resource pressures."[142] Moreover, skimming the public sector profits and channeling it toward the war effort had the direct effect of limiting government investment, which comprised a significant percentage of all investment funds.[143] This would have both an adverse effect on future economic growth and provide an additional stimulus for discovering a different economic formula.

Because the government avoided any major alteration of its revenue structure, the tax burden was disproportionally shouldered by the masses. The Central Bank of Egypt captures nicely this dimension:

> The structure of taxation remained unchanged since the introduction of the first tax legislation in Egypt (Law No. 14 of 1939), i.e. relying upon indirect taxation, especially consumption duties which could be easily levied despite their conflict with social justice which all tax legislation maintained through the exemptions afforded. They represented a burden on the consumer in general and on limited income groups in particular although carrying the burden of taxation during this period was a necessity of war preparation to which all Egyptians were entitled.[144]

Commodity taxes accounted for the bulk of the state's revenue, business taxes and foreign trade ranked second, and only a minor share of its receipts derived from personal income taxes. Although these modest steps failed to narrow the resource gap, particularly so after 1970, the government, fearing societal resistance, failed to undertake any other efforts.

Although the government was reluctant to increase the domestic burden, this did not necessarily mean that it would abandon any effort to increase the revenue base through domestic measures. Nasser began to experiment with controlled economic liberalization and allowed a relatively small, but growing, capitalist class to reemerge. Dual reasons provoked this reexamination of the capitalist class: economic stagnation and corresponding fiscal crisis combined with the war effort, and Nasser's reconsideration of the contribution that this once castigated class might make toward alleviating the government's fiscal problems and bolstering its sagging political standing. The first important step came in the March 1968 Declaration when Nasser essentially abandoned Arab socialism; by doing so he hoped that the upper classes might take advantage of their economic resuscitation to do more than consume and to provide some additional political and economic support.[145]

Possibly the most important economic contribution the upper classes might make was to increase the government's foreign currency reserves, which had become dangerously low with tremendous implications for the government's ability to pay for its weapons imports.[146] The government moved to increase its reserves in June 1968 with the Law of the Encouragement of Capital, which included new provisions for exchange control regulations. This bill served two purposes. Similar to most of the government's policies of the period, this bill was designed to further its economic and political objectives. First, it increased the government's revenue base, which could then be used for military operations. Egyptian nationals working abroad and foreigners residing in Egypt were given the right to "maintain external non-resident accounts in foreign currency," but such holdings would be placed in the Central Bank (interest accrued on the bank accounts would be paid in Egyptian currency).[147] By allowing Egyptian citizens and foreign residents to repatriate their foreign exchange earnings in Egypt and forcing them to use the National Bank for their transactions, the government could potentially tap this foreign currency directly and thereby add to its pool of resources. Second, these economic measures would also protect the government's back from another disgruntled social group.[148]

The burdens of the June War, then, contributed to rethinking Arab socialism's virtues for meeting the current military preparation and future economic growth and strengthening those groups within the state apparatus that advocated such policies;[149] both measures led to a reappraisal of the upper classes. This procapitalist legislation did not mean, however, that even its staunchest supporters were ready to see a return of capitalist rationality. According to Higazi, an early champion of a more market-oriented economy, there was no possibility for the outright liberalization of the economy at this point, for this might undercut the government's primary objectives of satisfying the needs of the masses and ensuring the military's access to its needed supplies. Be that as it may, the emphasis was on economic reform as a way of generating more resources for defense.[150]

Because of the political and societal constraints, Nasser vigorously pursued an international strategy to fund his war effort.[151] The question was how to convince potential donors that they should contribute to the cause. One way was to heighten the regime's symbolic value in the international and regional system. This enterprise was particularly problematic with regard to the Arab World because Nasser's pre-1967 foreign policy was designed to undermine those very oil-rich states he now needed for financial salvation. To facilitate their potential generosity

Nasser changed his ideological position from champion of the pan-Arab movement and Arab radicalism to leader of the anti-Zionist movement, a position that should concern all Arab states. In short, preparing for the next Arab-Israeli conflict was a privilege to which all Arab states were entitled. In this way Nasser capitalized on Egypt's status as a front-line, confrontation state to secure additional funds. Other Arab states had to let Egypt off the financial hook; other regimes, such as Libya's Quadafi, could carry the torch of radical Arab politics.[152]

This new posture led to the Khartoum Agreement in Fall 1967, when the oil-rich Arab states (Kuwait, Libya, and Saudi Arabia) agreed to compensate Egypt to the tune of $266 million a year for the revenue lost due to the closure of the Suez Canal, the drop in tourism, and the capture of the Sinai oil fields. Nasser, in "exchange," agreed to withdraw his troops from the Yemen conflict.[153] The Khartoum Agreement, however, covered only about one-half of Egypt's capital imports during these first post-1967 years; the net loss was still $165 to $185 million.[154] In general, Nasser intended to bolster the regime's regional legitimacy to increase foreign assistance, which served his social welfare and domestic political interests as well as his security needs.

This initial act of compensation for Egypt's disproportionate burden, however, did not continue smoothly. The first sign of trouble came at the Rabat Summit in December 1969 when intra-Arab rivalry was high, and the Egyptian representative informed the Summit that Egypt's forces "were in no way prepared to face a war with Israel at that stage or in the near future."[155] Moreover, the Saudis were also suspicious of Nasser's growing ties with the Soviet Union. As a result, Saudi and other Arab assistance came, if at all, with only the greatest of difficulties.

It was fortunate that Nasser did not have to rely exclusively on his Arab brethren, for he could turn to his other savior, the Soviet Union.[156] To increase the flow of military goods from the Soviet Union to Egypt, Nasser's strategy included involving the Soviets more deeply in Egyptian affairs. This ensured "that they [the Soviets] felt Egypt's defeat was their defeat; that their prestige was bound up with that of Egypt's."[157] This was not a difficult enterprise because the lack of Soviet assistance during the June War potentially undercut its reputation and position throughout the Arab World.[158] Nasser also appeared willing to fully embrace the Soviet Union. Whereas before 1967 he demonstrated some reluctance because of concerns of too much dependence, he now seemed willing to abandon such fears because of the tremendous limitations on his ability to either rely on or mobilize from local resources.[159]

The total value of the Soviet assistance package depends on the amount Egypt actually paid for Soviet arms and the conditions that accompanied them. On this issue there is considerable debate. For instance, one source says that "Egypt paid only a small proportion of the payments to the Soviet Union, while other Arab countries made the rest of these payments on Egypt's behalf. Even if Egypt had made all of these payments itself, the actual burden was relatively small, if not insignificant."[160] By some Western estimates the total Soviet military contribution was approximately one billion dollars (the SAM complex alone cost half that amount).[161] Saad al-Shazli, Egyptian chief of staff during much of this period, gives the most accurate estimate when he argues that Egypt's contractual arrangements with the Soviets are an open question.[162] Although there are considerable differences of opinion concerning the final value of Soviet assistance, there is near agreement concerning its enormity and escalation after the 1967 War. Whereas during the 1963–1966 period the Soviets transferred approximately $424 million in weapons to Egypt, this figure expanded to $2.231 billion during the 1967–1973 period.

This increased aggregate total, however, masks the fact that Soviet generosity steadily declined over this period. Initially the Soviets were quite understanding of the Egyptian financial predicament. Egypt lost nearly 80 percent of its military equipment during the 1967 War, and the initial Soviet resupply efforts were viewed as a virtual gift.[164] Afterward the Soviets subsidized Egyptian arms purchases in three ways: selling weapons at discount rates; providing long-term, low interest contracts; and trading equipment for Egyptian commodities. Between 1967 and 1973 the discount ran 50 percent, with a ten- to fifteen-year payback period, low interest rates (usually 2.5 percent per annum), and repayable in Egyptian currency.[165] This continued the terms established under the first Soviet-Egyptian weapons agreement in 1955 in which Egypt financed its weapons partly by exporting cotton and other agricultural goods and partly by long-term debt financing at low interest rates.[166] And the Soviets were willing to extend a long payback period. By 1970 Egypt still had not paid for any of the Soviet arms since the June War, but at a Tripoli rally Nasser indicated that payments were to begin the following year: "We obtained these weapons on an installment basis. We will pay for them over ten years at a low rate of interest, starting in 1971."[167]

Soviet generosity, however, had its limits. In March 1972 the Soviets demanded payment in full and hard currency for all weapons, which, owing to the previous long-term, low interest rates, effectively quadrupled their price. There were two primary reasons behind Soviet actions. The first was the emerging Soviet-American détente. Standard wisdom in Egyptian foreign policy circles claimed that the Soviets treated the Middle East conflict as derivative of East-West conflict, and the

Soviets were now interested in placing a keener eye on Egyptian officials to ensure that their actions did not disrupt U.S.-Soviet relations.[168] This was particularly evident in Soviet arms policy, as it placed greater restrictions on the type of weapons sold and their delivery dates.[169] Détente, then, created a double bind. Not only did it imply a lessened ability by the Egyptians to exploit the conflict to their advantage, but it meant that they were being placed under tighter scrutiny by the Soviets. Second, the Kremlin believed that the Saudis and Libyans would pay for the weapons in hard currency, which the Soviets could then use to pay for their imports of Western technology and food.[170] Soviet assistance, critical for allowing Sadat to maneuver between the demands of political stability and battle preparations, was rapidly disappearing. Sadat had to find a way to increase both the flow of arms and his decisional autonomy.

The Soviets could not have chosen a more inopportune time to increase the restrictions on and costs for arms. The ultimate irony was that some oil-rich Arab states, notably Saudi Arabia, had dramatically curtailed their assistance program to Egypt because of its close relationship with the Soviet Union. And by early 1972 societal frustration was on the rise, the economy was in shambles, there were escalating balance of payments difficulties, and a skyrocketing foreign debt owed largely to the demands of war preparation.[171]

These various domestic challenges and the fact that Sadat was newly installed and constantly fearful of his domestic standing meant that he was an unlikely candidate to increase the societal contribution. To support his domestic coalition Sadat had to discover new methods for deflating societal pressures. One useful strategy was to offer material benefits to disgruntled societal actors (or at least minimize their pains). In fact, Sadat took a number of measures designed to bolster his political fortunes at the expense of fiscal responsibility. To placate the lower classes Sadat lowered the prices of such basic staples as tea, sugar, and cooking oil and attempted to improve the heavily used public transportation system. The upper classes were to be pacified by relaxing foreign exchange controls to allow for the limited importation of personal consumption items.[172] Although such policies were politically expedient, they could not conceivably narrow the resource gap.

Sadat was caught in a vise. He needed to go to war to escape the costs of inaction, answer his domestic critics, and propel the economy forward again, yet he was reluctant to preside over a 1967-type campaign. In other words, Sadat desperately had to increase the flow of financial resources so that he could both shield the regime from domestic challenges and prepare for the coming war. One can argue that the discrepancy between the government's domestic and foreign policy objectives and its available resources, along with Sadat's unwillingness or inability either to cut back his objectives or increase the domestic contribution, provoked him to become rather bold and adventurous in his foreign policy. In short, domestic factors contributed to Sadat's decision to initiate a series of diplomatic maneuvers that would both alter his relationship with Saudi Arabia and the Soviet Union and, he hoped, loosen the political noose by securing greater material assistance.

The most celebrated of these activities came in July 1972 when Sadat ordered the Soviets to reduce their advisers from their 15,000 contingent to under 1,000. Why evict the Soviet advisers given Egypt's dependence on the Soviets for its military and financial survival? Although this move could be interpreted as a gesture toward self-reliance,[173] the result of Sadat's diplomacy—with the Egyptians more heavily dependent on foreign sources—belies this conclusion. Arguably as plausible were the domestic political and economic bases of this move.[174]

Both Sadat and the Soviets took care to contain the damage that might erupt from the latter's eviction.[175] For instance, the Soviets retained their ability to use Egyptian naval facilities, and the Egyptians received some of the very weapons systems the Soviets had previously refused to supply. Whereas the value of Soviet arms shipments declined from $656 million in 1970 to $360 million the following year, the Soviet response to their expulsion was to increase the value of the arms transfers to $550 million in 1972 (and it is likely that the vast percentage of this amount arrived after the July expulsion) and $850 million in 1973.[176] Why did the Soviets choose to reward this public affront? Simply put, the Soviets were determined to maintain their superpower status.[177] "The result was that, like a gambler who has lost a throw, the Soviet Union decided to double its stakes. The military . . . argued repeatedly in the Politburo that there was no easy way out, and that the flow of military aid to the Arabs must be stepped up."[178] The military's arguments carried the day. Although the Soviets were less willing to supply Egypt with all its weapons needs on the same favorable terms, they reopened their arsenals to such an extent that Sadat could both boast that the agreement of early 1973 was the largest ever concluded with the Soviets and declare that "the Russians are providing us now with everything that's possible for them to supply. And I am now quite satisfied."[179] Sadat's public humiliation of the Soviets led to his enrichment.

Although the Soviets might be able to supply more arms on better terms, the Saudis could possibly supply the financial assistance Sadat desperately needed to pay for arms and, as important, quell societal discontent. Rubenstein, for instance, claims that "Sadat knew that expulsion of the Soviets would find favor with the deeply anti-communist Faysal."[180] Sadat was correct in his estimation when the Saudis responded to Sadat's overtures and his eviction of the Soviets by pledging further financial support,[181] which would enable him to finance the purchase of Soviet weapons and keep Egypt from economic insolvency. Increased Saudi and Kuwaiti oil money was made available at a special session of the Arab Defense Council in Cairo in January 1973, in which Egypt was allocated from $300 to $500 million in hard currency for weapons and $400 to $500 million in balance of payments support (in addition to the $266 million already stipulated in the Khartoum Agreement of 1967).[182] This approximately doubled the amount of Arab financial assistance received the previous year.[183] Moreover, the Saudis helped finance the record arms shipment from the Soviets in March 1973.[184]

The additional security assistance was crucial for allowing Sadat to maintain both political stability and battle preparations. There is no evidence that Sadat believed the eviction of the Soviets would entail greater societal sacrifice, and Sadat demonstrated no willingness to implement a restructural policy alongside the Soviet eviction.[185] This move, therefore, should not be interpreted as an attempt to increase Egyptian self-reliance. The Soviet eviction was a calculated, if not risk-free, strategy of increasing the amount of foreign support and decisional autonomy. And, this strategy apparently worked. By distancing himself from the Soviet Union, Sadat was able to increase the amount of security assistance from both the Soviets and the Saudis, assistance that was absolutely necessary for maintaining both his political longevity and battle preparations.

By mid-1973 it became clear that six years of war preparation had spent society's patience and the economy's remaining resources. Sadat, ever sensitive to the political climate, recognized that any further measures in the name of some "mythical" battle with the Israelis would likely expose him to tremendous societal turbulence. Moreover, a continuation of this "no-war/no-peace" policy meant economic ruin. The government continued to funnel precious resources to the military, funds that were, for all intents and purposes, being diverted from development possibilities, and there was no concrete evidence that Egypt was any closer to confronting the Israelis. By Fall 1973 the economy had reached a dire point. According to Sadat,

> Securing a loaf of bread in 1974 was not on the horizon. We had debts due for payment in December according to international regulations, and there was no way we could repay them. We did not have 1 mil's worth of hard currency. This was one of the factors that contributed to my decision to go to war, because if 1974 were to come with us in that state, Israel would not have needed to fire a single shot.[186]

Substantial pressures were building on the government. Although there was some opposition by the Egyptian chiefs of staff against initiating the October War, one chief counterargument used by Sadat was that if they did no go to war soon they would face widespread societal distur-bances.[187] Moreover, unless Egypt abandoned its current ambivalent stance toward the Israelis and went to war, the rich, Arab oil states would probably not bail out Egypt's fiscal mess.[188] Not only was Sadat confronted by a deteriorating economy from which no further resources could be extracted and which was beginning to undermine his domestic political support, but he also faced an unacceptable status quo with Is-rael that was creating even further discontent among an impatient public and limiting Arab willingness to continue their economic assistance. It was clear that something had to give.[189]

In summary, the interaction between the government's objectives and decision context produced a clear logic to the government's financial strategy. Neither Nasser nor Sadat was willing or able to change the tremendous imbalance between commitments and resources because the regime's basis of survival was based on maintaining those very inter-ests. Both Nasser the populist and Sadat the defender of the societal elite avoided placing too much of the defense burden on society's shoulders because of the imperative of maintaining political support, the economic reality that the already impoverished masses were an unlikely source of revenue, and the state's inability to monitor financial flows. In fact, the government made no concerted effort to raise taxes after 1969; rather, it relied most heavily on the public sector, commodities, and peasant crops delivered to the state: those sources to which the government had direct access could be shielded from the public eye were, as it happens, regres-sive in character. What deficit remained was financed by borrowing from domestic, including social security and insurance funds, and external sources, for this seemed a better alternative than extracting greater amounts from the Egyptian population. The resource gap widened con-siderably between 1967 and 1973, and Egypt was even more destitute than before.

The government's predilections are reflected in table 4.3. As Water-bury succinctly puts its, "The regime's will to save itself was invariably eclipsed by its will to survive."[190] Consequently, there was now wide-spread agreement that the experiment with Arab socialism had failed and that Egypt would have to more fully open itself up to outside influ-ence if it was to resuscitate economic development. Thus, the period of war preparation paved the way for Sadat's turn to the West and the open-ing of the Egyptian economy.[191] The road to military victory was paved with economic ruin.

TABLE 4.3
Total Deficit, Net Deficit, and Net External Borrowing, 1966/67–1973[a]

	Total Deficit	Net Deficit	Net External Borrowing
1966/67	95	75	57
1967/68	106	50	24
1968/69	54	48	−13
1969/70	47	80	−15
1970/71	5	79	—
1971/72	101	77	18
1973	310	183	51

Source: John Waterbury, *The Egypt of Nasser and Sadat*, 114.
Note: This represents the official budget, and a large percentage of both defense outlays and military debt is not included in these figures.
[a] In current Egyptian pounds.

Production Strategy

The government's mobilization of war material was ultimately constrained by physical barriers. As the single largest owner of the means of production and principal source of investment capital, the state, assuming that it had the capital, could determine authoritatively those sectors that would be developed and favored, but it could not as easily overcome the economy's meager development. Although the government would have preferred to rely on domestic sources of supply, thereby avoiding foreign manipulations, its arms industries had slipped into disrepair during the 1960s owing to a number of factors and, as a result, were limited to production for the civilian economy.[192] Consequently, the Egyptians had no choice but to increase their reliance on the Soviets. Soviet military assistance, which had begun in 1955, expanded rapidly after the 1967 War and continued steadily over the next seven years. As already mentioned, during the 1967–1973 period the Soviet Union transferred nearly $2.2 billion in arms, which represented a vast majority of its total weapons imports. Egypt's arms needs depended on Soviet goodwill.

Although the Soviets had never provided the Egyptians with all their requested military equipment, the problems associated with supplier dependence became particularly acute by late 1971. The Soviets were placing more controls and conditions on the type and use of the weapons and their delivery dates in an attempt to maintain influence over their client.[193] As already suggested, Soviet manipulations were one reason for Sadat's expulsion of the Soviets in 1972.[194] And although Soviet arms transfers increased soon after their eviction, this arms dependence led to considerable irritation and frustration.

The Egyptians were obviously quite frustrated with this state of affairs, particularly when placed against the backdrop that the Israelis outproduced the entire Arab effort by nearly four to one.[195] Consequently, Sadat took two steps to create the conditions for future military industrialization, both of which depended on foreign participation. First, by 1971 Egypt had successfully pressured the Soviets to assist in developing Egypt's arms industry, including the production of such weapons as anti-aircraft guns, anti-tank launchers, the AKM automatic rifle, ammunition, and spare parts for Egypt's air force and army. The Soviets also agreed to help finance and construct the factories.[196] Second, Egypt also proposed to the Arab states that they develop collective military industrialization. Eighteen Arab countries agreed to contribute 2 percent of their GNPs toward the goal of surpassing Israel's military production within five years.[197] This program was even less successful than the Soviet arms assistance, as most countries did not meet their financial pledge. It seemed that for the short term, dependent arms production offered no reasonable escape from supplier dependence.

Although domestic arms production was out of reach, the government did hope that the economy might make two contributions. The first was providing strategic inputs. "Military plans and defense preparations were somewhat initiated along the same lines as the development program."[198] Between 1967 and 1973 mainly those economic sectors—notably steel, pharmaceutical, cement, and food—integral to the war effort were favored (see table 4.4). Egypt hoped that by favoring these industries the government could make a significant contribution to the war effort. As Nasser commented, "The fight is between two economies."[199]

The second area in which the economy furthered the war effort was in the creation of hard currency; the government began to favor those export sectors that could potentially generate hard currency and repay the debts accrued from military imports.[200] Here the government pinned its hopes not on the public sector but rather on the private sector. Again, it is noteworthy that the urgency of generating foreign currency and exports stimulated a reconsideration of the private sector in the government's development and military plans. The decision to rely on the private sector was arguably produced by two factors: first, Egypt needed to involve all societal talents in the war economy; second, both Nasser, who as an economic pragmatist was rethinking the virtues of Arab socialism, and the techno-bureaucratic elite, who had replaced the military in key decision-making positions, desired to allocate investment resources along more profit-oriented criteria.[201] Although the government's na-

TABLE 4.4

Egyptian Gross Fixed Investment by Sector and Source, 1966/67–1973 (in percentages)

	1967/ 68	1968/ 69	1969/ 70	1970/ 71	1971/ 72	1972	1973
Agriculture	8.5	7.6	7.7	7.9	6.1	7.5	7.6
Irrigation and drainage	10.8	12.6	9.8	7.1	5.9	5.8	4.9
Industry, petroleum, and mining	27.6	30.3	35.1	35.4	38.4	31.6	33.4
Electricity	21.5	9.6	7.8	6.5	5.8	6.9	6.6
Construction	0.7	0.7	1.0	2.5	1.5	1.0	1.1
Transportation and communication	13.1	20.5	20.4	22.9	21.8	26.5	26.6
Trade and finance	0.2	1.0	1.0	2.7	3.0	0.8	0.6
Housing	14.3	14.1	10.4	7.5	8.1	10.6	8.7
Public utilities	1.4	1.6	3.1	4.7	4.7	3.4	4.9
Other services	3.7	4.5	5.1	4.5	5.9	6.9	6.3
Expenditures for land purchases	−1.8	−2.5	−1.4	−1.7	−1.2	−1.1	−0.7
Public sector	91.0	87.3	89.3	88.5	89.0	89.2	91.9
Private sector	9.0	12.7	10.7	11.5	11.0	10.8	8.1

Source: David Carr, *Foreign Investment and Development in Egypt* (New York: Praeger Press, 1979), 100–103.

tionalizations during the 1960s had reduced the size of domestic capitalist class, those remaining were located in the export sectors. For example, a significant proportion of the country's exports in such commodities as textiles, wooden products, metal works, chemical goods, and tourist items (in addition to nearly 80 percent of the country's construction industry) was generated by the private sector (see table 4.5).[202] To assist this once castigated sector, the government began to channel more investment funds to these key, privately owned, export industries.[202] Moreover, the government diverted precious foreign exchange earnings from public sector to private sector industries to increase the latter's export earnings.[204] Thus, the private sector was given an important, if limited, role in the government's plans. This turn of events is even more dramatic when one considers that in June 1966 Nasser announced his intention to nationalize all wholesale trade over the following three-year period and that prior to the June War the government manifested tremendous public display of radical intent and socialist "deepening."[205]

In summary, the Egyptian government had few choices when it came to procuring its weapons needs because its own arms industries had slipped into disrepair without any prospects for domestic arms production. To forestall a repeat of the present ills, Egyptian leaders attempted

TABLE 4.5

Relative Contribution of Private Sector to
Manufacturing Sector (Selected Enterprises), 1966/67 (as percentage of total)

	Number of Establishments	Labor Employment	Output
Mining and quarry	89.7	8.3	11.7
Food products	97.1	36.5	31.9
Textiles	98.7	16.7	9.6
Clothing and shoes	99.9	92.0	84.8
Wood and wood products	99.8	81.2	78.2
Paper and paper products	97.5	11.5	12.1
Leather and leather products	99.8	78.7	79.8
Petroleum refining and coal	45.5	0.0	1.0
Basic metal industries	97.1	9.7	8.2
Fabricated products	99.8	59.6	57.5
Machinery	97.7	27.5	25.7
Electric machinery	95.2	18.3	11.8
Chemicals	83.6	8.8	10.7

Source: Girgis, *Industrialization and Trade Patterns in Egypt*, 50–51.

to lay the foundations for military industrialization by both developing key strategic industries and attempting to enlist the assistance of the Soviet Union and other Arab states as a way of developing local arms production. If the local economy could not actually produce the military's weapons needs, then the government hoped that it could generate the hard currency required to pay for their importation. This was to be the private sector's chief contribution to military production—at least for the time being.

Conscription Policy

As Egyptian leaders searched for clues to the army's disastrous performance in the 1967 War, they obviously looked at the military's activities and composition. One criticism already discussed was the military's over-concern with administration and governance, its neglect of the annointed duty to protect the country's borders. Nasser was not only depressed by his army's performance, but he also was impressed by that of his rival, the Israeli army. Thus, although some Egyptian military officials pointed to either alleged U.S. influence, Israel's surprise attack, or faulty Soviet weapons for their mediocre showing, the officials also noted the character of the Israeli military, which was noticeably better educated and less class-determined than that of its Arab neighbors.[205] Given the high correlation between education and income, the policy of exempting the educated effectively excused the upper classes from military service. Not only did this hurt the quality of the Egyptian army, but it also limited the number of troops that could be mobilized. These issues were important as the government reevaluated its manpower needs and conscription policies.

The military's disastrous showing in the 1967 War provided more than enough motivation to alter the conscription policy. The question was whether this could be successfully implemented without jeopardizing political stability. The masses may have been dissatisfied with the regime's performance (or lack thereof) in the 1967 War, but the Israeli occupation of the Sinai produced a national sense of outrage and need for retribution. In short, all the makings for a restructural conscription policy were in place: tremendous societal cohesion; the state's relative autonomy; and the all too obvious evidence that the government's previous manpower policy had miserably failed to perform its mission to defend the state's territorial integrity. These factors gave Nasser the motivation and ability to alter the government's conscription policy. It is noteworthy, however, that the only real protest emerging from this new policy did not oppose service per se, but rather objected that such military service was not matched by political liberalization. Students were willing to fight for the state, but they expected to be treated as full citizens.[207]

The government's restructural policy, then, was designed to ensure that Egypt would have both the quantity and quality of conscripts needed for the next battle. Although demographically Egypt annually produced approximately 350,000 men of draft age, Shazli argues:

> In reality of those 350,000 only 120,000 satisfied the army's minimum education and health standards, leaving a significant shortage of 40,000 recruits. Thus, the army needed regular soldiers, approximately 160,000 a year. In order to fill the void the army took two measures. The first was to accept lower medical and education standards. The second was to allow women to serve in certain roles, for example secretaries and other service roles.[208]

The widening of the conscription net ensured that the military would receive its required numbers.

Because any future military success depended on increasing the number of combat officers, approximately 35,000 college graduates were immediately placed in the conscription pool after 1969. This had a number of immediate consequences for the country's military preparedness. First, the military would now benefit from the demilitarization of the bureaucracy because this would allow professional officers to concentrate on battle preparations rather than on administration. Second, the number of reserve officers was increased by expanding the pool of conscripted university graduates who entered the reserve officers college for training. Not only did the officers corps increase, but it also infused the army with a heretofore absent technological expertise. Moreover, by drafting the upper classes into military service it integrated all stratum of society to defend the country and promote the war effort, thereby evoking a sense of equality. Overall, the armed forces increased from 800,000 in 1971 to 1.2 million in 1973, largely a result of conscripting educated groups.[209]

Not only was the scope of service extended but also its duration. Those who entered the army after 1967 could expect to serve for an indefinite period of time, or until the Sinai was recaptured. This edict was blind to the conscript's level of education. Although initially these new and extensive requirements met with little overt resistance because of the general societal agreement that the Sinai should be retaken, it would not be too surprising if the combination of uninterrupted military service and no-war/no-peace with the Israelis produced an antigovernment societal outlash.

Although Nasser could overcome the military's societal bias, he could not as easily correct the lack of expertise. The Soviets, therefore, became critical for retraining the Egyptian army. Before the 1967 War approximately 500 Soviet troops were in Egypt on a principally advisory mission. Soon after the 1967 War, however, the Soviet presence expanded rapidly. By 1972 approximately 15,000 advisers were stationed in Egypt, including 6,014 Soviet field personnel, 870 advisers, 100 experts who trained the Egyptian air force and army on Soviet equipment, and their dependents.[210] Not only did Soviet presence expand but also its responsibilities. The Soviets initially rejected Nasser's request both in late 1967 that they participate directly in Egypt's air defenses and in 1969 for a mutual defense agreement "in which the Soviets would assume immediate but temporary responsibility for Egyptian air defense." At the height of the War of Attrition in January 1970, given considerable frustration and anxiety over Israeli bombardments of centrally located Egyptian positions and given Egyptian (and hence Soviet) prestige on the line, the Soviets now agreed to participate in Egypt's air defenses.[211] This move fulfilled Nasser's goal of making the Soviets see Egypt's defeat as their defeat. In the next two months the Soviets sent two air force brigades and an air defense division, and accompanying equipment, including eighty MIG-21 interceptors and twenty-seven surface-to-air missiles compounds.[212] Critical here is that Nasser's decision to turn to foreign manpower assistance was determined by both technical considerations and the desire to have the Soviet's prestige tied to that of Egypt's. Nasser's move was not directly effected by domestic political considerations. Although most Soviet advisers were expelled in 1972, they returned the following year to train the Egyptian troops with newly arrived Soviet equipment.

By 1972 there was growing evidence that the government's never-ending conscription policy was contributing to domestic instability. Although the first challenge came early in October 1969 when rioting students protested new regulations that "made it more difficult to graduate from secondary schools and enter college,"[213] events heated up considerably and ominously by late 1972, when on October 12 an army officer led some of his troops into a mosque in central Cairo and publicly demanded immediate war with Israel. More ominous perhaps was a renegade group of military officers intent on arresting the top Egyptian leadership, including Sadat, motivated largely by the nonending nature of war preparation.[214] The army's impatience with the no-war/no-peace situation mirrored that of society's; thousands of students protested the situation, and hundreds were arrested. Moreover, the Writers Association and other intellectuals wrote an open letter in which they argued that students could look forward to being drafted into the army for an indefinite period of time, while an enormous amount of financial and human resources were being channeled toward a war that seemed nowhere nearer.[215] The government's conscription policy was tipping an already delicate state-society balance against it.

Sadat moved in two directions to release this conscription-induced pressure. Most important, he released some of society's steam by discharging some conscripts because of economic and "morale" considerations. Not surprisingly, those in the army for six years or more who were university graduates were the first to be discharged. Egypt now had a reserve system. This reserve system was itself a product of domestic security political considerations. Lt. General Shazli considered three types of reserve systems: the Israeli, the Swedish, and the Swiss. "The Swiss system I discarded. It allows a reservist to keep his uniform and personal weaponry at home, something our political authorities would never accept."[216] And because the Israeli system is an amended Swiss model, it too was inappropriate. In the end the Swedish system, which calls for the army to stockpile all weapons, was amended for Egypt's military and political needs. By October 1973 the army had placed nearly 100,000 officers and enlisted in the reserve pool.[217] This reserve pool added to the strategic surprise upon which the Egyptian command was depending in defeating the Israelis, in hopes that the Israelis would take the demobilization of troops as a sign of lacking Egyptian will.[218]

The second, decidedly less significant, move was international. No fewer than eight nonfront-line Arab states sent forces to support the Egyptian war effort.[219] Their primary contributions, however, were psychological relief and giving the Arab countries a feeling of common purpose. Key figures in the Egyptian high command were reluctant to include Arab forces for two reasons. First, the Egyptians wanted to feel as if they were alone in bringing about the coming victory. Second, the potential contributing Arab leaders wanted the request for forces to come immediately prior to war initiation, which obviously would have undercut the military's surprise strategy.[220] Be that as it may, the primary mechanism in which Arab forces were mobilized was through the Arab Collective Defense Treaty of 1950. Before the 1970s, however, the international organization had been mainly used for financial assistance because interpersonal relations and inter-Arab politics had previously upset any collective effort against Israel. This problem subsided substantially in 1973, as Egypt benefited from reinforcements sent by Algeria, Libya, Iraq, Morocco, Sudan, Kuwait, and Tunisia.[221]

In summary, the shock of the 1967 War caused the government to examine the root causes of the military's ineffectiveness. It was quickly determined that if Egypt was to defeat the Israeli army, it must emulate them in some important respects, not the least of which was with respect to its policy of conscripting the educated and upper classes. This policy was instituted rather smoothly, in part because of widespread societal agreement with the government's objective of recapturing the Sinai. Moreover, the Soviets lent their expertise and support until these newly enlisted conscripts could be trained in the ways of modern warfare. After years of military service with no apparent war in sight, both society in general and the conscripts in particular became more restless. This caused the government both to create an active reserve system and to search more actively for manpower support from other Arab countries.

Between 1967 and 1973 the government embarked on a course of action designed to mobilize society for war. Because of the intensified and determined nature of this action, no segment of society was excused from contributing to the effort. This war mobilization process, however, was not problem-free: the economy was already undergoing tremendous strains and stagnation; and the government feared that the masses, who already demonstrated real signs of discontent, would openly revolt and shake the government's foundations. Consequently, the government attempted to accumulate the required resources for war while maintaining its political basis. This meant, for instance, giving the upper classes new obligations, as they were expected to serve in the army, and new opportunities, as they were given a new role in the government's economic plan. It also meant assuring that private consumption did not decline too rapidly and that domestic extraction came from those areas least visible, such as public sector profits. By 1973 the economy was devastated from years of subordinating its needs to those of the government's objectives of war preparation and political stability. These war preparation strategies directly reflected an emerging security, economic, and political realignment. Much would hinge on the outcome of the 1973 war.

FROM VICTORY TO SELF-DEFEAT, 1973–1977

> By 1974 the government's economic power was nil, no
> revenue and no resources, and little ability to do anything.
> Defense preparation, in addition to welfare policies designed
> to quell civil conflict, had bankrupted the state.
> (*Ismail Sabri Abdallah, minister of planning, May 14, 1987*)

> In order to pay for defense you have to play
> Arab politics correctly.
> (*Tahseen Bashir, Nasser and Sadat adviser, January 7, 1991*)

The War of Ramadan was a momentous event in modern Egyptian history. With the crossing of the Suez Canal, Egypt erased twenty-five years of military humiliation and defeats at the hands of the Israelis, upset the current stalemate in the Arab-Israeli conflict, and began a process whereby it eventually reclaimed the occupied Sinai Peninsula. No matter that Israeli troops now sat on both sides of the Canal and that Egypt's postcrossing military performance belied the claims and exaltations from the Arab World, for Sadat had recast the image of the inept Arab soldier and the invincibility of the Israeli army. Domestically Sadat crossed more than the canal, for he was hailed a hero, thus firmly established in his legitimacy with the Egyptian people. "The crossing of the Suez Canal became the mandate to create his new kind of Egypt ('restore' may be a better word) and to move from his predecessor's shadow. . . . Nasser's Egypt stood for defeat, socialism, Arabism; the new, triumphant Egypt for a 'free economy,' a more responsible order, an Egyptian Egypt."[222]

Now that Egypt's military stature was reestablished and Sadat's personal legitimacy was solidified it was important that he seize the moment to pave new directions for Egypt. It was both fortuitous and necessary that such military successes produce new opportunities, for Egypt could not afford to rest and savor its battlefield and psychological victories. The first order of business was ending the state of belligerency with the Israelis and rebuilding the army. Egypt had no more resources with which to renew the conflict. After all, the Egyptian economy had been spent for this limited military victory. There seemed little alternative, at least from Sadat's viewpoint, to a negotiated settlement. A cessation of the constant state of belligerency with the Israelis would (theoretically) allow Sadat to redirect scarce resources from the military to the economy and to regain Egypt's three principal sources of revenue—the Suez Canal, the Sinai oil fields, and tourism.

This change in strategy had important implications for Egypt's Arab and superpower relations. By deciding to seek a negotiated solution, Sadat placed himself at odds with the dominant Arab thinking, and certainly with Syria, his compatriot in the 1973 War, who continued to sponsor a rejectionist stance. Consequently, Sadat had to abandon a comprehensive settlement of the Arab-Israeli conflict and seek a separately negotiated agreement with the Israelis. In general, before 1973 Egypt's Israel strategy was premised on a collective Arab effort and the adoption of confrontational actions and policies; after 1973, however, Sadat opted for a solitary diplomatic stance. The first move that signaled Sadat's determination to strike out on his own came in late 1973 when the Egyptians signed a separate agreement with the Israelis for the exchange of each side's prisoners of war. A series of agreements that led to the eventual Israeli withdrawal from the Sinai and the formal cessation of hostilities followed: from the reopening of the Suez Canal and the Israeli withdrawal from the Sinai passes in 1975, to Sadat's trip to Jerusalem in 1977, to the Camp David Accords in 1979. The moderate successes of war enabled Sadat to make peace.

This change in foreign policy tools was related to a change in superpower relations. Although the Soviets were relatively adept at supplying Egypt with the money and material required for battle, they were less useful when the Egyptian strategy shifted from the battleground to the diplomatic round. Only the American secretary of state could "deliver" the Israelis; consequently, Henry Kissinger became integral to Sadat's postwar reconstruction. Although the Soviets attempted to carve out a role for themselves in the ensuing diplomatic dialogue through the Geneva Talks in 1974, they increasingly found themselves on the periphery of the negotiations and had to console themselves with a closer relationship with Syria. Sadat's willingness to join the American camp, something that all previous American administrations since 1952 had attempted but ultimately failed to accomplish, was a remarkable development from the American, and no doubt as well from the Soviet, perspective. The Soviets looked upon Sadat's closer ties to the United States with a combination of disbelief and anger.[223] The Soviet-Egyptian relationship, which had spearheaded the Soviet involvement in the Third World, became increasingly ill over the next few years, until it died an unceremonious death in 1976 with the termination of the Soviet-Egyptian Friendship Treaty. Sadat's hope was that as he distanced himself from the Soviets he would be compensated by his new friends in the West.

Although the diplomatic negotiations with the Israelis were portrayed as providing a respite from the security burden, Sadat continued to emphasize and privilege national security. Defense outlays hovered at 1973 levels over the next four years, and as a percentage of the GNP they actually increased to a high of 37 percent in 1976.[224] Over the next few years, then, Egypt spent enormous sums on national defense. For instance, whereas between the Czech arms deal of 1955 and 1975 Egypt spent nearly $2.2 billion on arms imports (of which $500 million had been repaid), from 1975 to 1981 Egypt purchased nearly $6.6 billion worth of equipment. In other words, Egypt spent three times on arms in six years as it had in the previous twenty.

There were compelling domestic political and national security reasons for maintaining such high levels of defense spending. First, while it was true that the Israeli threat had diminished, Egyptian defense officials, like their counterparts most places, based their defense needs on the enemy's capabilities, not its intentions (not to mention the simple fact that a peace treaty was not signed until 1979).[225] And because Israeli capabilities expanded rapidly after the 1973 War, so too must Egypt's. Second, a Soviet menace emerged and surrounded Sadat and threatened his regime. The Soviets replaced the Israelis as the new provocateurs, accused of causing Egypt's domestic unrest and instability and backing Libya's provocations on Egypt's western border. Whether real or not, Sadat consistently used the (so-called) Soviet threat to justify his U.S. arms requests and continued defense expenditures; this phenomenon became more pronounced in the late 1970s.[226] Third, Sadat's regional concerns included such actors as Somalia, Sudan, and Iran.[227]

Fourth, Sadat had to replenish a military arsenal, exhausted from the Yom Kippur War, with Soviet supplies and with Western weapons when the Soviet option was no longer available. And U.S.-made weapons systems tended to be much more expensive than those produced by the Soviets. As Sadat adviser Tahseen Bashir noted, "A period of realignment carries with it extra cost. . . . And now you get the U.S. 'mercedes.' "[228] Fifth, a strong military was also designed to serve an important economic function. Sadat's premise was that Egypt would only be able to attract foreign capital and financial assistance if it was an important regional and global player. One indicator of such geostrategic importance was both a visible foreign policy and a military that could support his regional ambitions. Finally, defense spending would also further Sadat's power base. Although he was in the process of demilitarizing the cabinet, keeping the army complacent and quelling any societal opposition meant supplying the army with new weapons.[229] In sum, there was no shortage of reasons to maintain a high level of security expenditures. This trend, however, challenged the government's ability to meet simultaneously social welfare, development, and defense. Such defense outlays, whether designed to confront a real or fictitious enemy, had very real consequences.

Sadat's plan was to use his military accomplishments and newly won legitimacy from the 1973 war to redirect Egypt's domestic and foreign economic policy. In other words, whereas in the interwar period the government had sacrificed the economy for national security, it was now hoped that Egypt's battlefield accomplishments could provide some new economic vitality and possibilities.[230] Sadat's economic policy was known as al-infitah (literally "the opening"): the government attempted to open the domestic economy, welcome and encourage foreign and domestic capitalist investment, and signal its commitment to private capitalist accumulation.[231] To remove any lingering doubts concerning its sincerity toward capital, the government introduced a number of policies, laws, and directives that openly benefited and supported its interests.[232] Notable was the Law on Foreign Investment no. 44 (1974), which gave greater freedom for foreign exchange transactions and modifications in the income tax law for foreign investors and revamped a banking sector that had been devastated by the nationalizations of the previous decade.[233] As Ismail Abdallah summarized it, the general attitude or motto was distinctly "what's good for business is good for the country."[234]

What were the forces behind al-infitah? The excessive burden of the national security figured prominently. All of the country's economic ills—little economic growth, a spiraling foreign debt, a balance of payments crisis, and depleted foreign exchange reserves—had been made irreparable, if not actually caused by, the Yemen War and six years of war preparation. The man in charge of presiding over most of Sadat's policies as prime minister made clear the crux of the problems: "Egypt's revised economic policy was based on a cold calculation of its desperate economic conditions, strained by continuing military expenditures and massive external debt."[235] Moreover, as I have already suggested, the signs of al-infitah can be traced to the post-1967 period, as a more pragmatic Nasser moved away from certain features of Arab socialism and toward a more important role for the private sector.[236] Second, the international economy had undergone tremendous change in the previous year, stimulated in large part by the new-found oil power of Egypt's

Arab brethren, who now controlled tremendous wealth. If only Egypt could tap this potential resource pool and become both the banking center for the Arab World and a source of investment opportunities, then its development prospects would be quite favorable. Third, Egypt's trade pattern also caused some concern; it had become one of essentially exchanging its exports for Soviet military imports. The government viewed this pattern as partly responsible for Egypt's low rate of capital investment and growth because it foreclosed the option of trading its exports for Western technology.[237] "The West had the technology, so you had to go to the West. . . . Arab petrodollars, combined with Western technology, could send Egypt into a new era of economic growth and expansion."[238]

Fourth, these economic ideas and orientations were promoted by a distinct set of elite interests. The composition of the state elite had begun to change after 1967, and even more so after 1973, as it shifted from the military to technocratic elite. Sadat and other key officials who comprised the "right-wing" of the July 1952 Revolution became more visible and active after 1973 and more insistent in their determination to include the private sector in the government's economic plans. Moreover, many state managers that had once benefited from Arab socialism now supported infitah; by the late 1960s they had become disillusioned with the former's track record and wanted a more market-oriented economy from which they themselves could benefit. In general, while this procapitalist group became more influential under Nasser and Sadat after 1967, the government was unable to move decisively toward liberalization because it lacked legitimacy (particularly so for a more market-leaning Sadat) and needed to provide for both political stability and battle preparations. Sadat's new-found legitimacy, however, handed him the power to push through these economic reforms.[239]

In general, Sadat's economic policy of al-infitah hinged on peace with Israel (though not necessarily a lighter defense burden), which would bring investment capital from the West and increase foreign (Western and Arab) aid.[240] Egypt's reliance on external actors for its capital and resource needs would not change; only who was supposed to do the funding would change. The "winners" were the oil-rich Arab states and the United States.

Sadat's third objective of maintaining political control and popular support appeared unassailable—at least for the time being. As "hero of the crossing," Sadat was rewarded with a great deal of legitimacy and support for both himself and his policies. In fact, his political power seemed so secure that by the mid-1970s he even began to experiment with controlled political liberalization and greater freedom of expression.[241] Moreover, the Parliament began to serve as a locale for interest articulation for the upper classes, as a source of limited government oversight in some areas, as a forum for limited policy debate, and as a channel for elite recruitment.[242] The Parliament's augmented decision-making powers, however, did not extend to Sadat's privileged domain of defense and foreign policy. In most respects, then, Sadat's pre-1973 centralized and highly personalized decision-making style continued unabated.

The class basis of the Sadat regime accurately reflected its economic policy, as he both constructed a coalition from and articulated the interests of the upper classes and procapitalist forces. There were definite winners and losers in the change from Nasser's Arab socialism to Sadat's infitah. Whereas Nasser rewarded army officers, managers, and technocrats, Sadat privileged big landlords and businessmen and allowed these and other members of the capitalist classes greater access to the policymaking process,[243] not as much through institutionalized channels but rather by a general definition and admission of their interests into the core elite. Hinnebusch nicely summarizes the contrast between Nasser and Sadat:

> Nasir, a populist who sought to build mass support in the face of opposition from the haves, frequently chose to put the expectations of his mass constituency above the interests of the bourgeoisie. Sadat, in contrast, rested his rule and his policies on the support of the bourgeoisie and the Western powers; the need to accommodate their demands introduced powerful influences potentially, although not always, in contradiction with the expectations of the have-nots. . . . [This] also shifted the balance of sympathy in elite circles in favor of the haves. The structures of mass-elite linkage also biased the distribution of political influence.[244]

Under Sadat there was a conscious attempt to admit the demands of the upper classes. The best families in Egypt were once again in favor, able to recapture the important institutional ties between the state and society—the president's attention.[245] Sadat was the capitalist class's medicine to the Nasserite fever.

Although Sadat was able to rework the regime's class basis, he still had to contend with the legacy of Nasserism, one that had mobilized the masses and led them to expect the state to act as provider of last resort. Consequently, regardless of how much Sadat wanted to emphasize efficiency over equity, there were limits to how much the former could displace the latter.[246] In other words, although Sadat's political and economic policies favored the upper classes, it would be political suicide if the masses felt that their own economic welfare were being sacrificed for the wealthy few. Sadat, like Nasser before and Mubarak after him, had to concern himself with lower-class resistance. When he seemed to ignore or run roughshod over their interests—as was the case in 1975 and more dramatically in the January 1977 food riots—the regime met with fierce and violent resistance. Although Sadat dismissed these outbursts as "uprisings of thieves" and attempted to convince the populace that accumulation of wealth was not something to be feared,[247] he had to ensure that his regime was not undercut from below. As a result, the government's welfare and subsidy policies expanded.

Consequently, the post-1973 Egyptian government faced the same dilemma as had the pre-1967 one: a rather costly set of defense, development, and welfare objectives quickly outstripped its domestic resource base. In fact, Sadat's policy of al-infitah, his security posture, and particularly so his stance toward the Israelis hinged on the participation of foreign actors. Although an outward-looking strategy was not new, it was noteworthy that the Soviets were no longer considered either an appropriate development model or principal source of financial support. The United States held the key to Sadat's economic and security objectives. Only the United States was positioned to mediate a peace between Egypt and Israel, and only the United States had access to capital markets and could deliver international economic institutions such as the International Monetary Fund.

In summary, the political noose that had slowly tightened around Egypt's political and economic neck was loosened after 1973. The "crossing" bolstered Sadat's personal power, legitimacy, and image in the Arab World and Egypt and provided him with an aura of bravado and courage. If Sadat reigned supreme in Egypt, he reigned supreme of a bankrupt and stalled economy, mortgaged for his military preparations. Be that as it may, Sadat's new-found legitimacy gave him a license with which to rework Egypt's economic and foreign policy direction. This permit, however, extended only so far as it did not expect too much from the masses. In many ways, then, Sadat, his military success notwithstanding, was in the same vise as Nasser had been in 1952: the need to rebuild the army and resuscitate development while placating the masses and distributing rewards to the upper classes. The vise was somewhat tighter than during this earlier period, however, because of the now desperate straits of the economy.

The combination of the tremendous domestic pressures and costly governmental objectives caused Sadat to adopt a combination of accommodational and international war preparation strategies. Sadat was in no position to ask society to contribute further to the country's security needs; after all, he had decided to sue for peace and was realizing, however slowly, the Egyptian goal of reclaiming the Sinai. Moreover, Sadat's economic policy was premised on providing a warm and enticing business climate, which implied that the government would confer upon them the required benefits. In sum, because the masses were spent and Sadat's economic policy called for providing material rewards for the upper classes, his financial strategy embodied a series of highly limited accommodational measures and a very active international strategy. Indeed, Sadat's military victory was intended to increase the flow of resources for his political and economic needs. The government was still in much the same predicament as it had been before with regard to weapons procurement: a desire for military independence without the necessary socioeconomic ingredients. Thus, Sadat emphasized an international strategy. Finally, the combination of war termination and Sadat's economic policy led to a partial demobilization that favored somewhat those classes that provided for both the class basis of the regime and its economic prospects, though these classes would not enjoy the same exemptions they once had. In general, Sadat's post-1973 Egyptian war preparation strategies looked strikingly like Nasser's 1952–1957 war preparation strategies.

Financial Strategy

The burden of progress and construction must fall principally
on the shoulders of the Egyptian people. . . . [Yet] we still
have a great need for foreign resources.
(*Anwar Sadat*, October Paper)

When you cannot expand the national cake, then use the
military to project power abroad to get more money
from foreign sources.
(*Tahseen Bashir, adviser to Sadat, December 28, 1990*)

Although the Yom Kippur War proved a major benefit to Arab prestige and Sadat's legitimacy, it did not come cheaply. The costs of war, approximately $3.7 billion, were truly extraordinary, particularly when situated against Egypt's bankrupt status. Alongside a national debt that totaled approximately $10 billion, the annual deficit expanded from EL 1.25 billion in 1973, to EL 670 million in 1974, and averaged around EL 1.3 billion in 1975 and 1976, owing in no small part to the high demands of national security.[248] The issues were: Who would pay the bill? How would the government stop, let alone narrow, a widening resource gap?

The government, though wary of imposing a still greater financial burden on society, capitalized on the tremendous popularity it had acquired from the "crossing" to make a limited attempt at raising taxes and strengthening control over and increasing compliance with the existing tax laws. The government imposed Jihad taxes on movable, agricultural, and rented properties, industrial, commercial, and professional profits, entertainment, drink, cigarettes, and all but third-class trains (which service the poorest Egyptians); raised income taxes by 12 percent on the upper-income brackets and increased the stamp tax; expanded the social security system, which represents a tax of sorts, to include another 500,000 employees; and expanded the compulsory savings for public sector employees from three-quarters to one-day's pay per month. As a result of these extraction policies, the government increased disproportionally the burden on the middle and lower classes.

For all intents and purposes this was the limit of Sadat's accommodational policies. The government chose not to raise direct taxes because its economic policy called for lavishing material rewards on the bourgeoisie and the state apparatus was renown for its inability to extract revenue.[249] Sadat's determination to reorient Egypt's economic direction and introduce a new economic policy dependent on capitalist investment was visibly reflected by his tax policy. The social power of the capitalist class and business interests generally expanded during the period of infitah, and one of its first effective lobbies was in the area of taxation. A new bias in the policy process favored the wealthy.[250] The Central Bank of Egypt records that

> it was natural that legislation would be passed and formal guarantees be given to the private sector as a means of protection against non-commercial risks and extraordinary measures such as sequestration, confiscation, and nationalization. For this reason the state abandoned direct methods previously applied in bridging incomes, and adopted a trend that called for social justice by expanding labor opportunities through indirect methods, such as public expenditure, carrying on the subsidy policy, enlarging and improving free services, taxation and pricing policies.[251]

The government was attempting to encourage productivity, investment, and savings by reducing the tax burden on the capitalist classes, and it hoped that the regressivity of the tax structure would be made up by combining welfare transfers and economic growth ultimately to benefit the masses. Even the Ministry of Finance, worried by its narrowing resource base, often vocalized strong support for tax reductions for the upper classes (though by 1978 the Ministry of Finance, concerned with its lack of revenue, led a rebellion to rescind some tax concessions).[252] The outcome of the government's policies was that the tax system lost any propensity toward progressiveness, a general concession toward capital and a consequence of the high degree of evasion practiced by the elite.[253] As a result, the state's collection of direct taxes as a percentage of GNP declined over this period.[254]

Because the government balked at raising direct taxes, only a small percentage of the tax was based on the ability to pay, and the rural and lower classes contributed disproportionally to the government's outlays. For instance, the agricultural sector's contribution rose from 15 percent in 1972 to 30 percent in 1975 and directly reflected both the lack of political power among the landed classes and the peasantry and the state's ability to more easily monitor commodity movements.[255] Yet Sadat was leery of burdening the masses too much for fear of domestic rebellion. His fears were well-founded. On New Year's Day, 1975, thousands of workers stormed through Cairo to protest high prices and low wages. Although the government made the standard observation that such riots were instigated by communist and leftist forces, it took a number of immediate economic actions to redress the situation. Specifically, the government implemented the previously suspended wage increases and promotions in the public sector, increased the wages for university graduates, and restored its subsidy program.[256] More dramatic were the Food Riots in January 1977, which left 73 people dead and 800 injured. These riots were a direct result of the government's decision to follow the International Monetary Fund's conditionality program: in return for balance of payments assistance it required Sadat to raise the price of basic food stuffs. Sadat responded to these mass demonstrations by immediately restoring the subsidy program. These societal pressures forced a steady budgetary expansion, as Sadat was committed to both placating the masses with subsidized goods and services and rewarding the upper classes for their support and contributions.[257]

Sadat exhibited greater enthusiasm at cashing in his new-found legitimacy with foreign actors. It was well understood that Egypt's financial needs could be met only through external financing because of Egypt's meager resource base, a war-depleted economy, and, more important, Sadat's political and economic objectives. Sadat argued, not unlike Nasser, that Egypt's key strategic and political position "would make it possible to obtain these resources in a way to strengthen our economy and speed up development. Hence the case for an outward-looking policy."[258] Sadat made his intentions known: Egypt's regional importance would serve its financial needs.

Initially Sadat viewed the Arab countries as Egypt's best financial hope:

We know from the memoirs and revelations of some of Sadat's close associates that there was an urge to prove Egypt's capabilities to other Arabs, a realization that other Arab states were not going to help Egypt so long as the country did not perform its role as the Arab world's principal fighting force. That is why the first shot had to be fired and the crossing accomplished before Sadat dispatched Sayyed Marei, one of his closest associates and a pillar of the Sadat regime, to Saudi Arabia and other oil states. There Marei and his delegation were to put before the oil states Egypt's accomplishments and needs. As Marei recalls it, he was under instruction from Sadat not to ask for any specific sums of money: Other Arabs had to be made to face their obligations.[259]

Sayyed Marie's trip was a relative success: the oil-rich Arab states offered to defray the costs of the 1973 War. The first assistance came when Arab governments subscribed to the new Jihad taxes, offered by the Central Bank of Egypt at inconvertible currency at home and abroad. This helped finance Egypt's largest ever trade deficit and attracted an estimated LE 28 million by October 20, 1973.[260] Moreover, the Saudis, Libyans, and the oil-rich Gulf states contributed over one billion dollars in direct payments to the Soviets for Egypt's arms purchases and reimbursement toward the costs of war.[261] In fact, Israeli sources calculated that Egypt received in outright grants nearly $4.2 billion between October 4, 1973, and April 1, 1975, from the oil-producing countries, which contrasted with the paltry $22 million it received between 1955 and 1967 and $1.8 billion between 1967 and 1973.[262] The Arabs, genuinely enthusiastic about Sadat's achievements, were willing to reward him accordingly.[263]

These perks began to disappear, however, once Sadat went ahead with his separate peace negotiations with Israel in 1975. Consequently, while the initial burst of enthusiasm for Sadat's achievement garnered him $1.25 billion in financial assistance, this figure tapered off to $988 million in 1975 and $625 million in 1976. Sadat's sense of betrayal ran high, for Egypt had provided the Arab army at a significant cost only to have the Arab states now run roughshod over his economy in its time of need. This view became even more pronounced after the January 1977 food riots.[264] The Egyptian press relayed the government's official view:

> Egypt lost in a quarter of a century 40 billion Dollars [sic] as a result of its undertaking to defend Arab land and to resist enemy encroachments in four successive wars. Egypt bore this nationalist and common burden with as little support from the Arabs as the sum of four billion Dollars. The Arabs failed to rise to their historic responsibility by sharing equally the burden of a common cause.[265]

This dissatisfaction with the paucity of Arab financial support and Egypt's deteriorating economic conditions was arguably an important force behind Sadat's peace initiative and visit to Jerusalem in November 1977.[266] It can be noted, then, that whereas in 1973 Sadat moved against Israel militarily to arrest a deteriorating economic condition, four years later the same forces caused him to gravitate once again toward the Israelis; but this time he approached with an olive branch rather than a gun. Financial support from the oil-rich Arab states dissipated with Sadat's journey and evaporated completely after he signed the Camp David Accords in 1979.

The Arab states were not the only group that became visibly displeased with Sadat's behavior, for the Soviet Union also lost patience and grew visibly upset with his diplomatic manueverings and closer ties with the Americans. Accordingly, the Soviets were less willing to subsidize Egypt's defense burden. The first sign of trouble came soon after the 1973 War, when Egypt requested that the huge debt owed the Soviets be renegotiated, but the Soviets responded that under the current climate they would do no such thing.[267] In general, the Soviets steadfastly refused to reschedule the debt that, according to one Egyptian official in January 1976, stood at $4 billion in nonmilitary and $7 billion in military obligations. Relations continued to deteriorate until the final break in March 1976, when Sadat unilaterally terminated the Soviet-Egyptian Treaty of Friendship, citing the Soviet unwillingness to supply either arms or financial assistance as the primary reason.[268]

Sadat hoped that the financial penalty imposed by the Arab states and the Soviet Union for his enrollment in the American-sponsored peace process would be offset by Egypt's newest financial benefactor, the United States. In fact, as Soviet and Arab assistance declined the United States contribution increased. Although little aid came immediately after the Yom Kippur War, by 1977 Sadat was being generously rewarded by the United States for his participation in the peace process and anti-Soviet stance. For instance, while the Arab states refused to mitigate Egypt's economic woes following the 1977 food riots, the United States responded quickly by shifting nearly $190 million committed for capital investment to commodity imports (out of a total aid package of $750 million); this certainly made the United States a much more attractive ally.[269] The Americans seemed only too happy to demonstrate to Sadat the benefits that could be gained from joining the Western camp and breaking with Egypt's historical mission of shouldering the burden of the Arab-Israeli conflict. Thus, after 1973 the United States took up the role once played by the Soviet Union and began to provide Egypt with injections of economic and military aid (see table 4.6).

In summary, although the Yom Kippur War and Sadat's decision to make peace with the Israelis was owing in part to the tremendous costs of the warfare, Sadat continued and in fact escalated the amount spent on defense. The question was how to finance such expenditures. Sadat's economic strategy and political basis depended on privileging the upper classes, who received immediate financial benefits and rewards, particularly evident in Egypt's tax policy. The middle and lower classes could not—nor were they expected to—make up the residual. In fact, to con-

TABLE 4.6
U.S. Financial Assistance to Egypt, 1975–1978 (in millions of U.S. dollars)

Fiscal Year	Obligated	Sub-Obligated	Expended	Unexpended Obligations
1975	370.5	334.9	307.1	63.4
1976	984.6	733.3	427.3	557.3
1977	892.3	672.1	445.1	447.2
1978	516.3	401.1	116.4	399.9
Total	2,763.7	2,141.6	1,295.9	1,467.8
Grants	409.3	208.0	113.5	295.8
Loans	514.3	143.7	3.6	510.7
Commodity import program loans	1,155.0	1,114.8	570.3	584.7
Total AID funds	2,078.6	1,466.5	687.4	1,391.2
PL480				
Title I	641.4	641.4	581.3	60.1
Title II	43.7	33.7	27.2	16.5
Total	2,763.7	2,141.6	1,295.9	1,467.8

Source: Wein, *Saudi-Egyptian Relations,* 77.
Note: Terms are defined as follows:
   Obligated—Agreement signed.
   Sub-Obligated—Letter of Commitment issued.
   Expended—Funds dispensed or goods shipped.
   Unexpended Obligations—Obligations minus expenditures.

vince them to acquiesce to his economic policies, he increased their sub-sidies. Because Sadat displayed a reluctance either to hold back any in-centives to capital or impose any further burdens on the masses, Egypt's external borrowing and reliance on Arab and American generosity ex-panded dramatically. As a result Egypt's foreign debt exploded (see table 4.7). Since the early 1970s a large percentage of Egypt's budget has derived from foreign sources. Sadat, unwilling to either sweat in-creased savings and extraction from the population or jeopardize his domestic political and economic objectives, relied instead on foreign loans and aid.

Production Strategy

Soviet arms continued to be delivered through November 1973; how-ever, the following month the Soviets halted new supplies of sophisti-cated equipment and haggled over the terms of payment. The Soviets, who were willing to keep open the flow of arms through the October

TABLE 4.7

Total Deficit, Net Deficit, and Net External Borrowing,
1971/72–1979 (in millions of EL)

	Total Deficit	Net Deficit	Net External Borrowing
1971/72	101	77	18
1973	310	183	51
1974	560	380	119
1975	1,388	731	210
1976	1,265	437	488
1977	1,532	374	464
1978	2,149	332	705
1979	3,195	1,197	690

Source: John Waterbury, *The Egypt of Nasser and Sadat*, 114.

War, began to reconsider their previous level of generosity once Sadat demonstrated his ability to be seduced by Western vices. Syria, who remained loyal to the Soviet Union, experienced none of these difficulties. Obviously such developments caused Sadat tremendous displeasure.[270] Sadat could not afford to alienate fully Soviet goodwill, however, for his army was Soviet-equipped; moreover, Western arms could not replace Soviet weapons, the Egyptian army could not retool and retrain that quickly, and domestic production was not going to replace foreign imports in the near future.

Soviet arms deliveries became sporadic and unpredictable, a shadow of the general deterioration in Soviet-Egyptian relations. For instance, in 1974 Egypt was unable to obtain the spare parts for its existing Soviet-built arsenal. Soviet deliveries came sporadically throughout the early part of 1975, as Sadat acknowledged, "thanks to the purchases by my friend President Boumedienne, as well as equipment from West Europe paid by King Faisal."[271] By Fall 1975, Sadat delivered another public lashing of Soviet arms policy. The Soviet-Egyptian arms relationship continued to deteriorate until the final in November 1977 when the Egyptian Foreign Minister Ismail Fahmy was sent to Moscow to query once again about Soviet arms policy. He told Premier Brezhnev:

> spare parts and replacements for arms that had been promised Egypt but had not been delivered; "no doubt," he added, "owing to some bureaucratic hold-up, which you, Mr. Chairman, will be able to overcome." Brezhnev looked at him. "That was not the result of any bureaucratic hold-up," he said, "it was the result of a political decision." "Who took it?" asked Fahmy. "I did," said Brezhnev. "The implication of the policies pursued by your government is that in no circumstances is Egypt going to fight. So what do you need these arms for?"[270]

Soon thereafter came the final rift when Sadat froze Egyptian debt payments, including any interest payments, to the Soviets.[273]

Sadat was not keen on having the military's weapons needs subject to such manipulations. Although he had no choice for the moment because of the fundamental fact that Egypt had few arms industries, he pursued two arms policies designed to diminish Egyptian arms dependence. First, he sought to diversify Egypt's source of arms. The initial indication of Sadat's intention to move in this direction came in April 1974 with the "October Paper."[274] The diversification scheme registered its first success in January 1975, when Sadat signed an arms agreement with France worth an estimated one billion Egyptian pounds and included such military hardware as Mirage jets and tanks.[275] Sadat added insult to Soviet injury when in late 1975 he received a gift of thirty MIGs engines and spare parts from the Soviet's chief rival, China.[276] And although the carrots Kissinger offered to Sadat were U.S. arms, nothing more than a symbolic shipment of twenty C-130 transport planes arrived before 1977.[277]

The second policy designed to lessen Egypt's arms reliance on the Soviets was another attempt at military industrialization. This most recent effort, begun soon after the 1973 war, was a direct product of the Soviet disinclination to finance or maintain arms deliveries. Sadat's image of arms production differed from that of Nasser's in two respects. First, where Nasser attempted to promote full-scale military industrialization, Sadat aimed for specialization in certain hardware.[278] Second, Nasser's motives for military production were linked to Egypt's national security and prestige. Sadat, though fully appreciative of the potential security benefits from military production, was more attracted to the potential economic rewards. Not only did he regard military industrialization as an important step in general economic development, but he also believed that a successful effort would promote exports, relieve Egypt's balance of payments difficulties, solve the foreign exchange crisis, and provide employment for the huge pool of recently demobilized conscripts. These economic motivations were articulated by Defense Minister Abou-Ghazala: "Military industry is one of the most important sectors of any national economy. The French revenues from arms exports are almost $80 million. The USSR has also become the most important arms exporter. Why not us too?"[279] The current military industrialization bid, like all post–World War Two efforts, was the exclusive domain of the public sector. The private sector, except foreign capital, was excluded from partaking in production owing to the lack of financial capital and national security concerns.[280] In many respects Sadat's vision of military industrialization was a microcosm of his infitah policy: Western technology would be imported, Arab oil would finance the effort, and Egypt would contribute labor and some financial support.[281]

Before 1973 Egypt had conducted some preliminary negotiations with other Arab states concerning the possibilities of collective Arab military production. Additional consultations took place after the Yom Kippur War. Egypt submitted a proposal for pan-Arab production at the Arab Summit in Algiers in November 1973, but not until April 29, 1975 did Egypt, Saudi Arabia, Qatar, and the United Arab Emirates agree to form the Arab Industrial Organization (AIO), of which the Arab Military Industrial Organization (AMIO) was the showcase and major venture. The goal of the AIO was to provide each party access to military hardware without interference and manipulations from the superpowers. In this effort each country contributed $260 million, while Egypt paid in kind with its missile and aircraft factories, bringing the AMIO's initial assets to $1.04 billion. The AMIO commenced immediately, and a number of joint ventures were concluded with Western multinationals. Although there were constant tensions between the four participating countries, they were contained until Egypt and Israel signed the Camp David Accords, at which time only Egypt remained in the consortium.[282] At present the AIO continues to operate, but solely under Egyptian guidance.[283]

In summary, once Sadat evidenced his desire to seek détente with the Americans and place his economic eggs in the capitalist basket, the Soviets let it be known that they would no longer perform their past philanthropist role. Consequently, Sadat took two courses of action: he diversified his arms supply; and he promoted arms industrialization with foreign assistance. Because the fruits of such efforts would not accrue for some time, Egypt was forced to switch its arms dependence from East to West. Again, the domestic limitations forced Egyptian officials to pursue an international strategy.

Conscription Strategies

Egypt's battlefield victories are rightfully accredited to the changed composition and size of the military. The inclusion of the upper classes had provided the army with a tremendous infusion of educated conscripts that could both operate the sophisticated military equipment and expand the depleted officer's corps. The Egyptian army had just cause to feel proud.

Despite the success with the army's "new look," there were tremendous pressures to modify the current conscription formula. The upper classes, along with everyone else for that matter, were tired of a never-ending service, and wished to pursue their civilian careers. Consequently, the first conscripts to be demobilized derived from the upper classes. Moreover, after 1973 the conscription formula was revised to lessen the burden on the upper classes. Those who went up to (technical) high school served for three years; those who graduated from high school served one and a half years; college graduates served one year. College graduates had the option of joining as a reserve officer or a soldier. Because of the different time commitments, one year for a soldier and two for an officer, most college graduates elected to become a soldier. This relatively light burden was subsequently reviewed because of the additional manpower pressures and the fear that the army was losing its quality conscripts. Although the government considered the possibility of either adding an additional year to the college graduate's tour of duty or providing greater financial rewards for these individuals to reenlist,[284] because there was no immediate national threat, no change was forthcoming.

Two important considerations, however, precluded any move to revert to the pre-1967 policies that exempted the upper classes. First, with the switch from the Soviets to the Americans came a move from a more labor-intensive to a more high-tech weapons posture. This meant that a more highly educated and technologically adept Egyptian solider was required. Second, one important factor for Egypt's battlefield victory was the army's new demographic profile; the military insisted that it be given the troops it required to maintain Egypt's military preparedness.[285] The implication was that the upper classes would not be able to cash in their renewed social standing for an exemption from military service.

The next four years were, in many respects, a repeat of Nasser's first years in power after the July Revolution. The government had overcommitted itself—rebuilding the army, subsidizing the welfare of the masses, and increasing capital investment, while relying more heavily on the private sector for economic development. Consequently, Sadat looked to foreign sources to relieve the security burden. His ability to pursue successfully an international strategy was certainly fostered by Egypt's military victory in 1973 and general importance in superpower relations. If the post-1973 period began as one of promise, it soon turned into something very different.

Far from constructing their national security and domestic policy in separate spheres, Egyptian leaders consciously tailored their war preparation strategies to correspond to their domestic objectives. Throughout the examined period there was an implicit, if at times wary, recognition of and respect for how national security was integral, and possibly detrimental, to the government's other goals of development and political stability. The Egyptian state was situated in both the international and domestic realms, and the government's war preparation strategies reflected this basic fact.

Egyptian leaders' three basic objectives duly affected their war preparation strategies. First, national security at various times consumed both the passion of Egyptian officials and their budgetary resources. Second, political stability had a multidimensional character. On the one hand, it included conferring and distributing rewards to those economic actors that were to be part of the government's development plan and ruling coalition. On the other hand, regardless of the class basis of the regime, no Egyptian leader, whether a self-proclaimed populist such as Nasser or defender of upper-class privileges such as Sadat, could ignore the minimal needs and requirements of the masses. Finally, Egyptian officials sought economic development, which witnessed a steady change: from private capital accumulation, to state capitalism, to a hybrid of the two. These three objectives profoundly shaped the government's war preparation strategies.

Even under the best of circumstances these various objectives would have been difficult to accomplish. The domestic economic and social structure that had been profoundly affected by colonialism, however, added to the difficulties. Simply put, the legacies of colonialism limited the state's ability to extract the few resources there were, and to be sure, there were few material resources. This was nowhere more evident than in the simple fact that owing largely to British colonial practices the economy did not contain the industrial sectors required for arms production. These various state and social structural characteristics, then, implied that the trade-offs for war preparation, political stability, and economic development would emerge very quickly.

These rather costly objectives and significant constraints produced an ever present tendency toward significant resource gaps, which would manifest themselves in dramatic fashion during moments of heightened security pressures. In other words, war preparation provoked an expanded cost of its budgetary commitments, and not any concerted effort to bring its commitments into line with its available resources. Rather than attempting to increase their extraction efforts, Egyptian officials demonstrated a strong propensity to capitalize on any systemic opening that would thereby relieve them from undertaking otherwise controversial and government-threatening measures. These sorts of concerns, considerations, and constraints pushed successive Egyptian governments toward an international war preparation strategy. Notable, then, were not the supposed opportunities that might befall an authoritarian government, one that also controlled a vast and expansive public sector,

TABLE 4.8
Summary of Egyptian War Preparation Strategies

	Fiscal	Production	Conscription
1952–57	international/ accommodational	international	accommodational
1957–67	international	international	accommodational
1967–73	international/ accommodational/ restructural	international/ restructural	restructural/ international
1973–77	international	international	accommodational

allowing it both access to another resource pool and the ability to determine investment patterns by its own criteria; notable, instead, was one that faced significant constraints limiting its ability to penetrate and extract from society.

Egypt's war preparation strategies can be divided into two distinct periods (see table 4.8). During the first period, from 1952 to 1967, national security was a top, but not exclusive, goal, and development took its place alongside the defense of the realm. Then came the Six-Day War. Egypt was thrown off the Sinai, and Nasser was left facing a victorious Israel on the eastern bank of the Suez and a stunned and agitated Egyptian society on the western bank. As a result, the government's overriding objective was to recover the Sinai from the Israelis while protecting itself from antiregime violence. Despite society's widespread agreement for retribution, there were even greater barriers to the government's claims on societal resources. To acquire the means of war while meeting the needs of the masses, development was suspended, and the economy was placed at the behest of security. The successes from the 1973 war did not offer a respite from the extraordinary defense burden, given the still significant security and systemic demands. Over the entire twenty-five-year period the single constant feature of Egyptian of life was the attempt to rely on foreign actors for much of the government's security-related needs. A restructural policy emerged on two different occasions: when it became abundantly clear that past security practices had not satisfied the government's military needs and when it was assumed to produce more resources and/or protect the government's political back.

Financial Policy. Rarely did Egyptian officials attempt to fund their military activities with anything short of an international strategy. The decision to make this a constant feature of Egypt's financial strategy in each period was owing largely to the fact that this solution enabled the government to fund its military activities alongside its other domestic political and economic objectives. This strategy was available because of Egypt's symbolic importance in each superpower's containment policy.

From 1952 to 1957 Nasser established a populist image and a reformist economic policy, which meant that the masses were the basis of his political fortunes while foreign and domestic capital were his economic basis. When defense costs began to rise in 1955 the government was reluctant to jeopardize either its development policy, which depended on the goodwill of foreign and domestic capital, or its populist image and political basis. Consequently, Nasser raised taxes only slightly; he opted to expand domestic and foreign borrowing to supplement any budget deficit. Although these early externally directed tendencies were not too troubling in modest amounts, it gave both the government and society a taste for exporting—that is, delaying—the costs of war.

Although the wave of nationalizations from 1957 to 1961 restructured the government's development policy and operating constraints, as it moved from private to state capitalist accumulation and increased its relative autonomy, respectively, it ceased to include the capitalist class in its fiscal struggles. Consequently, the state's tax policies became even more regressive. This bias, which began in the 1950s when the government's development policy depended on the capitalist classes, continued throughout this period; it accurately reflected the state's limited fiscal capacities, which necessitated that it rely on indirect means— those financial flows, for example, agricultural production, foreign trade, and public sector activities—that it could most easily monitor and shield from the masses' attention. Such indirect efforts signified that the masses would shoulder an unequal tax burden. There were definite limits, however, to these regressive policies. Not only were the masses extremely poor and therefore unable to contribute anywhere near the government's fiscal requirements, but Nasser had to maintain an appearance, at the least, as the consummate populist to protect his regime from society's wrath, and he was sincerely interested in improving their economic condition. Although the fiscal crisis that developed in the mid-1960s, in no small part a consequence of the costs of the Yemen War, might have prodded Nasser to contemplate a different fiscal course of action, societal disturbances quelled any momentary thoughts of greater extractive measures because such measures would most likely have translated into greater societal hardships and resistance. Once again, the Soviet Union absolved any need to choose between competing objectives.

The government's fiscal troubles looked tame compared to what occurred after 1967. Now the regime was caught in a vise, for it was determined to militarily confront the Israelis, yet unable to mobilize the domestic resources necessary because of the state's limited extractive capacities and the government's populist image and past policies. The government essentially maintained its previous fiscal path. Domestically, the government more fully exploited those domestic sources, notably public sector activities, that were both indirect and invisible. To ensure that the masses' standard of living did not decline to politically dangerous levels, the government maintained private consumption at around pre-1967 levels. At the same time a "pragmatic" Nasser emerged and exempted the upper classes, no longer because of his inability to impose greater burdens on them, but rather because of their important role in generating more revenue and shoring up his declining political condition. The government's reliance on indirect methods alongside a subtle shift in the accumulation dynamic (though for the most part there was little attempt to have any capital accumulation during this period) caused the fiscal burden to become even more regressive. Because these cautious domestic measures could not possibly satiate the state's ravenous appetite, both Nasser and Sadat increasingly turned to and relied upon foreign panaceas, notably the Soviet Union and the Arab countries.

These fiscal trends intensified after 1973. Although Sadat was realigning Egypt's political, economic, and strategic allies, there was little fiscal realignment. Sadat attempted to open up Egypt's economy and shift the capital accumulation dynamic away from its weight on an exhausted public sector and toward the capitalist class. The upper classes, therefore, were able to decrease their offerings to the government's coffers. Moreover, although the class basis of the regime shifted from Nasser's populism to Sadat's elitism, Sadat had to contend with the legacies of Nasserism and its commitment to the masses' welfare. This meant that alongside a decrease in the financial contribution from the upper classes came an increase in governmental welfare transfers and subsidies. The result of such expensive objectives, Nasserite legacies, and current political and economic realignments was an expending resource gap. Fortunately, the United States and other foreign patrons were more than willing to allow Egypt to expand its foreign obligations.

In summary, throughout the post-1952 period each Egyptian government constructed a fiscal policy that was a function of its objectives of war preparation, political mobilization, the dominant mode of capital accumulation, and socioeconomic constraints on its actions. This meant that an international strategy became the preferred method of closing the gap between commitments and resources. For instance, Nasser and Sadat exploited the rewards to be collected by a regional power that closed ranks with a superpower benefactor and thus mobilized additional financial resources; they thereby relieved themselves of the choice of either furthering, probably controversial, domestic measures or bridling their objectives. The financial binds supposedly alleviated through external borrowing only transferred these troubles to some future date.

Production Strategy. The government's strategy for mobilizing the instruments of warfare also relied on an outward-looking policy. International actors were prominent in Egypt's production policy whether to provide the actual instruments of warfare or to create the conditions for future domestic arms production. The government undertook a modest attempt at military industrialization during the early 1950s, a move through which the government hoped to service all the military's weapons needs and be independent of foreign influence. However, because of the limited economic base and meager financial resources, Egyptian leaders held no illusion that domestic arms production was an immediate possibility. Consequently, they sought a reliable foreign, preferably Western, source, but settled on a willing Soviet sponsor by 1955. Although Egypt garnered its required military equipment on highly favorable terms—never in the quantity and types that it so desired—it meant forfeiting what remained of its arms producing capacities, for the Soviets were unwilling to assist Egypt's military industrialization efforts in hopes of creating an Egyptian dependency. Consequently, Egypt's domestic arms industry steadily declined into nonexistence by the late 1960s.

In the early 1970s the government renewed its concern with Egypt's arms dependency and the possibility for domestic arms production, produced in large part because of the Soviet Union's manipulative actions. At this time Egypt, unable to undertake military industrialization by itself, successfully pressed the Soviets to sponsor and build a number of arms factories in Egypt. The strategy here, like that of Egypt's fiscal policy, was to use superpower assistance to its maximum benefit; Egypt thereby sought to erase the constraints of an underdeveloped economy while avoiding the obvious costs of being a "client" state. After the 1973 war Sadat took two additional measures to reduce Egypt's susceptibility to foreign manipulations. First, he undertook military industrialization with the assistance of other Arab countries and also agreed on coproduction with some Western firms. Second, he diversified Egypt's foreign suppliers. Although neither cured Egypt's addiction on foreign sources, both provided an acceptable and necessary first step toward greater arms independence.

Conscription Policy. Whereas military production was constrained primarily by physical features of the economy, the government's conscription policy derived from socioeconomic factors. When the Free Officers took power in 1952 they inherited a conscription policy that weighed the heaviest on the lower classes and the lightest on the upper classes—an accurate representation of the state's class basis. Despite Nasser's populist and egalitarian claims and the demand for a larger and more powerful army to match the government's regional plans, the military's conscription policy continued to burden disproportionally the lower classes, most likely reflecting the government's development policy and reformist (not radical) tendencies. In addition, there was no crisis to provoke a major rethinking. Although Egypt's involvement in the Yemen War placed even greater manpower pressures, particularly for officers, on the military, there was no change in the government's policy except for a small increase in the number of university graduates drafted. The government's conservatism can once again be attributed to, first, the government's development plans, which, though no longer relied on the capitalist classes, still required the educated groups, and, second, the absence of a military crisis that would demand these groups be allocated to security.

Then came the June War. The lessons of the June War, in addition to the government's intensified battle preparations, produced a reconsideration and revision of past enlistment procedures. The Egyptian government believed that one major reason for the Israeli army's impressive performance—and the opposite for the Egyptian army—was because the latter had exempted its cream from military service while the former had not. By including the better educated groups the military's quality would improve, and professional soldiers could be released from their administrative tasks and concentrate on combat-related duties. Finally, the government believed that all societal groups should contribute to the honor of recapturing the Sinai; this national effort should include all groups. Thus, the government now conscripted all eligible males, including university graduates, for an indefinite period. The tremendous shock to the system motivated the government to alter its conscription formula, while the state's tremendous legitimacy and the societal cohesion that followed the war enabled it to initiate what otherwise might have been a highly contentious and controversial move. Be that as it may, when it became clear that years of uninterrupted (and seemingly never-ending) military service was increasing societal instability, the government moved to demobilize many conscripts—the first targeted were the upper classes—and to establish Egypt's first reserve system. This measure both enabled the government to meet its military requirements and maintained political stability.

Despite the expanded numbers and increased quality of the Egyptian army, Egyptian leaders had to look outward for manpower relief for two reasons. First, although the Egyptian army now had a more highly educated and technologically adept profile, it would take time to adequately train and instruct them in the ways of modern warfare. In the meantime, the Soviet Union contributed logistic and training support until the Egyptians could adequately perform the task. That the Soviet Union willingly involved itself in a process that it recognized could easily turn into an open-ended commitment can be attributed to the fact that its prestige was also on the line. Nasser had successfully tied the Soviet Union's future strategic life in the region to what happened to Egypt. Second, the inclusion of the forces from other Arab states lent tremendous symbolic, if not military, support.

Although the military's successes in the 1973 War were partially attributed to these manpower changes, once the national emergency was over and Egyptian society was vindicated, the army demobilized in large numbers and partially reverted to its old policies wherein the upper classes once again were relieved of as heavy a burden and the lower classes once again provided the bulk of the manpower. Demobilization was certainly justified on the grounds that the military objective had been attained and a large army was no longer required, but it is not coincidental that those first targeted for demobilization—and subsequently given a lighter military duty—were also part of Sadat's class basis and viewed as instrumental to infitah. Be that as it may, it was impossible to revert fully to the pre-1967 formula if only for the simple fact that the army now had, and benefited from, a new technological look—and one that only the upper classes could fully provide.

The government's security policy was not solely determined by narrow strategic considerations but rather by a combination of systemic and societal forces and the government's objectives in the international and domestic spheres. Systemic factors were most prominent in Nasser's and Sadat's strategies of promoting its regional and global importance both to expand its meager resource base and relieve it of the need to undertake highly painful and controversial domestic measures. This was particularly evident after 1967. Unable to undertake massive battle preparations by itself, Egypt wedded its prestige with that of the Soviet Union. The Soviets believed themselves to have bought a strategic ally in the Middle East, while the Egyptians believed themselves to have bought a willing superpower patron that would allow the government to prepare for war while relieving society of the otherwise painful contributions.

These systemic windows were particularly important given the tremendous societal constraints owing to the country's meager resources, the state's limited infrastructural capacities, and the government's unwillingness to undertake the necessary steps to mobilize more domestic resources for war because of its other costly objectives of political stability and economic development. These windows became even more important when the government's objectives came into even more direct confrontation with each other after 1967. The government answered by paving over the economy with security and political stability, as the country's economic future was mortgaged by depleting the public sector of its available investment capital, borrowing tremendous sums from foreign sources, and increasing subsidies to the masses. After the 1973 War Sadat continued, and in fact intensified, this course of action. Defense expenditures maintained a steady upward direction, the upper classes were exempt from contributing to the state's coffers, and the masses received increased subsidies—all a result of the government's combined security, development, and stability requirements. The outcome was a chronic budget deficit and, consequently, a spiraling foreign debt.

These war preparation strategies had tremendous consequences for state-society relations, the subject of Chapter 6.

CHAPTER FIVE.

Explaining Israeli War Preparation Strategies

ALTHOUGH Israel's security posture has been the subject of intense scholarly scrutiny since its initial campaign for statehood in 1948, relatively neglected has been Israeli leaders' ability to mobilize resources for a seemingly never-ending chore of war preparation. This omission is rather puzzling because the government's mobilizing capacities certainly represent a significant reason for the country's battlefield successes. This neglect may be due to a couple of factors. First, the realist tradition dominates security scholarship and assumes an autonomous state with direct and perfect access to societal resources. Second, the common wisdom holds that the Israeli state is strong vis-à-vis society and thus has little difficulty in mobilizing societal resources. This characterization of the Israeli state is correct in its implicit recognition that the government has demonstrated significant prowess at extracting resources because of the state's capacity, autonomy, and legitimacy, though these features of the state that provided it access are never specified. At this same time this portrayal is misleading. It does not adequately recognize how the government's war preparation strategies reflected its foreign and domestic policy goals. In addition, the assumption of an omniscient state ignores how Israeli leaders have been increasingly constrained by societal pressures and demands. This is especially true since the Six-Day War. Israeli war preparation practices were summarily shaped and influenced by security pressures, features of the state and society, and domestic political objectives.

This chapter investigates and explains Israeli war preparation strategies between 1948 and 1977; its three discussions correspond to those periods of Israeli history in which the government perceived itself under substantially different security pressures and demands (see table 5.1). The first period covers the War of Independence through the 1956 Suez War and incorporates the state's monopolization of the means of violence and the institutionalization of state-society relations. The second period examines the years between 1957 and 1967. Because of the military's success during the 1956 War and the lack of any severe or immediate Arab challenge, the government remained confident that its current practices were sufficient to rebuff any military challenge and therefore

TABLE 5.1

Israeli Defense Spending, 1950–1978

	Defense Expenditure as % of Governmental Expenditure	Defense Consumption as % of GNP	Defense Consumption as % of Total Net Resources
1950		9.1	7.4
1951		7.6	6.3
1952	23.0	6.0	4.8
1953	19.7	5.8	4.7
1954	19.0	6.3	5.2
1955	21.8	7.7	6.1
1956	34.9	14.2	11.0
1957	21.6	9.2	7.4
1958	23.2	8.5	7.0
1959	22.0	7.9	6.7
1960	21.9	7.9	6.8
1961	22.6	8.7	7.4
1962	27.4	10.5	8.4
1963	28.8	10.8	8.9
1964	32.5	9.3	7.5
1965	31.8	9.5	7.9
1966	31.2	10.4	9.0
1967		17.7	15.3
1968		18.2	15.2
1969		20.2	16.4
1970		25.7	20.3
1971		23.6	19.0
1972		20.9	17.3
1973		32.4	23.7
1974		30.8	22.6
1975		33.8	24.7
1976		29.6	22.6
1977		23.1	19.1
1978		25.8	20.0

Sources: First column derives from Yaacov Lifshitz, "Defense Expenditures and the Allocation of Resources," 94. Second and third columns derive from "Defense Expenditures in Israel, 1950–1983," *Monthly Bulletin of Statistics, Supplement* (Jerusalem: Central Bureau of Statistics) 35 (7) (July 1984): 10.

made little move to deviate significantly from its pre-1956 posture. The third period includes the tumultuous decade between 1967 and 1977, in which Israel participated in the Six Day War, the War of Attrition, and the Yom Kippur War. The combination of the government's objectives and the enabling and constraining features of the decision context sent

Israeli officials searching both domestically and internationally for their desired security resources. These post-1967 developments would profoundly alter the nature of the Israeli political economy in general and Israeli state power in particular.

MOBILIZATION AND INTEGRATION, 1948–1956

As David Ben-Gurion succinctly put it, "Security unarguably comes first."[1] While the War of Independence demonstrated the young state's rather surprising war-making capacities, Israeli leaders viewed the 1949 armistice as a temporary respite from, not a solution to, the Arab-Israeli conflict. Israel's borders were far from secure or recognized. Indeed, the years preceding the 1956 war were marked by numerous raids and counterraids between Israel and Egypt, Syria, and Jordan, which created both a permanent state of tension and a sense that it was only a matter of time before the next war erupted.

Accordingly, during these first years security considerations loomed mightily and overshadowed most other state concerns. Israeli leaders had a difficult time conceptualizing any policy—economic, urban, immigration, settlement, or education—without questioning how it would further the country's national security. The Israeli government evaluated nearly all of its programs and policies according to how well they would contribute to its principal goal of territorial defense. For instance, absorption centers were placed in the periphery so that the Arab states would not be able to deal a devastating blow by attacking one part of the country; agriculture was encouraged because of the necessity of food self-sufficiency in times of war; industrial and manufacturing sectors were developed because they were essential for any arms-producing complex; and a strong educational base would produce a scientific community crucial to any future autonomous military industrialization program.

Relatedly, the government's broad security goal was to create a self-sufficient country, free from foreign influence. This interpretation of security was not owing solely to the Israeli leaders' understanding of the anarchic character of the interstate system. The lesson of Jewish history, reinforced by the experience of the Holocaust and further reinforced by the state's relative isolation in world affairs during this period, was simple: a Jewish state must not depend on outsiders for its survival.[2] To depend on non-Jewish actors for Jewish survival was to forget these lessons of history and to negate a primary need for the Jewish state and a central tenet of Zionism. It was a self-help system for both the Jewish people and the Jewish state.[3]

The government's broadly conceived definition of security was infused in all other governmental objectives, particularly so its other principal objectives of immigration and development. While the government was attempting to secure the state's borders, it also had to concern itself with absorbing its many immigrants. In the three short years following Israel's independence its population nearly doubled from little more than 700,000 to over 1.4 million, owing primarily to the tremendous immigration flows. Most of these immigrants were refugees from the Arab lands or survivors of the Holocaust, which meant that they arrived with little or no means for reproducing their very existence or for providing their basic needs. The state, therefore, had to take ultimate responsibility for their care. Such a heavy welfare burden meant that the country's prospects for economic growth depended upon its ability to absorb successfully the population and remove them from the state's trust. The option of temporarily limiting Jewish immigration, no matter how desperate the military and economic situation, was unthinkable, for the government could not waiver from its proclaimed responsibility of sheltering the many Jewish refugees without calling into question a fundamental reason for the state's very existence. The state's viability and legitimacy depended on the economic and cultural integration of these immigrants into Israel's emerging social fabric. Although the immigration deluge severely strained local resources, it also represented a tremendous boon to the state's security, as it added mightily to the country's military strength. Tom Segev's revisionist account of Israel's first years contends that Ben-Gurion's promotion of immigration was only secondarily motivated by "saving Jews." Rather, the "most vital reason for promoting immigration was for the sake of the state's national security and military might, and it was that which mattered most." According to Ben-Gurion, "We might have captured the West Bank, the Golan, the entire Galilee, but those conquests would not have reinforced our security as much as immigration. Doubling and tripling the number of immigrants gives us more and more strength."[4] Immigration was the most immediate way to expand the country's manpower pool and to strengthen the country's military power.

The third governmental objective, economic development, was often viewed as subsidiary and complementary to the first two objectives. "Beset by political and military problems of crucial importance, the new administration perhaps viewed the economic aspects of independence as secondary; but gradually the understanding emerged that political and military problems cannot be disassociated from the economic setting."[5] Initially the government had no real economic plan, but proceeded along in a piecemeal fashion. Not until 1951, when immigration had slowed, the state's borders were more secure, and the economy was beset by a series of tremendous economic problems that included strict rationing, a rampant black market, a galloping inflation rate, a tremendous budget deficit, and a severe balance of payments problem, did government officials sit down to produce an economic strategy.

The centerpiece of the government's plan, the New Economic Policy (NEP), was intended to redress these economic maladies and then some. Specifically, the NEP was designed to narrow the government's budget deficit through demand reduction and to curtail the trade deficit through devaluation and import restrictions. Alongside these broad macroeconomic objectives, the government's economic policy was also intended to encourage and develop those economic sectors that would further the country's national security (more on this later). According to Zvi Dinstien, "the general attitude was that a sound economic policy and general development is the only way with which to pay for the heavy defense requirements of the country. . . . From the beginning the army was intertwined with everything."[6] In true neomercantilist fashion, the government demonstrated a willingness to use the economy to further its national security needs, as many of the government's economic policies were often undertaken not with the objective of realizing an economic profit but with furthering Israel's self-sufficiency and independence in strategic economic sectors and industries. Simchas Soroker, director of the budget during this period, reflected the mood of the time when he commented:

> You can really see the state's general orientation when you examine these early years. The state's resources went to two things: agriculture and defense. The Jews were attempting to resettle the land, to cultivate the soil. However, they were in a hostile territory and therefore also found it necessary to defend themselves. We had a ploughshare in one hand and a gun in the other. This attitude carried over into the first years of the state.[7]

These early Israeli governments explicitly recognized that the state's security was serviced by a rapidly developing economy, and that the latter could be tailored to meet the defense requirements of the state.

Political popularity, while always on the minds of Ben-Gurion and his Mapai travelers, was the least of the cabinet's troubles and worries. The biographies of David Ben-Gurion, Levi Eshkol, Moshe Dayan, Golda Meir, and other Mapai luminaries read like the biography of the State of Israel. Their lives were bound up with the Zionist project, and they were viewed as the direct descendants of Herzl, the creators of the Jewish state. Mapai was identified with almost all the important symbols and institutions of the Jewish state—the kibbutz movement, the Histadrut, the Haganah. Consequently, Mapai easily made the transition from guardian of the Yishuv to guardian of the state in 1948. This should not imply that the government was cavalier concerning its need for popular support, for it certainly was not. Israel's elected officials were no different than those from any other country, and they often constructed policies intended to satisfy their electoral aspirations. Be that as it may, though Mapai never won an absolute majority and was thus forced to form a series of coalition cabinets, it never really feared the possibility of being turned out of office. Mapai's level of popular support and status as the dominant party virtually assured its hegemony for years to come.[8]

Mapai's popular support, however, could not assure intra-elite tranquility. Many of these divisions revolved around Israel's security, its posture toward the superpowers, and its reprisal policy against the Arab states.[9] The Lavon Affair, however, represented the most important chapter in Mapai politics during this period. Pinchas Lavon was the minister of defense under Prime Minister Moshe Sharrett when several Israeli agents were caught bombing select foreign-owned, primarily U.S. and British, properties in Egypt. Those Israeli officials in charge of the operation were hoping to make it look like the handiwork of Egyptian nationals, a plan to embarrass Nasser and distance him from the rest of the West and, in the process, increase Israel's importance and value to the West. When the Israeli agents were caught, Lavon denied all knowledge and responsibility, though others, notably Ben-Gurion's protégé Shimon Peres, named him as fully aware and supportive of the plan. Lavon was forced to resign from his post, and Ben-Gurion returned from his desert retreat to take over. This chapter remained closed until 1960, when its reopening ripped apart the Mapai party.

These objectives of immigrant settlement, defense, and development required tremendous resources and energies under the best of circumstances. For a newly developing country with few economic resources, however, these various demands were overwhelming. Yet the government's tasks were facilitated by two key features of the state: its relative autonomy from society and tremendous legitimacy. Briefly, in chapter 3 I argued that the state was relatively autonomous from society because of its control over much of the economy, either directly through state-owned firms and investment capital or indirectly through Histadrut. This autonomy was strengthened by the transfer of more than one billion dollars to the Israeli state during this period, capital that passed through the relatively unrestricted hands of Israeli officials. For instance, at a high point in the early 1950s, the state was responsible for nearly two-thirds of all domestic investment, and even by 1960 it was still accountable for over half.[10] As a result, the government could channel investment in such a way that it facilitated its other objectives. Moreover, unlike other postcolonial countries of the time, government officials did not have to worry as much about whether their dictates and laws were viewed as legitimate by the local population. The Israeli state was based on tremendous societal consent, and this affirmation of the Zionist state certainly eased the tremendous burdens and challenges facing the government in the coming years.[11] The government could expect society to make the required sacrifices for this historic event. This would be particularly evident as the government prepared for war.

Similar to leaders in most postcolonial states in the post-war era who were overwhelmed by the burdens of state building and the lack of domestic resources, Israeli leaders anticipated that attaining their objectives depended heavily on the state's relationship to the international system. Since Herzl's initial overtures toward the Ottomans, the British, and the German kaiser, the Zionist movement has appealed to international actors for recognition and support of its legitimacy and attainment of its goals. The Ben-Gurion government was no different in this regard, for although Israeli leaders were determined to remain impermeable to foreign influence there was still room for international goodwill and support, particularly so if it arrived with few conditions.[12] During the immediate postindependence period a key cabinet debate on its stance toward the East-West conflict determined both its possible security alliances and position in the international economy. Although initially the government attempted to maintain a policy of neutrality that must allow it to capture resources from both the East and the West, it became evident that local and global developments were forcing it to take a definite stance. The determining factor was whether the East or the West could best satisfy Israel's defense, economic, and political needs.[13]

A number of reasons recommended adopting a pro-Soviet stance. First, Mapaam, Israel's most ardent socialist party and an important coalition partner in the first cabinet, was a vocal supporter of the Soviet Union and intended for Israel to take its place next to its socialist comrades. Israel's founding fathers were quite explicit in their socialist intentions. Second, the state already controlled a great deal of the economy, either directly through its control over investment capital and public sector corporations or indirectly through its control over the Histadrut. Thus, Israel's economy more closely resembled, and had more to learn from, Soviet-style socialism than from American-style capitalism. Moreover, Israel's unstable border situation meant that foreign direct investment was not likely (nor was there much activity anyway). Finally, most Israelis recognized that the Soviet Union, by allowing Czechoslovakia to send desperately needed shipments of airplanes and ammunition in 1948, was the outside party most responsible for creating the state. Such actions were particularly significant against the backdrop of a United States-constructed Western arms embargo of the Middle Eastern confrontation states. As such, powerful arguments—rooted in the economy, ideology, and security—favored the Soviet Union.

At the same time, the Western capitalist democracies also held some luster. Foremost, the United States and world Jewry, who resided primarily in the United States, were providing a substantial amount of unilateral transfers to the new Jewish state. No such desperately needed aid was forthcoming from the Soviet Union. Moreover, despite the Soviet Union's initial military assistance, its future relations with Israel were cool and reserved, if not at times openly hostile. Furthermore, many of early Israeli elite were themselves political refugees from Russia and thus held no delusions of Soviet-style socialism. The Soviet Union's notorious anti-Semitic campaign, which culminated in the Doctor's Plot of 1953, created a great deal of antipathy toward the Soviet Union and resolved any lingering doubts concerning the nature of the Soviet government. Finally, Israel's leaders intended on constructing a Western-style democracy with a strong socialist flavor and, therefore, viewed the Western European states as a more appropriate model for political development.

As is well known, Israel quickly sided with the West. Regardless of the final cause for this move, this decision was, in many respects, as much a result of the Soviet Union's decision to side with the Arabs and unrelenting hostility as it was a conscious policy of the Israeli cabinet to shift its international allegiance. Israel's vote in support of the pro-United States position on the U.N. resolution concerning the Korean conflict is viewed as the moment Israel became firmly embedded in the Western camp.[14] In Cold War politics Israel adopted an openly pro-U.S. foreign policy strategy and, equally important, looked toward the West for financing its development and security needs.[15] Despite Israel's open sympathy for the West and many Western countries' sympathy for the new Jewish state, the tangible rewards were relatively few and slow in coming. The Truman administration was willing to confer diplomatic recognition and some development assistance but not much else, while the Eisenhower administration labored under the belief that a closer U.S.-Israeli relationship would jeopardize Dulles's containment plans where the Arab states were considered strategically central. This meant that although Israel could count on Western diplomatic support and some financial assistance, government officials overwhelmingly believed that Israel's survival depended on its actions alone. This drive for self-sufficiency, implemented through various neomercantilist policies, colored the government's war preparation strategies for many years.

The combination of the government's defense, welfare, and development objectives, features of the state and society, and position in the international system led Israeli decision makers to pursue the following war preparation strategies. The Israeli government's predisposition toward a self-reliant security posture, relative geopolitical isolation, and the state's relative autonomy and legitimacy would dispose it toward a restructural financial and manpower policy during this initial period. The government's costly objectives, however, eventually overwhelmed the domestic resource base and any attempt to adhere to a self-reliant posture forced state officials to construct an international strategy. Although the country could manufacture its most rudimentary weapons and ammunition needs, the government had no choice but to pursue an international strategy for its more sophisticated requirements. In general, the government implemented a restructural policy to rely on its own society when the material conditions permitted, but it constructed an international strategy when they did not and the systemic conditions permitted such an opening.

Financial Strategies

There are two certainties in every Israeli's life: war and taxes. Accordingly, it is unsurprising that they emerged simultaneously. One of the government's first official acts was to increase taxes by 100 percent for all income groups because of the emergency situation. Although there was some discussion and concern that such high tax rates would be detrimental to the state's future economic policies because they might discourage private investment and personal initiative, at this early stage the need to finance the war overrode all other policy considerations.[16] The tax rates remained at these higher levels and decreased only after the influx of foreign transfers from world Jewry and the United States.[17] The government's motivation behind the tax increase was more than purely economic, for it was also intended to demonstrate to the watching world that the new state had control over a population that was willing to sacrifice for the Zionist state.[18] At least initially, a relatively high degree of compliance, a rather good indicator of the state's legitimacy and, to a lesser extent, the state's capacities, were inherited from the mandatory period.

After the 1949 Armistice Agreement the government began to consider more long-term fiscal strategies,[19] but it soon discovered that its financing options were rather limited. The budget was already under expansionary pressures, and it seemed as if no part could be cut. Defense expenditures could not be slashed without potentially jeopardizing the existence of the state. Social welfare, the other large expenditure, was also considered unassailable, for the government could not shirk its responsibility of providing for the basic needs of the immigrant population. The government could further raise taxes; however, taxes had already been increased to a point considered both economically counter-productive and uncollectible. (After 1949 high rates of taxation had directly translated into equally high rates of evasion, which was implic-itly encouraged by the government's inability to demonstrate resolve and strength in the pursuit of tax evaders.) Moreover, the relatively poor population could not be expected to finance the government's opera-tions. In short, the government was in the bind of having to fulfill its ideological and security mission without the necessary resources. Ac-cordingly, the government turned to a third option, printing money, which promptly sparked an inflationary spiral and eroded the living stan-dards for most income groups.

The government's preference for deficit spending ceased in 1951, as it attempted to redress the situation and decrease the inflation rate, by shifting from an expansive to a restrictive money supply, principally through reductions in both government borrowing from the Bank of Israel and governmental demand in general and defense spending in particular.[20] Ben-Gurion's decision to cut defense by one-sixth resulted in streamlining the IDF, the dismissal of 8,000 regular army men and another 10,000 civilians employed by the IDF, and the resignation of the IDF's Chief of Staff Yigal Yadin.[21] "The idea [was] to cover the De-fense Budget by taxes and loans without further recourse to new Trea-sury Bills. Indeed, the government was met with some early successes during this period, for between April and August not a single Treasury Bill was issued."[22] And by 1953 Ben-Gurion believed that Israel's bor-ders were reasonably secure for the next few years; hence, the govern-ment could cut defense and channel the released funds toward economic development.

In general, during these first years the government moved from a re-structural policy to a series of accommodational gestures. From now on Israelis could accurately boast about being among the most heavily taxed people in the world, though there would few dramatic, mainly incre-mental, increases. And while the government was relatively successful in its extractive methods, it was less successful in evenly distributing the burden. Notwithstanding the progressivity of the Israeli tax structure, the burden fell the heaviest on the middle-income classes and the light-est on the lower- and upper-income classes. Lower-income groups were the principal beneficiaries of the welfare state. Upper-income groups were expected to contribute most; however, tax evasion was widespread among these groups because they were salaried, employed primarily in the private sector, and thus could more easily evade surveillance. Be-cause the middle classes dominated the ranks of the civil service, the state could more easily monitor their compliance. "While people with low incomes pay their taxes on the whole correctly and regularly, the richer classes frequently practice evasion and delay in their tax payments."[23] Moreover, corporations were taxed lightly to encourage capital investment. In general, the tax incidence was a product of the government's attempt to lessen the load on the lower-income groups and the lack of state capacity to monitor the compliance of upper-income groups.

Direct taxes could not solve the government's fiscal woes; hence, indirect taxation could be a more deft vehicle because it had the advantage of easier collection at decreased cost. However, Histadrut blocked its adoption in greater force because indirect taxation was perceived as indiscriminate and would hurt everyone equally, which was against both the government's and Histadrut's progressive orientation. Moreover, the government's protectionist trade policy after 1952 cut the volume of imports, which limited the amount that could be collected from this avenue. Accordingly, by the end of 1955 most of Israel's domestic revenues derived from four major sources: approximately 35 percent from direct taxes, 16 percent from luxury taxes, 12 percent from custom duties, and 20 percent from taxes on tobacco, liquor, and fuel. Despite such extraction successes, total expenditure continued to double collected revenue.[24]

The government, therefore, was in a perpetual bind: high domestic expenditures and an insufficient domestic resource base. Consequently, the government relied on an international strategy to supplement its domestic resource base. The government benefited from three major foreign benefactors. The first was world Jewry. Moshe Zambar, a former governor of the Bank of Israel, said that the government "always considered the Jewish people and Israel the same," so that unilateral transfers from world Jewry were perceived as "part of the family."[25] Although a significant amount of these transfers were delivered as grants and donations, those that were loans came on very friendly terms. The second source was U.S. foreign assistance. The United States began extending aid to Israel soon after Israel's independence. During the first years between 1952 and 1954, the United States provided assistance exclusively in grant form and earmarked funds for the purchase of fuel, food, raw materials, and spare parts. In 1955 economic assistance was comprised of both grant and loan, repayable at friendly rates of 4 percent interest over forty years.[26] Between 1952 and 1957 Israel received $233.7 million in grants and $42.5 in loans from the United States.[27]

In 1953 these two primary sources were joined by a third. Reparations payments came from West Germany to both individual victims of the Holocaust and the Israeli government for the cost of resettling these survivors. Ben-Gurion's highly controversial decision to accept what

Menachem Begin termed "blood money" was clearly motivated by the prime minister's understanding that the Israeli economy faced severe resource limitations, particularly sources of capital investment, and that Germany should not benefit financially from its destruction of European Jewry. Ben-Gurion's decision to sign a reparations pact with West Germany, however, brought the Israeli state close to civil war. Menachem Begin led a violent demonstration on the Knesset that was only turned away through the use of force. In hindsight it is clear that the state benefited tremendously from these government-to-government transfers, as it received both liquid and primarily industrial capital, which it was able to funnel to its preferred areas. In total, West Germany transferred some $700 million directly to the Israeli government and another $120 million via Israel to other worldwide Jewish organizations during these early years. The impact of these funds cannot be overstated. For instance, in 1953–1954 one-quarter of the development budget was funded by reparations payments, and the following year this percentage rose to nearly half; thereafter it declined. In general, until 1966 German reparations funded no less than one-fifth of the development budget.[28] Many of these funds found their way to Israel's industrialization and arms-building program.

In general, capital transfers, Israel's major source of investment capital and revenue enhancer throughout the 1950s, represented nearly 18.7 percent of all resources available to the government.[29] Most important, the state incurred no, or relatively few, obligations from these foreign injections of capital, and thus its autonomy from foreign forces remained in tact. Moreover, most funds were channeled through the state, which freed it from the demands of those that controlled investment decisions.[30] In general, the state's autonomy from both societal and foreign forces was enhanced by these unilateral transfers.

In sum, this period established the parameters for the government's future fiscal choices. The government had successfully implemented a restructural policy that entailed a heavy financial burden. This was made possible by the policy-making apparatus that had been built during the Yishuv years and the tremendous societal cohesion and legitimacy bestowed upon the state. This restructural policy was quickly institutionalized and followed by a series of incremental moves. The state's extractive arm, however, touched some groups more heavily than others. The middle classes bore the brunt of the domestic burden, while the upper and lower classes became accustomed to a relatively lighter incidence. Although the government, given its newly developing status, was comparatively successful at resource extraction, no doubt owing to the state's legitimacy, its efforts could not nearly satiate governmental expenditure. As a result, the government adopted an international solution and located a number of foreign patrons who contributed vast sums and needed relief without imposing any major financial or political obligations on the new state. The tremendous amount of unilateral transfers alleviated the government's need to undertake more dire choices, which might otherwise have forced society either to shoulder a heavier burden or to circumscribe one of its other objectives, such as economic development.

Production Strategies

Locally manufactured materials could only supply part of the
army's needs. Such military items as tanks, heavy artillery,
planes, naval vessels had to be bought abroad.
(*David Ben-Gurion*, Ben-Gurion Looks Back)

With the establishment of our military industry,
we experienced for the first time the limitations and
opportunities for interlinking security
and economic affairs.
(*Shimon Peres*, David's Sling)

It was quite natural during this early period to ensure that
some aspect of national security was included
in all aspects of production.
(*Simchas Soroker, director of budget, June 12, 1987*)

These quotes accurately reflect the disposition of the government's material policy during these early years. During the War of Independence the Israeli government was relatively self-sufficient in small weapons production and ammunition because of the creation of "ta'as," the Yishuv's arms-producing consortium.[31] But, as Ben-Gurion noted, because of the economy's limitations local efforts could not meet the military's immediate weapons needs. Consequently, Israeli representatives were sent out to locate official and clandestine suppliers. Israel's initial military campaign was aided by surplus World War Two equipment and, more famously, by the Soviet Union's assistance through its Czechoslovakian proxy.[32] This route was not long-lasting, for soon thereafter the Soviet Union shifted its support from Israel to the Arab states. Israeli emissaries were therefore sent out once again to procure used armaments. "The method of the day was to purchase the hardware wherever it could be obtained and only then worry about its compatibility with the prevailing mode of combat."[33] This was not a strategy of choice but rather of necessity, for Israel was unable to obtain arms from any major powers. The signatories of the 1950 Tripartite Declaration (United States, Britain, and France) attempted to regulate and enforce a regional balance of power by controlling the flow of weapons to the area.[34] These experiences taught Israeli leaders a painful lesson in dependence and convinced Ben-Gurion that Israel should do whatever it needed to remove itself from this vulnerable and exposed position.

While the government's desire for autonomy was a powerful reason to develop an arms industry, other, notably economic, factors also propelled the government in this direction. "The Israelis believed that this industry had been a major factor in turning France from a basically agricultural country into an advanced industrial state."[35] Moreover, domestic production could potentially prove cheaper than expensive imports.[36] Arms production offered numerous benefits.

The government, accordingly, moved in two different directions to establish the foundations for an arms industry. The first was to create Israel's first arms industries. This move required Ben-Gurion to override cabinet opposition, for military experts, industrialists, and economists argued that the domestic and international market was too small to support an efficient domestic arms industry and that Israel had more pressing needs for its scarce capital.[37] His ability to overcome domestic opposition is a testimony to Ben-Gurion's forceful presence and his successful wielding of the security argument. Although some companies received their start from the repair and maintenance of weapons purchased abroad, there was little capital available for any intensive military industrialization effort during the country's first years.

The breakthrough for the Israeli defense industry came in 1953 with the West German reparations agreement. The unilateral transfer of nearly one billion dollars now allowed the government to use fully Israel's civilian economy for defense-related purposes.[38] During this period many of Israel's major defense companies got their initial capitalization. For example, Bedek, which later became Israel Aircraft Industries (IAI), currently Israel's largest defense industry, was founded in 1953 for the purpose of maintaining Israel's fledgling air force; Tadiran, one of Israel's premier electronics industry, also received its start during this period with Defense Ministry funding.[39]

The second move was to create a diversified manufacturing and industrial base, one that could boast those sectors—such as chemicals, steel, and engineering—that were integral to arms production. The government's plan was facilitated by two factors: import-substitution policy of 1951 and governmental control over production and investment capital.[40]

Although the government had the broad intention of encouraging domestic production in various economic sectors through a mixture of exchange-rate controls, investment subsidies, and trade barriers, those sectors that served both the country's industrialization and militarization programs received a substantial amount of attention. Protectionist policies were justified on a number of traditional grounds—defender of infant industries, enhancer of revenues, and diminisher of imports—but it is noteworthy that nearly half the state's protectionist efforts were directed at those sectors considered integral to national security.[41] Three sectors in particular, considered basic to any future military industrialization, received the greatest amount of protection: chemicals, metals, and machinery.[42]

The government could do more than protect domestic industries that would provide the foundations for arms production, for it could also confer upon them tremendous resources provided by the German reparations agreement. This leads to the second factor. The government's control over production and investment capital allowed it to dispose of and channel funds in an unrestricted fashion to its preferred economic sectors. For instance, the metals industry received nearly 30 percent of German reparations during this period.[43] Two routes were most favored: the defense budget and Histadrut-owned financial company, Hevrat Ha'Ovdim, which owned Koor industries, which, in turn, owned "civilian" companies like Tadiran.[44] Both recipients were under the strict control and direction of Mapai officials.

It is significant that there was no real expectation that security-related industries would be able to reap a profit in either the near or the distant future. Michael Michaely reflects the disposition of many Israeli officials during this period:

> The expectations inherited from [the Yishuv] period were not only that the central organs of the community would play a role in economic activities, but also that these activities would not necessarily be undertaken for the sake of profit making. Sometimes, the latter notion has even taken the extreme implicit assumption that when profits are made the national cause must have been subverted. Similarly, a substantial fraction of the population as well as many policy makers maintained at the beginning that economic laws do not hold in Israel.[45]

Further evidence of the government's desire to promote these defense-related industries was its willingness to sacrifice its other objective of labor absorption because it was not as rapidly attainable in these capital-intensive industries.[46] While Ben-Gurion was again accused of placing scarce capital into economically inviable enterprises, he argued that as long as Israel was surrounded by hostile neighbors it was necessary to avoid dependence in the event of war.[47] And while Ben-Gurion and Peres often conceded that these enterprises might (at this juncture) be a burden on the government's budget, industrial development was consistent with both the government's development plan and security needs.[48]

The government's ability to maintain a rough balance between itself and the Arab armies through imports and a small defense industry proved sufficient until 1955. That year, however, witnessed the signing of the Egyptian-Soviet arms agreement. The deal created a panic in the Israeli cabinet and reinforced the need to cultivate a Great Power sponsor and steady arms supplier. The government identified four possibilities. Sweden would not relent because of its scrupulous policy of not exporting weapons to areas of tension. The United States was also closed because the Eisenhower administration had decided to abstain from selling Israel weapons for fear of jeopardizing its ties with the Arab World.[49] Great Britain was another possibility, but it would not endanger its relationship with Egypt and Saudi Arabia by selling arms to Israel.[50]

That left France.[51] Both France and Israel had a common enemy in radical Arab politics; France was then becoming engaged in a bitter struggle in Algeria (and Egypt was selling arms to the Algerian rebels), and Israel's concerns were quite evident. The United States gave its blessing, and the French now began selling weapons to the Israelis. A friendship of convenience soon formed, and as the French-Algerian struggle grew increasingly more bitter the French-Israeli friendship grew increasingly more friendly. Although the Israeli government considered the first weapons shipment from France in 1955 a major breakthrough, the turning point in the relationship was the 1956 war, in which France, Britain, and Israel coordinated their attacks on Egypt. Thereafter the French-Israeli relationship developed to the point where Israel was granted coproduction of some French weapons systems. This arrangement afforded Israeli scientists and engineers invaluable experience, thus providing a critical foundation for Israel's future military industrialization program.[52]

In summary, because the state was unable to rely on its own wherewithal for its military hardware it was forced to construct an international strategy and turn to foreign patrons wherever they could be found, a wholly unsatisfactory policy. To decrease the likelihood of a replay of this episode, many governmental economic policies were undertaken, not with the objective of realizing an economic profit, but with the hope that it would lead to Israel's eventual self-sufficiency and independence in security-related industries. That the government could build these foundations must be largely attributed to the tremendous unilateral transfers it received and its ability to disperse these funds to its preferred economic sectors. And by 1955 Israel ended a period of uncertainty concerning its arms reservoir, as it established a fledgling relationship with France that would provide it with both the knowledge needed to manufacture military hardware and a secure source of arms until it could achieve its more distant objective of autonomous production. In general, Israel began a long-standing attempt at dependent military industrialization, a conscious strategy to become dependent on a Great Power so that it develop its own arms industry that might lead to future arms independence.

Conscription Policies

The civilian is a soldier on eleventh month leave.
(Yigal Yadin, Israel's first chief of defense)

The government waged two separate battles during the War of Independence: control over its borders and control over society. Although the former process has been the more enduring and threatening of the two challenges, this should not lead us astray from the process of monopolizing the means of violence.

While the Israeli leadership was consumed with the task of fending off the invading Arab forces, it also had to extinguish the other Jewish military organizations that had arisen during the British mandate and thereby establish a monopoly over the means of coercion. The Haganah, the "official" military arm of the Jewish community, consisted of approximately 46,000 reserves and 500 regulars and represented the future Israel Defense Forces (IDF). Other notable military units were the Palmach, the kibbutz movement's military arm, and Etzel and Lehi, representatives of rightist Zionist movements. In other words, each guerilla organization represented an important political faction in the Yishuv. For this reason alone it was important that the government quickly collapse all rival military units under its rule.

This problem of multiple military organizations was resolved promptly, if not dramatically. At the time of statehood the Haganah and the Palmach were quickly and easily absorbed under the state's authority.[53] Etzel and Lehi, however, were more suspicious of their rival's attempt to dismantle their military force. This set the stage for one of the more critical threats from Jewish elements to the new state's command. Etzel and Lehi had arranged to receive a shipment of desperately needed military equipment during the early weeks of the War of Independence. It arrived on the cargo ship *Altalena*, but Etzel refused to turn the arms over to the government. Ben-Gurion interpreted this as a flagrant assault on the state's sovereignty and its potential military power and, rather than allow Etzel to take consignment of the desperately needed war material, he made the difficult decision of destroying the cargo of arms and, in the process, extinguishing the lone private military challenge to the state's authority. A violent clash between the Israeli army and Menachem Begin's forces left many dead, destroyed a cargo of arms, and initiated a lifelong feud between Ben-Gurion and Begin. Soon thereafter Etzel and Lehi transformed themselves into political parties; the more famous was Herut, the predecessor of Likud.[54]

Given the immediate security demands at independence, the administration quickly and unanimously decided to mobilize all segments of society for military service. Universal conscription seemed necessary given the population's small size; the state could ill-afford to exempt certain groups. Moreover, not only was fighting for and defending the Jewish state considered a privilege, but by burdening all citizens equally with military service the government also furthered its ideological goals of socialism and equality. If Ben-Gurion could easily contemplate arming the vast majority of Israel's citizens, a move unthinkable for other postcolonial leaders of the period, it was only because of the state's tremendous legitimacy. Once the draft was announced in 1948 the government was able to mobilize around 50,000 soldiers; by 1949 that number had doubled to 100,000, approximately 18 percent of the population. There was little if any opposition to conscription, as almost all societal elements identified with the goals of the state.[55] In short, the state's legitimacy provided the preconditions for a restructural policy.

Neither did the state's ideological legitimacy stop at its borders nor, consequently, did its source of manpower. Thousands of overseas volunteers flocked to Israel to fight for the state's creation. Two groups were most prominent. After World War Two there were a large number of Jewish refugees held in limbo in the displaced persons camps in Europe and Cyprus. They neither wanted to (and in most cases could not) return to their prewar homes, nor were the immigration doors open in any Western country. Israeli representatives recruited these refugees to immigrate to Israel and to help fight for and build the Jewish state. Nearly 20,000 of these recruits literally went directly from the ship to the army. This rag-tag force was joined by a second, more professional, set of volunteers, known as MAHAL (Mitnadvey Hutz La'aretz—Foreign Volunteers in the War of Independence). Approximately 4,000 to 5,000, primarily from Anglo-Saxon countries, enlisted for mainly personal ideological reasons. They principally contributed to Israel's air campaign. There were few Israeli pilots, and this group contained nearly 300, many of whom had experience with either the ASAF or RAF.[56] Subsequently many stayed to help establish and reorganize the Israeli Air Force.[57]

After the Armistice the cabinet had to reconsider the proper size of the IDF. Here one clearly sees how Israeli war preparations were a product of both national security and domestic political objectives. Two issues stood out. First, the government sought to align the army with what was economically sustainable. By the end of the War of Independence the army comprised approximately 10 percent of the population, and it was clear that the labor force was badly needed for civilian activities.[58] Second, during the recent campaign it took the army months to achieve full strength, something that might prove militarily disastrous in the future. As such, the government wanted an army that was both economically affordable and almost always at full strength. As Ben-Gurion noted, he wanted to have his cake and eat it, too.[59] That is, the government was searching for a way to reconcile its various domestic and foreign policy objectives into a coherent and workable manpower formula.

After some debate the cabinet decided to establish a small standing army and a large reserve army.[60] Henceforth military service was compulsory for almost all citizens: men served for three years, and unmarried women for two.[61] To relieve the economic burden of a large standing army while meeting the military's manpower needs, the government established an extensive and lengthy reserve system, modeled after the Swiss method wherein the bulk of its army consists of reserves permanently assigned to military units and allowed to take home their personal military equipment.[62] Every male participant could be called up for thirty-one days of annual reserve duty until the age thirty-nine, and those between the ages of forty and fifty-five years of age were eligible for twenty-one days;[63] during periods of national emergencies the military could demand an almost unlimited military service of every citizen. In general, the government attempted to instill the reserve system with universalistic qualities and ensure that an individual's status in society would not prejudice the amount of time dedicated to the reserves.

The army's responsibilities extended beyond its strict security function to include important ideological and economic goals as well. Article F of the Defense Service Law stated: "The first twelve months of regular service of a recruit will be devoted, after preliminary training, primarily to agricultural preparation as shall be determined in the regulations, except for a recruit sent to serve in the air force or navy."[64] This law was the outcome of both societal pressures and governmental objectives. The Defense Service Law reflected societal demands, as the agricultural sector, notably kibbutz interests, wanted to serve but also argued that military obligations would increase the strains on an already labor-scarce environment in the rural sector.[65]

More important than societal pressures, however, were the government's security interests. The government wanted to establish "peripheral defense" by placing settlements in the outlying regions so that they would absorb the first blow of an Arab attack and stall its advance until the IDF could be fully mobilized. Shimon Peres reflects:

> It would have been difficult to defend Israel's lengthy borders if it were not for the frontier kibbutzim, smallholding farm settlements and villages. In the absence of strategic depth, border settlements serve as Israel's shock absorbers deterring, holding, or absorbing the first wave of incursion or attack. . . . Without a regional defense system of border settlements the army would have to disperse its troops along the borders, which would leave it with only a small concentration of force to carry out its main task of dealing with the basic defense problems of the state.[66]

Zeev Schiff also writes:

> During the War of Independence the High Command of the IDF was convinced that the best defense for the young state lay in the agricultural settlements, since these settlements, and especially the kibbutzim, formed obstacles to the invading armies. Whenever an Arab force came up against agricultural settlements it had to fight much harder and risk heavy losses. Consequently, after the War of Independence the IDF tried to continue filling in the gaps on the borders with these settlements. The problem was that manpower was lacking for the rapid construction of settlements. So it was decided to create settlements with soldiers.[67]

Constructing agricultural settlements for defense also served Ben-Gurion's vision of the IDF as a farmer's army, which "was influenced by early Zionist thinkers who stressed the redemption of Jews was to be found in labor of their historic homeland."[68] Nahal was the end product of this vision. Nahal soldiers were sent to work these settlements for a period of at least a year, and at the end of the year these individuals were given the option of staying at the holding settlement and, if they did, acquiring the settlement's property.[69] Nahal, then, "combines the 'civilianization' of the army and the 'militarization' of farming to serve the double aim of strengthening defense and extending farm settlements."[70] In general, the government hoped that by requiring each recruit to toil in the periphery they would adopt kibbutz-like values, develop the land, create new settlements, and protect the country's borders. In other words, the kibbutz and these other agricultural settlements were charged with the ideological mission of transforming the Jewish individual, but the location of this transformation, on the periphery, also met the state's defense requirements.

The dream of making the IDF into a farmer's army subsided by 1950, as it became obvious that full-time training would be required if Israel was to have a progressive and technologically proficient military.[71] As such, a number of amendments to the Defense Service Law freed both professional soldiers and those who entered past the age of twenty-five from agricultural service. The final, inevitable, move was the abolition of agricultural service soon thereafter.[72] Moreover, although regional defense partially compensated for Israel's shortage of manpower, lack of territorial depth, and (potentially) the time it would take to mobilize reserves, its importance has lessened since the 1967 War.[73]

As noted, the government's restructural manpower policy was a nearly all-inclusive affair motivated largely by the fact that only an expansive policy would fulfill the government's security needs. In this way, then, the government attempted to distribute the burdens of war fairly evenly and without regard for the individual's status in society. Thus, Israel's military, like most militaries, reflects some broader patterns of state-society relations. Similar to many Third World militaries, the IDF derived its elite forces from the dominant groups in society. Unlike many Third World militaries, however, this occurred not because an unpopular government feared domestic threats, but rather because the state manifested a tremendous legitimacy. This phenomenon reflects the commitment to the state, not to any set of leaders who happen to occupy its offices. Military service and the army in general are also seen as reflections of societal stratification and elite group privileges; service defines who is an accepted member of the community and who remains peripheral. For example, the better educated elites declare exemption with less frequency than do other members of society.[74] Furthermore, serving in the elite corps requires a greater dedication of time, but generally the rewards and prestige associated with this service more than offset the unequal duration.[75] Finally, the type and length of military service is used to distribute rewards in society, as it can provide: (1) a sense of ability to influence decision making; (2) accessibility to restricted or classified material, which can provide general status and greater influence over policy making; and (3) attachment to more common central goals through the actual performance.[76]

Because conscription is nearly universal and thus most individuals do not gain prestige from serving, a group's peripherality in society is defined by its unwillingness to serve or its exclusion from service.[77] Two groups were excluded from conscription. The first were students of religious institutions. Their exemption came after Ben-Gurion received substantial pressure from religious authorities, who claimed that they should be given special privileges in the Jewish state.[78] The second group exempt from military service were Israel's Arab population; the government believed that such policy would both keep guns away from a potentially hostile minority and absolve them from a dual loyalty—to the Jewish state and to their fellow Arabs in the neighboring states.[79] "For the majority of nonconscriptable social groups, nonconscription is used as an indicator of marginality, or partial membership. Consequently, a social group's (or its representative's) demand for conscription is a demand for full membership."[80] The penalty for not serving in the military can be severe, meaning a loss of prestige, influence, and rewards for life beyond the military.[81] In general, the government's manpower policy reflected the simple but important fact that it could trust most societal groups with access to the state's weapons and not fear that they would be turned against the state managers. Those excluded from such access were those who did not accept the state's existence, though only Israel's Arab community was viewed as a security risk.

Although the government had nearly maximized the country's manpower potential, it believed that Israel could benefit from a Great Power protector and ally. In some ways this recalls the days of Herzl, but this "pre-independence alliance policy was diplomatic rather than strategic. A patron was sought primarily for purposes of international recognition, not effective participation in a balance-of-power game of nations."[82] Now the Jewish state searched for a protector to offset Arab strategic advantages.

As already discussed, by 1950 the Israeli government placed its sympathies and hopes on the West. Neither arms nor alliances, however, were immediately forthcoming. It was not for lack of Israeli interest or determination.[83] Britain had initially expressed some interest, but it became clear to Israeli leaders that Britain wanted the logistic benefits offered by Israel's geostrategic location without any real commitment to Israel's security.[84] Similarly, neither the Truman nor the Eisenhower administration was willing to enter into an alliance agreement. In fact, Dulles's Soviet containment policy included the Arab countries but excluded Israel. Israel's strategic isolation during this period is nicely captured by the following story. Nasser had told the United States that for him to consider Egypt's participation in any future Western alliance system Israel would first have to cede part of the Negev. "Both Secretary of State Dulles and British Foreign Secretary Eden, who rarely saw eye-to-eye on any topic, concurred that the demand was worth exploring. Thus, not only was the Israeli request for a security guarantee turned down, but Israel was also made to understand that it might have to pay with its own territory for the consolidation of the U.S-British-led strategic alliance from which Israel would be excluded."[85] It became clear to Israeli leaders that any security guarantee would come at its expense. For the time being Israeli leaders would have to be content with a reliable arms supplier.

Israel was now a "reality" despite the significant odds and the dire predictions concerning its viability. The government had nurtured and directed the country through a difficult period, and after a particularly worrisome first few years, it appeared to be steering society and the economy in a positive direction. The increased series of border raids before 1956 notwithstanding, Israel seemed to have solidified its existence among the community of states.

Clearly there was a dynamic relationship between the government's war preparation strategies and its postindependence stance vis-à-vis society. The independence campaign could only have been won with tremendous societal support and dedication. The government capitalized on the state's legitimacy, capacity, and autonomy to implement a restructural strategy and mobilize societal resources, which, in turn, contributed to and institutionalized the state's solid presence in the post-1948 period. This relationship was particularly evident in the government's manpower and fiscal policies. The government was not only able to draft and arm most of society, a rare feat for postcolonial states, but these conscripts also performed important state-building tasks during the next few years. Moreover, the government was able to extract revenue through direct means, without nearly the same degree of trauma or outright opposition evidenced in other postcolonial countries, which, in turn, contributed to its ability to deepen the state's extractive capacities. In general, the government's initial restructural policy was quickly followed by a series of accommodational gestures.

Because of the significant domestic constraints the government was unable to maintain a self-reliant stance and serve all of its required war-related resources. Despite the government's strident desires to remain independent from external influence and its relative success in mobilizing society for defense, Israel's expanding defense, welfare, and development commitments in a postcolonial environment implied that it would have to rely on foreign sources for the difference between these pledges and its domestic resources. Luckily, the state received many unilateral transfers that came with few strings or conditions; these first enhanced the state's relative autonomy, and second enabled the government's attempt to create a solid foundation for autonomous military industrialization. The government's material policy did register a modicum of success: not only did it establish the foundations for future military industrialization, but it also broke through its strategic isolation and formed a relationship with France, from whom the country hoped to learn the basics of military industrialization. Until that day arrived, however, the Israeli government had to remain content with a reliable source of arms. In general, the government's concern for external autonomy was overwhelmed by its need for external sources of support. Such divergence between the government's goals and its actions repeated itself with increasing alarm once security demands became overwhelming after 1967.

IN THE EYE OF THE HURRICANE, 1957–1967

The decade following the Sinai War witnessed Israel's consolidation both abroad and at home. Notwithstanding Nasser's ability to capture the moral highground in the Sinai War and the United States' direct confrontation with the Israelis over their postwar occupation of the peninsula, the campaign brought relative peace to Israel's borders, halted the fedayeen raids, demilitarized the Sinai, and reestablished Israel's right of passage through the Straits of Tiran. In fact, it was Israel's most peaceful decade. That this was so was not strictly Israel's doing. The Arab World was engulfed in a bitter intra-Arab conflict, provoked in large part by Nasser's attempt to export his brand of politics and the Yemen War from 1962 to 1967. Even without these intra-Arab distractions, it was less than evident that the Arab states wanted to challenge Israel militarily in the near future. Nasser's opinion was that the next Arab-Israeli war should be fought at the Arab's behest, not at Israel's convenience. These developments led the Israeli government to estimate that there was little likelihood of a third Arab-Israeli war in the immediate future.

Israel also broke through its strategic isolation during this period. Although the French-Israeli relationship deepened considerably over this period, more important for Israel's strategic future was its relationship to the United States. The United States was still reluctant to openly embrace Israel's possible role in a strategic alliance, but the latter's importance grew with each U.S. setback in the Arab world. Most important was the overthrow of the pro-American Quassim government in Iraq in 1958 and the continued tensions between Nasser and the United States. Israel quietly capitalized on these developments, for although the United States still refused to sell weapons directly to Israel, it did begin to channel some hardware through European allies.[86] The United States finally upgraded its covert relationship in 1962 when Kennedy sold Israel the Hawk missile system. Lyndon Johnson was more openly sympathetic, and in 1964 he agreed to the first shipment of offensive weapons systems.

Finally, Israel began to establish relations with other Third World countries. Israelis rejoiced and greeted enthusiastically this development, for it shattered their feeling of isolation and exclusion in the international system. Israel, itself a major recipient of foreign aid, began to venture into the field of foreign assistance itself, as many Israelis volunteered and served as development advisers. Israel's first foray was Burma, and this friendship was quickly succeeded by other affiliations in Southeast Asia, Africa, and Latin America. These assistance programs were designed to expand Israel's commercial ties and, possibly more important, symbolize Israel's acceptance in the community of states. In general, it was clear that at the political, strategic, and symbolic levels Israel had arrived on the world scene.

Given the relative quiet on Israel's borders during this period, the government placed its efforts on achieving rapid development. At this it seemed quite accomplished. The Israeli economy expanded at a tremendous rate over the next decade, achieving growth rates approximating 10 percent annually. Industrial development grew ninefold from 1953 through 1967, and industrial exports as a percentage of all exports climbed from 60 percent in 1953 to 81 percent in 1967. Moreover, unemployment steadily decreased throughout this decade until there was an actual labor shortage in 1964.[87] Two major economic developments occurred during this period. First, in 1962 the government began to dismantle its protectionist barriers (begun in 1952) and liberalized trade by relaxing import controls. The government intended to rid the economy of its inefficiencies and to open the door to export-led growth. Second, a severe recession from 1965 until 1967, partially caused by the government's attempt to narrow the import surplus, marked the only interruption in an otherwise steady economic expansion. The recession aside, the Israeli government had overcome the early dire predictions concerning its economic future. In fact, Israel had become one of the success stories in the Third World, and many other countries were now anxious to apply its lessons locally.

With such economic, military, and diplomatic successes the government could feel optimistic about the future. The various uncertainties that surrounded its early existence seemed to have given way to a bold, vibrant future. An economic success story, Israel had demonstrated its ability to defend itself; it had become a development model for other Third World countries. Israel seemingly became the West's "new protégé."[88]

Yet ominous clouds darkened the government's horizon. Although the state retained its central role in the economy, there were warning signs that the government's once unassailable position would soon be challenged. During this period the state became the country's largest employer,[89] which had both positive and negative consequences for its control over society. On the one hand, the added personnel meant that the state's ability to monitor society was strengthened. On the other hand, the expansion undermined some of the most important common elements of solidarity.[90] Previously, the upper echelons of the bureaucracy depended on political considerations; however, over time these positions were allocated along more professional considerations. This was not a uniform development, however, for different elements of the state apparatus were more susceptible to changes in class patterns and elite formation. For instance, in the finance, military, diplomatic, and judiciary bureaucracies, more professional appointments were made, not dictated as much by party considerations. This weakened the internal homogeneity and cohesion of the state elite, for these new appointments were not as concerned with the state's adherence to socialist-Zionist norms.[91] The above tendencies produced substantial changes in the relationship between the elite and society. Whereas once the bureaucracy had been an extension of the party leaders, it since had grown into an organization with interests and policies distinct from the party in power.[92] By implication, then, the government's ability to use the state apparatus for its own interests was diminished.

The professionalization of the bureaucracy and the "loosening" of the state structure corresponded to the first signs of Mapai's weakening political control. A number of developments contributed to this stumble. First, Mapai's initial dominance was partially owing to its symbol as pioneer. Over time, however, the monopolization of this image weakened, and other groups, most notably the military, began to share this symbol with Mapai. Second, as more immigrants were absorbed into society, the privileged position of the agricultural sector, and the kibbutz in particular, was diminished.[93] New economic sectors, not as tied to the old guard, came of age and importance.

There was also a subtle, yet important, change in Histadrut-state relations.[94] By the late 1950s Histadrut managers began to develop their own political and economic interests, distinct from those of state managers. This was accentuated by developments of the mid-1960s, as Histadrut's enterprises, owing in part to the government's protectionist policies, had become increasingly inefficient. Histadrut Secretary General Yitzhak Ben-Aharon attempted to instill new energy into these enterprises by introducing a whole new generation of Histadrut managers, essentially technocrats (as opposed to party bosses) who had a greater private enterprise orientation. These new managers began both to cooperate with private capital more frequently and to look toward foreign capital for investment. The questions emerged: Could Mapai control Histadrut? Could Histadrut leadership control its corporate managers? By the early 1960s Histadrut had become more autonomous and represented a potential threat to the interests of Mapai and the state.

Moreover, there was growing internal rivalry and fractionalization within Mapai.[95] The genesis of the division was the Lavon Affair of 1955, which had initially created tremendous intra-Mapai conflict but was seemingly halted by the resignation of Minister of Defense Lavon and his replacement by Ben-Gurion. This chapter was reopened in 1960, however, as Lavon became the new secretary-general of the Histadrut and wanted his name exonerated and divorced from the Lavon Affair. A committee of seven cabinet ministers was formed, and it subsequently granted Lavon absolution. Ben-Gurion was infuriated by this decision and, even though Lavon was forced to resign his position at Histadrut, pressed for a judicial inquiry. The result was a fierce intra-Mapai struggle, and the ethereal alliance between Ben-Gurion and the old guard collapsed. The issue was more than simply Lavon's responsibility for this affair, but rather the future of Mapai. Ben-Gurion offered himself and his protégés Moshe Dayan and Shimon Peres, while the rest of the Mapai leadership was content with the old guard. In the end Ben-Gurion departed from the party, and Rafi was formed in 1965. Contrary to Ben-Gurion's hopes, Rafi won only ten seats in the 1965 election and found itself outside cabinet politics. Eshkol became the new prime minister, and Ben-Gurion retreated to his desert kibbutz at Sde Boker. In general, this episode of Mapai politics left the party divided and weaker than ever before.

A final development that potentially threatened the government's control of society and economy was the role of private capital in its development plans. In the mid-1960s Pinchas Sapir, the minister of industry, became the minister of finance and began to emphasize the role of private sector in the government's economic plans. By doing so Sapir hoped to demonstrate the government's sympathetic attitude toward private capital, thereby attracting foreign capital, particularly from the United States and U.S. Jewry. Second, after a long period of labor surplus, by the mid-1960s there was full employment. Labor became scarce, which increased Histadrut's political power because of its status as labor's official representative. Again, there was some question concerning Mapai's future political base, and whether the Histadrut could be trusted to play Sancho Panza to Mapai's Don Quixote. By turning to private capital, Sapir believed he might offset Histadrut's political and economic power. Finally, there was a general opinion that increased competition promoted greater productivity and efficiency, which corresponded to the state's new economic policy. The best way to introduce competition was to insert the private sector into the economy.[96] Although this projected enlarged role for the private sector was a minority viewpoint during the mid-1960s, it was an omen of an increasingly prevalent attitude within the party and the state apparatus. Be that as it may, in Chapter 3 I noted that although the private sector always controlled a fairly significant portion of the economy, it was weakly organized and located in the marginal sectors of the economy, that is, not in industrial or manufacturing areas. Domestic capital had a few more routers in the state apparatus, but this feature of its political weakness did not change significantly.

In general, the economic structure and state structure underwent greater differentiation during this period. Although the immediate implication was that the government might be unable to implement its policies as easily as before, Mapai was still the beneficiary of a large amount of popular support, and its officials controlled most unilateral transfers and, hence, investment funds. Therefore, the state still had a significant amount of control over society and the levers of the economy.

What might be expected of Israeli war preparation strategies during this period? Because this decade witnessed only occasional war-threatening events, few indications that the Arab states were actively planning war in the immediate future, and no domestic political challenges, there was little pressure for Israeli leaders to rethink their current war preparation strategies. Under such circumstances, little change could be expected. Israeli leaders could be expected to remain true to their past mobilization practices and thus rely on a combination of accommodational tactics when domestic resources were available and an international strategy when they were not.

Fiscal Strategies

After absorbing the initial costs of the Suez War, Israeli defense spending consumed a relatively constant portion of the budget until 1962, when Israel began to move full-swing into a high-technology military posture and received its first consignment of U.S. weapons (see table 5.1).[97] These comparatively modest increases in the defense bill did not sound a fiscal alarm, for the country was experiencing a period of rapid economic expansion (at least until 1965 recession) and continued to receive a substantial amount of unilateral transfers from world Jewry, the United States, German reparations, and other foreign loans.[98] Under such circumstances there was little pressure to alter the government's financing schedule.

The continued reliance on foreign financing and capital imports, however, caused many government officials to worry that Israel was becoming too dependent on foreign patrons. Given the expanding economy and the increasing defense needs, for a short-lived moment the government considered shifting more of the burden onto society. Significant political pressures, however, precluded any revision of the state's current income tax arrangements,[99] which reinforced its fidelity to an accommodational policy. An increasing percentage of the population consisted of immigrants and children, which implied those with little or no income. Histadrut also stood by as guardian of the workers and precluded any tax increases on middle- and lower-income groups. Moreover, there was a widening income disparity between these income groups, and increased taxation might have heightened social tensions and class conflict. Although the upper-income groups might have borne a greater burden, they were relieved of such responsibility because they tended to be highly trained professionals whose skills could be demanded internationally.[100] Moreover, raised tax rates might not necessarily translate into increased revenue given this group's adept ability at tax evasion.[101] Finally, there was an acknowledged difficulty of monitoring and imposing effective controls over the larger private and public corporations, owing in part to the state's administrative weakness.[102]

Not only did the government avoid raising income tax rates, but it also found significant deterrents to increasing indirect taxes. "Mr. Eshkol's [the minister of finance] present dilemma . . . is that raising indirect taxes on luxuries and semi-luxuries is a policy which becomes self-defeating after a time, while raising indirect taxes on necessities is politically difficult."[103] In other words, duties on luxury imports, intended to promote welfare and distributional objectives, were not as effective at raising revenue, while Histadrut could ensure that its members' interests were shielded from the government's attempts to raise the price of essential commodities. Moreover, the trade liberalization policies of the following year (1962) meant that import duties were the last thing the government wanted to raise.

Thus, the government's tax strategy changed little before 1967, for the government was both stymied in its efforts to raise the percentage of resources derived from domestic sources and unwilling to place undue hardships on those groups deemed central to its development efforts. Consequently, the tax structure continued to weigh heaviest on middle-income groups. "Both tax policies, with their limits on the upper brackets of income tax levels, and the de facto wage policy greatly favored the upper brackets of the upper-middle groups."[104]

Because societal pressures effectively precluded the government from changing its fiscal policy, foreign aid relieved the government of difficult choices.[105] Again, world Jewry, German reparations, and U.S. assistance were the most important sources of capital transfers. The terms attached to U.S. assistance, however, underwent an important change over this period. In 1958 the U.S. assistance program was restructured and divided between "special aid," a grant for the purchase of U.S. agricultural products, which totaled around $30 million by 1962 when it ceased, and loans from the Defense Loan Fund, given to the Israeli government for the purchase of U.S.-made products. In addition, these loans were on friendly terms and repayable in Israeli pounds.[106] In 1962, however, the United States no longer allowed the repayment of loans in Israeli currency, and henceforth made them repayable in dollars only. Consequently, Israel's foreign debt rose dramatically. In general, the flow of grants from the United States was fairly steady during the 1950s and declined during the 1960s; it ceased completely in 1968 and resumed in 1972. This debt would have expanded further had it not been for the continued flow of capital imports (see Appendix 7). Israel's reception of a tremendous amount of unilateral transfers enabled it to undertake what, under normal circumstances, would have been an overcommitment to defense, welfare, and development. An international strategy, then, offered a fairly reasonable alternative to the limitations imposed by societal constraints.

Production Strategies

As a result of both the fear caused by the rapid development of Egypt's defense industry and the increased defense cooperation with the French and the Germans, the government's objective of military industrialization took tremendous strides during this period. However, it was still confronted by a situation in which its eyes were larger than its economic infrastructure or scientific know-how. As a result the government's strategy was to diversify its source of supply while developing the basis for expanded military industrialization. In other words, although an international strategy was required because of the economy's lack of the appropriate infrastructure, the government hoped such a strategy of dependent militarization would provide the Israeli economy with the necessary tools for autonomous militarization.

The key to Israel's hopes in both the importation of military weapons and development of military industrialization was its quasi-alliance with France.[107] This post-1956 period marks the "second phase" of Israeli defense production. Israel's progress in arms production had been aided by its refurbishing and redesigning of weapons designed for the European theater for the Middle East context, but the real breakthrough came when the French agreed to licensed coproduction.[108] The French-Israeli relationship exceeded all Israeli expectations. After years of isolation and searching for a Great Power patron, France began to supply Israel with the arms, technology, and scientific expertise it desperately needed. This relationship, however, was always limited and never achieved the status of a full-fledged alliance, where both countries pledged assistance and support in the event of war. In fact, once the Algerian conflict was settled in 1962, the French began to act more coolly toward the Israelis, to the point where they broke off their arms relationship prior to the 1967 War. Be that as it may, the Israeli quest for an autonomous arms program received a substantial boost from its association with the French.

Although the French relationship served many of Israel's needs, the government attempted to diversify its source of support. Two countries received the bulk of Israel's hopes. Beginning in 1958 the Israeli government began to explore more fully the possibility of reaching some sort of security pact with West Germany, and soon thereafter Israel received some military assistance.[109] Israel also hoped to expand its ties with the United States. The United States had begun to reevaluate Israel's potential contribution to U.S. security policy after the collapse of an Arab-centered U.S. Middle East policy in the late 1950s and the reconstituted belief that Israel might act as an important regional balancer and status quo force.[110] The breakthrough from the Israeli perspective, the 1962 sale of the Hawk anti-aircraft missile system, represented the first time that the United States agreed to the official sale of an advanced weapons system. Israel hoped this sale represented an important foundation upon which it could build.

This propulsion toward military industrialization, however, occurred solely under the state's authority, a continuation of the pre-1956 policy.[111] The Defense Ministry's policy, guided and supervised under the watchful eyes of Shimon Peres and Moshe Kashti, placed most defense production under its jurisdiction. Shimon Peres, who was then in charge of the state's defense companies, began to favor and bolster this sector for a variety of reasons. First, a debate raged within the Mapai leadership between the old guard, which tended to defend the interests of Histadrut, and the new guard, best represented by Moshe Dayan and Shimon Peres, who articulated Ben-Gurion's statist view of the economy. By favoring arms production under the state's guidance, Peres promoted this etatist vision and potentially developed a new power base. It also served the bureaucratic interests of the Defense Ministry and the political interests of Mapai, both of which were credited with expanding the state's national security apparatus.[112] Finally, only the state had the required capital to undertake such a substantial commitment of resources. Histadrut, because of its close association with the state elite, was given some military contracts and coproduction with public sector corporations. The private sector, however, was virtually excluded from this potentially profitable sector of the economy.[113]

In summary, the government's desire to promote an autonomous arms industry progressed tremendously during this period. There were two integral parts to Israeli military development. First, the tremendous inflow of capital imports, most notably from German reparations payments, helped to account for not only Israel's rapid economic growth but also the capitalization of many important Israeli defense industries. Second, the relative autonomy of the state allowed government officials to channel these unilateral transfers and distribute resources in a manner that corresponded to their objectives. Indicative of the expansion of the arms industry was the rise in exports, which grew from around $7 million in 1956 to around $30 million in 1967.[114] This modest growth aside, it was clear that the capitalization of local arms industries and French-Israeli collaboration provided a solid foundation for further military industrial expansion after 1967.

Conscription Policies

Because the state's borders remained relatively calm, there was little pressure to alter the manpower requirements. What remained uncertain, however, was the performance of the new Israeli army under battlefield conditions. Since 1948 a greater percentage of the army's reserves and regulars were now IDF-trained, no longer a motley group of civilians, but a highly trained professional fighting force. The 1956 War had demonstrated to IDF planners that the reserve system could work effectively in battle. Indeed, "an army of civilians, whose only previous battle experience had been in a slow-moving, defense war, revealed itself capable of fighting a brief, intensive war based on a decisive-victory concept. Starting from this assumption, IDF architects had no reason to change the overall regular/reserve ratio [or] the call-up system."[115]

Although there was no attempt to extend the scope or the length of military service, there were attempts to enlist the support of foreign governments in Israel's defense. The success of the French relationship led to a debate among Israeli officials of the benefits and importance of strategic alliances. Moshe Dayan once again argued for a policy of "defiant self-reliance," as he saw little value of alliances. Others, notably Abba Eban, were early and staunch advocates of an alliance with the United States; Shimon Peres, the main architect of the French-Israeli relationship, also saw the value of distributing Israel's security eggs in various baskets and exploring the expansion of French and West German security ties. The debate was for the most part irrelevant because there were no respondents to Israeli feelers. No doubt these rebuffs would have caused greater concern had Israel not just experienced a tremendous lift from its battlefield successes in the 1956 War. In general, Israel had to resign itself to less formal and less public security arrangements for ensuring Israel's access to strategic minerals (e.g., oil and uranium) and weapons.[116]

That there was little change in the government's war preparation strategies can be attributed primarily to two factors. First, that systemic environment gave Israeli decision makers few reasons to reevaluate their mobilization practices. Israel's borders were relatively secure and calm, a direct consequence of both the Sinai War of 1956 and the subsequent period of intra-Arab struggle. Second, the government not only still faced few domestic challengers, but also the country underwent a period of tremendous economic expansion that added to its resource base. In short, the absence of either systemic or domestic threats meant that Israeli leaders, reluctant to challenge the status quo, were satisfied with the current formula. If the period between 1957 and 1967 appeared calm, it was only in comparison with what had just taken place and what was about to occur.

LIFE DURING WARTIME, 1967–1977

As Israeli leaders surveyed the regional and domestic scene on June 10, 1967, they had every right to believe that they had recorded a momentous victory. As Israeli writer Amos Elon has observed, the victory marked the Israeli passage from self-doubt to self-assurance, for "when most was at stake, they could stand up and shape their own future. They proved it to others, but above all to themselves. The 1967 War was a military victory; the psychological effect was even greater. For Israelis it marked the transition from adolescence to maturity."[117] The Zionist experiment and its institutional mold had worked, vividly demonstrated by the tremendous military victory. Jerusalem, the symbol of Zionist aspirations and the seat of the Israeli capital was united and, as far as most Israelis were concerned, never to be divided again. Israel's victory in the recent war appeared to signal the superiority of its way of life over its Arab neighbors in almost all imaginable categories—intellectually, economically, militarily, and politically. At least that was the conclusion some Arab intellectuals and nearly all Israeli leaders reached.

Yet this initial euphoria lasted a scant few months and was soon succeeded by "the new fatalism,"[118] caused by the realization that Israel would not be able to trade the captured territories for peace as initially envisioned by most Israelis. Rather than responding to the 1967 War by making the "phone call" to negotiate that many Israeli leaders were expecting (because it was clear to them that they could not be moved militarily), the Arab states convened at the Khartoum Conference in Fall 1967 and committed themselves to the policy of no direct peace negotiations with Israel and the task of reclaiming the occupied lands through force and, along with it, Arab honor and pride. Now it seemed that the next war was only two to three years away, just as soon as the Arab states could rebuild their demolished armies and demoralized societies. This was not to be the war to end all wars.

Consequently, although Israeli leaders had always placed national security as a, if not the, top priority, the decade following the 1967 War was unprecedented in its heightened security awareness and its associated costs (see table 5.1). Whereas during the 1958–1966 period defense expenditures had remained relatively stable, after the 1967 War they escalated in a seemingly uncontrollable fashion: defense costs that equalled 15 percent of national income in 1967, hovered near 20 percent between 1968 and 1972 and hung around 30 percent after the Yom Kippur War.[119] A number of factors precipitated this increase. First, during this decade Israel proceeded to fight two more wars, the War of Attrition and the Yom Kippur War. Second, immediately following June 1967 both the Israelis and the Arabs began to resupply their spent armies and prepare for the next round, and neither side seemed to tire from the task of absorbing increasing numbers of weapons. In a related issue, each side's respective superpower provided weapons that were some of the latest, and costliest, in its arsenal. Third, once the AOPEC countries successfully raised the price of crude oil, their ability to underwrite the frontline Arab states increased dramatically. This was a double blow to the Israeli economy, for Israel attempted to maintain a regional balance of power while paying more for oil imports. Fourth, the IDF's mission expanded; added to its normal responsibility of defending the country's borders was the problem of policing the occupied territories. Finally, Israel had to respond to a new military threat, the PLO. Briefly, before 1967 the PLO was a semi-autonomous entity whose actions were highly dependent on its host country and subordinate to Arab "grand strategy." The crushing defeat of the Arab armies in 1967 had a significant impact on the Palestinian movement, as its leaders proceeded on the assumption that if they were to wait for the Arab states to realize its dream of an independent state, they would have to wait a very long time. The PLO, therefore, began to display more independence and to organize terrorist missions aimed at Israeli civilian targets at home and abroad. This became even truer after 1970 when the PLO took up residence in Lebanon and established an autonomous existence on Israel's northern border. Israeli leaders had to confront familiar and new security challenges in the post-1967 era. The June War, rather than handing Israeli leaders the peace they were hoping for, gave them more of the same—and then some.

One systemic change did offer Israeli leaders some respite and relief from these security challenges: Israel's closer relationship with the United States. After the 1967 War the United States replaced France as Israel's closest ally and guardian in the international system. Although this friendship was slow in developing, it grew at an amazing rate after 1970 and particularly so after the 1973 War. According to Safran, the United States' commitment was solidified by its support of Israel's demand for a full and comprehensive peace settlement after 1967.[120] Perhaps more important, Israeli officials had convinced the United States of Israel's strategic value, its ability to act in accord with U.S. interests in the region and to play a stabilizing role in the Middle East (this was particularly visible in September 1970, when Israeli actions were credited with stopping Syria from intervening on behalf of the PLO against Hussein of Jordan). Israeli leaders now assumed that they could count on the United States for its survival, and notwithstanding the absence of an explicit security commitment, that the United States would dispatch American troops to Israel should they be required. In fact, Israeli leaders now rejected U.S. feelers for an explicit alliance pact, something they had only dreamed of since 1948, because they believed that they would gain little—the United States was already acting in this fashion—at some cost, given Israel's expected withdrawal from the captured territories without any peace treaty.[121] From now on the United States seemed committed to funding Israel's expanding security needs and defending Israel's existence, with or without the presence of an official alliance pact. Israel's constant, but heretofore fruitless, search for a Great Power protector had been realized.

Added to the increased security pressures and burdens were major societal changes and domestic challenges. Prime Ministers Eshkol (1967–1969), Meir (1969–1974), and Rabin (1974–1977) would preside over an increasingly weakened Labor government.[122] This downhill slide culminated in the "upheaval" of 1977, when Likud's Menachem Begin usurped Labor's control and the latter became the opposition party for the first time in Israeli history. Among many factors four contributed significantly to Labor's demise and Likud's rise. First, Labor was increasingly unable to claim that it could best guarantee the state's security. While the IDF had risen to the occasion in the 1967 War, the same could not be said about the Eshkol government. Indecision appeared to reign supreme in the weeks prior to June 4 and was resolved only when Moshe Dayan was named minister of defense in the last week of May.

Moreover, the "government of national unity" formed immediately prior to the Six-Day War legitimized the opposition parties as responsible governmental officials.[123] Although Labor, the dominant coalition partner, was credited with the successes of 1967, its junior partners were able to capitalize on their inclusion and association with the tremendous battlefield feat.

The 1973 War further eroded Labor's support. The Yom Kippur War stimulated the first public demand for a review of the government's handling of security and defense issues in general and its failure to detect the surprise attack in specific. The Arganat Commission was established in 1974 to look into these matters, and although the Commission did not finger Prime Minister Meir and Defense Minister Dayan as the principal culprits, as was widely expected, it did lead to their eventual resignations, an undermining of societal confidence in Labor's ability to meet the Arab threat, and the formation of the final Labor party government under Yitzhak Rabin.

Second, although the Six-Day War seemed to give Israel the territorial security and prospects necessary for forging peace, it also ripped apart the territorial compromise concerning the nature and scope of the Jewish state. A key debate during the prestatehood years was the proper size of the future Israeli state: should the Zionist leadership press for all of biblical Israel, which would include both sides of the Jordan River, or should it accept something less? As is well known, the Yishuv leadership accepted the much smaller two-state solution, and the 1949 Armistice lines ended any meaningful debate over expanding Israel's ideal size. Israel's 1967 victory and occupation of the territories (particularly the West Bank), however, reopened this chapter and controversy. The Israeli Right's dream of having a Greater Israel reawakened, and the process of redefining the state occurred once again.[124] If a central feature of any state is its territoriality, then the proper scope of Israel's borders would be questioned by both foreign and domestic actors.

Third, during this period the split between European (Ashkenazi) and non-European (Sephardi) Israelis forcefully emerged. Briefly, the Ashkenazi Jews, who dominated the ranks of the Mapai party, were credited with creating the state; they were also responsible for overseeing a state-building project that viewed the Sephardim as a group to be integrated into the dominant and superior European mold. This peripherality of the Sephardim eventually led to tremendous resentment, as the Sephardim claimed that the benefits of development were accruing disproportionally to the Askenazim and that they were the target of an oppressive and highly arrogant Ashkenazi-run state bureaucracy. After 1970 Sephardic hostility against the establishment visibly emerged and crested in a wave of riots in Jerusalem in March 1971, as they directly challenged the government's priorities that seemingly placed social services, housing, and other Sephardic concerns on the back burner. More demonstrations followed over the next number of years.[125] The Sephardim, adding insult to injury by voting for Likud in record numbers, could take credit for bringing Menachem Begin to power.

Finally, the post-1967 economic boom contrasted decidedly with the economic stagnation that characterized the post-1973 economy. The 1967 War, coming on the heels of a recession, stimulated a tremendous growth spurt in the Israeli economy. What might be understood as a policy of military Keynesianism, the government's increased defense spending and defense-related capital investment energized various economic sectors and lowered the unemployment rate. The country's GNP grew by approximately 7 percent per annum during the interwar years, industrial exports rose exponentially, private consumption increased, and Israel seemed to have entered into a period of economic affluence. All this abruptly halted in 1973, as the double shock of the Yom Kippur War, which cost one year's GNP, and the oil price rise had a tremendous impact on the economy's performance. The government presided over a series of increasing budget and balance of payments deficits, which translated into a number of related economic headaches and a declining standard of living for many Israelis. Although Finance Minister Yehoshua Rabinowitz made some modest attempts to address the deteriorating economic situation by attempting to cut capital imports through an austerity budget and a devaluation of the Israeli pound, the Rabin government viewed such economic belt tightening as political suicide. As Sachar comments,

> The premier himself issued no forceful call for the nation to accept additional sacrifices. Rather, in this period, Israel was plagued by a wave of strikes, most of them organized not by blue-collar workers but by salaried professional groups—engineers, physicians, teachers—who proved remarkably adept at immobilizing vital public services. The government for its part seemed to look on helplessly, and in the end to surrender to the strikers' demands.[126]

In short, the Sephardim, who made up the lower classes and lower occupational positions, were defecting from the Labor party in droves, while the professional groups, Labor's main source of support, were equally contentious. There was no rest for the weary.

In general, the Labor party's political future was being whittled away by its symbolic status as the protector of the European Jews, its activities during the 1967 and 1973 Wars, and its inability to solve the country's economic woes. During this entire period, then, Labor became less confident of its continued popularity, and this duly effected its evaluation of which policies were politically feasible. Even in the best of times such tremendous security pressures subjected Israeli leaders to tremendous strains. And these were certainly not the best of times. Nadav Safran writes:

> Altogether, then, the changes wrought by the immediate aftermath of the Yom Kippur War unraveled the configuration of the political system that took shape in the wake of the Six-Day War but did not produce one that seemed better adapted to dealing with the crucial issues confronting the country. It can be said, without much exaggeration, that if *unwillingness* to make decisions and incur the risk of divisions characterized the previous configuration, inability to make decisions because of a particular pattern of political division in the country, the government, and the dominant party was the hallmark of the new configuration.[127]

It would not be surprising, then, if the government's war preparation strategies reflected these very domestic pressures. For instance, Yaniv writes of this period:

> Israeli society was changing in a manner that increased the inevitable tension between domestic demands and external needs. With a significant change in the social basis of politics also came a gradual change in the political array of forces, in the rules of the game, in the texture and pace of domestic politics. It also added up to an immeasurably greater difficulty in insulating national strategy from the warp and hoof of the domestic political process.[128]

These tremendous systemic and domestic pressures posed grave new challenges to Israeli officials.

The Israeli government's mobilization of financial, productive, and manpower resources was highly dependent on systemic openings, societal constraints and opportunities, and governmental objectives. The following discussion contends that Israeli officials, capitalizing on a "strong" Israeli state and motivated by the existence of a salient national security threat, political struggles, and new development concerns and attitudes during the 1967–1977 period, moved to liberalize the economy to increase the material base but, cognizant of their political future, relied more heavily on the U.S. strategic alliance for much of their financial need. This outcome depended on the objectives of state actors, their decision context, and systemic openings. Although the state continued to benefit from tremendous societal legitimacy, the government's conscription policy could hardly be expected to expand significantly beyond the pre-1967 formula that was designed to maximize the country's manpower needs while minimizing the economic strain. These restructural and international policies, as I argue later, led directly to the devolution of Israeli state power.

Financial Strategies

Before 1967 Israeli leaders attempted to mobilize the required resources necessary for meeting their objectives without jeopardizing the state's external autonomy.[129] Of importance was the fact that Israel incurred no obligations from its foreign sources of financing, and therefore its independence remained intact.[130] Although Israel benefited from a tremendous amount of unilateral transfers, such transfers alone could not adequately fund the government's welfare, warfare, and development objectives. Consequently, there was heavy societal extraction as well. In general, before 1967 the government was able to fund its expensive budgetary commitments through a combination of unilateral transfers and heavy societal extraction.

For several reasons the 1967 War did not provoke any major reexamination of the government's fiscal strategy, even though national security became both more salient and more costly. First, the government's initial reaction was accommodational; that is, it relied on tried and true policies during times of conflict: increasing indirect and direct taxation and imposing a special defense tax.[131] Although income tax rates were raised for all income classes (relatively less so for lower-income groups), Finance Ministry officials anticipated that the upper classes with their greater propensity for evasion would therefore escape a major part of the state's taxation efforts. Such behavior was tolerated because this class was considered instrumental to the state's development needs.[132] Again, the middle-income groups bore the burden.

The need to undertake more drastic measures between 1967 and 1970 was mitigated by rapid economic growth and continued capital imports.[133] The state's coffers expanded rapidly, which diminished the necessity either to increase its external financing or to raise substantially the domestic burden. Halevi argues:

> The heavy defense burden in 1970–71 did not prevent general prosperity. One reason is that the growing allocations to defense after the Six-Day War came at a slack period for the economy; in fact, they supplemented the policies adapted to regain full employment. A second factor is that the balance-of-payments implications have become much more serious in recent years. Israel increased the share of resources going to defense, not by cutting the absolute amounts going to other uses, but primarily by increasing total resources—partly by a growth in GNP, and partly by an increase in the import surplus.[134]

The economic expansion proceeding the 1967 War spared the government of imposing additional financial pains on society.

The outlook changed in late 1970, however, when the budget was severely underfinanced owing to both an economic slowdown, which meant a smaller than projected collection total, and increasing defense costs. Although the government moved to raise modestly import, purchase, and direct taxes, it was painfully obvious that such accommodational measures would hardly meet the government's expanding budgetary commitments. At this point "defense expenditures became too big for Israel and the Jewish people together,"[135] and the government identified its dominant financial strategy.

The government's principal solution, to seek external sources of financing, broke with its long-standing policy of avoiding foreign financial entanglements. A number of factors, both external and internal, prodded the government toward an international strategy. First, the emergence of a new international security alignment provided new financing opportunities at relatively little risk.[136] The United States seemed willing to subsidize Israel's expanding defense needs given its newly awarded status as a U.S. strategic asset, a bulwark against communism and Soviet expansion. Accordingly, the percentage of foreign financing in the Israeli budget increased during this period, and this began the government policy of exporting the costs of war preparation.[137]

A second reason for shifting the burden to foreign sources was the mounting societal pressures. Beginning in 1970 the Sephardic community took to the streets to protest against the Ashkenazi-dominated Labor government and directly challenged the government's priorities; these groups were no longer willing to pay for defense from welfare.[138] Such public demonstrations reinforced the government's belief that society would not tolerate an increased burden and that extraction had reached its limit.[139] Thus, the government perceived the direct trade-off between an increased domestic burden that might minimize Israel's growing financial dependence on the United States and political popularity, and came to value the latter objective over fiscal responsibility. Many prominent officials of this period argued that the government, more concerned with getting reelected than with fiscal sanity, therefore moved to minimize the extraction effort and maximize its electoral chances.[140]

In fact, the government not only avoided increasing the domestic burden, but it also responded to these societal pressures by allocating more funds for social services. For example, as a percentage of GNP, government transfers to individuals went from 6.7 percent during the 1962–1966 period, to 8.7 percent during the 1968–1973 period, and to 16.2 percent during the 1974–1980 period, and the government's taxation-to-transfers ratio significantly decreased over the 1962–1980 period: from 24.2 to 19.9 to 14.0, for 1962–1966, 1968–1973, and 1974–1980, respectively.[141] Thus, after 1972 the combination of increased welfare transfers and defense expenditures promoted an inflationary spiral, indicative of the government's weakening control over the society and the economy.[142] "Until 1971 we were able to keep the lid on a boiling pot; in 1972 things start to break apart"; then, in 1973, "on this boiling level, the worse situation . . . oil shock and the war."[143]

The Yom Kippur War was a tremendous shock to the Israeli government, the society, and the economy. The government had misjudged the Arab threat, leading to a general societal reevaluation of Labor's ability to be trusted with the state's security.[144] Although the cost of the June War was considered astronomical (a rate of $100 million a day), it seemed modest compared to the unparalleled costs of the Yom Kippur War (the equivalent of one year's GNP). Although the government may have failed in its task, there was a near societal consensus that national security demanded an even greater commitment of societal resources. According to Arnon Gafni, "the generals were all excited. . . . No one had the guts to say no [to increased defense spending]."[145] The military had a blank check.

The increased societal cohesion following the war convinced Israeli leaders that they could increase the societal financial burden, albeit in a less than restructural manner. Before 1973 the cabinet's perception was that society's appetite for taxation was satiated, but Arnon Gafni noted that "the best time to increase taxes is during war, since hardly anyone objects and people know that they are giving toward the war effort. We may argue that such measures are temporary, but these temporary measures stay on years after the war is over. Therefore, we take advantage of the situation and raise taxes when we can, and meet little opposition."[146] A number of measures were implemented to pay for the immediate effects of the war, including increased taxation, a "voluntary" war loan, and a state loan (essentially a tax, but repaid after fifteen years).[147] Finally, the government attempted to reduce its budgetary commitments. Finance Minister Sapir took advantage of the situation by slashing price subsidies on a number of basic commodities.[148] "Much of the public accepted the [price] rises with a stiff upper lip and teeth-grinding, but poorer sections, especially large families, were particularly bitter."[149] There were limits, however, to how far the government could move against those areas of the budget that had strong societal support. Its principal target was that part of the budget with no real constituency: public sector investment. The Development Budget, essentially public investment, was cut by almost 50 percent, which also saved foreign currency reserves and cut capital imports.

These post-1973 measures, however, could not narrow the budget deficit, which consequently stimulated an inflationary spiral.[150] The government attempted to reduce the inflation rate, which reached 50 percent in 1974 and 40 percent in 1975, by moving to increase taxes and to restrain any future wage hikes, but these actions were met by tremendous unrest throughout entire country.[151] This standoff, with society ready to make the government pay electorally for any increased financial burden, continued over the next number of years. This was particularly true by 1975: memories of war had faded, and most Israelis were not as willing to sacrifice their own well-being for that of the country's. The government, conscious of its less than perfect performance during the 1973 war, was reluctant to impose further financial burdens, and challenges from Likud dampened Labor's willingness to introduce the tough but needed economic reforms. There were definite limits to what the government was either willing or able to do. Safran squarely blames Labor party officials:

> Much of the failure [to restrain the economic deterioration], however, was due to weaknesses in the government and the Labor party. The defense minister, for example, opposed any meaningful reduction of the huge defense budget and was able to have his way. Lack of solidarity in the government ruled out firmness in the face of unauthorized strikes, and the lack of harmony and coordination between Labor leaders in the government and the Histadrut either pitted the two against each other or undermined the latter's ability to control its unions. . . . The result was not only that the government failed to keep a lid on wages and prevent a wage-price spiral but also that its authority and credibility suffered heavily. And as in all such situations, the unorganized, the weak, and the poor were the ones who suffered most. Matters came to such a point that on one occasion in May 1976, slum dwellers in Tel-Aviv took to the streets, threw up barricades, battled the police with firebombs and grenades, and were subdued only by tear gas.[152]

The government's limited domestic moves were the product of political expediency.

Because the government's accommodational measures could not fund its expanding budgetary commitments, its principal solution was to request, and receive, additional security assistance from the United States (see table 5.2).[153] Again, an international strategy was made possible by the new strategic alignment, and it arrived at a time when Israeli leaders were more willing to depend on foreign financing because of domestic political pressure.[154] Such trends, of course, provided the basis for many of Israel's problems after 1973. As Zambar stated, "although in the first twenty years we were able to finance everything domestically, now be-

TABLE 5.2
U.S. Assistance to Israel, 1972–1978 (in millions of dollars)

	Direct Grants	Loans			Defense	
		Received	Repaid	Gross	Net	Imports
1972	71	330	125	401	276	−490
1973	820	369	118	1,189	1,071	−1,253
1974	672	301	155	973	818	−1,225
1975	642	1,361	148	2,003	1,855	−1,846
1976	1,176	892	215	2,068	1,853	−1,496
1977	977	656	253	1,633	1,380	−942
1978	1,181	1,004	226	2,185	1,959	−1,612

Source: Bank of Israel, Annual Report (1978), 113.

cause the burden . . . was so heavy, we requested a huge amount from the United States. Israeli leaders knew that the United States would cover any additional costs, and we were not as motivated to scrutinize the budget. . . . It is easier to spend more if you know someone is going to pay for it. . . . Now we base our policy on foreign financing."[155]

Because of the government's preference for an international solution Israel's external debt expanded rapidly after 1967 (see Appendix 11). Between 1955 and 1966 both the external debt and national product climbed at similar levels, at an approximately annual rate of about 9.5 percent. Between 1967 and 1973, however, while the national product grew at its previous level, the debt proliferated at an annual average of 20 percent. Then, from 1973 to 1976 the national product declined to a point of stagnation, while the external debt accelerated to around 23 percent per year. Moreover, the composition of the debt also deteriorated, as the proportion of short-term debt rose and the grant element declined.[156] One final indication of the government's eroding financial position is that an estimated 37 percent of the Israeli defense budget is financed by U.S. largess, a tremendous increase over 1960 figures.[157] Such trends would have sent Ben-Gurion, a staunch advocate of maintaining Israel's financial independence, reeling.

In summary, the government's financial strategy underwent a dramatic change, as it abandoned its concern for financial autonomy and increased its reliance on foreign sources of financing. This was a direct result of the government's dual objectives of political popularity and war preparation. Although the government was willing to increase modestly the already heavy societal burden through a series of accommodational measures, the government's principal solution was international. This period can generally be seen as a struggle over the distribution of the burden, with the middle-income groups and the state's future financial solvency the primary losers. The upper classes continued to benefit from a relatively inefficient state collection system while the lower classes were relatively protected by the welfare system. The middle classes, however, had neither escape and found their living standards further eroded by the inflationary spiral unleashed by the war and the oil shocks of 1973. When challenged by stiff domestic opposition to its policies, the government attempted not to redistribute the burden more evenly, but to increase the amount of resources by expanding its foreign debt. And so, as domestic constraints increased the government moved toward an international solution to save its political neck. Fortunately, Israeli leaders were able to translate their new symbolic role as a U.S. strategic ally into substantial material benefits.

Production Strategies

Prior to 1967 the government obtained its armaments from, first, its fledgling domestic arms industry under the state's auspices, and, second, its quasi-alliance with France. The post-1967 strategy was designed to deepen military industrialization, but it differed from past policies in one very important respect: it now included nurturing a previously unheralded capitalist class. The reason for the government's deviation from its past policies can only be understood by examining the systemic environment, the state's autonomy, the development of the economic infrastructure, and the government's objectives of national security, development, and political stability.

The government's satisfaction with the pre-1967 weapons policy was undermined by a number of factors. First, a series of events alerted Israeli officials to the danger of arms dependence. Probably the most dramatic was the French embargo of Israel before the 1967 Arab-Israeli war. This sent shockwaves through the Israeli leadership, created uncertainty over the reliability of Israel's future arms suppliers, and reinforced the belief that Israel must not depend on outside sources for its national security needs.[158] Israel's experience during the Yom Kippur War further reinforced its wariness of dependence. As the Israelis saw it, Kissinger purposefully halted the arms resupply effort to Israel at the outset of the war in order to increase Israel's openness to Kissinger's suggestions and willingness to support (however reluctantly) his strategic goals. This experience was followed by the Ford-Kissinger reappraisal of U.S. Middle East policy in 1975, which included a temporary ban on arms shipments to the principal participants, primarily Israel. That this new arms embargo came on the heels of a U.S. guarantee of long-term arms shipments and seemed more punitive than anything further increased the government's desire for military independence.[159]

Becoming arms independent also made good economic sense. Israel's import bill grew exponentially, and nearly half of its balance of payments deficit in 1968 was attributed to rising defense costs; and this figure excludes raw materials and machinery for Israel's growing defense industry.[160] This deficit was a principal cause of the economy's troubles, including a rapidly expanding budget deficit and external debt, a galloping inflation rate, and a depletion of scarce resources. The expansion of a domestic defense industry would not only decrease the import bill, but would also yield jobs for a growing scientific community, provide important spin-offs for the civilian sector, and save precious and dwindling foreign currency reserves.[161]

Israel hoped that establishing and encouraging those industries and enterprises, notably chemicals, steel, optics, engineering, and computers, would further the country's defense needs, serve the country's economic future, and advance an export-led development strategy.[162] In general, during this period the government continued to sing the familiar neomercantilist tune that economic development and national security were inseparable and mutually compatible goals. As Zvi Dinstien commented, "Industrial development and defense requirements are intertwined."[163]

Although Israeli leaders favored greater defense production, three important ingredients enabled such an undertaking. The first was Israel's strategic relationship with the United States. Israel's defense industries had profited immensely from its association with France,[164] and now the hope was that much the same would occur under the aegis of the United States. Part of the developing relationship included the transfer and infusion of important military technology, with some guarantees for coproduction and financing.[165] This strategic partnership was solidified by the 1975 Memorandum of Agreement, which provided for transfering sophisticated technology to Israeli defense industries.[166] In other words, the dependent militarization strategy begun under France continued with the United States. The second enabling development was the maturation of the economy and the development of certain strategic industries, primarily electronics, chemicals, and engineering; those industries, the target of the government's protection and support over the previous twenty years, made military industrialization a possibility.[167]

Perhaps most important to the government's objective of military industrialization was its relative autonomy from society. The government in general and the Defense Ministry in particular controlled a large amount of unilateral transfers that it could dispose of in a relatively unhindered manner. It is difficult to overstate the importance of this factor. The following figures tell part of the tale. Between 1966 and 1972 the government increased by 300 percent the funds for research and development in security-related fields.[168] Consequently, from 1965 to 1977 real growth in these industries was 12 percent, while others industrial sectors weighed in at 7.9 percent.[169] Furthermore, domestic defense industries received approximately 20 to 33 percent of the defense budget, which amounted to nearly one billion dollars per year and represented nearly one-third of all domestic investment.[170] In general, the government was intent on promoting these security-related industries because of their critical contribution to the government's goals of increasing military independence and boosting the state's exports, hard currency, and economic prosperity.[171]

A number of important factors, therefore, provided Israeli leaders with the both the motivation and the ability to deepen military industrialization. Specifically, a restructural production strategy was made possible by the state's substantial relative autonomy and industrial infrastructure. Thus, the external shock provided the stimulus to the government at a time when it was reasonable to expect the economy to handle the requirements of a sophisticated arms industry. Yet it was still unclear whether the government would proceed toward greater centralization over the economy or a new policy of decentralization. This depended heavily on the objectives of Israeli officials and their ideas about the most efficient route.

Given the government's past etatist stance and control over defense production, as well as salience of national security, one might expect Israeli officials to maintain, if not expand, their control over the economy. And to a degree this policy was continued after 1967. It was previously argued that a major reason for the Defense Ministry's control over military industries before 1967 was the absence of an industrial base; only the state was able to undertake the massive commitment of resources. According to Pinchas Zusman, the Defense Ministry official perhaps most responsible for the government's investment policy during this period, the ministry used "objective criteria" when awarding defense contracts. The first consideration was whether a company already produced the needed product or could reasonably be expected to produce it in the near future; for example, the larger Histadrut and state-owned enterprises (e.g., Koor and Israel Military Industries, respectively) were considered important to military industrialization and received further funding. Thus they solidified and increased their market share.[172] These larger Histadrut and state-owned enterprises were considered integral to military industrialization given their prior level of development, resources, and investment capital. If the project was too large and beyond the means of an existing company, the Defense Ministry would build the necessary plants, provide the financing, and assume ownership and control.[173]

Simultaneously, however, the government began to deviate from its pre-1967 policy of excluding the private sector from defense production.[174] In fact, now the private sector often found itself openly courted and favored. If the required capital was not prohibitive and a public sector corporation did not have a monopoly over production, then the government would turn to private capital. According to Tzvi Tropp, although "all companies are equal" and the objective criteria of cost, quality, and delivery (in that order) should be considered when deciding upon a bid from a number of companies, an unwritten rule was that, everything else being equal, the defense ministry favored the *private sector firm over the public sector firm.* Its policies were in effect to "put the seeds in the small plants of defense industry in Israel" and thereby provide the foundation for a larger and more expansive private sector. For example, El Bit and El Op, both private sector companies, received their initial investment capital from the Defense Ministry. Tropp continued, "In general, if it was possible to have military production done by the private sector we would do it there."[175] The private sector now had an important role, given the government's decision to move away from etatism and toward economic liberalization.[176]

Why the enthusiasm for private capital? Israel was founded by a socialist-minded elite suspicious of, if not outright antagonistic toward, private capital, the government had pursued an etatist development policy, and there was a significant national security threat; thus, one might expect the government to maintain a tight control over military industries. But the government coalesced around and promoted the private sector for economic, ideological, and political reasons.

The government believed that Israel's development prospects, and hence its security, depended on the economy's decentralization and exposure to greater competition. Officials thought that decentralization, essentially equivalent to the development of the private sector, would increase competition, lead to more efficient production, and thereby promote exports. This promarket attitude had been bolstered by the recession of 1965–1967, which was partially attributed to inefficient industrial and manufacturing sectors, a consequence of both the government's excessive protection of these sectors from foreign competition and a lack of domestic competition. Defense Ministry officials also believed that its previous policy of limiting production to the public sector had jeopardized Israel's security and was inappropriate for the changing environ-

ment and circumstances. In addition, they assumed that greater technological spin-offs could be generated by those companies that produced
for both the defense and civilian markets, as opposed to those companies
that produced exclusively for defense. Efficiency considerations also
were prominent, as state officials believed that private sector firms
should specialize in certain products, thus increasing efficiency and profitability. Moreover, by encouraging production for export markets and
exposing the national economy to the international economy, the government could "assist" the domestic firms' transition toward economic
efficiency.[177]

These economic motivations were bolstered by a growing ideological
belief that an economy guided by state intervention was inferior to one
shaped by market forces. There was an interesting transformation in the
composition of the upper reaches of the bureaucracy as it became staffed
by officials sympathetic to capitalism.[178] A whole generation of economists, educated and trained in neoclassical economics, had attained key
ministerial positions. Many in the Defense and Finance Ministries believed that less government intervention was needed for a more productive economy. According to Dinstien, "These were the ideas of [Finance
Minister] Sapir and [Prime Minister] Eshkol. We [at the Finance Minis-
try] did everything we could to develop this [private] sector. . . . This
was the same philosophy in the Defense Ministry . . . [where] there was
also a belief that a decentralized economic environment was the best way
to produce what the military needed."[179] The Defense Ministry's belief
was that if a firm was insulated from competitive pressures, the pricing
mechanism would become distorted. This was true of those firms that
produced only for the military and retained a monopoly position over
production. The "discipline of the market" was preferred because "every
company becomes as inefficient as allowed by its environment."[180] Although this promarket attitude among ministry officials surfaced shortly
before the 1967 War, it became increasingly prevalent and overt
throughout the 1970s.

Political considerations also figured prominently in the move toward
the private sector. The government's weakening political foundation required some bolstering. Dispersing defense funds to as many groups as
possible would broaden Mapai's political base and win the loyalty of domestic capital.[181] Coalition politics was also important because the General Zionists, who had always advocated a decreased state role in the
economy and greater capitalist initiative, were then part of the government coalition and could assure that the private sector would benefit
from defense contracts. Finally, there was also an element of bureaucratic politics. Because the Defense Ministry controlled the public sector military industries, other ministries believed that its bureaucratic

rival would become too powerful if past trends continued unabated. The only way to offset current patterns was to funnel additional funds to the private sector and promote exports, which would lessen the public sector's dependence on the Defense Ministry for investment funds and thus promote the former's autonomy; it would also relieve the state's investment burden.[182]

Because the private sector was relatively malnourished, the government used a number of policy tools to sponsor its development. First, the Ministry of Defense established the Procurement and Production Administration, which was designed to "facilitate and streamline the transfer of orders from the IDF to local civilian industries. This policy was carried out in conjunction with the Ministries of Finance and Commerce and Industry."[183] The military was a captured market, from which government officials could guarantee a large demand. This was accomplished, for example, by channeling investment, placing long-range orders, and providing investment subsidies and tax breaks. In this environment private companies could plan while minimizing market uncertainty. Moreover, the public sector was actively encouraged to undertake joint ventures with private companies. If the public sector was still unresponsive, the Defense Ministry took the additional step of creating a number of firms for the exclusive purpose of facilitating the transfer of public sector operations into the private sector. For example, Galram was a Defense Ministry creation, designed to ease the coordination of public and private sector activities. Less subtle strategies included those instances when the Defense Ministry said it would go exclusively to private capital unless the public sector acceded to its participation (this happened in the case of Tadiram and IAI).[184]

Given the general favoring of domestic capital, it is obvious that the government's criteria for awarding defense contracts did not always follow "objective" criteria. Personal connections often played an important role in its investment decisions. Steff Vertheimer, now a major entrepreneurial figure in Israel, began his career under the auspices of defense contracts granted through personal connections.[185] Such was the case for many private firms, whose efforts had been consistently blocked by the Defense Ministry before 1967; they now discovered their requests approved with greater frequency through these informal networks.[186]

Despite the fact that this restructural policy was highly successful at paving the way for military industrialization, the economy still could not produce the more sophisticated and technologically advanced military hardware needed for modern warfare owing to a lack of industrial infrastructure, financial resources, and scientific know-how. As a result, in addition to the restructural policy the government also adopted an international strategy and came to depend wholly on the United States for its supply of advanced military hardware, particularly fighter planes. Between 1966 and 1972 the cost of Israeli defense imports per annum (in U.S. dollars) increased nearly fivefold, and then in 1973 it more than doubled over the previous year and resided at around that level for the next decade.[187] Israel was more dependent than ever on U.S. security assistance.

The government's production strategy was a function of its objectives—mobilizing defense production, ushering in a new development phase, and bolstering its political base—and opportunities open to it. Rather than centralize its control over the economy, the government moved toward liberalization, a shift enabled by the high degree of state autonomy. A number of spirited officials, with autonomous control over substantial resources, channeled "seed" money to the private sector and promoted its growth. As a result of this policy, three different arms-producing consortiums emerged: (1) a state-controlled sector; (2) a large number of joint ventures between Israeli groups and foreign partners, often encouraged by the state (a relatively new phenomenon because prior to 1967 most MNCs were uncertain of Israel's physical survival); and (3) a large and growing number of companies wholly owned by private sector interests.[188]

Despite the tremendous growth of the domestic defense industry, Israel still relied on the United States to supply those weapons it could not produce domestically and to fund the expansion of the military industrial sector. Consequently, by the end of the period Israel relied more heavily on the United States for satisfying its defense needs than it did at the beginning. The government's increased reliance on the United States and the development of a more autonomous and powerful set of domestic economic elites had significant implications for Israeli state power.

Conscription Strategies

Not surprisingly, Israel's involvement in three separate wars and occupation of the captured territories increased its manpower needs. Briefly, Israel's conscription policy before 1967 was established in the "Defense Service Law," which stipulated that every citizen serve two years in the military (one year for women) and every permanent resident be subject to annual reserve duty for thirty-one days until the age of thirty-nine and for fourteen days between the ages of thirty-nine and fifty-five.[189]

Because conscription was already nearly universal before 1967, only an incremental change was likely. After 1967 the Ministry of Defense and the religious establishment arranged for religious Jews to join the army, primarily through the Nahal (the army's agricultural unit), and stationed them principally on the West Bank. This extension of conscription served the interests of both the Defense Ministry, which sought to extend the scope of conscription, and the religious community, which wanted to participate in defense and the political struggle over the occupied territories.[190] In addition, service for male conscripts was lengthened from two to three years, and the annual reserve duty was raised to two or more months, while many over-age reservists were reactivated.[191] Immediately before the 1973 war, however, the length of service was reduced to thirty-three months and reserve duty reverted back to the pre-1967 standards. This was a result of government's confidence in the air force's ability to deter any possible Arab attack.[192] Such cutbacks were premature.

The Yom Kippur War reintroduced even greater manpower pressures. The government and the IDF were determined not to be caught again by a surprise attack, and Israeli estimates of the manpower balance between itself and the Arab states projected a decline from 2:3 in 1977 to 1:3.5 in 1984. Consequently, the government lengthened the reserve time required of most Israeli conscripts, and in some cases this meant reserve units were not demobilized until April 1974, six months after war termination. Although these changes placed tremendous financial pressures on the state and the individual, the government viewed these moves as justified by the security threat.[193]

The army did benefit from a strong societal feeling of patriotism and the belief that the state was in mortal danger, which led to an increased reenlistment rate for reserve officers.[194] Patriotic fervor alone could not sufficiently meet Israel's manpower needs. However, to lengthen the service period placed it beyond the pre-1967 standard, which was maximizing the military's needs while minimizing the economic costs. The IDF therefore began to review the conscription registry for those who had dodged or had never been called up. Although this consumed considerable energy, it did increase the manpower pool by a few thousand men.[195] The military also rechecked the original criteria for exemption and attempted to enlist those originally exempted. Although initially such exemptions applied to only a few hundred, by the 1970s they covered 10,000 to 14,000 men.[196] Finally, the government modified its pattern of military service for women. Previous to 1973 most women served in offices and relatively safe positions far removed from the battlefield. The expanding defense needs after 1973, however, forced the IDF to involve women in combat training and instruction, and eventually led to their participation in the rear bases of combat units.[197]

In addition to these accommodational measures, the government pursued a limited restructural policy as it attempted to increase the country's manpower through a return to the notion of "spatial defense." This policy was initially introduced during the first years of Israeli independence, as the government armed the peripheral settlements so that in the event of an attack, and if the army could not mobilize quickly enough, they would absorb the first blow. (Between 1956 and 1973 the concept was for all purposes abandoned owing to a lack of resources.) The IDF debated the utility of training Israeli settlers for paramilitary duties on the West Bank in case of another 1973-type invasion, and Chief of Staff Rafael Eitan, a strong advocate of a Greater Israel, created civilian groups on the occupied territories capable of using force if the IDF could not respond quickly enough to security threats in the occupied territories. "This created an anomaly whereby civilians in the occupied territories, especially in the West Bank, become authorized vigilantes."[198] This important development in the government's manpower strategy later became a controversial, and sometimes unpredictable, coercive arm of the state.

As Israel's security needs became more demanding and costly after 1967, its war preparation strategies underwent tremendous change. The Israeli case demonstrates that even in so-called "strong" states, with high legitimacy, extractive capacity, and control over production, significant domestic constraints affect its ability to mobilize security resources. To explain fully Israeli war preparation strategies it was necessary to incorporate the government's other domestic objectives, which included creating a sound economic environment and protecting the government's political base, and the constraints on its actions. How both the government's objectives and decision context produced its war preparation strategies is most evident in Israel's production strategy, which changed from an etatist stance to one that incorporated the previously excluded domestic capitalist class. This shift was motivated by the private sector's role in strengthening the government's security, political, and economic objectives, and the government could initiate such a significant change in the country's economic organization given the state's autonomy. But, despite such military industrialization efforts, domestic sources alone could not produce all the state's required military hardware, thus requiring it to supplement its restructural orientation with strategic assistance from the United States. The government's financing strategy also underwent radical change, as Israeli officials quickly jettisoned their pre-1967 policy of maintaining financial autonomy and began to depend heavily on the United States. This international strategy was both a reaction to Israeli society's unwillingness to absorb the mounting costs of war without extracting a pound of flesh, and the result of the opportunity created by the new U.S. alliance that allowed Israeli decision makers to export these costs. As a result, budgetary constraints were relaxed, and the government lost the political will to impose further demands on society. Because conscription had already been nearly universal and lengthy, a product of the state's tremendous legitimacy, it changed largely at the margins.

———————

Since the establishment of the state, Israeli leaders have been involved in the simultaneous process of solidifying and defending the territorial existence alongside the process of state building. Unlike the history of most postcolonial states, however, the latter was definitely the easier of the two challenges. If Israeli leaders stood fearful and wary of their presence in the international system, then they stood hegemonic and powerful vis-à-vis their own society. This domestic stature was instrumental in allowing Israeli leaders to counter their weakness in the interstate system.

This did not mean, however, that its war preparation strategies represented the singular outcome of national defense. Rather Israeli leaders often constructed their war preparation strategies with the belief that such policies would further their objectives in both the domestic and the international sphere. Moreover, after 1967 the interstate system became more filled with conflict, and domestic elements grew less pliable. Consequently, the decade following the June War found Israeli leaders becoming more conscious of how their war preparation strategies should further their objectives of political stability at the most and ensure that they did not further erode their political standing at the least. Although fortunes reversed from the pre- to the post-1967 periods—for it seemed that as the Israeli state was becoming a permanent fixture on the Middle East map, Mapai was becoming an increasingly expendable element— Israeli governments always leaned heavily on an international solution. An international strategy became more important as the domestic costs associated with resource extraction increased.

Israeli war preparation strategies follow a characteristic pattern (see table 5.3). Israel's war preparation strategies can be divided into two periods. First, from 1949 to 1967, the Israeli state initially restructured its relationship to society to gain direct access to its required security resources. The state's ability to perform such penetrating feats was enabled by its tremendous legitimacy, control over investment decisions, and developing institutional capacities. By the 1950s, however, Israeli leaders were satisfied with their mobilization practices and thus settled on accommodational tactics. If this policy was acceptable, it was largely because no imminent crisis provoked a rethinking. This was particularly evident following the 1956 War when the Israeli Defense Forces per-

TABLE 5.3
Summary of Israeli War Preparation Strategies

	Fiscal	*Production*	*Conscription*
1948–49	international / restructural	international / restructural	restructural / international
1949–56	international	international / accommodational	accommodational
1957–67	international	international	accommodational
1967–77	international / restructural	restructural / international	accommodational / restructural

formed admirably and the Arab Front was anything but congealed and primed for another round. An international strategy, however, always maintained a rather heavy presence because of the government's rather expensive and limited resource base.

The second period begins with the 1967 War. Israel's military feats provided only a short respite. Increased security pressures were derived from the Arab states rejectionist stance, and new security concerns accompanied the occupied territories. Alongside these systemic challenges were domestic ones as well. Mapai's unwillingness to impose even harsher domestic measures was owing to the belief that its once unassailable hold over the electorate was becoming less so, as its control over both the economy and the polity was experiencing greater cracks and challenges. Israeli officials were expected to defend the country's security but denied the domestic, principally financial, resources with which to undertake such actions. The role of the United States, then, was political and economic savior.

Financial Strategy. Israelis can boast that they are among the most taxed in the world, but it is important to recognize that this tax structure was established relatively early in Israel's fiscal history and since has mushroomed from a series of accommodational actions often times coming on the heels of a war. Mapai, the benefactor of tremendous legitimacy and societal cohesion, implemented a tax structure that, while unable to satiate the state's budgetary commitments, was rather successful when compared to the experience of other postcolonial polities. Although the newly formed state had little infrastructural capacities with which to enforce its policies, there was a solid foundation upon which future efforts could expand.

Such virtuous efforts, however, could not satisfy the government's defense, welfare, and development commitments. Israel's taste for foreign assistance came early. Although Israel was neither a strategic asset nor a regionally important power—one that would become the object of superpower attention and financial rewards—it was able to mobilize tremendous external resources from its symbolic status as the modern Jewish state. Most important, these capital imports—derived from West German reparations, world Jewry, and U.S. assistance—arrived with few strings or future obligations and were left to the political discretion of Israeli officials. Although Israeli state managers benefited from fairly unconditional sources of financial transfers, their arrival was somewhat of a mixed blessing. These transfers enabled Israeli governments to accomplish the impossible task of expanding both development and defense in a postcolonial environment, but the high level of capital imports established a societal addiction for foreign injections rather than greater personal sacrifices.

The problems associated with funding the government's objectives with external assistance became clear following the 1967 War. Although the first few years following the war saw high economic growth rates and increased revenues, by 1970 the rate of economic growth shrunk and so did the state's revenue. The problem was that society, grown accustomed to have both security and increasing standards of living, was reluctant to break this habit without extracting a pound of political flesh. This was especially true after 1973 when the public was particularly unforgiving because of the government's recent performance in the Yom Kippur War and the economy nosedived because of the combined costs of the war and oil shock. Consequently, Israeli leaders, pressed between an unforgiving domestic and international environment, chose what they considered the most politically expedient route: reliance on U.S. largess. The difference between these foreign transfers, however, and those of earlier years was that these more recent consignments came with greater restrictions. The principal injury here was to Israel's debt burden, which continued to expand rapidly over the 1970s. In general, although Israeli state managers might have been in a position to extract more from society because of the state's relative autonomy and capacity, the perceived political pains associated with such extraction attempts and the availability of U.S. offering was more than any prudent politician could resist.

Production Strategy. Israel's movement toward autonomous military industrialization has been a slow, calculated, dependent, and relatively successful process. Although the country was relatively self-sufficient in its most basic weapons needs, it had to rely on foreign suppliers for its more sophisticated requirements. To fulfill this latter need the government moved in two directions. First, it constructed a neomercantilist policy, attempting to develop a modern, industrial, and sophisticated economy. And, like many neomercantilist policies of the past, the state, its chief architect and protector, prized and privileged those economic sectors deemed critical to the national security and future military industrialization.

Second, the government engaged in a policy of dependent military industrialization, wherein Israeli officials consciously fostered a policy of dependence on France to further its military independence through a process of learning and doing. This relationship provided Israel with not only a relatively secure source of armaments but, more important, a series of coproduction agreements that gave Israeli engineers and scientists the know-how through which to deepen military industrialization. The French more than adequately served as a strategic ally. A Great Power protector was needed for a second reason, for only a Great Power could supply Israel with its required military equipment; at this early juncture Israel's defense requirements could not be produced domestically.

The 1967 War was a major turning point in Israeli production strategy. Abandoned by France before the June War, convinced that its etatist framework had hindered the pursuit of independent arms production, dissatisfied with its current economic path, and confronted by increased security pressures, Israeli state managers liberalized the arms production policy and more fully included the capitalist class in its efforts. Alongside the continued provision of investment funds and subsidies to those Histadrut and public sector enterprises involved in defense production, the Israeli government simultaneously nurtured a domestic capitalist class through similar investment measures and promoted greater capitalist rationality among these other state-owned and Histadrut enterprises. Israeli leaders were able to implement a restructural policy and introduce a greater element of market forces because of the state's relative autonomy.

Although Israel made rapid strides toward military industrialization, it was unable to supply all its military hardware, particularly advanced aircraft. For these items Israel capitalized on the tacit strategic alliance with the Americans. Israel, hoping that the reliance on American hardware would soon be succeeded by an autonomous domestic arms program, continued a pattern of dependent military industrialization established during its first twenty years. In general, the common theme of Israel's production strategy was to use momentary dependence on a Great Power to further its long-term goal of security independence.

Conscription Policy. Because of its high degree of legitimacy, the Israeli government was able to implement a restructural manpower policy and institute universal conscription during the War of Independence with only temporary opposition from some peripheral elements. Once the Armistice was signed in 1949, a less economically draining conscription policy was developed, one that centered around an all-encompassing reserve system. To further the state's territorial defense the military developed a policy of spatial defense that spotted the rural sector with agricultural settlements. Although initially exempted from military service, Israeli Arabs and the religious community were considered either a potentially hostile minority (e.g., the Arabs) or relatively peripheral (e.g., the orthodox community).

It would be difficult to expand upon such efforts in the future because of the universal quality of the government's initial conscription policy. Further manpower pressures after 1967 and 1973 were met by modest changes at the margins, such as extending the number of days in the reserve system. The only notable change was the revival of territorial defense after 1967 when Israel captured the West Bank from Jordan. Here settlers on the West Bank were given the means of coercion and began to operate as a quasi-autonomous security force.[199]

Although Israeli leaders made no move to enlist the assistance of foreign troops in its immediate defense, successive Israeli governments continuously searched for a strategic ally to provide psychological support and a secure military depot in the event of another Arab-Israeli war. No such explicit alliance was ever forthcoming, though both the French and the American strategic relationship can be categorized as alliances. These implicit alliances, particularly in the American case, were extraordinarily valuable to an Israeli government that found itself increasingly pinched by both domestic and security pressures.

Never the product of strictly narrow, strategic considerations, successive Israeli governments consciously tailored their war preparation strategies to meet their other domestic objectives. This was as true during the first twenty years when Israeli leaders were able to capitalize on a relatively strong state and implement a series of policies designed to further the state's military power and the government's other domestic objectives as it was during the ten years following the 1967 War when they consciously avoided numerous domestic measures because of their perceived associated costs. In addition, another feature of Israeli security policy loomed: whether because of material limitations or because of political and economic constraints, foreign benefactors played a key role in allowing Israeli officials to meet their rather costly domestic and security objectives. These war preparation strategies were instrumental in bringing about substantial changes in Israeli state-society relations and state power.

CHAPTER SIX

War and the Transformation of State Power

THE EGYPTIAN and Israeli experiences confirm and refute the views of both those scholars that contend that war enhances state power and those that assert that war undermines state power. In fact, not only did Egyptian and Israeli state power evidence tendencies in both directions, but, in fact, it also appears as if both states chartered parallel courses. Specifically, both the Egyptian and Israeli states experienced an expansion of state power between the beginning of each country's respective time period and 1967, owing in part to the legacies of war preparation. After the 1967 War, however, intensified war preparation was central in eroding state power in both countries. In neither case is this erosion captured by the state's institutional capacity alone because the reliance on foreign financiers alleviated the government's need to move more forcefully domestically; rather, the state's changed structural relationship to the economy provides a more dramatic and arguably more accurate indication of the changing nature of state power. The important point to keep in mind, however, is that the expansion of the state's military power came directly at the expense of its power vis-à-vis society. A Dorian Gray image surfaces, for the expansion of each state's external strength came at the expense of its own internal health. And, like Dorian Gray, governments in both countries knowingly made the bargain without realizing the full costs of their actions.

Three important issues concerning the causal relationship between war preparation and state power must be highlighted and reiterated. First, I have assumed that the causal link between war preparation and state power derives from the government's mobilization of material resources. My discussion of the relationship between the government's war preparation strategies and state power relies on identifying the government's dominant strategy—whether accommodational, restructural, or international—and making explicit how these war preparation strategies effected state power. I argued in chapter 2 that both accommodational and international policies prodded state power down its demarcated path. This can mean either the exacerbation of already entrenched tendencies or the intensification of existing contradictions. In sum, either of these two strategies reinforces state power's current condition.

A restructural policy, however, one that attempts to transform state-society relations to increase the societal contribution to the war preparation effort, contains the very real possibility for altering state power. I previously argued that four features are central to the transformative relationship between war preparation and state power: (1) the government's ideas about the "efficiency" of various policies for increasing the societal contribution; (2) the strength and demands of societal actors that oppose the government's attempt to alter the state-society compact; (3) the bargain struck between state and society for access to these desired means of war; and (4) the outcome that these constraint-shaped decisions have on the trajectory of state power.

State power can either decrease or increase depending on how the government compensates the contributing societal actors for their efforts and, relatedly, the effect this compensation has for the state's institutional strength and relationship to societal actors. In this way the state's intrusion into society can be seen as a dialectic: while allowing for either the state's increased control over societal resources and/or greater societal contribution, the government may, at the same time, sacrifice some of its political and economic autonomy to these societal groups. Another possibility goes beyond the simple fact that major policy innovation derives solely from societal pressure and influence. Here the interest is in the evolution of new ideas about what policies might be most efficient for accomplishing the government's objectives. After all, it is now taken for granted that under certain conditions the government can itself stimulate societal change, change not reducible to the actions and demands of societal groups; these actions may be the product of either governmental learning or the introduction of new groups with different sets of ideas into the decision-making process. Both aspects, and particularly the latter, were evident in the Egyptian and Israeli cases. The primary focus throughout, then, is on the government's restructural policy, its ideas about the efficiency of various policy alternatives, the bargain struck between government and society for access to security-related resources, and the consequences this bargain has for the state's ability to penetrate society and maintain its autonomy from societal actors.

The second issue concerns the evaluation of state power. State power is linked to the state's ability to penetrate and govern society and its autonomy from societal actors. I pointed to two sets of measures as a way of gauging change in state power. The extractive capacity of the state included both its use of those policy instruments that enable it to directly penetrate and extract from society and the extent of tax evasion that isolates the intensity of the state's monitoring capacities. Another set of indicators examines the state's structural relationship to the economy, its role in the capital accumulation process, and its source of revenue. I assert that both sets of indicators are important for capturing complementary and necessary facets of state power.

The third issue was that state power and other macrohistorical concepts can be treated as an outcome of "causal complexity." That is, they are shaped historically by an interaction between various socioeconomic processes and, therefore, cannot be fully accounted for by any single variable, whether war preparation or the domestic political economy. This incorporates my assertion that the government's war preparation strategies reconcile both domestic and foreign policy objectives. In no instance do I argue that war preparation alone accounts for the major changes that occurred in Egyptian and Israeli state power. For instance, the 1967–1973 period was an important point of transformation for Egyptian state power because Nasser (and later Sadat) was compelled to provide a greater role for the private sector in war preparation processes in light of his own domestic political concerns and Egypt's economic bankruptcy. Reference to both war preparation and features of the domestic political economy, then, are necessary for explaining change in state power. Although I am not evaluating the "potency" of war preparation in a narrow statistical sense, I am intending to identify the *conditions* under which war preparation policies might have transformative properties. These conditions are linked to the nature of the state's mobilization policies and the historical dynamics in each case. In this way this explanation avoids the structural determinism evident in many other interpretations of state power and demonstrates how changes in state power are products of the intended and unintended consequences of the government's war preparation strategies.

EGYPTIAN WAR PREPARATION STRATEGIES AND STATE POWER

In chapter 4 I categorized Egyptian war preparation strategies in a four-part scheme (see table 4.8). There are three distinct periods of Egyptian war preparation history. During the first period, between 1952 and 1967, Nasser maintained a consistent policy of attempting to export the costs of war. From 1967 to 1973 Nasser and Sadat embarked on a (albeit rather limited) restructural strategy. Although the Egyptian government was wary of placing too great a security burden on society, its limited domestic maneuvers instigated a period of rapid change in state power. Third, between 1973 and 1977 Sadat reverted to Nasser's pre-1967 strategy of depending fully on foreign sources for national security resources. Because changes in state-society relations that occurred as a

result of the 1967–1973 war preparation strategies became institutionalized during this post-1973 period, I collapse both periods into one long
decade to better gauge the relationship between war preparation and
state power.

1952–1967

Egyptian state power at the time of the July Revolution was meager because a history of colonial policies both restricted the state's institutional
capacities and created a dependent economy dominated by foreign and
domestic capital. The handicaps imposed on the Egyptian state from
Britain's colonial policies were most evident in Egypt's fiscal policy and
relationship to economic elites. Before 1930 the government was precluded from raising either tariffs or taxation without the prior agreement
of foreign powers. Consequently, tax receipts derived mainly from foreign trade and other indirect methods. The state's lack of institutional
capacity was duly reflected by its reliance on indirect methods in general
and its pre-1952 fiscal history in general.

The state's institutional weakness was matched by its lack of autonomy
from societal actors. Although the government was no mere appendage
of a monolithic capitalist class, it was severely constrained from the types
of policies it could pursue given its interests. An accurate reflection of
this feature was that the landed classes and foreign capital were privileged by the government's initial tax policies and subsequent reforms.
Moreover, the state apparatus was staffed by individuals both derived
from and sympathetic to capitalist class interests. In general, the state's
reliance on indirect taxes for its revenue accurately reflects both the absence of more direct and sophisticated tools for revenue enhancement
and the state's lack of autonomy from domestic and foreign capital.
When the Free Officers gained the mantle of leadership in July 1952
they inherited a state that had relatively little infrastructural capacity or
autonomy from societal forces. In short, the simple fact that the guard
changed in the Royal Palace had no effect on state power.

Although the Free Officers' movement was a partial response to their
collective experience in the 1948 War, once they came to power their
primary security concern was saved for Britain's continued occupation of
the Suez Canal. After this most visible affront to Egypt's sovereignty was
removed in 1955, Arab-Israeli tensions escalated and began to cause
greater anxiety among Egyptian leaders. Unwilling and unable to mobilize the security requirements from society, Nasser established a strategic alliance with a Soviet Union that was only too willing to leapfrog over

the U.S. containment effort and establish its presence in the Middle East. This arrangement enabled Nasser to meet his expanding defense commitments while continuing to both shield society from the financial pains of war and maintain his capitalist development plan. Although the Soviets opened their arms depot to the Egyptians, they balked at providing any assistance to Egypt's military industrialization program; this policy, as probably intended, sent Egypt's modest arms industry into disrepair and Nasser into the Soviet's arms. Egypt's conscription policy also remained intact, continuing to burden the lower classes and absolve the upper classes. In general, the shortened and comparatively modest national security threat between 1954 and 1956 that was answered with a series of accommodational and international measures would not be expected to cause any significant change in state power.

Neither the militarily calamitous Suez War nor the Yemen expedition caused Nasser to alter his war preparation procedures, though one might have imagined the latter in particular to provoke some concerted domestic response by Nasser. Not only did it expose the many apparent deficiencies in Egypt's war-fighting capacities, particularly with respect to the army's conscription policy, but it also occurred at a time of, and dearly exacerbated, a downward economic trend. Nasser seemed unwilling to undertake the domestic reforms required on either the domestic or the foreign front and essentially maintained the status quo. In general, between 1952 and 1967 Nasser responded to an increased security threat by exporting the expanding costs of national security onto his Soviet benefactor.

In this reading war preparation did not significantly alter, only advanced, the path of state power between the 1952 and 1967. Nasser's standard response to security demands was to rely on the status quo; he purposefully avoided placing too great a burden on society because of a combination of the state's limited infrastructural capacities and the perceived political repercussions associated with increased hardship. These limited efforts were consistently followed by a turn to the Soviet Union (see table 6.1). As long as Egypt's security cradle existed externally little sustained effort was extended toward the state's extractive capacities. Nasser's refusal either to include new societal groups or to increase dramatically the societal burden led to little change in the state's infrastructural capacity.

Although the state's capacity as measured through its extractive prowess changed little over this fifteen-year period, there was a significant change in the state's autonomy from foreign and domestic capital. In 1952 the state comprised approximately 5 percent of all industrial investment; by 1959 nearly all industrial investment was undertaken by the

TABLE 6.1
Egyptian Extractive Capacity, 1952–1967

	Share of Total Taxes		Share of Direct Taxes		Tax Collection (% of GNP)	Direct Taxes (% of GNP)
	Direct	Indirect	Business	Personal		
1952/53	26.3	73.7	8.1	6.3	14.5	2.6
1953/54	22.4	77.6	7.5	4.5	14.5	2.1
1954/55	25.8	74.2	7.3	4.3	13.9	1.8
1955/56	20.3	79.7	8.2	4.6	13.9	1.8
1956/57	23.3	76.7	8.5	6.8	13.8	2.2
1957/58	24.9	75.1	10.5	5.4	13.2	2.9
1958/59	32.8	67.2	8.0	4.9	13.1	2.5
1959/60	20.4	79.6	8.2	5.1	12.2	2.1
1960/61	28.2	71.9	13.3	6.1	12.3	2.4
1961/62	24.8	75.2	11.2	5.6	12.2	2.1
1962/63	22.8	77.2	14.8	4.8	12.7	2.5
1963/64	23.2	76.8	15.8	4.8	—	—
1964/65	26.5	73.5	16.8	5.1	—	—
1965/66	32.0	68.0	20.2	5.2	13.9	4.0
1966/67	31.4	68.6	20.7	4.7	16.6	5.0

Sources: Columns one through four taken from El-Edel, "Impact of Taxation in Income Distribution: An Exploratory Attempt to Estimate Tax Incidence in Egypt," 140–41. Columns five and six are computed from Donald Mead, *Growth and Structural Change in the Egyptian Economy* (Homewood, Ill.: Richard D. Irwin, 1967); and M. Abdel Fadil, *The Political Economy of Nasserism* (Cambridge Department of Applied Economics: Cambridge University Press).

state.[1] Although domestic capital continued to contribute to nonindustrial activities, the state sector overshadowed private sector activities throughout the 1960s. Once Nasser was convinced of both his ability to move against the capitalist class without sustaining any debilitating political or economic setback and the public sector's ability to contribute to the development process, any potential systemic threat to his regime was immediately translated into concentrating more economic power under the state's domain and shifting it away from private economic elites. This was particularly evident with the nationalizations of 1958 and 1961, which not only provided the state with a vast financial base but also insulated it from the power of capital. The change was reflected by the various slogans used to label the state's role in the economy, from Patrick O'Brien's apt phrase of "guided capitalism" to describe the 1957–1961 period to the period of Arab socialism from 1962 to 1967.[2] In general, Egyptian state autonomy increased with the destruction of domestic and foreign capital and its corresponding insulation from these economic interests.[3] There is a near consensus that the decade between the Suez and June Wars was a time of steady expansion of state power, and this observation is substantiated by the change that occurred in the state's role in the capital accumulation and investment process.

The implication of the foregoing analysis is that other factors—including a developmentalist economic policy, bureaucratic inertia, and personal ambitions—are most responsible for the major changes in state power that occurred during this fifteen-year period. This conclusion, however, is premature. What is largely considered to be a turning point in Egyptian history was a consequence of war, but not directly associated with the state's mobilization practices per se. The 1956 Suez War gave Nasser the courage and pretext to nationalize the holdings of foreign capital. These nationalizations, more than any other event of the period, derailed Nasser's reformist stance and propelled him towards state capitalism. From this moment on the state regulated the pulse of the economy and controlled a significant percentage of investment capital that could be distributed according to the state's political, not capitalist, objectives. Although generally frustrated with the lack of economic assistance provided by capital for Nasser's development aspirations prior to 1956, there is little evidence that he seriously considered any break with his reformist stance. The Suez War punctuated the equilibrium, reversed the hierarchy between the capital and the state that had characterized the pre-1956 period, and institutionalized a new set of state-society relations. And as the events of 1958 and 1961 demonstrated, after 1956 Nasser answered foreign challenges by stripping his domestic enemies of their economic resources. Therefore, war preparation cannot account for the most significant change in state power, but neither can more conventional approaches. The major change in state power occurred more because of Nasser's improvisation than because of structural determination.

In general, although war preparation did not substantially effect state power, the Suez War established a new state-society arrangement that directly affected the future direction and tone of Nasser's security and economic policies. Despite greater access to society and the reduced power of capital during the late 1950s and early 1960s, Nasser continued to rely on the Soviet Union for meeting his expanding security, welfare, and development commitments. Consequently, the Egyptian state's infrastructural power increased only modestly, and there is little evidence to suggest that the state's ability to survey and monitor society expanded substantially over this period. In general, state power did expand rapidly during this period, but the expansion was owing primarily to the galvanizing impact of the Suez War and the steady increase of the state's role in the economy in general and importance of domestic investment in particular.

1967–1977

The war preparation processes of the pre- and post-1973 period simultaneously rebuilt a devastated Egyptian military and eroded a once relatively powerful Egyptian state. Although the 1967 war forced Nasser to reconsider his ineffectual policy of shielding society from the costs of national security and relying principally on the goodwill of the Soviet Union, his increased security-related demands came in the midst of a dramatic economic downturn at a time when society was already expressing severe doubts about the government's ability to handle the country's economic and security affairs. The combination of a fiscal crisis of the state, domestic challenges to the regime, and a heavy defense burden caused the government both to follow a series of accommodational and international strategies that were intended to alleviate the domestic burden and, at the same time, to introduce a modest restructural strategy to help loosen the state's control over the economy and society. The government retreated in the face of various domestic challenges, and accordingly, so did Egyptian state power.

The notable feature of this period of sustained war preparation was that rather than attempting to centralize political and economic power, which had been the standard response after the foreign-threatening events of 1956, 1958, and 1961, Nasser planted the seeds of the state's weakening control over economy and the reemergence of the private sector. One early victim of the June War was the government's 1966 plan to deepen socialism, as Nasser was reluctant to risk angering another societal group. The government soon followed on this action with two policies that demonstrated its disposition, however reserved for the present, toward the economic and political resurrection of domestic capital. One policy introduced the first legislation in nearly a decade that provided some benefits to the capitalist class for its potential economic contribution to the state's coffers. The principal move here was to ease the foreign currency restrictions and, in the process, attract more hard currency into the Central Bank, which could then be used to purchase military items from the Soviets. The second policy provided investment subsidies to those private sector firms that dominated the export markets. By assisting their activities the government hoped to redress the tremendous balance of payments crisis owing to its considerable military imports. Therefore, these export-oriented private sector firms became more important for the immediate goal of war preparation.[4] Although these modest measures could not be interpreted as an outright embrace of a free market economy, they set the tone for more dramatic gestures in the future. These moves represented the government's initial attempt to make peace with the bourgeoisie and enlist their services in the government's economic policies and war preparation strategies. It is worth repeating that unlike past occasions the government had decided that further economic centralization was no longer the remedy to its fiscal troubles and security needs.

There is no evidence that these concessions to domestic capital occurred because of either the structural or the behavioral power of capital, for it had been marginalized both economically and especially politically during the Nasser years. What, then, was the source of this change? The fiscal and political crisis prodded Nasser to rethink past policies and their appropriateness for the present era. After 1967 Nasser shifted the composition of the cabinet from a dominance of the pro-Arab Socialist forces to an increased role for the new technocratic elite and others who were more sympathetic to capitalism. These new cabinet voices argued that few resources could be generated by bleeding dry what remained of the private sector and that a better and possibly more profitable option in the long-run offered some select incentives to renewed private economic activity. In short, a new set of state elites whose arguments carried more weight because of the current economic crisis and delegitimation of Arab Socialism acquired greater influence over economic policy making. These restructural policies emerged, not because of any explicit bargain struck between the government and capital, but rather because the government changed its understanding of politically savvy and economically wise policies. If the state's diminution was not immediately evident, this period of sustained war preparation assembled the foundations for a dramatic reversal in state power.[5]

These various trends were solidified and extended after 1973; two forces directly traceable to the interwar preparation strategies pushed the political economy toward al-infitah and in the process weakened state power. First, the state's fiscal exhaustion resulted from seven years of sustained war preparation. This problem was aggravated after 1973 because Sadat continued to expend considerable resources on defense for various reasons, not the least of which were the needs to diversify his arms supply after he parted ways with the Soviet Union and to maintain a prominent regional role in the Middle East as a way of attracting U.S. financial assistance. According to Sadat's plan, the heavy security burden and lack of capital would be solved by the anticipated tremendous infusion of Western capital and Arab petrodollars. Because Sadat refused to increase the domestic savings rate by slashing the state's heavy welfare burden, al-infitah placated (at least temporarily) the masses and the capitalist class; the masses were not expected to return all the gains they had made under Nasser, and the capitalists were now closer to the pre-1956 model than they had been for nearly fifteen years.[6]

Accordingly, the fiscal crisis of the state continued and in many respects expanded after 1973, for increased revenues could not be expected from an economy that was near stagnation and a government that had cut the tax rate for the upper classes and refused to increase the burden on the masses. Foreign and domestic borrowing was the only answer. While Sadat maintained Nasser's policy of relying on internationalist practices, though shifting his allegiance from Moscow to Washington, he solidified Nasser's move away from Arab socialism and fully inaugurated his "economic opening."

The second factor that contributed to transforming state-society relations was the government's restructural conscription policy. Because Nasser accepted the premise that the army's dismal performance during the most recent campaign was partially caused by a conscription policy heavily skewed toward the uneducated masses and away from the educated elite (i.e., the upper classes), he extended military service to include this once privileged group. Except for the selected demobilization during 1972, these new draftees served continuously from 1968 until 1974. After the Yom Kippur War, however, most conscripts in general and the elite in particular, not surprisingly, were demanding a return to civilian life. Sadat was quick to oblige. Then the question was: What were these demobilized troops going to do? It would be political and economic suicide to allow these unemployed to sit idle in a potential "devil's playground." But because the war effort had ravaged the economy, it could not absorb the demobilized masses. Moreover, although traditionally the public sector had acted as a depository for excess educated labor, even the state could not accommodate these multitudes. The only possible salvation was an expanding private sector, one that had responded positively to the breathing space it was allowed during the interwar years. Therefore, he hoped that this growing private sector might not only rejuvenate the economy but also provide employment opportunities for the newly demobilized.

There is an additional interpretation of the relationship between the state's conscription policy and the private sector's rising status. In Western European history the state's conscription of new groups has normally included a "favor" in return, often new political rights and protections. Al-infitah could be interpreted in much the same way. The elites, who had interrupted their careers and lives for the state's military objectives, were now demanding compensation. Unlike their West European counterparts, however, they were not demanding greater political rights be-

TABLE 6.2
Egyptian Extractive Capacity, 1967–1978

	Share of Total Taxes		Share of Direct Taxes		Tax Collection (% of GNP)	Direct Taxes (% of GNP)
	Direct	Indirect	Business	Personal		
1967/68	26.8	73.2	15.8	5.0	16.2	4.0
1968/69	29.7	70.3	18.8	4.9	17.0	4.7
1969/70	29.7	70.3	19.2	4.8	17.2	5.0
1970/71	29.9	70.1	19.7	4.8	17.6	5.0
1971/72	30.5	69.5	19.9	4.3	17.0	5.0
1973	29.8	70.2	20.4	5.1	16.2	4.7
1974	28.5	71.5	20.3	4.9	16.3	4.7
1975	24.5	75.5	19.6	3.2	19.5	6.1
1976	28.7	71.3	23.0	4.1	21.5	5.9
1977	29.8	70.2	25.3	3.8	24.8	6.1

Sources: Columns one through four are taken from El-Edel, "Impact of Taxation in Income Distribution: An Exploratory Attempt to Estimate Tax Incidence in Egypt," 140–41. Columns five and six are computed from Ikram, *Egypt*, and Abdel Fadil, *The Political Economy of Nasserism.*

cause they were already well-represented by a capitalist-leaning Sadat. Instead, these societal elites were demanding new economic opportunities, privileges, and the ability to start their careers that had been suspended because of their service to the state. As Tilly notes with reference to the Third World, "participants in the war effort, including military personnel, acquired claims on the state that they deferred during the war in response to repression or mutual consent *but which they reactivated at demobilization.*"[7] Sadat, already sympathetic to their interests, was further convinced of his need to introduce an economic opening because of this additional factor. Two important reasons governed Sadat's decision to strengthen the private sector after 1974: the government's interwar fiscal policy had bankrupted the economy and its conscription policy.

That state power eroded as a result of the government's war preparation strategies can be seen in two dimensions. First, the Egyptian government intentionally avoided any sustained extraction effort because of the political repercussions associated with such a visible tax and the state's limited institutional means. Thus, there was relatively little change in the state's institutional capacities. Because of the government's reliance on foreign financing, those measures of state power that focus exclusively on the state's extractive capacity would (prematurely) conclude that war preparation had only a modest, if any, observable effect on state power (see table 6.2). Whether state capacity is measured in direct taxes as a percentage of either total taxes or GNP, the consistent conclusion here is that the state's control over society increased only modestly during this period.[8] Although direct taxes in absolute terms and as a percentage of the GNP rose steadily after 1967, this was owing more to the state's increased extraction from public sector activities. Moreover, although as a percentage of GNP the government's revenue extraction increased dramatically after 1976, this was because of the re-claimed Suez Canal and the Sinai oil fields, not necessarily any enhanced institutional capacity. Most important, not only did income taxes as a share of total taxes change little over the entire post-1967 period, but also after 1973 their percentage actually declined, an accurate reflection of Sadat's procapitalist orientation.

Although the state's ability to extract from and monitor society changed little, the state's autonomy from societal actors rapidly eroded. In other words, any measure of state power based on the extractive ca-pacity of the state would (prematurely) conclude that the state's control over society changed little during this period. This reading, however, ignores some major trends emerging in the Egyptian political economy, trends that offered live testimony to the government's war preparation strategies. To appreciate fully these changes, we need to direct our at-tention away from the extractive capacity of the state and toward the state's relationship to economic activity and its source of revenue. These dimensions present a very different picture of the effects of the govern-ment's war preparation strategies on Egyptian state power.

Two major factors vividly demonstrate an Egyptian state that is increasingly constrained by domestic and foreign forces: the first is the source of the state's income; the second is the state's budget activ-ities and role in the capital accumulation process. With regard to the first issue, the state's principal source of income since the early 1970s changed tremendously; a greater percentage of the budget was no lon-ger self-financed but rather derived from foreign assistance. The Egyp-tian government attempted to avoid the perceived economic and politi-cal costs attached to further domestic extraction and looked to finance their growing budget deficits with foreign and domestic borrowing. The government tended to relieve these increased budget pressures through borrowing (see table 6.3). Consequently, whereas approximately 22 per-cent of the 1966 budget was funded by borrowing, that figure expanded to 40 percent in 1973, a high of 53 percent in 1975, and 41 percent in 1978. Not only was an increasing percentage of the budget financed by domestic and foreign borrowing, but after 1973 a growing percentage of this borrowing was used to purchase military- and consumption-related items rather than to increase the amount of capital available for eco-nomic growth.[9] In contrast to the pre-1967 period, a smaller percentage of the state's revenue derives from its extraction efforts.[10]

This massive increase in foreign assistance, owing largely to the mili-tary burden of the post-1967 period and the economic exhaustion that

TABLE 6.3
Average Inflow of Loans to Egypt, 1956–1960 to 1976–1978 (in millions of dollars)

Loans	1956–60	1961–65	1966–70	1971–75	1976–78
Medium- plus long-term loans	71.5	77.2	81.2	424.5	1446.2
Western countries	45.0	16.0	21.1	46.0	649.0
Eastern Bloc	26.5	36.4	51.2	41.1	−14.3
Arab countries	—	24.8	8.9	337.4	811.5
World Bank and IDA	6.2	2.5	−4.3	15.2	85.9
Suppliers' credits	20.0	32.2	22.1	64.6	−10.0
Eurocurrency loans	—	—	—	45.2	100.0
Banking facilities	2.8	14.3	5.0	215.8	−242.0
Total	100.5	126.2	104.0	765.3	1380.1

Source: Ikram, *Egypt*, 359.

followed as a result, produced an explosion in Egypt's debt burden. For instance, in 1970 Egypt's medium- and long-term debt stood at $1.64 billion, but it expanded to $2.5 billion in 1973, to $5.1 billion in 1975, to $10 billion in 1978,[11] and to nearly $50 billion by June 1986. Although the major change in the absolute debt burden occurred after 1978, both the propensity to mortgage the future and the highest rate of annual change occurred over the post-1967 decade. Moreover, a full 25 percent of the total debt load is military related,[12] which represents 30 percent of all debt servicing and amounts to $650 million out of an annual debt schedule of $2.2 billion; this figure equals Egypt's revenue from its two largest income-producing sources, petroleum production and the Suez Canal.

Until recently foreign actors in general and the United States in particular have not been totally sympathetic to the Egyptian government's predicament, and the U.S. has generally refused to reduce the interest rate on the military debt for fear of establishing a bad precedent. Furthermore, Egypt does not have the option of "unilateral rescheduling" the debt because there is a 4 percent surcharge on missed payments, and delays of more than a year are met with a suspension of all aid.[13] There was a major change in 1990, however, as Egypt benefited financially from the Iraqi invasion of Kuwait that year. In gratitude to Egypt's pro-U.S. position, the United States canceled $7.1 billion in military debt, which translates into a savings of $700 million a year in repayments.[14] Although those international agencies and states to whom Egypt is obligated financially have demonstrated a reluctance to force Egypt to make regime-threatening structural adjustments,[15] their increased control over Egypt's financial stability has not been painless.

The second issue concerns the changes in the state's principal activities and role in the capital accumulation process, both of which can be accounted for by forces associated with and unleashed by war preparation. Although before 1967 the Egyptian economy was evidencing serious economic difficulties, the state was still chiefly responsible for economic growth and capital investment. The state's centrality for capital investment began to change during the interwar period, particularly once the government relieved the public sector of much of its investment capital, concentrated more on providing both welfare and warfare, and gave greater breathing space to the private sector as a way of relieving the shortage of capital funds. This changing state role was solidified after the 1973 war when the budget was increasingly consumed with defense, public works, welfare, and debt redemption.[16] Indicative of the government's changing priorities is the ratio of defense spending to total investments. Immediately prior to the Yemen War defense spending represented 32 percent of total investment, between 1967 and 1970 this percentage averaged nearly 80 percent, and from 1972 through 1974 this yearly average was approximately 110 percent.[17]

As the government became more concerned with meeting its welfare and warfare objectives it expected domestic and foreign capital to play a greater investment role. As a result, the state is now more dependent on domestic and foreign capital for capital investment.[18] Private sector investment as a percentage of all domestic investment has more than doubled between 1970 and 1980. Not only does the private sector account for nearly 25 percent of all investment, but also a greater percentage of state investment goes to nonprofit-making activities,[19] those areas less attractive to the private sector. Robert Bianchi argues that whereas before 1973 the state was the senior partner and private capital the junior, by the early 1980s investment in joint ventures was evenly divided between private and foreign capital, "with the state acting as a junior partner," and in some economic sectors the private sector represented the primary source of investment capital.[20] Roy adds that "the new economic policy points to the creation of a more 'mixed' and less regimented and centrally controlled economy in which both the private sector and foreign capital are permitted to play a more active and competitive role."[21] Although the economy never quite shifted toward strict capitalist rationality, and one can argue that it never intended to, the economy was decidedly more mixed than ever.[22]

In a related matter, the function of the public sector has changed. Sadat's attempt to use the public sector to attract foreign and domestic investment has created a situation whereby the state is now objectively less coherent and unified than it was before, more oriented toward the private sector and a free-market direction, and more tied to the fortunes of capitalist sectors that were allowed to permeate and expand their po-

litical and economic power over the 1970s.[23] Handoussa writes that "with
the introduction of the open door policy, the state has moved toward
decentralising control over public sector enterprises by abolishing the
general organizations which supervised their operations and by giving
an important measure of freedom to management in making incentive
payments to employees."[24] Because of this bias, public sector officials
have negotiated with domestic and foreign capital for joint venture activities.[25] Moreover, whereas the public sector used to be heavily involved
in profit-making activities, it has increasingly shifted its operations to
less lucrative activities such as infrastructure and communications.[26] Bianchi summarizes this trend in the following manner: "In general, the
participation of state capital seems geared *not to establish public control
but to supplement local private investment* and ensure that control of
nearly all categories remains in Egyptian hands."[27] A new set of institutional arrangements and expectations is in place that signals a decreased
role for the state and its weakening control over society and economy.

In general, war preparation was central in promoting four factors instrumental in eroding state power. War preparation led to: a decrease in
the amount of capital available to the public sector; a deepening of the
fiscal crisis of the state as a result of a heavy defense burden that began
with the Yemen; a government that became more consumed with welfare, warfare, and debt redemption and less with continuing its past role
as the dominant source of investment capital; and the undermining of
those actors associated with Arab socialism and the promotion of those
who championed capitalist and market rationality.

There is little doubt that Egyptian state power has eroded since the
mid-1960s. The state's ability to penetrate and monitor society changed
little over the post-1967 period because of the government's war preparation strategies, both accommodational and international. Yet its autonomy substantially eroded as the budget became more dependent on
foreign sources and the state occupied a less central role in the capital
accumulation process.

Between 1952 and 1967 the state's accommodational and international
orientation had little direct effect on state power, tending more often
than not to reinforce previous state-society relations. The major change
in state-society relations during this period was a consequence of the
Suez War, not directly traceable to either war preparation per se or political economy processes. Although after 1967 the government shifted
only slightly from its internationalist proclivities, the continued accommodational practices and modest restructural policies heightened the
already existing economic crisis and reintegrated domestic capital's potential contribution to ease the fiscal crisis. Sadat moved more forcefully
toward liberalization after 1973, in part because of his own ideological

disposition and geostrategic plan, but more decidedly because of the economic bankruptcy following seven years of sustained war preparation and the government's restructural conscription policy that fully involved the upper classes for the first time. After 1973 Sadat's war preparation strategy reverted to Nasser's 1952–1956 policy of attempting to attract foreign and domestic capital while shielding the masses from the pains of development and security. The government's restructural and international strategies combined to create the scenario whereby the government's infrastructural capacities changed little but its autonomy from nonstate actors eroded substantially. Thus, the Egyptian state's budget has become more dependent on foreign largess, its debt burden has increased dramatically to finance a growing budget deficit, and the state has become more dependent on private capital accumulation. While these war preparation strategies enabled the Egyptian government to build an impressive military machine, they also championed an impressive erosion of state power.

ISRAELI WAR PREPARATION STRATEGIES AND STATE POWER

> In many respects Israel under what we termed the "system
> of 1948" may be considered a limiting case of extreme state
> autonomy vis-à-vis capital. . . . However, . . . by the
> 1970s this relationship has been turned on its head.
> (*Michael Shalev, "Israel's Domestic Policy Regime"*)

In Chapter Five I portrayed Israeli war preparation strategies in tabular fashion, noting its division into three distinct periods (see table 5.3). The first period includes the War of Independence, when the quasi-governmental and centralized features of the Yishuv were transferred to the institutions of the sovereign state. Most important, this period institutionalized the state-society parameters within which future Israeli governments would have to operate. The second period between 1950 and 1967 is characterized by the state's accommodational and international practices. Therefore, war preparation is not expected to produce any major change in state power during this phase. The third period is the decade following the 1967 War when national security became a consuming goal of successive Israeli governments. The government deviated from its past war preparation practices and attempted to obtain self-sufficiency in some areas (production), increase its reliance on foreign actors in others (financial), but always tried to protect its political back. The consequences of these strategies were enormous: they eroded the very foundations of Israeli state power and thus established a narrower set of governing parameters for future Israeli governments.

War of Independence

Confronted by a three-front war, isolated militarily in the interstate system but empowered by a high degree of legitimacy, the first Israeli government was able to extract society's financial and manpower resources for the task of security without any real societal strife; the only notable opposition to the state's centralizing moves was the *Altalena* incident. Working from a shadow state apparatus that had been developed during the British mandate, the new Israeli government moved quickly to put some muscle on the skeleton bureaucracy and implemented a tax and conscription policy that both represented the state's supposed egalitarian principles and mobilized the needed financial wealth and manpower for its independence campaign. With the state's survival at stake, almost all societal groups willingly volunteered both lives and finances to the country's defense. In addition to such domestic efforts, the state also benefited from tremendous financial and modest manpower support from world Jewry. Although the Yishuv had developed some limited arms production, the meager industrial base forced the state to rely on the consignment of surplus World War Two equipment from arms merchants and the Soviet Union. In general, the state's interventionist role, already institutionalized by the pre-1948 Yishuv compact and an ideology of socialist-Zionism, was given a boost by the tremendous security demands. The goal of establishing a Jewish state, a motivating and galvanizing experience supported by the vast majority of the population, institutionalized a dominant role for the state in both economy and society.

1949–1967

After the War of Independence the government mobilized its required men, money, and material through accommodational and internationalist measures. Although never complacent about defense, the Israeli government could take comfort from the fact that its security had been strengthened over this period because of the presence of tremendous capital imports and unilateral transfers that it could then channel to its preferred economic sectors, the willingness of the French to assist Israel's fledgling military industrial complex, the demonstrated strength of the Israeli army during the 1956 War, and the political fragmentation of the Arab World. Consequently, there was little attempt to restructure the state's relationship to society and economy for the task of national security.

State power expanded over this period, as the state's extractive capacity and autonomy from society both improved and stayed at a relatively

TABLE 6.4
Israeli Extractive Capacity, 1955–1967

	Direct	Indirect	Tax Collection (% of GNP)	Direct Taxation (% of GNP)
1955	38.1	61.9	20.6	7.86
1956	41.9	58.1	23.07	9.68
1957	—	—	—	—
1958	43.5	56.5	21.1	9.19
1959	40.7	59.3	21.76	8.86
1960	35.8	64.2	26.2	9.4
1961	34.3	65.7	27.49	9.45
1962	39.8	60.2	26.78	10.66
1963	43.06	56.94	26.2	11.3
1964	43.8	56.2	26.9	11.8
1965	44.04	55.96	25.68	11.3
1966	45.58	54.42	27.3	12.45
1967	46.07	53.93	26.19	12.06

Source: Bank of Israel, *Annual Reports*, various years.

high level, respectively; but in neither case can the argument be made that war preparation was the single most important factor for these outcomes. Rather, the government's war preparation strategies seemingly reinforced and corresponded to already present tendencies that were strengthening the state's hand. This can be seen in the state's ability to penetrate and extract from society and its autonomy from societal actors. In the first place the state's extractive capacity did evidence considerable improvement over this period (see table 6.4). Although by 1966 the Israeli tax structure continued to rely on indirect taxes for its revenue, there was a move to change this pattern and derive a greater share of the state's revenue from direct taxes. Although the salience of national security provided both the government with greater motivation to enforce its tax policies and the population with greater reason to adhere to them as closely as possible, the trend toward greater fiscal competence is also noted among other developing countries. Pack observes:

> This is consistent with the experience of most underdeveloped countries in which administrative bottlenecks limit the reliance on more sophisticated forms of taxation. However, the rapidly growing administrative competence has permitted a major transformation of the tax system from one relying primarily on commodity taxation to one in which income taxation has become increasingly important; indeed the increase in the aggregate tax rate has been almost entirely attributable to the growth in direct tax rates. . . . It provided the government with greater flexibility in adjusting its revenue policies to the necessary structural changes in the economy.[28]

In general, although a relatively stable but heavy security burden acted as a constant motivation for making the tax system more effective, arguably more forceful factors in increasing the state's extractive capacity were the structural changes in the economy and administrative learning. If the state was satisfied with an accommodational orientation, it was because the continued high level unilateral transfers and capital inflows relieved it of any urgency to alter its fiscal strategy.

The state's substantial relative autonomy continued throughout this period. Not only did the state continue to hold sway over a rather large public sector and Histadrut activities, but its control was also furthered by the presence of a large amount of unilateral transfers and, relatedly, the state's centrality in the capital accumulation process. Indicative of how war preparation interacted positively with these other state-enhancing processes was its arms production policy. The government built the foundations for military industrialization through the provision of the economic infrastructure and industrial base. This statist attitude paralleled the government's developmentalist orientation in other key economic sectors, though it provided greater benefits and protections to defense-related industries.[29]

In general, the government's consistent set of accommodational and international war preparation strategies bolstered state power during this pre-1967 period. The state's infrastructural capacities continued to develop throughout this period because of the salience of international conflict and other developmentalist and institutionalist features, and its autonomy was enhanced by the continued infusion of unilateral transfers that were channeled to state-controlled economic sectors. In sum, war preparation, though not the primary cause, reinforced those already present socioeconomic processes to further the path of state power.

1967–1977

State power, rather than being strengthened by this period of intense security activity, moved decisively in the opposite direction. After the 1967 war the government deviated substantially from its previous war preparation strategies and initiated a process that would loosen the state's control over the economy and society, a move best reflected by an increase in the structural power of capital, by the state's dependence on foreign financing on more restrictive terms, and by an erosion of the state's control over the means of violence. Although some evidence that I present is rather tentative, particularly so with respect to the state's conscription policy, the combined findings from these three dimensions form a vivid picture of war preparation creating a post-1977 Israeli state considerably more constrained than the pre-1967 state.

TABLE 6.5
Israeli Extractive Capacity, 1967–1980

	Direct	Indirect	Tax Collection (% of GNP)	Direct Taxation (% of GNP)
1967	46.07	53.93	26.19	12.06
1968	45.9	54.1	28.6	13.16
1969	45.6	54.4	31.0	14.15
1970	49.1	50.9	33.3	16.38
1971	46.6	53.4	36.79	17.16
1972	44.4	55.6	37.2	16.5
1973	43.38	56.62	37.2	16.79
1974	44.6	55.4	37.6	16.78
1975	47.59	52.41	39.9	19.0
1976	49.3	50.7	48.6	24.0
1977	50.06	49.94	47.5	23.79
1978	51.5	48.5	44.7	23.07
1979	51.76	48.24	46.9	24.28
1980	55.6	44.4	46.58	25.9

Source: Bank of Israel, *Annual Reports*, various years.

Although the government's immediate response to the security burden after the 1967 War was to increase its extractive efforts, any further measures were absolved by the expanding revenue base (due to the economy's growth) and the high level of capital imports. The combination of an economic downturn in 1970 and continued defense burden, however, caused the government to turn to a willing United States to relieve it of any substantial increase in its extraction efforts. This policy continued unabated after 1970, except for one brief moment following the 1973 war, when, in the words of Arnon Gafni, "we increased taxes because during a period of national emergency we can do such things."[30] So long as the United States was willing to subsidize the Israeli war effort there was little incentive for Israeli state managers to impose a greater share of these costs on society and thus possibly jeopardize their political support.[31] Although the economy took a severe downturn because of the combined economic shocks of the Yom Kippur War and increased oil prices, such economic hardships in no way equalled the real costs to the economy. The Labor government strove to protect society from the full pains of structural adjustment for fear of accelerating its declining political fortunes.

One expects, because the government preferred international and accommodational strategies, there should be little change in state's extractive capacity (see tables 6.5 and 6.6). Yet the trend was in the opposite direction, for the state's capacities appear to have increased substantially throughout this post-1967 period. There are two reasons, however, to

TABLE 6.6
Percentage of Israeli Taxes by Source

	Wages	Companies	Other[a]
1970	15.9	8.8	11.25
1971	14.18	7.67	10.35
1972	13.17	7.69	9.8
1973	13.56	8.74	9.01
1974	13.04	9.22	7.65
1975	12.78	10.54	8.33
1976	13.23	11.83	10.65
1977	14.48	8.99	11.19
1978	13.91	9.42	12.14
1979	15.5	9.23	11.9
1980	17.9	7.7	14.17

Source: Bank of Israel, *Annual Reports*, various years.
[a]Includes self-employed, company directors, members of cooperatives, and deductions at source.

question this conclusion. First, the state's increased extractive capacity can be partially accounted for by the fact that this was a period of relatively high inflation, which effectively pushed many lower- and middle-income groups into higher tax brackets. Second, this extractive measure lacks some reliability as an indicator of the state's ability to penetrate from and monitor society because of the dramatic increase in the black market economy (see Appendix 13). Although there is no unanimity concerning the size of the black market economy, according to one estimate the black market nearly doubled during the 1970s. In general, there is reason to doubt the conclusion that the Israeli state has experienced a substantial increase in its capacity to extract from and monitor society throughout this post-1967 period.

Although the state's capacity improved little during this period of sustained war preparation, its autonomy underwent tremendous erosion because of the government's international financial strategy and restructural production policy. A good indication of how the government's changing revenue base dramatically increased the government's operating constraints is provided by Shimshoni's portrayal of the finance minister:

In the 1970s the worsening economic situation did not allow for maneuvers in the old style, while it demanded changes in direction and method. A number of factors prohibited the political and economic flexibility enjoyed by [the Minister of Finance Pinchas] Sapir. *The growing influx of foreign funds arrived in the form of official government and or loans, allowing less discretion in their use than formerly when donations or grants predominated.*[32]

TABLE 6.7
U.S. Assistance to Israel (in millions of dollars)

	Total U.S. Aid	Soviet Jewry Resettlement	Economic Loans	Economic Grants	Military Loans	Grants
1968	76.8	—	51.3	0.5	25.0	—
1969	121.7	—	36.1	0.6	85.0	—
1970	71.1	—	40.7	0.4	30.0	—
1971	600.8	—	55.5	0.3	545.0	—
1972	404.2	—	53.8	50.4	300.0	—
1973	467.3	50.0	59.1	50.4	307.5	—
1974	2,570.7	36.5	—	51.5	982.7	1,500
1975	693.1	40.0	8.6	344.5	200.0	100
1976	2,229.4	15.0	239.4	475.0	750.0	750
TQ[a]	278.6	—	28.6	50.0	100.0	100
1977	1,757.0	15.0	252.0	490.0	500.0	500
1978	1,811.0	20.0	266.8	525.0	500.0	500
1979	4,815.0	25.0	265.0	525.0	2,700.0	1,300
1980	1,811.0	25.0	261.0	525.0	500.0	500

Source: Leopold Laufer, "U.S. Aid to Israel: Problems and Prospects," 127.
[a]Transitional quarter.

The finance minister's increased operating constraints are representative of what happened to state power. Before 1967 most foreign assistance was transferred to the Israeli government with few if any strings attached. The trend after 1967 was substantially different, however, as there was a "decline of *discretionary* capital inflow and the rise of nondiscretionary gifts tied to Israel's military commitments."[33] Because a growing percentage of Israel's external resources were tied to certain restrictions and conditions, Israeli state managers became more susceptible and vulnerable to external demands.

The change in the composition of Israel's capital flows is most visibly seen in the U.S.-Israeli financial relationship. Between 1949 and 1970 U.S. military assistance was relatively modest (and virtually nonexistent until 1962), but economic assistance, which came in terms of relatively soft loans or grants, financed nearly 20 percent of Israel's import surplus (see tables 6.7 and 6.8). A quantum increase occurred after 1970, when U.S. military aid increased from $30 in 1970 to $545 million in 1971 to a peak of $4.0 billion in 1979. Although the proportion of military assistance that comes in grant form has increased, most of this aid must be spent in the United States. "In other words, because of Israel's role as a regional power wedded to the United States (a role which Israel has of course embraced with enthusiasm), the burden of the state's military spending is far in excess of the gifts it receives from the U.S."[34] During most of the post-1973 period U.S. financial assistance has exceeded arms

TABLE 6.8

U.S. Government Aid and Defense Imports, 1972–1980 (in millions of dollars)

	Grants (1)	Loans Received (2)	Loans Repaid		Total Aid		Direct Defense Imports (7)
			Principal (3)	Interest (4)	Gross[a] (5)	Net[b] (6)	
1972	71	330	125	32	401	244	490
1973	820	369	118	52	1,189	1,019	1,253
1974	672	301	155	74	973	744	1,225
1975	642	1,361	148	86	2,003	1,769	1,846
1976	1,176	879	215	99	2,055	1,741	1,555
1977	977	656	253	155	1,633	1,225	1,084
1978	1,181	1,004	226	200	2,185	1,759	1,612
1979	1,214	1,004	228	268	2,218	1,722	1,225
1980	1,454	1,454	222	363	2,836	2,251	1,713

Source: Bank of Israel, Annual Report, 1980, 212.
[a]Gross = 1 + 2.
[b]Net = 5 − 3 − 4.

imports by an average of only 10 percent. This, obviously, does not include domestic defense expenditure.[35] During the late 1950s the state benefited from foreign aid receipts equivalent to approximately one-sixth its GNP (which would have covered the entire defense budget *and* most of the investment from the entire business sector) that came with few strings, but by the mid-1970s most foreign assistance derived from the U.S. government was tied directly to the purchases of American military equipment.[36]

The consequences of these developments were enormous. As argued earlier, the state's autonomy is strengthened when it generates its own source of revenue and/or it has access to a resource base that does not restrict its use and dispersal. Whereas before the 1967 War the Israeli state had a fair amount of capital with which to allocate to domestic actors at its discretion, such foreign aid from the United States now returns to the United States, and, more accurately, to American defense contractors. In general, since 1967 the Israeli state's ability to distribute these funds according to its own standards and agenda has steadily eroded, and the government must now spend most of its foreign aid on U.S. military items. A major source of the state's relative autonomy before the 1967 War, its unconditional control over foreign transfers, is now absent.

In addition, Israel's debt burden has expanded since 1967 (see table 6.9). "These [loans from the U.S.] are less convenient for the country than other sources such as unilateral transfers or capital investments, since loans must be repaid at specified dates."[37] A growing percentage of the Israeli budget is comprised of debt servicing. Although most of this

TABLE 6.9
Israel's External Liabilities, 1967–1977

	Total ($m)	Change from Previous Year	Short-Term	Bonds	National Income	Total Resources	Exports	State Budget
					External Debt as Percentage of:			
1967	1,391	14.0	0.5	53.4	—	—	—	—
1968	1,553	11.4	0.7	52.8	—	—	—	—
1969	1,858	16.9	1.1	47.5	5.8	5.7	13.6	15.4
1970	2,407	27.6	2.9	42.3	6.4	5.7	12.6	14.9
1971	2,926	33.4	3.2	40.9	5.9	6.1	14.4	15.3
1972	3,308	18.1	1.7	41.8	9.0	8.0	15.2	20.3
1973	4,003	17.8	2.3	43.5	10.0	7.7	15.1	15.7
1974	4,686	26.9	3.0	40.6	11.2	8.0	14.4	17.7
1975	6,197	13.4	1.1	32.9	11.7	8.1	14.3	16.8
1976	7,311	12.7	2.0	30.1	14.8	9.8	14.3	19.0
1977	8,119	22.6	2.3	29.3	24.3	15.3	16.8	26.5

Sources: Sella and Yishai, *Israel: The Peaceful Belligerent*, 59.

debt is long-term and held by the U.S. government, which might mean greater freedom than if held by private financial institutions, Israel's debt burden has risen substantially since 1967; this leaves the uniform impression that its financial stability and life are now in the hands of foreign actors.[38] Between 1955 and 1966 both the debt and the national product climbed at the same rate of about 9.5 percent. A tremendous change occurred between 1967 and 1973, however, for while the national product maintained its previous growth rate the debt expanded at an annual average of 20 percent. This trend continued between 1973 and 1976, as the national product declined to stagnation levels while the debt expanded 23 percent a year.[39]

In general, since 1967 two major changes in Israel's capital imports have eroded Israel's financial autonomy. First, a growing percentage of Israeli capital imports are tied to defense expenditures, and most are targeted at U.S. defense imports. This implies that a major source of the state's autonomy, the tremendous amount of unilateral transfers that flowed into Israel between 1948 and the mid-1960s, has dissolved. In addition to the change in the composition of the aid came an increase in the national debt that far outstripped its economic growth. The Israeli state is now more beholden to foreign actors to stabilize its financial life.

Alongside this revolution in the state's financial life was a major change in its relationship to the economy in general and its relative autonomy in particular because of its strategy for mobilizing defense production. Although the government promoted military industrialization because of its potential contribution to the state's security, Mapai's political fortunes, and the country's economic direction, the state is now beholden to those actors who it initially sponsored to further its own interests. By no means is the state captured by a capitalist class or a military-industrial complex, but it is now more dependent on their actions for continued economic development and capital accumulation.[40] What is important, then, is that the state's involvement in the economy, according to aggregate indicators such as the public sector expenditure as a percentage of the economy, would not necessarily detect this subtle difference of the nature, role, and function of the state in the economy. Although the state still controls a significant share of capital investment, which potentially provides it with considerable political and economic power, this should not cloud the fundamental issue that the state still heavily structures and conditions capitalist relations while acting in ways that benefit private capital accumulation.[41]

That the government's post-1967 production policy lessened the state's autonomy can only be understood in the context of other ongoing processes in the Israeli political economy. The first real signs that some Israeli officials were displeased with the state's heavy presence in the economy came during the 1965 recession. The government, dissatisfied with import-led growth and its general dependence on capital imports for continued economic growth, wanted to rid the Histadrut and public sector companies of their inefficiencies and thereby pave the way for export-led growth.[42] As noted in Chapter 5, during the mid-1960s a new set of Histadrut and public sector managers were installed that were supposed to bring with them a capitalist spirit and further an atmosphere that favored a decrease in the state's involvement in managerial decision making.

This was the economic milieu when the 1967 War elevated security to the top of the government's concerns. Many of those very defense officials, including the likes of Shimon Peres, who had championed Ben-Gurion's etatist economic vision and had excluded the private sector from defense production, began to reconsider their statist direction. Not only were these state managers no longer confident in their ability to provide for the country's future economic growth and national security alone, but they also labored under the impression that their pre-1967 policy of excluding domestic capital from military industrialization had hampered their goal of arms independence. In short, there was both a changed economic orientation of some state officials who had previously championed etatism and the emergence to power of others who were already convinced that the Israeli economy must become more market-oriented. Both groups, then, shared the belief that a restructured state-economy relationship would better fulfill the state's security and economic objectives than would a continuation of past practices. And similar to the Egyptian case, there is no compelling evidence that this new economic posture was the product of either the behavioral or structural power of domestic capital. In sum, Israeli state managers coalesced around a new set of economic principles to pursue its two major goals of military industrialization and a high-tech, market-disciplined economy.

The government pursued these two objectives by directing a tremendous amount of resources and investment capital to those high-technology industries that would provide the foundations for a progressive, export-oriented economy and widescale military industrialization. Therefore, such industries as computers, electronics, and engineering received a significant amount of the government's attention. Because of the public sector and Histadrut's previous industrial size, scope, and political connections, they were able to maintain if not augment their dominance in the economy. Be that as it may, a monopoly of any kind, whether public or private, only created a large and relatively inefficient domestic industrial base; therefore, the government moved to instill greater market discipline on these firms by decreasing political interference, emphasizing the importance of capitalist production criteria, and sponsoring the development of domestic capital to increase competitive pressures. The Israeli military-industrial complex consists of three concentric circles: the public sector at its core, the Histadrut in the middle, and the private sector at the outermost circle. According to Mintz and Maman, "there are also numerous mediating factors which blur the distinction among these subsectors, including joint initiatives, the involvement of foreign companies and investors in the military-industrial sector in Israel and interdependence among various sectors in the military industrial economy."[43] A second way of restructuring the economy was to increase foreign investment, which would also create greater competitive pressures on domestic producers. In general, to promote arms independence and economic growth the government sponsored a military industrialization program that enhanced the managerial autonomy and profit-oriented behavior of the large defense contractors and encouraged the development of a more prosperous and important private sector.[44]

Israeli state managers were quite successful in their goals of promoting military industrialization, increasing managerial autonomy, and enlarging the private sector. Israel has become self-sufficient in a vast array of military hardware, including such sophisticated and technologically difficult to produce items as the Gabriel missile, the Kfir jet, and the Merkava tank.[45] Furthermore, Israeli state managers were only too successful in promoting managerial autonomy and domestic capital; a military-industrial complex (MIC) of some significance has developed as a result of these governmental policies.[46] Many of those same officials responsible for this process now openly question the state's ability to control the military-industrial complex. For example, Pinchas Zusman, former director general of the Defense Ministry, said:

> There is less political control and a weakening of political authority, which is primarily due to 1973. There is an erosion of authority, confidence, and trust. . . . Now public and private interests are more wedded, they find that they have more in common than they used to, particularly with the growth of defense expenditures and that their fortunes are tied to the defense economy. . . . They began to cooperate sometime around 1977, but before then there was more conflict between these groups than there was cooperation. They found that if they could cooperate they could use their resources more efficiently for economic purposes, and could wield greater political clout. There was some fighting, but like all marriages they found that their interests overrode any other bad times. *Now it really is that the monster has grown larger than the creator. The state has less control over society, especially when compared to before 1967.*[47]

Zusman's attitude is not exceptional, for his sentiments were expressed by many other prominent government officials of the period. Although the state may have created the monster, by no means can the state control it. These observations underscore how the state's decision-making autonomy has lessened over recent years because of its arms production policy.

Moreover, the state-sponsored military complex now occupies a central position in the economy. For instance, the defense corporations now: represent three of Israel's top five corporations, consume 40 percent of all metal demand and 50 percent of all electronics demand, comprise nearly one-third of all Israeli exports, and represent 43 percent of all governmental commercial operations.[48] Because of its centrality in the Israeli economy, the MIC can now make demands on state managers by virtue of its structural position in the economy.

As the scope and size of the defense industry has grown, so too has its autonomy. The emphasis on the export market and the recent decline in Israeli defense expenditures has given a further boost to this independence. To increase their economies of scale and maintain their profitability and viability in the context of a decline in domestic demand, the Israeli government has encouraged its defense industries to locate and export to foreign markets. This move has lessened the dependence of these companies on the government for a significant proportion of their capital, and they have thus developed their own autonomous source of funds. Mintz notes that "when budget cuts are considered the relative strength of the defense industries becomes especially evident, as these industries are the only component in the military-industrial complex that is less dependent on the local allocations than on income generated by exports."[49] The state is no longer able to sanction these military industries because of their relative size, centrality in the Israeli economy, and autonomous source of investment capital.[50]

The MIC points to a more general set of issues concerning the relationship between the state and economy. A growing number of Israeli scholars have argued that the state's control over the economy has been considerably weakened, owing in large part to the defense burden and the development of a war economy.[51] Shalev aptly terms this the "sorcerer's apprentice effect," wherein the state-sponsored military industrial sector has become a center of power that can now make greater demands on the state's resources. Shalev's argument is that initially the Israeli political economy could be characterized as "pluralistic," in which the Histadrut and public sector companies dominated the economic landscape with some room for the private sector. A defining feature of this pluralism was that the state in general and Mapai in particular had the instruments with which to control the economy and steer capital, not to be controlled by it. Because Mapai dominated both the state and the Histadrut, this control was owing to both political and economic (investment capital) instruments. After 1973, however, the lines between these various sectors became blurred to the extent that they are better characterized as closely linked "pillars."[52] A defining feature of this post-1973 economy was a growing concentration of capital that has included an integrative role for the public sector, the Histadrut, and domestic capital.[53] There now clearly exist "complex ownership/control ties among the holding groups, reciprocal buying and selling arrangements, financing relations among the banks, the government and the industrial groups, property rights enjoyed exclusively by the largest groups and, finally, explicit collusion."[54] Given the state's heightened dependence on capital and capital's growing economic and political autonomy, the state is no longer able to use capital's dependence as a source of leverage.[55]

In general, the state-sponsored drive for military industrialization and economic revitalization, premised on greater market measures, produced both an impressive self-sufficiency in a wide array of military hardware and a military-industrial complex that "has grown larger than the state." The general concerns over the MIC and its ever-growing powers are microcosms for other more generalized developments in the Israeli political economy. The state's budget is more consumed with debt redemption, social services, and warmaking; meanwhile its source of financing has become increasingly restricted. In short, the state is more dependent than ever on foreign and domestic actors for its financial life and the country's future economic growth.

The state's post-1967 conscription policy also undercuts Israeli state power. After 1967, and particularly after 1973, there were renewed manpower pressures. One act by the state extended the length of military service for both initial conscripts and reserves. Because conscription was nearly universal, however, few additional measures were available to the state to expand the manpower pool. The only groups exempt from military service were religious students and Israeli Arabs. Israel's Arabs could not be drafted without potentially arming a hostile minority, but the students could possibly be included in some fuller measure. Moreover, religious authorities were now actively soliciting their inclusion, making this route even more possible. The religious community's change of heart was partially motivated by its perception that by exempting itself from military service it had damaged its ability to translate its interests into state policy.[56] The "Arrangement Yeshivoth," which incorporated the religious students into the military, was a result of a special compact between the minsters of Defense and Religion, whereby some members of the religious schools (yeshivoth), who were primarily connected to the National Religious party, would serve nineteen months in the army within consolidated and autonomous units. Subsequently they would complete four years of military service without pay as students of the yeshiva.[57] More critical is that they requested of, and were granted by, the Labor government the right to establish some settlements on the West Bank.

> Approximately ten such Arrangement Yeshivoth exist, with almost all located on territory captured by Israel in the 1967 War. . . . This combination of combat and religious studies is a fairly recent phenomenon in Israeli society. It stemmed from the desire of elite religious youths to participate actively in the defense effort and in the internal political struggles that focused on the future of the occupied territories. The prestige (and at times the organizational know-how) acquired during military service was converted into political power.[58]

The government and the religious community were furthering their own respective goals. The religious groups were pursuing their messianic dream of settling the West Bank, while the army was reviving the concept of peripheral defense, outpost settlements that would provide important manpower support and act as a shock absorber in the event of a surprise attack. Therefore, the Labor government, on record for wanting to trade land for peace, began to arm a religious minority who was fundamentally opposed to negotiating away what it considered its biblical homeland.

Although initially the state could rest assured that it was establishing, funding, and supporting the creation of a new paramilitary unit that it could control, there is occasional evidence that these groups have become quasi-vigilante organizations that may not view as legitimate the state's goals in general and attempt to control them in particular.

The main right-wing active opposition to the government's policy on the occupied territories, beginning in the early 1970s, was executed by the groups of religious youth (Gush Emunim). They constituted part of the elite military units and were originally educated by the National Religious Party's Youth Movement. *This group, in opposition to the government's policy, established, through violent political struggles, several settlements in the occupied territories in order to establish faits accomplis.*[59]

It is questionable whether the government would have the ability to disband these newly armed religious zealots if it found it in its interest to do so. Therefore, if a key definition of the state is its monopoly over the means of violence, the state has, in effect, been responsible for its own diminution by decentralizing control over the means of coercion. It is interesting to speculate as to what problems such conscription policies might hold for future Israeli governments.

One additional feature of the state's conscription policy provides further evidence for the claim that there has been an important change in state-society relations. In Chapter 2 I argued that the state's ability to conscript widely indicates its overall legitimacy.[60] In this respect there is a subtle, undocumented, but widely perceived change in the willingness of certain societal groups to fulfill some of the IDF's current roles and duties.[61] Although outright objection to military service is nearly nonexistent, there is an increased objection to carrying out some of the military's current tasks. This change is particularly noted in the Left's attitude toward the army. While the Left was overrepresented in the elite branches of the military officer corps,[62] during the past two decades the Left's support for the military's new-found responsibilities has undergone a slowly accelerating erosion.

Five events since 1967 contributed to the altered character of the Israeli army, its duties, and perception by the Left. The first event, the 1967 War, created the problem of occupying and enforcing discipline among a hostile population. The army was transformed from a defensive unit that protected the state's border's to one now charged with functions for which it was previously untrained or unprepared. The second event, the Yom Kippur War, shattered the belief that Mapai could best serve the state's security interests. Moreover, the Agranat Commission, which investigated the causes of the IDF's lack of readiness and mobilization prior to the Yom Kippur War, pinpointed limited corruption and indecision among many of the state's elite and military commanders. Both of these events enhanced the security alternative offered by Mapai's chief political rival, Likud, which stressed the need to retain the West Bank for security and nationalist reasons.

Third, in 1977 Likud's victory challenged the "rules of the game." Whereas previously the state's objectives and strategies were fairly well-defined, Likud brought to power a different vision of society and security. The Left now perceived that not only were their interests and attitudes unwelcome but that their vision was now openly challenged by the new political elite.[63] Until this point, however, there was no significant challenge to the military's role and duties on the West Bank and Gaza. It is not coincidental that the first extraparliamentary movement that emerged from the military did so at this time. Peace Now was founded by nearly 350 reserve officers in early 1978, just months after Sadat's visit to Jerusalem. Not only did the signatories argue against a Greater Israel, but also, more significantly, they wrote that " 'real security can be achieved only in peace. *The real strength of the Israeli army grows out of the citizen-soldiers' identification with state policy.*' "[64]

The Israeli invasion of Lebanon, however, shattered the hegemonic status of the military. For the first time groups openly challenged and objected to the state's military policies during wartime. The army was now seen as engaging in offensive, as opposed to purely defensive, operations. Although few individuals refused to serve outright, there are now the first instances in which conscripts balk at participating and serving in those areas and activities they considered illegitimate and contrary to their interests—that is, Lebanon, the West Bank, and Gaza. This represents a fundamental, qualitative change in the unchallengeable role of the IDF in society. The final event is the intifada, arguably the most cataclysmic and upsetting event of the post-1967 period. Now more groups, notably *Yesh Gvul* (there are borders), which originated in the Lebanon War but took on greater stridency because of the intifada and the perceived abuses of the Israeli army in the territories, openly challenged the IDF's current mission. A growing number of soldiers, openly defying military orders, have refused to serve in the West Bank and Gaza. Whereas before 1982 those that dissented from the received security wisdom and role of the IDF remained secretive, since Lebanon protest has become more acceptable. Although few soldiers have gone to jail for outright refusal, more significant and commonplace are "gray refusniks," those who avoid service by activities such as feigning illness and going abroad for a few days when they expect to be called up.[65]

In general, the Left's and the Right's attitudes reflect two alternative visions of the army. On the one hand, the Left has begun to distance itself from certain policies of the state, particularly with respect to its behavior in the occupied territories and Lebanon. This manifests itself in such behaviors as *rosh keton* (little head), implying that the conscript take as little responsibility and initiative as possible, and "jobnik," seeking out those desk jobs that absolve the soldier from such active and "dirty" duties as patrolling the West Bank and Gaza. There is an opposite trend, however, among many on the Israeli Right and the Sephardim.

These individuals, widely viewed as occupying the lower social stratum in Israeli society, have become more enthusiastic about military service. This trend is signified by the term *tor etzba*, willing to do in West Bank what was done in Lebanon, and by their increased willingness to reenlist and become career officers. In general, the relationship between various societal groups and the military reflects some more generalized trends in state-society relations.

Although Israeli state power certainly increased as a result of war preparation between 1948 and 1967, the continued centrality of the state was owing more to the institutionalized role of the state in the economy and other processes involving development than it was to security procedures. The Six-Day War, a major demarcating event, signaled the willingness of the state to devolve its control over the economy in order to further its economic, political, and security objectives. The state's decision to sponsor a military-industrial complex to service its defense needs and the replacement of discretionary capital from foreign sources by conditionally tied U.S. financial assistance and an exploding foreign debt have combined to lessen the state's relative autonomy. Finally, there is evidence, however tentative, that the state's control over the means of coercion has become less certain for the first time since 1948.

The ebbs and flows of Israeli and Egyptian state power demonstrate remarkable similarity. Both Israeli and Egyptian state power maintained a relatively steady march toward aggrandizement during the pre-1967 period. Although war preparation undoubtedly helped prod such movements, the major reasons behind such tendencies were unique to each case. In Egypt, the effects of the Suez War and the nationalizations of 1957 were decisive. This restructured state-society relations and reconstituted the state's relationship to the economy. In Israel, the pre-1948 compact, with Mapai in control over the polity and the economy, was institutionalized in the apparatus of a sovereign state. Unquestionably, the fact that neither Israeli nor Egyptian state managers restructured state-society relations for national security is the principal reason why the state's war preparation strategies did not have a significant effect on state-society relations prior to 1967. In an interesting mirroring of economic histories, just prior to the Six-Day War both the Egyptian and Israeli economies demonstrated some signs of exhaustion in its import-substitution strategy. Whereas the Israeli government debated and tested the virtues of liberalization, Nasser signaled his intention to carry out a socialist "deepening."

Although there was a hint that these two countries would go separate economic directions before 1967, the 1967 and 1973 wars caused both Israeli and Egyptian governments to restructure their relationships to society and economy to increase their military power. That war preparation is the primary cause for the decline in Israeli and Egyptian state power counters the common wisdom that war almost always leads to the state's expanded control over society. Instead, both Israeli and Egyptian state power declined as a result of each government's war preparation policies. This decline is attributed to not only the state's attempt to restructure society but also to the historical context in which the security demands emerged. As important regional powers confronted by tremendous security demands, possible domestic turbulence, and profound questions concerning the viability of a statist economic path, both governments began to liberalize their control over the economy and society, as they reevaluated the role the private sector could play in the state's war preparation strategies. Israeli state managers were more spirited in their efforts as they actively sponsored the rise of the domestic capitalist class; the Egyptian government limited its liberalizing tendencies to some subsidization of important export industries and a relaxation of foreign currency controls. Sadat's liberalizing trends, which came to the fore after 1973, were made necessary by the post-1967 security burden that had effectively bankrupted the economy.

The decline in Israeli and Egyptian state power was seen from two angles. First, an examination of the state's foreign debt reveals a fundamental turn from the pre-1967 period when both countries either produced a significant amount of their own revenue (as in Egypt) or were the beneficiary of tremendous amount of unilateral transfers and capital imports (as in Israel). Second, although in neither case has the absolute size of the public sector subsided, it has become more autonomous and more bound up with foreign and domestic capital. In general, as both states have become more consumed with fulfilling a welfare, security, and debt redemption function, they have become more dependent on foreign and domestic capital for capital accumulation. These trends leave the clear impression that Israeli and Egyptian state power has become increasingly circumscribed by both foreign and domestic actors. Although the state's autonomy reversed itself, the state's capacity, as measured by its extractive capacity, changed little because state managers in both Israel and Egypt relied on a strategic ally that absolved them of imposing greater financial hardships on its society. Not only did this outward propensity cause an explosion in each country's debt burden, but it also sensitized their societies to avoiding the financial pains of war.

Both the Israeli and the Egyptian states now face greater operating constraints given the intended and unintended results of war preparation. Although the Israeli and Egyptian governments successfully promoted their military power in the interstate system, they were equally adept, though less intentioned, in their ability to promote the state's diminution in the domestic system.

CHAPTER SEVEN

Egypt and Israel in Comparative and Theoretical Perspective

MACROHISTORICAL concepts, often derived, formulated, and refined in other geographical regions, can enhance our understanding of various processes such as war preparation and state formation in the Middle East. Fred Halliday has suggested that the study of the Middle East has been dominated by those who argue for "analytic particularism," that "categories used to describe these societies must themselves be specific to the region."[1] This entails both the construction of sociological categories and concepts particular to the region itself and not necessarily appropriate to other regions and the rejection of Weberian, Marxist, and other sociological favorites of Western academics. Analytical particularism is contrasted with "historical particularism, according to which the specificities of the contemporary Middle East can only be comprehended in the light of the particular historical formation of the societies and politics of the region."[2] In this second approach the Middle East is distinct not because the categories used here are necessarily inappropriate for the analysis of other social formations outside the region,

> but because of the specific processes of historical formation through which all Middle Eastern states have gone. The particularity of the Middle East is therefore to be seen in the manner in which its contemporary social formations have emerged: these particularities are, however, to be grasped in terms of analytic categories that are universal, and that may be all the more relevant precisely because they *are* of general comparative application.[3]

The obvious attraction of this approach is that it rescues Middle Eastern studies from its segregation within the comparative enterprise and demonstrates not only how these categories can be fruitfully transferred to the Middle Eastern context but also how our knowledge of the Middle East as informed by these categories can, in turn, contribute to understanding these more enduring themes.

That this study adopts such an approach contrasts decidedly with most scholarship that has attempted to explain Israeli and Egyptian war preparation strategies and the changing fortunes of state power. I have argued that the processes associated with both can be comprehended through the assistance of the same theoretical framework, a framework derived substantially from the West European and Third World historical experiences. The framework for investigating the government's war preparation strategies was premised on: a limited number of assumed governmental preferences, the relevant decision context that acted as a set of enabling and constraining conditions on its ability to mobilize societal resources, and the impact of these strategies on state power. The usefulness of such a framework is similar to other sorts of macrosociological research strategies: it makes explicit the relevant structural properties and variables privileged and selected by the researcher in his or her historical inquiry. Not only can Israeli and Egyptian history be sensitively approached in a comparative manner, but their experiences can also be instructive for theory building.

THE CONSTRUCTION OF THE GOVERNMENT'S
WAR PREPARATION STRATEGIES

The enduring problem confronting Israeli and Egyptian leaders, and this was never more evident than during periods of intense systemic pressures, was how to attain their very costly objectives of national security, political stability, and economic growth in a resource-scarce, postcolonial setting. Too often, however, many observers of the Egyptian and Israeli politics implicitly argue that, although these are resource-poor countries, mobilizing existing resources should be easily accomplished because these are relatively strong states. Egyptian leaders, however, were constrained by various aspects of the state and social structure, handicaps often the result of colonial legacies and the problems associated with late industrialization and the political consequences associated with a too heavy extraction effort: An economy dominated by agricultural production implied that it was ill-suited for arms production; the state's institutional capacity had been stilted by British control over its economic and political life until after World War Two; and the state had little autonomy from foreign and domestic capital, until the nationalizations of 1957. These various features of the Egyptian state and social structure implied that state officials would have a difficult time mobilizing domestic resources for national security in either a frictionless manner or a way that did not undercut their other objectives.

The Israeli state is often characterized as a near classic case of a strong state. And there is much truth to this observation. The Israeli state inherited a relatively strong state apparatus as a result of the Yishuv's relationship to British mandatory authorities, embodied a Zionist ideology that espoused a large, omnipresent role for the state, articulated an etatist economic policy, received a steady stream of unilateral transfers that substantially increased its relative autonomy, and contained a dominant party in every sense of the concept. These factors produced a state that was both relatively autonomous from domestic economic actors and demonstrated an impressive ability to penetrate and extract from society when compared to the record of other postcolonial states. Although no one can doubt the impressive record accumulated by Israeli officials in gearing and mobilizing society and economy for war, its war preparation maneuvers were still circumscribed, initially because of the lack of domestic resources and a relatively undeveloped state bureaucracy and later because of political and economic constraints. In other words, even during periods of intense security pressures, when we can expect both the government to be more forceful in its actions and societal actors to be more giving because of societal cohesion, there were real limits on the government's mobilizing capacities. Government leaders were severely tested as they attempted to mobilize men, money, and material, and during times of war both the state's strengths and its limitations were revealed.

Because each government's objectives were rather costly and there were significant constraints on its actions, the constant tendency toward an ever widening resource gap, in turn, produced real dilemmas for state officials. What happens when the government's objectives of war preparation, political stability, and economic growth conflict? How do leaders respond when they are facing increased pressures from the domestic and the international environment? In *Of Rule and Revenue* Margaret Levi provides one way of thinking about these matters. She suggests that the issue is whether leaders have high discount rates, where they value the present over the future and are thus likely to extract as much revenue as possible, or low discount rates, where they value the future over the present and are thus likely to be moderate in their extractive propensities. One critical factor that affects a leader's discount rate is whether he feels secure in his rule; a leader who is relatively more secure is more modest in his requests because the "shadow of the future" is long and one can anticipate a future stream of benefits, but a leader who is relatively less secure is more ravenous in his demands. According to Levi, war or a warlike atmosphere profoundly affects a ruler's discount rate by causing him to privilege the present over the future and therefore become more predatory.[4]

Most visible was how government officials in both countries attempted to avoid any shortening of the domestic shadow during periods of intense security pressures.[5] When the shadow appeared to be receding because of domestic forces, government officials relied primarily on two types of countervailing measures. The first were accommodational strategies. If one fears that there is already a high level of domestic dissatisfaction, then the last thing a government leader is likely to do is adopt those policies that increase discontent. This reliance on an accommodational strategy, however, had one major implication: because the government's prewar mobilization policies tended to reflect the underlying distribution of societal power, the burdens of security tended to be borne disproportionally by nondominant societal actors. For instance, after the June War the Egyptian government's domestic financial extraction was reserved for those indirect areas that consequently tended to burden the masses. This became even truer after 1973, when the percentage contributed by the capitalist class actually declined from pre-1973 levels because it was both the class basis of the regime and a central actor in its development prospects.

The second way to lengthen the domestic shadow was to engage in various sorts of distributional policies that inevitably privileged the short term over the long term. This was most dramatic with regard to the changes in the government's investment policies. There was a direct trade-off between investment and consumption in Egypt after 1967 and in Israel after 1971. The state, which was a central source of investment capital, began to channel fewer resources in this direction (which translated into real declines in future economic growth) and more toward the masses through welfare transfers, subsidies, and other policies designed to raise their standard of living and, therefore, the government's approval rating. In a very real sense, then, as the discount rate rose government leaders became more short-sighted, more predatory, and more willing to sacrifice future benefits for more pressing demands.

This meant that leaders did not always become more ravenous or predatory as they became more insecure. In fact, as leaders became increasingly convinced that their days were numbered they took steps to reverse the process. This entailed various sorts of measures, from tapering their extractive efforts (e.g., the Egyptian case after 1967), changing their foreign policy orientation toward others (e.g., Sadat's decisions to go to war in 1973 and sue for peace after war termination), funneling greater material benefits to the masses (e.g., the Israeli case after 1970), to granting key societal groups such as a relatively marginalized private economic elite greater material rewards in exchange for anticipated political support (e.g., both the Israeli and Egyptian cases after 1967). In fact, although the government may have become more predatory to the extent that it consumed a greater percentage of national resources, not only did a greater percentage of its revenue derive from foreign sources but it also sponsored the withdrawal of its control over some economic areas. In other words, the government's shadow was shortened by both domestic and foreign threats, and turning to domestic actors to confront the foreign challenge only accelerated its domestic demise.

Leaders, then, face real dilemmas in attempting to forestall any short-ening of either the foreign or the domestic shadow. The problem con-fronting leaders during periods of security pressures is determining which system, the domestic or the international, is the more forgiving. Recently a number of writers have suggested that in the contemporary era sovereignty has essentially guaranteed the survival rate for states.[6] If this is true then even during times of war government leaders should take actions that reflect this basic fact. The Egyptian case does suggest that leaders judge the domestic system more threatening to their politi-cal survival. Sadat's stance prior to the Yom Kippur War provides, how-ever, one counterexample as he knowingly flirted with his own political survival to extend war preparation. In this episode Egyptian society grew increasingly impatient with the delay in material progress and the constant pronouncements that war with the Israelis was soon at hand. Be that as it may, Sadat went to war in October 1973 in no small part be-cause Saudi financial assistance, which was stifling an increasingly perni-cious Egyptian populace, would cease unless he militarily confronted the Israelis; moreover, the Egyptian population would no longer con-tinue to tolerate the situation of "no war/no peace." In other words, Sadat preferred to take his chances with the Israelis rather than with his own society. That domestic actors are less forgiving than are international actors is historically dependent and more relevant to the contemporary era where few states face the threat of territorial extinction (though from the Israeli perspective they are a notable exception), but many state managers do. This finding is consistent with the experiences of World War One Germany, Iraq, and Iran, where state officials often subordi-nated their military campaigns to domestic politics and survival.[7] Sover-eignty, which might guarantee the state's survival in the interstate sys-tem, has no domestic corollary for government officials in the domestic system.

The principal method of avoiding the choice between reducing the country's military preparedness and raising the domestic burden was to seek an international strategy. Although Egyptian and Israeli leaders expressed real concerns about external dependence, any wariness was overwhelmed by the potential costs associated with increased domes-tic mobilization. To justify their material requests officials in both coun-tries had to portray and construct themselves as important players in the Middle East. Egyptian and Israeli leaders consistently attempted to convince their targeted superpower benefactors of their value as a stra-tegic ally in a region of immense geostrategic importance, which in-cluded the maintenance of rather large and expensive militaries. This move, however, was nearly self-defeating and led to certain unforeseen consequences. For instance, to receive greater military and development assistance from the Soviet Union, Nasser emphasized Egypt's strategic importance in the Middle East and world politics. An impressive military was a central component of this drama, but one that could easily be interpreted by the security-conscious Israelis as a revelation of Nasser's aggressive intentions, which would subsequently fuel Middle Eastern passions in general and Israeli security fears in particular. Once these regional tensions escalated, Nasser had to continue to privilege the military, which drained more and more resources away from development. The paradox, then, was that Nasser, who accentuated Egypt's military importance in order to attract Soviet assistance, was caught in a dynamic that increasingly stressed security to the detriment of development. This story was reinterpreted by Sadat after 1973, as he could make the strategic switch from the Soviet Union to the United States only because the United States viewed Egypt as a desperately sought after prize. Israeli officials read the same script with a Western slant, as they tried time and again, with varying degrees of success, to convince the Americans of their strategic value. This is not to argue that security tensions, border conflicts, and security dilemmas were derivative of, for instance, Egyptian leaders' use of the military to attract more resources for its other objectives, for these security tensions were real and in no way reducible to other phenomena; but I simply argue that leaders in both countries recognized the nonstrategic benefits to be gained by a strong army. Both Egypt and Israel, willing participants in the East-West conflict, exploited it to their advantage to increase their pool of material resources and further their own domestic and foreign policy objectives.[8]

The immediate implication, then, is that alliances are formed and alignment patterns tightened not simply to confront external threats. Although one can undoubtedly find particular alliances traceable exclusively to systemic forces, and perhaps others arising primarily from domestic factors, a complete understanding of international alliance formation must include both systemic and societal variables. The systemic component largely specifies the degree of the perceived external security threat, the availability of international alliances, the nature of the strategic guarantees and economic or military resources that might be provided, and the autonomy costs that must be sacrificed in return. But systemic variables alone are insufficient for explaining the alignment behavior of states. The domestic objectives of state actors and the social, economic, and political constraints that limit the availability of resources in society and the government's access to those resources at acceptable costs must also be considered. This is particularly true in the contemporary Third World, where domestic threats to governmental stability are often perceived as greater in magnitude and immediacy than are external threats to national security and where alignments are often valued as much for their contribution to internal economic and political stability as external security. And if domestic politics profoundly influenced the Egyptian and Israeli states—which have been routinely characterized throughout this period as strong, ruling over a relatively homogeneous and cohesive society, and confronted by serious external threats—then there are good reasons to believe that state-society relations must be central in the explanations of the alliance behavior of other Third World states as well.[9]

There were limits, however, to what either the Soviet Union and the United States were willing to supply and what the Egyptians and the Israelis were willing to request. Although material support was forthcoming, potential donors and recipients alike were hesitant about sending and receiving troops, respectively. There is no evidence that the Israelis ever requested the assistance of foreign troops in their immediate defense.[10] The Egyptians, however, did obtain some manpower support during the Yemen Campaign and between 1967 and 1972 from the Soviet Union and some Arab assistance prior to and during the Yom Kippur War. Noteworthy is not the material contribution of manpower support but the symbolic importance assigned to such assistance. Nasser was quite vocal that the involvement of Soviet forces was desired not only because of technical shortfalls but also because he wanted the Soviets to see their prestige as bound up with Egypt's; he hoped that tie would make it easier for Egypt to continue an internationally directed war preparation strategy in the future. The Soviets, however, were rather reluctant to commit their prestige more than they already had, and they recognized that this very slippery slope could send them into greater involvement.[11] Moreover, Soviet support was a sensitive subject among the Egyptians because of the colonial legacy and the implicit indictment this raised of Egyptian capabilities; therefore, as soon as Egyptian troops received the required technical training they were to relieve the Soviets of their positions. Arab troop assistance prior to 1973 was important for much the same reason: it served as a symbolic gesture because Egypt understood itself to be fighting on behalf of the entire Arab World, and therefore it was only just that its Arab brethren also donate. Because there was a mutual reluctance by the Great Powers to supply, and the Egyptians and Israelis to request, foreign troops, both the Israeli and Egyptian governments had to rely on their own societies for their manpower needs.

An accommodational strategy could not satiate the government's expanding resource needs, and there were limits to what Israeli and Egyptian leaders could expect or cared to request from their superpower sponsors; therefore, they reconsidered the utility of the current societal contribution for the war effort and implemented a restructural strategy. The primary motivating factor behind a restructural strategy was the presence of an international crisis. Postwar periods of acute security threats forced government leaders to confront the outcome of their past mobilization efforts for adequately meeting the state's security needs. The exigencies surrounding crisis politics contain a number of characteristics that facilitated the search for new policies. First, during the environmental drama society becomes more accessible and permeable as a result of cohesive processes. Thus, a primary deterrent to change, anticipated and manifested societal resistance to the government's movements, becomes less salient. This was, for instance, particularly true in Egypt after 1967; the June War, more than a military defeat, provoked an ideological, political, and economic crisis as well. Second, crises are not normally confronted by the habitual, but rather by the extraordinary. Because of inadequate standard operating procedures, decision makers more thoroughly search the environment for various alternatives and responses and more easily override both bureaucratic inertia and societal opposition. Relatedly, wars (and other crises) create policy "elasticity"; they open up the policy process and allow new groups to express alternative policy proposals. [12] Crises discredit old policies that failed to confront the present challenge and instigate a search for new solutions. In sum, state and societal actors recognize that crisis politics demand a deviation from the routine to satisfactorily confront the exceptional challenge.

Although a crisis or war-threatening atmosphere might motivate Egyptian and Israeli leaders to adopt a restructural policy, such a policy was permitted by the presence of the state's relative autonomy, legitimacy (conscription), capacity (taxation), and economic structure (production). In the Egyptian and Israeli cases the most important factors were the state's legitimacy and its control over financial resources; these two factors gave societal actors a reason to contribute to the state's security and insulated the government from the retaliatory measures of domestic economic elites, respectively. Consider Nasser's move to conscript the upper classes following the June 1967 War. The government was able to move in this direction because tremendous cohesion followed the war and both state and societal actors believed that the state's legitimacy was under attack and threat. The absence of either state legitimacy or state autonomy would undoubtedly have precluded Nasser from widening the conscription net as easily as he did. The same was true for the Israeli government's conscription policy during the War of Independence. Ben-Gurion capitalized on the Israeli state's substantial legitimacy to construct quickly and easily a citizen's army. Mass conscription was (and continues to be) a rarity among many postcolonial states; it took place only because of the state's ideological stature. In general, the Israeli and Egyptian governments' abilities to centralize their control over society and economy was owing primarily to the state's legitimacy and relative autonomy.

It should be immediately noted that the Israeli and Egyptian cases might be relatively uncommon for many Third World states because each secured a fair degree of legitimacy and autonomy from society. Many Third World states stand alien from their societies, therefore unable to conscript widely or construct policies that do not respect the demands of dominant economic elites. But these cases, particularly Egypt, are probably more representative of the dilemmas confronting Third World state leaders where the colonial process leaves Third World states routinely characterized by a lack of state capacity and an economic structure dominated by agricultural and commodity production. Therefore, most Third World governments have a difficult time either extracting money or producing their own source of armaments. Systemic factors in general and the colonial process in particular created a situation whereby most Third World states tend toward an international war preparation strategy.

The government's adoption of a restructural policy cannot be understood by solely examining either the underlying structural conditions that allow action to take place or the motivational dimensions behind the government's movements. Both features are required. The identified structural factors may be most appropriate at explaining the original formulation of the government's policy and its wholescale reevaluation rather than its modification and changes at the margin during moments of "normalcy." These constraint-shaped policies become institutionalized by rendering them rather impervious to radical alteration until the next crisis.

I want to consider in detail the Israeli government's decision to adopt a restructural production strategy following the 1967 war, for this episode highlights a number of important theoretical issues. It is important to recognize at the outset that this move would have been near impossible had it not been for the tremendous relative autonomy of the Israeli state, its control over an independent source of revenue. Because the Israeli government was able to undertake a restructural policy without worrying about societal opposition, governmental preferences and ideas became the driving forces behind the content of its policy. In other words, Israeli officials might have been interested in pursuing a set of policies that they hoped would further the state's arms independence, and the state's high degree of relative autonomy and its control over much of the public sector enabled it to move in either a centralizing or liberalizing direction. Specifically, the interesting issue was that the government moved to relax, rather than strengthen, its hold over the economy. This is particularly curious for it occurred at a crucial time: when a warlike atmosphere would have placed the discount rate at its highest (precisely when government officials are supposed to be most possessive); when the state already controlled a substantial percentage of the economy, including the commanding heights; when the state had already pursued an etatist development policy; and, when few societal, particularly private sector, elites were positioned to challenge the state's authority. Why would the state relax its direct control under these circumstances? Why were Israeli officials not more predatory? Was it strictly because of politically motivated calculations or an overestimation of society's volatility?

To gain a better handle on these questions we must move away from the objective set of constraints included in the theoretical framework and return to a more careful consideration of the government's intentions and motivations. Israeli leaders were influenced by not only the present decision context but also their expectations and desires: How did they envision the future? What kind of society did they want? And, most important, what kind of organizing principles did they think would best guide the economy and generate more resources for war? Israeli officials intimated that the economy was entering a new, differentiated, and more complex phase, one that would certainly outstrip the government's planning abilities.[13] Moreover, these same officials suggested that although a state-led economy had been appropriate during Israel's first economic phase, the decision to limit the private sector had unfortunately limited the evolution of new ideas and sources of economic growth required to meet the myriad demands emerging after 1967. In short, government leaders were influenced by changing conceptions about what would best solve the country's security needs and what economic organizing principles would best serve future economic growth. The government was profoundly influenced by not only the objective constraints but also an evolving set of ideas about the future and the policies thought most efficient to meet these objectives.

Can a rational choice framework handle these issues? Only in part. Although rational choice approaches do not exclude the possibility that constraints are subjectively constructed, that learning occurs, or that ideas matter, preferences are taken as given and exogenously derived. Consider the Israeli liberalization policy after 1967 in greater detail. Israeli leaders pursued a liberalization policy that they believed would secure their various political, security, and economic objectives. It is less than clear that the government's various objectives would have been substantially undercut in the short term had it maintained its past production policies or that, for instance, it was immediately evident their past procurement policies had proved so disastrous. In other words, no overwhelming information signaled to state leaders that promoting liberalization was immediately superior to their past practices. The policy choice was highly dependent on the government's conception of which economic principles it thought would best satisfy its goals. According to Michael Taylor, "thin rationality is relative to *given* aims and beliefs, and that the agent's actions are *instrumental* in achieving or advancing the given aims in light of the given beliefs."[14] The Israeli government opted for a liberalization policy because of certain beliefs they held about economic activity and the mechanisms and principles that flowed from that set of beliefs. In short, Israeli officials adopted a different understanding of the instrumental.

One possible way to approach this issue is through the literature on learning.[15] Some defense ministry officials commented that they turned to the private sector because they believed that past Defense Ministry policies, which excluded private sector participation from the defense economy, had injured the state's security. This realization caused them to abandon the status quo and adopt new practices. This was not adaptive or simple learning but rather complex learning, for it involved changed norms and ideologies.[16] The government appeared not only to have lost faith in the utility of a state-led economic policy but also to have gravitated toward market-oriented principles. This required a substantial change in how government leaders approached and understood the world around them.

Not all Israeli officials learned or adopted new ideologies at the same rate. States are complex organizations where political power is fractionated and "shifts in social structure and political power determines whose learning matters."[17] Many of these officials, articulating a new set of economic norms and ideologies, were placed strategically in the state apparatus—relatively autonomous from other bureaucratic agencies and societal forces and armed with substantial financial assets. In short, they were ideally situated, both temporally and spatially, to implement their new economic ideologies. Eisenstadt suggests that parts of the Israeli bureaucracy, notably the defense, judicial, and finance ministries, were reorganized along rational, technocratic lines, while other ministerial posts, such as education and religious affairs, continued to be allocated along political lines.[18] Officials in the Defense Ministry and the Finance Ministry, given their bureaucratic power and access to substantial capital, were ideally placed to champion their new understanding of the instrumental.[19] A state as rational and unitary actor approach, then, does not adequately capture the government's liberalization policy, for this policy was highly dependent on both a changed set of beliefs and who in the state apparatus did the learning, respectively.[20]

In general, the government's evolving notion of what would best fulfill its objectives in general and beliefs about the instrumental in particular decidedly shaped its adopted war preparations. And these issues were highly important when situated in the context of the tremendous policy latitude given to officials in both countries generated by the underlying state and social structure. Israeli and Egyptian officials turned to the private sector after 1967 and 1973, respectively, not because of capital's current political and economic power, but because, alternatively, a new generation of state elites who articulated different norms came to positions of influence, state elites who had advocated a market-oriented policy found that their previously rejected ideas were now embraced, or the same state elites who had once promoted the old vision now adopted new understandings and ideologies because of a learning process. In any case, changing norms and ideologies are critical for understanding issues of preference formation, subjective constraints, and their respective change. These issues, which stand outside most standard rational choice perspectives,[21] must be included for understanding changes in the government's policies in general and its war preparation strategies in specific.

In summary, Egyptian and Israeli war preparation strategies evidenced certain themes. Leaders in both countries were primed to capitalize on any societal opening but quick to revert to their well-worn caution at the first signs of domestic resistance. Unable or unwilling to move beyond a modest accommodational stance to secure their required security resources, the principal mechanism exploited by both Egyptian and Israeli governments was superpower support. In other words, when security became more intense and increasingly conflicted with its other goals government officials sought to export the burgeoning costs of war. This desire was a product of each country's limited resource base, the political and economic constraints on the government's access to those existing resources, and the willingness of foreign actors to sponsor these costs. Although Israeli and Egyptian officials were rather wary of relying on outside actors for their survival, this seemed a better option than extracting more from a potentially explosive domestic society. By recognizing that Israeli and Egyptian state managers were both enabled and constrained by features of the state and society, the attempt here was to strike a balance between volunteerism and determinism and to recognize that leaders have choices but not necessarily in the context of their own choosing. Adopting a theoretical framework that identifies a set of structural categories assumed to condition the goal-oriented activities of government officials has been relatively instructive in explaining not only how and why state managers constructed their war preparation strategies in the way that they did but also how Israeli and Egyptian leaders adopted similar policies.

WAR PREPARATION AND STATE POWER

The second principal objective of this project was to establish the micro-foundations for macrohistorical change, to demonstrate the linkages between governmental actions and changes in state-society relations. One important finding should come as little surprise: the state was a motor force of social change in general and redefining the state-society compact in particular. After all, the state's central role in promoting important domestic changes has been a standard observation in the state literature for over a decade. Nor should it be astounding, though generally under-appreciated and underspecified, that war and its associated activities were central to this change. And given that over the past decade we have seen "power-seeking" state officials call for the state to trim its size and interference in the economy, the observation that the state might promote its own withdrawal from the economy should also raise few eyebrows. Be that as it may, I want to conclude by speaking to the issue of war and institutional change. That is, how do the Israeli and Egyptian cases correct and modify the conventional understanding of the relationship between conflict processes and state power?

Although our theories of state formation and state-society relations have incorporated the role of both domestic and international political economy for shaping the various forms of the state, most studies have failed to acknowledge that the state is also embedded in an interstate system placing security demands on its energies. All too often national security and security-related processes are relegated to residual categories evoked only when more accepted explanations—notably political economy processes and the self-aggrandizing actions of state officials—are exhausted. Here I attempted to demonstrate that war and war-related processes are significant causal factors in their own right, but I sought to do so in such a way that I incorporated how they interacted with other dynamics and causal forces to produce the observed outcome in state power.

To provide a more explicit understanding of how war preparation affects state power, I argued that the state's broadly defined mobilization strategies—whether accommodational, international, or restructural—had various implications for state power. The first two strategies were assumed either to leave state power unchanged or prod it down its established path, which also included the possibility for heightening existing state-society contradictions. A restructural strategy, one that attempts to reorganize society to increase the societal contribution to the war effort, and often does so by striking a bargain with societal actors for access to these resources, serves most directly to transform state-society relations.

In this study I intended, however, to leave open the possibility for either an increase or a decrease in state power as a consequence of these mobilization practices. There is "no sense in which history is an *immanent* process. Nothing which happens was 'inevitable' even though once it happens it can be explained as a causal outcome of the fused structured processes."[22] Although I posited a set of tendencies that might arise in the government's war preparation strategies owing to an idealized set of state-society relations and governmental preferences, these were always understood as distinct tendencies, not mere conformations of some prewritten historical script.

Accommodational and international strategies could heighten already existing state-society contradictions to a crisis-inducing point of transformation, but the government's restructural strategy was most responsible for the major alteration in state power. Crisis politics creates the conditions for institutional change and innovation. As Ikenberry notes, "the institutional approach . . . gives special attention to specific historical junctures when economic or political crises reshape social relations and the institutions of policymaking. 'Critical junctures' or episodic events refer to unanticipated and exogenous events that drive institution building. . . . Depression and war are critical catalysts of change from this perspective."[23] It is important to recognize that the change in and devolution of state power occurred not only because of the "bargaining power" of private actors, as exchange theorists and rational choice advocates often propose, but also because state officials, guided by new conceptions of economic organization, wanted to redefine and redesign the state's relationship to society and institutional norms, broadly understood, to further their ideas of the instrumental. In short, what constituted the national interest did not change, but its path did. These officials were able to change this path given the state's substantial autonomy.

These institutional innovations, however, were not spontaneous; rather, they were structured by the previous historical path. Although war might have stimulated a search for new policies by both the Israeli and Egyptian governments and set the foundation for institutional change, these changes were structured by historical dynamics. For instance, after 1967 Israeli officials searched for new ways to increase the societal contribution to the war effort while also pursuing their economic and political objectives. This period solidified new opportunities for the domestic capitalist class and decreased the state's autonomy from society because of the nature of the Israeli political economy prior to the 1967 War and the ideological disposition and objectives of state managers, some of whom, like Finance Minister Pinchas Sapir, had been championing capital's cause before 1967 but only now found their ideas more enthusiastically received.[24] This was also evident in Nasser's reevaluation of the private sector after 1967 (and particularly noticeable after 1973), as he became more receptive to a reappraisal of its role because past policies had been discredited and offered no real solution to present ills. The military and economic crises discredited old policies and those associated with them and enhanced the position of those who offered fresh alternatives and ideas.

Because the direction of state power as a consequence of the government's war preparation strategies depends on both the prewar preparation state-society relations and the government's objectives, this analysis stands in contrast to the prevailing characterization of the relationship between war and state power, which is based on the following scenario. A security threat forces the state, owing to its pivotal role as defender of the country's borders, to mobilize the required material and human resources, and to take extraordinary measures, both politically and economically, to confront these foreign challenges. The end of hostilities does not, however, signal the state's withdrawal to its prewar stance, as these new-found procedures became a permanent part of its policy arsenal and thereby contribute to the expansion of the state apparatus and its control over society. This interpretation of the relationship between war and state power, then, tends to assume that the state's power over society is a beneficiary of war and that this is best evaluated by examining its capacity to implement and extract from society.

There are three significant deviations from this traditional characterization of the relationship between war and state power in both the Israeli and Egyptian cases during the post-1967 period. Many studies that plot the relationship between war and state power argue that the most important changes have derived from the state's increased extraction and control over societal resources. This was not necessarily true for either Israel or Egypt during this period. Because of the presence of superpower benefactors, the domestic limitations on the state's access to society, and the government's other objectives, the government in each country increased its foreign and domestic borrowing; that is, each chose to mortgage its financial life to foreign actors and thus leave relatively unchanged its extraction capacities. In short, the bargaining process between government and society that often proceeds a major change in the state's extraction capacities was basically absent in both cases. This is consistent with the experience of many medieval European states, where a weak state apparatus precluded the government's intervention in society's fiscal matters.[25] Israeli and Egyptian leaders are not the only ones accused of preferring foreign financing over making tough economic choices; both Presidents Johnson during the Vietnam War and Reagan during the "new Cold War" have been interpreted as engaging in a similar type of behavior.[26]

There is a second deviation from the common characterization of the relationship between war preparation and state power; in both Israel and Egypt the major alterations in state power occurred not because of the government's intervention in society, but rather because of its *withdrawal*. After 1967 both Israeli and Egyptian governments attempted to promote the fortunes of the domestic capitalist class in order to increase its contribution to both the war effort, governmental stability, and the economy's fortunes. In the Israeli case this liberalization also included the additional feature of increasing the public sector's managerial autonomy. That the government chose to relax its control over economic activity and increase the role of market mechanisms for allocating resources during a period of security tensions must be attributed to the historical dynamics that preceded and interacted with war preparation. Specifically, both countries had suffered an economic crisis prior to the 1967 War; in Israel, a recession lasted from 1965 to 1967, and in Egypt there was a balance of payments crisis. In addition to an increasing dissatisfaction with this state-led economic policy was the emergence of state officials who had different economic ideas about the proper organization of the economy and new search by old state elites; and the recognition that war was not going to be immediate but sometime in the future implied that state officials might be more interested in creating the conditions for generating resources rather than simply extracting those resources already present. War and its related tendencies, however, must be viewed as instrumental in bringing about this change. There is absolutely no basis to argue that such changes would have taken place absent such security pressures or that they only accelerated changes already present in the system. That sort of argument conforms too closely to a narrow, economic deterministic, and teleological vision of history.

Moreover, the Israeli case forsakes traditional neomercantilist thought in an important respect. A standard wisdom in economic nationalist thought is that the state should control the "commanding heights of the economy," and societal interests should be subordinated to some conception of the national interest. During the first twenty years the state maintained an overpowering hold over the economy in general and military industries in particular, but a subtle yet important reversal after 1967 as the government's neomercantilist policies led not to the state's increased control over society and economy but rather just the opposite—to its very erosion. This was a consciously produced strategy, as Israeli leaders believed that excessive state intervention had actually stymied the state's security interests. Although the state still owns many of the country's most important military industries and industrial enterprises, it both increased the state-owned enterprises' managerial autonomy and devolved its control over other economic levers that were intimately bound up with its ability to shape, not be shaped by, economic forces. That the state's attempt to increase its economic and security goals would lead to its diminution is a possibility overlooked by most economic nationalists' writings. Although it was impossible for Israeli leaders to conceive of the economy and security as anything besides interrelated, their understanding of that relationship could, and did, change significantly.

Third, the decline in state power is traced through the state's relative autonomy. Changes in state power were uncovered not in the realm of the state's tax effort and extraction capacity, but rather in the state's restructured relationship to foreign actors and domestic economic elites. The erosion of the state's autonomy was both an intended and unintended consequence of its actions. It was certainly intended by virtue of the fact that many Israeli and Egyptian officials believed that the economy would operate in a more productive and efficient manner once the state divested some of its authority and control over investment and production decisions. Once these decisions were made, however, neither Israeli nor Egyptian officials could predict the direction or force it would take. For instance, although Israeli leaders believed that a less prominent state would enhance the country's production of wealth and its military industrialization program, many officials did not entertain the idea that a state-sponsored military-industrial complex of such force would emerge, later challenging the state's decision-making autonomy. The state's slipping autonomy implied that its governing parameters were more constrained and limited as it became more dependent on private actors for continued capital accumulation and contribution to the state's revenues. In other words, the changes in state power were most accurately observed not by the government's actions, not by what it did, but rather by what it was unable to do. Too often past indicators of state power have taken their cues from the state capacity tradition, which tends to rely on the observed actions of government officials for evidence of state strength. Although this captures part of what is central to state power, the state autonomy tradition adds the necessary feature that state power is also shaped by what governmental actions are prohibited. The infrastructural capacity of the Israeli and the Egyptian states has not changed significantly, but both are more constrained than they once were because of the rise of domestic economic and political actors that substantially control their revenue base and the economy's investment decisions. Confronting the costs of war, then, was not simply economic but political as well.

In general, the common wisdom that war and war preparation increase the state's control over society and that such control can be accurately traced through the state's extraction of resources can be highly misleading. Although war and its related tendencies undoubtedly reinforced the state's centralizing tendencies before 1967, after the June War the state's fortunes in both countries began to recede in the face of various societal and systemic pressures. This study, therefore, challenges both the common characterization of the relationship between war and state-society relations and how it is evaluated. State power in both the Israeli and Egyptian cases was undercut by war preparation, and this is observed via its relationship to concepts derived from reading the political economy. Again, I am not attempting to substitute an overly economistic and endogenously derived analysis of state power with a security-centric one. The state, situated in both domestic and international structures, attempts to pursue wealth and security while maintaining its political stability. War preparation interacted with other macrohistorical processes to produce the observed outcomes in state power.

A theme here is that the current Israeli and Egyptian states are products of governmental choices, strategies, and ideological orientations. And although it was possible to unravel the causal logic that produced these outcomes, there was nothing predetermined about either the war preparation strategies of Egyptian or Israeli leaders or the effects these policies would have on future state-society relations in both countries. Some of the most important policies that weakened the state's hand resulted from forces that depended on various factors, from the government's objectives and beliefs to the domestic and international constraints and opportunities it faced in the pursuit of those goals. Structural change is ultimately a product of both structural dynamics and the idiosyncratic.

The Janus-faced state is alive and well and living in the state's security policy. Government officials are concerned with their reproduction in both domestic and international structures; therefore, they construct their policies with an eye toward both ends. As the government is concerned with both its international and domestic opposition and viability, processes in both spheres shape and transform the state and its relationship to society. Just as the European state system was a product of and shaped by both the logic of capital accumulation and interstate violence, these themes and processes continue to be important factors in shaping the experiences of Third World states in the modern era.

Appendixes

APPENDIX 1
Jewish Investment and Capital Inflow, 1932–1939 (LP thousands)

	Land	Farming	Public Works Construction	Industry and Crafts	Other	Total	Capital Inflow
1932	150	1,400	1,000	1,100	200	3,850	4,570
1935	1,700	1,000	5,750	1,600	650	10,700	10,840
1937	400	1,000	3,000	1,000	600	6,000	5,540
1939	380	900	2,000	900	620	4,800	6,870
Total 1932–1939	5,450	10,000	24,600	8,400	4,350	52,800	60,060
Percentage	10.3	19.0	46.6	15.9	8.2	100.0	

Source: Halevi and Klinov-Malul, *The Economic Development of Israel*, 22.

APPENDIX 2
National and Public versus Private Jewish Capital Flow to Palestine, 1918–1937

	In Millions of Palestinian Pounds	Percentage
National and public capital	20	21
Private capital	75	79
Total	95	100

Source: Kimmerling, *Zionism and Economy*, 30.

APPENDIX 3
Summary of Fiscal Operations, 1962/63–1978 (in millions of Egyptian pounds)

Item	1962/ 63	1963/ 64	1964/ 65	1965/ 66	1966/ 67	1967/ 68	1968/ 69	1969/ 70	1970/ 71
Total Revenue	458	527	598	660	753	643	675	750	869
Central govt. revenue	359	440	514	560	666	510	565	658	726
Tax revenue	214	272	317	342	423	414	451	524	564
Transferred profits[a]	68	71	84	86	69	26	32	40	101
Other nontax revenue	31	44	44	50	46	55	48	56	56
Investment self-financing	68	43	40	50	41	78	62	36	87
Total expenditure[b]	710	896	906	1022	971	894	880	956	1063
Subsidies	—	—	—	—	—	1	—	—	3
Public authority deficits	na	na	na	na	na	14	6	—	41
Investment	273	369	294	300	271	268	312	352	358
Emergency fund deficit	na	na	na	na	na	na	na	na	na
Overall deficit	−252	−369	−308	−362	−218	−251	−205	−206	−194

Source: Ikram, Egypt, 408–9.
[a]Mandatory transfers under the legal requirement that 65 percent of net profits after tax and depreciation be transferred to the Treasury.
[b]Excludes Emergency Fund deficit.

APPENDIX 4
Soviet-Egyptian Military Aid Accounts (in millions of dollars)

Year	Total Value	Subtotal Discount	Before Discount	Value After Grant	Accumulated Debts	Alleged Payments	Residual Debts
1955–59	581	581	387	—	387	387	—
1960–66	965	956	965	460	183	64	119
1967–73	6259	5378	537	—	2689	672	2017

Source: Efrat, The Egyptian Defense Burden, 98.

APPENDIX 5
Arab Financial Assistance to Egypt, 1973–1976 (in millions of dollars)

	1973	1974	1975	1976
Kuwait				
Concessional				
Commitment	210.16	449.63	324.81	118.12
Disbursement	194.99	244.62	439.23	60.38
Nonconcessional				
Commitment	171.93	123.67	955.00	327.38
Disbursement	—	102.00	566.94	332.52
Qatar				
Concessional				
Commitment	—	15.00	105.36	25.47
Disbursement	—	15.00	55.18	75.55
Nonconcessional				
Commitment	20.00	3.41	1.75	1.70
Disbursement	—	13.41	11.75	1.70
Saudi Arabia				
Concessional				
Commitment	370.00	471.00	1262.91	489.99
Disbursement	170.00	471.00	948.91	496.84
Nonconcessional				
Commitment	60.00	102.57	5.00	—
Disbursement	—	31.00	36.57	20.00
United Arab Emirates				
Concessional				
Commitment	30.65	130.04	372.57	307.26
Disbursement	20.73	120.66	284.05	349.54
Nonconcessional				
Commitment	60.00	—	—	—
Disbursement	—	30.00	30.00	—

Source: Wein, *Saudi-Egyptian Relations*, 48.

APPENDIX 6
Capital Imports to Israel, 1950–1967 (in millions of dollars)

	Loans and Investments (net)		Unilateral Transfers Payments		Total		
	Public	Private	Public	Private	Public	Private	Total
1950–54	57.8	33.6	150.2	21.8	208.0	55.4	263.4
1955–59	57.6	16.2	155.6	86.6	213.2	102.8	316.0
1960–64	70.6	128.4	143.5	193.4	214.2	321.8	536.0
1965–67	140.6	78.3	175.6	207.6	316.3	286.0	602.3
1950–67	75.1	62.6	154.1	118.4	229.2	181.0	410.2
Total	135.2	1,126.8	2,773.8	2,131.2	4,125.6	3,258.0	7,383.6

Source: Prime Minister's Office, *Israel Economic Development*, 172.

APPENDIX 7
Share of Capital Imports in Total Resources and Gross Investments, 1950–1967 (in millions of dollars)[a]

	Total Loans, Investments, Grants	Total Resources	Gross Domestic Investment	Ratio of Capital Imports to Resources	Ratio of Capital Imports to Investment
1950–54	274	1,157	394	17.6	69.5
1955–59	398	2,071	497	19.2	80.1
1960–64	697	3,165	667	22.0	104.4
1965–67	805	4,399	834	18.3	96.5
1950–67	515	2,620	572	19.7	90.0

Source: Prime Minister's Office, *Israel Economic Development*, 174.
[a]Figures show total and annual averages.

APPENDIX 8
Investments by Branch in the Economy, 1950–1967[a]

	1950–1954	1955–1959	1960–1964	1965–1967	1950–1967	Percentage Distribution in 1950–1967
Agriculture	628	1,056	894	428	3,007	14
Water and irrigation	405	266	526	219	1,417	7
Industry, mining, and construction equipment	1,055	1,192	2,131	1,091	5,469	26
Electricity	178	440	346	292	1,257	6
Transportation and communication	626	874	1,912	1,458	4,869	22
Business, hotels, and personal services	171	161	421	273	1,026	5
Public institutions (services)	395	800	1,630	1,316	4,141	20
All branches (except housing)	3,458	4,790	7,860	5,078	21,185	100
Housing	2,198	2,431	3,748	2,275	10,652	
Total investment in fixed assets	5,656	7,221	11,607	7,354	31,837	

Source: Prime Minister's Office, *Israel Economic Development*, 101.
[a]Figures rounded to nearest million Israeli pounds.

APPENDIX 9
Gross Investment in Fixed Assets,
by Investing Sector, 1952–1966 (in percentages)

	1952	1954	1958	1960	1962	1964	1966
Public sector	34	50	45	41	48	43	41
Private sector	66	50	55	59	52	57	59

Source: Prime Minister's Office, *Israel Economic Development*, 103.

APPENDIX 10
Capital Imports to Israel, 1967–1977 (in millions of dollars)[a]

	Loans and Investments (net)		Unilateral Transfers Payments		Total		
	Public	Private	Public	Private	Public	Private	Total
1967	291	27	267	254	558	281	839
1968	151	40	104	331	255	371	626
1969	137	49	112	346	249	395	644
1970	515	67	206	443	721	510	1,231
1971	477	141	151	612	628	853	1,481
1972	410	314	281	773	691	1,087	1,778
1973	635	366	1,396	780	2,031	1,441	3,175
1974	458	173	967	771	1,425	943	2,768
1975	1,383	123	1,031	723	2,415	846	3,261
1976	869	177	1,527	683	2,396	860	3,315
1977	533	110	1,271	810	1,805	921	3,256

Source: Bank of Israel, Annual Report (various years).
[a]Numbers are rounded.

APPENDIX 11
Indicators of Debt-Servicing Burden, 1969–1978

	1969	1970	1971	1972	1973	1974	1975	1976	1977	1978
1. Interest payments	109	141	147	179	262	389	530	552	620	757
2. Principal payments, long and medium term	250	248	330	432	420	469	534	622	726	882
3. Total debt servicing (1 + 2)	359	389	477	611	682	858	1,064	1,174	1,346	1,639
4. Exports of goods and services	1,290	1,402	1,875	2,222	2,784	3,634	3,825	4,566	5,664	6,634
5. Unilateral transfers	464	650	792	1,059	2,190	1,718	1,770	2,210	2,082	2,429
6. Ratio (3/4)	27.8	27.7	25.4	27.5	24.5	23.6	27.8	25.7	23.8	24.7
7. Ratio 3/(4 + 5)	20.5	19.0	17.9	18.6	13.7	16.0	19.0	17.3	17.4	18.1

Source: Bank of Israel, Annual Report (1978), 127.

APPENDIX 12
Investments in Industry by Branch

Year	Food	Textiles	Wood and Paper	Mining and Minerals	Chemicals and Plastics	Metals, Electronics, and Transport
1968	11	18	7	14	19	31
1969	10	15	10	10	20	35
1970	11	15	11	10	16	37
1971	11	12	9	9	20	39
1972	11	17	12	8	12	31
1973	11	16	12	8	12	41
1974	14	13	11	7	12	44
1975	11	12	13	9	15	40
1976	11	9	7	11	21	41
1977	11	9	7	11	19	45

Source: Naftali Blumental, "The Influences of Defense Industry Investment on Israel's Economy," in Z. Lanir, ed., *Israeli Security Planning in the 1980s* (New York: Praeger Press, 1984), 170.

APPENDIX 13
The "Underground" Economy in Israel: Various Estimates
(in percentage of GNP)

Year	Ben-Shahar, et al.	Mishory and Tal	Unger and Zilberferb	Nadel
1955			0.7	
1960			1.4	
1965			5.1	
1970	4.2	5.6	9.3	
1971	6.7	7.3	8.6	
1972	7.8	4.2	7.8	
1974		4.3	9.3	18
1975			10.6	
1977			15.0	

Source: J. Rowley, S. Bichler, and J. Nitzan, "Some Aspects of Aggregate Concentration in the Israeli Economy, 1964–1986," *Department of Economics Working Papers* (McGill University, 1988), 25.

Notes

Chapter One
War Preparation and State Power

1. The relationship between the state's war-related activities and its control over society is well documented historically. War is considered central to understanding the formation of the Western European states and state system. See Perry Anderson, *Lineages of the Absolutist State* (New York: Verso Press, 1974); Richard Bean, "War and the Birth of the Nation State," *Journal of Economic History* 33 (March 1973):203–21; John Brewer, *Sinews of War* (Boston: Unwin Hyman, 1989); Otto Hintze, "Military Organization and the Organization of the State," in Felix Gilbert, ed., *The Historical Essays of Otto Hintze* (New York: Oxford University Press, 1975), 180–215; Charles Tilly, ed., *The Formation of the National States in Western Europe* (Princeton: Princeton University Press, 1975); Charles Tilly, *Coercion, Capital, and European States* (Boston: Basil Blackwell, 1990); and Aristide Zolberg, "Strategic Interactions and the Formation of Modern States: France and England," *International Social Science Journal* 32 (1980):687–716. War also figures prominently in the development of capitalism. See Douglass North, *Structure and Change in Economic History* (New York: Norton, 1981); Michael Mann, *States, War, and Capitalism* (Boston: Basil Blackwell, 1988); and John Hall, "Introduction," in John Hall, ed., *States in History* (London: Basil Blackwell, 1987), 1–21. See Arthur Marwick, *War and Social Change in the Twentieth Century: A Comparative Study of Britain, France, Germany, Russia, and the United States* (New York: St. Martin's Press, 1974); Anthony Giddens, *The Nation-State and Violence* (Berkeley: University of California Press, 1985); and Karen Rasler and William Thompson, *War and Statemaking* (Boston: Unwin Hyman, 1989) for good studies of the relationship between war and change in capitalist states. See Arthur Stein, *The Nation at War* (Baltimore: Johns Hopkins University Press, 1979), for the U.S. case.

2. See Gabriel Ardant, "Financial Policy and Economic Infrastructure of Modern States and Nations," in C. Tilly, ed., *The Formation of the National States in Western Europe* (Princeton: Princeton University Press, 1975), 164–242; Michael Howard, *War in European History* (New York: Oxford University Press, 1976); Charles Tilly, ed., *Formation of the National States in Western Europe* (Princeton: Princeton University Press, 1975); Tilly, *As Sociology Meets History* (New York: Academic Press, 1981); Tilly, "War Making and State Making as Organized Crime," in P. Evans et al., eds., *Bringing the State Back In* (New York: Cambridge University Press), 169–91; Giddens, *The Nation-State and Violence*; A. F. K. Organski et al., *Births, Deaths, and Taxes: The Demographics of Political Transitions* (Chicago: University of Chicago Press, 1984); and Ted Robert Gurr, "War, Revolution, and the Growth of the Coercive State," *Comparative Political Studies* 21 (April 1988):46–65.

3. See Jürgen Kocka, *Facing Total War* (Cambridge: Harvard University Press, 1984), for the German case; and Theda Skocpol, *States and Social Revolutions: A Comparative Analysis of France, Russia, and China* (New York: Cambridge University Press, 1979), for the Russian case.

4. Charles Tilly, "Shrugging Off the Nineteenth Century Incubus," in J. Berting and W. Blockmans, eds., *Beyond Progress and Development* (Aldershot: Avedury Press, 1987), 73.

5. Douglass North, *Structure and Change in Economic History* (New York: Norton, 1981), chap. 11.

6. See Alan Milward, *War, Economy, and Society, 1939–1945* (Berkeley: University of California Press, 1979), and William McNeill, *The Pursuit of Power: Technology, Armed Forces, and Society since A.D. 1000* (Chicago: University of Chicago Press, 1982). This is a relatively recent and geographically restricted phenomenon, only becoming prevalent among advanced capitalist countries since the mid-1800s. See Donald MacKenzie, "Militarism and Socialist Theory," *Capital and Class* 19 (1983):33–73.

7. Mary Kaldor, "Warfare and Capitalism," in E. P. Thompson, ed., *Exterminism and the Cold War* (London: New Left Books, 1983), 261–88; MacKenzie, "Militarism and Socialist Theory"; and Martin Shaw, "Introduction: War and Social Theory," in M. Shaw, ed., *War, State, and Society* (New York: St. Martin's Press, 1985), 1–22.

8. Tilly, *Coercion, Capital, and States*, 5–12.

9. Ibid., 10. Both Weberian and Marxist-inspired accounts err in the same direction; they tend to focus on internal, to the exclusion of external factors, and also tend to place economic forces as primary to their explanation, though Marxist explanations generally fall closer to this position. Weber himself defined the state as including a monopoly of the means of coercion, yet he was less specific about the effects of employing that coercion in the interstate arena on the development of the state and preferred instead to rely on internally generated factors. While Weber and sympathetic followers have been willing to recognize that war has shaped the development of the modern state, they are too willing to subordinate the role of international conflict to domestic forces. See, for example, Giafranco Poggi, *The Development of the Modern State* (London: Hutchinson Press, 1978); Ellen Trimberger, *Revolution from Above: Military Bureaucrats and Development in Japan, Turkey, Egypt, and Peru* (New Brunswick, N.J.: Transaction Books, 1978); Frank Parkin, *Marxism and Class Theory: A Bourgeois Critique* (New York: New York University Press, 1979; and Steven Skowronek, *Building the New American State* (New York: Cambridge University Press, 1982). Fred Block, "The Ruling Class Does Not Rule: Notes on the Marxist Theory of the State," *Socialist Revolution* 33 (1977):6–28; Theda Skocpol, "Bringing the State Back In: Strategies of Analysis in Current Research," in P. Evans et al., *Bringing the State Back In*, 3–37; and other Weberian-influenced scholars have also called for greater attention to the state's role in interstate relations in general and periods of conflict in specific.

Marxist scholars, preoccupied with the state's role in capitalist society, have also neglected how war has shaped the modern state. For instance, in capitalism the state has the responsibility for maintaining societal cohesion and tranquility during periods of disarticulation and crisis. See James O'Connor, *The Fiscal Crisis of the State* (New York: St. Martin's Press, 1973); Nicos Poulantzas, *State, Power, Socialism* (London: Verso Press, 1978); and Goran Therborn, *What Does the Ruling Class Do When It Rules?* (London: New Left Books, 1978). To forestall such turmoil, the state expanded its activities and functions, which resulted in its increased control over society and an enlarged state apparatus. Phillip Corrigan, ed., *Capitalism, State Formation, and Marxist Theory* (London: Quartet Books, 1980); Boris Frankel, "On the State of the State: Marxist Theories of the State after Leninism," *Theory and Society* 7 (1979): 199–242. Bob Jessop, *The Capitalist State* (New York: New York University Press, 1982); and Michael Hechter and William Brustein, "Regional Modes of Production and Patterns of State Formation in Western Europe," *American Journal of Sociology* 85 (1980): 1061–94. Marxist scholars have been too concerned with crises associated with capital accumulation and too little interested in crises associated with military competition. See Shaw, "Introduction: War and Social Theory"; Anthony Giddens, *The Nation-State and Violence*; Martin Shaw and Colin Creighton, "Introduction," *The Sociology of War and Peace* (New York: Sheridan House, 1987), 1–13; and Jeffrey Isaac, *Power and Marxist Theory: A Realist View* (Ithaca: Cornell University Press, 1987), 198–208, for good critiques of this overly internally directed tendency in Marxism.

10. Tilly, *Coercion, Capital and European States*, 6. For instance, an influential account of the growth of state power is the power-seeking activities of the government. This approach is adopted almost exclusively by those social scientists that utilize rational actor models of governmental behavior. See Margaret Levi, "A Predatory Theory of Rule," *Politics and Society* 10 (1981): 431–65; and Levi, *Of Rule and Revenue* (Berkeley: University of California Press, 1988); North, *Structure and Change in Economic History*; and Organski, Kugler, et al., *Birth, Death, and Taxes*. These scholars assume that government officials are power-seeking agents, who will capitalize on any and all opportunities to increase the resources under their control. The only barrier between power-starved officials and societal resources is domestic resistance. War figures prominently in their explanations.

11. This literature is obviously quite expansive and well-developed. Thomas Callaghy, *The State-Society Struggle: Zaire in Comparative Perspective* (New York: Columbia University Press, 1984) provides a good example of predatory theories; Dietrich Rueschemeyer and Peter Evans, "The State and Economic Transformation," in P. Evans et al., eds., *Bringing the State Back In*, 44–77, offer a good example of the state's role in the capital accumulation process; and Immanuel Wallerstein, *Historical Capitalism* (London: Verso Press, 1983) is representative of one vision of how the global political economy shapes the nature of state power. Su-Hoon Lee, *State-Building in the Contemporary Third World* (Boulder: Westview Press, 1988), for instance, argues that Third World state formation has been profoundly influenced by industrialization and transnationalism; international conflict, though discussed at some length, is viewed as derivative of these more primary causal forces. See Peter Evans, "Predatory,

Developmental, and Other Apparatuses: A Comparative Political Economy Perspective on the Third World State," *Sociological Forum* 4 (1989): 561–87, for a good overview of past approaches to Third World state formation.

12. Samuel Huntington, *Political Order in Changing Societies* (New Haven: Yale University Press, 1968), 122–23. Quoted from Rasler and Thompson, *War and Statemaking*, 2.

13. Joel Migdal, *Strong Societies and Weak States* (Princeton: Princeton University Press, 1988), xvii, n. 6.

14. Marwick, *War and Social Change*, in an extension and test of Stanislav Andreski, *Military Organization and Society* (New York: Routledge and Kegan Paul, 1954), argues that the effects of war are a direct function of the proportion of society that is mobilized for war. This book contrasts decidedly with Andreski's approach when I argue that the direction is highly dependent on the objectives of governmental officials and prewar preparation state-society relations.

15. Tilly, "War Making and State Making as Organized Crime," 181.

16. Huntington, *The Common Defense* (New York: Columbia University Press, 1961), 1.

17. Among political scientists the former has received much more attention than the latter. Jack Levy, "Domestic Politics and War," *Journal of Interdisciplinary History* 18 (Spring 1988): 653, in a review of the literature on the domestic foundations of war, writes that "it is difficult to read both the theoretical literature in political science on the causes of war and historians' case studies of the origins of particular wars without being struck by the difference in their respective evaluation of the importance of domestic political factors." Much the same can be said of the domestic foundations of security mobilization. Although theoretically oriented political scientists have failed to highlight the friction that ensues between the state and societal actors for control over security-related inputs, numerous historical accounts and many case studies and overviews of the evolution of the U.S. national security doctrine have incorporated the role of state-society relations. For specific cases, see Howard, *War in European History*; Milward, *War, Economy, and Society*; McNeill, *Pursuit of Power*, and John Godfrey, *French Capitalism at War* (New York: St. Martin's Press, 1987). For the American case, see John Lewis Gaddis, *Strategies of Containment* (New York: Oxford University Press, 1982); and Arthur Stein, "Strategy as Politics, Politics as Strategy: Domestic Debates, Statecraft, and Star Wars," in R. Kolkowicz, ed., *The Logic of Nuclear Terror* (Boston: Unwin and Hyman, 1987), 186–210. The importance of state-society relations on the U.S. security doctrine is underscored by Truman's decision to rely on nuclear weapons for the U.S. deterrent force. The decision to embrace a capital-intensive security policy was motivated as much by the administration's fear that continued conscription would necessitate raising taxes and thus challenge its political popularity as it was by the Soviet Union's security posture. See Robert Pollard, *Economic Security and the Origins of the Cold War, 1945–1950* (New York: Columbia University Press, 1985), 228–30. Gaddis, in concluding his study of U.S. postwar security policy, argues that "the economic orientations of particular administrations, defined in the light of domestic priorities, do have profound influences on na-

tional security policy." *Strategies of Containment*, 356. Such observations reinforce the importance of recognizing the state as situated in, constrained by, and pursuing its objectives in both the international and domestic spheres simultaneously. Although these studies are not implicitly concerned with theorizing about the nature of these constraints, they are *assumed* to exist and are addressed where deemed appropriate.

18. See Otto Hintze, "Military Organization and the Organization of the State"; Skocpol, "Bringing the State Back In"; Fred Halliday, "State and Society in International Relations: A Second Agenda," *Millennium* 16 (1987): 221; Robert Putnam, "Diplomacy and Domestic Politics," *International Organization* 42 (Summer 1988): 427–60; and Michael Mastanduno, David Lake, and G. John Ikenberry, "Towards a Realist Theory of State Action," *International Studies Quarterly* 33 (Winter 1989): 457–74. Also see Stephen David's concept of "omnibalancing," which recognizes that Third World leaders balance domestic and foreign threats. "Explaining Third World Alignments," *World Politics* 43 (January 1991): 233–56.

19. Lawrence Freedman, *The Price of Peace: Living With the Nuclear Dilemma* (New York: Harry Holt and Company, 1986), 7.

20. The security literature has been relatively inattentive to constraints on governmental action. See Joseph Nye and Sean Lynn-Jones, "International Security Studies: A Report of a Conference on the State of the Field," *International Security* 12 (Spring 1988): 24. Notable exceptions are offered by A. F. K. Organski and Jacek Kugler, *The War Ledger* (Chicago: University of Chicago Press, 1980): Alan Lamborn, "Power and the Politics of Extraction," *International Studies Quarterly* 27 (1983): 125–46; and Jacek Kugler and William Domke, "Comparing the Strength of Nations" *Comparative Political Studies* 19 (April 1986): 36–39.

21. Michael Barnett, "High Politics is Low Politics: The Domestic and Systemic Sources of Israeli Security Policy, 1967–1977," *World Politics* 42 (July 1990): 529–62.

22. In *Theory of International Politics* (New York: Addison-Wesley, 1979), Waltz concedes that societal variables shape the state's military potential, but he downplays the importance of this insight. Richard Ashley's (1981) distinction between practical and technical realists is useful here. "Political Realism and Human Interests," *International Studies Quarterly* 25 (June 1981): 204–36. Whereas "technical" realists such as Waltz have failed to adequately incorporate state-society relations, many "practical" realists, have concerned themselves with the societal dimension, notably Klaus Knorr, *The War Potential of Nations* (Princeton: Princeton University Press, 1956) and *Power and Wealth: The Political Economy of International Power* (New York: Basic Books, 1973); Klaus Knorr and Frank Traeger, eds., *Economic Issues and National Security* (Lawrence: University Press of Kansas, 1977); and Hans Morgenthau, *Politics Among Nations*, 5th ed. (New York: Alfred A. Knopf, 1978). For instance, on page 1 Samuel Huntington began his classic *The Common Defense*, with the following note: "The most distinctive, the most fascinating, and the most troublesome aspect of military policy its Janus-like quality. Indeed, military policy not only

faces in two directions, it lives in two worlds. One is international politics, the world of balance of power. . . . The other world is domestic politics, the world of interest groups. . . . The currency here is the resources of society." Despite the welcome attention given by "practical" realists to the societal bases of the state's military policy, they have not put forward any coherent framework for understanding the societal constraints on security mobilization. Organski and Kugler, *The War Ledger*, develops a systematic treatment of the state's relationship to society and war-fighting capacity; however, the approach fails to adequately account for the multiple objectives of government officials and to specify the exact nature of the societal constraints.

The economic nationalist tendency to construct an autonomous state is well-represented by Stephen Krasner, *Defending the National Interest* (Princeton: Princeton University Press, 1978); Jacob Viner, "Power versus Plenty as Objectives of Foreign Policy in the Seventeenth and Eighteenth Centuries," *World Politics* 1 (October 1948): 1–29; E. H. Carr, *The Twenty Years Crisis, 1919–1939* (New York: Harper & Row, 1964); Robert Gilpin, *The Political Economy of International Relations* (Princeton: Princeton University Press, 1987); and Paul Kennedy, *The Rise and Decline of the Great Powers* (New York: Random House, 1987). Finally, most quantitative approaches to international conflict also posit an autonomous state. For example, in the Correlates of War project, the state's power in the international system is a composite of the country's demographic, military, and industrial features. See J. David Singer, Stuart Bremer, and John Stuckey, "Capability Distribution, Uncertainty, and Major Power War, 1820–1965," in J. David Singer et al., eds., *Explaining War* (Beverly Hills: Sage Press, 1979), 159–88. Unquestioned is whether the state has access to these resources or how these resources are to be mobilized in the event of international conflict.

23. Ernest Mandel, *The Meaning of the Second World War* (London: New Left Books, 1986). Two additional traditions do investigate the domestic foundations of the state's security policy. The first examines how defense spending is both constrained by the government's other budgetary priorities, namely the trade-off between "guns and butter," and affected by interest groups coalescing around defense because of economic motivations that result in a "military industrial complex" and an "iron triangle." See Emile Beniot, *Growth and Defense in Developing Countries* (Lexington, Mass.: Lexington Books, 1973); Alex Mintz, "The Military-Industrial Complex: American Concepts and Israeli Realities," *Journal of Conflict Resolution* 29 (1985): 623–39; and Gordon Adams, *The Iron Triangle: The Politics of Defense Contracting* (New York: Council on Economic Priorities, 1981), respectively. Although at times this literature does identify instances wherein these domestic pressures have influenced the state's strategic policy, its principal purpose and concern is to document the societal demand for defense spending, and not so much the frictions that arise between the state and various societal actors over control of security-related resources.

24. For broad overviews of Marxist approaches to international conflict and military strategy see Bernard Semmel, *Marxism and the Science of War* (New York: Oxford University Press, 1981); and Sigmund Neumann and Mark von Hagen, "Engels and Marx on Revolution, War, and Army in Society," in Peter Paret, ed., *The Makers of Modern Strategy* (Princeton: Princeton University

Press, 1986), 262–80. More generally, Marxist writing is distinguished for its tendency to view defense spending as derivative of the needs of domestic capitalism. See, for instance, Rosa Luxemburg, *The Accumulation of Capital* (New York: Routledge and Kegan Paul, 1963), 454–67; Nikolai Bukharin, *Imperialism and the World Economy* (New York: Monthly Review Press, 1972); Paul Baran and Paul Sweezy, *Monopoly Capitalism* (New York: Monthly Review Press, 1966); and Michael Kidron, *Western Capitalism Since the War* (London: Weidenfeld and Nicolson, 1968).

25. Although neo-Marxist theories of the state have rid themselves of these quasi-instrumentalist views, such wisdom has yet to penetrate Marxist approaches to international conflict. Neo-Marxism's understandings of the state's security policy could be advanced if informed by these wider debates on the state. Chris Dandeker, "Warfare, Planning, and Economic Relations," *Economy and Society* 12 (February 1983): 109–10, is instructive here, as he recognizes that state managers have their own interests, separate from that of, and possibly antagonistic toward, the dominant class and the maintenance of capitalism, and that such divisions may come to the fore during times of war. Kaldor, *Warfare and Capitalism*, 275, notes that although warfare may be an extension and necessary feature of capitalism, there are limits to what the working class will accept for capitalism's misadventures. Finally, MacKenzie, "Militarism and Socialist Theory," and E. P. Thompson, "Introduction," in E. P. Thompson et al., eds., *Exterminism and the Cold War* (London: New Left Books, 1982), 20–21, evoke similar concerns with Marxist approaches of militarism. MacKenzie notes that military expenditures can have dysfunctional consequences for capitalism, and E. P. Thompson argues that Marxist theory is unable to account for the importance of national security because it overemphasizes economic interests, fails to incorporate the significance of security interests and technologies, and ignores how socialist states have also contributed to the international system's militarized condition.

26. Because my goal is to construct a framework for investigation, not to posit a set of lawlike hypotheses and relationships, this project adopts the methods and aims of historical sociology. For good overviews, see Daniel Chirot, "Introduction: Thematic Controversies and New Developments in the Uses of Historical Material by Sociologists," *Social Forces* 55 (1976): 232–41; and Victoria Bonnell, "The Uses of Theory, Concepts, and Comparisons in Historical Sociology," *Comparative Studies in Society and History* 22 (1980): 156–73; Philip Abrams, *Historical Sociology* (Ithaca: Cornell University Press, 1982); and Theda Skocpol, ed., *Vision and Method in Historical Sociology* (New York: Cambridge University Press, 1984). Historical sociology selects and privileges certain events owing to a theoretical framework and attempts "to *theorize* history, to achieve a reasoned interpretation of the design of long-term historical change and to do so on the basis of arguments which integrate general social theory and detailed historical documentation rather than asserting the claims of either against the other." Abrams, *Historical Sociology*, 148. Much like historical sociology selects certain historical material according to the theoretical framework and concepts, one culls history discerningly, with an eye to those events appropriate to the question at hand. The object here is to discern those structural

features that both enable and constrain the government's policies. Therefore, the social structure represents the agents' causal powers, which "exist necessarily by virtue of the nature of the objects which possess them, it is contingent whether they are ever activated or exercised." Andrew Sayer, *Method in the Social Science: A Realist Approach* (London: Hutchinson, 1984), 99. Also see Anthony Giddens, *The Constitution of Society* (Berkeley: University of California Press, 1984), and Abrams, *Historical Sociology*, 3.

This approach is also similar to the "historical-structural" methodology of Enrique Cardoso and Enzo Falleto's, *Dependency and Development in Latin America* (Berkeley: University of California Press, 1979), and the "structured, focused comparison" of Alexander George and Timothy McKeown, "Case Studies and Theories of Organizational Decision Making," in R. Coulam and R. Smith, eds., *Advances in Informational Processing in Organizations, Research on Public Organizations*, vol. 2 (Greenwich: JAI Press, 1985). The comparison is structured because by "designing the study, defines and standardizes the data requirements of the case studies. This is accomplished by formulating theoretically relevant general questions to guide the examination of each case." It is focused "insofar as the researcher deals selectively with only those aspects of each case that are believed to be relevant to the research objects." George and McKeown, "Case Studies and Theories," 41.

27. Charles Ragin, *The Comparative Method* (Berekely: University of California Press, 1985), 24. Reminiscent of Mills's notion of "chemical causation," he refers to this as "causal complexity" (p. 25), wherein the produced change results from the intersection of the specific properties of the context.

28. Skocpol, *States and Social Revolutions*, 30.

29. See Alvin Z. Rubenstein, *Red Star on the Nile: The Soviet-Egyptian Influence Relationship Since the June War* (Princeton: Princeton University Press, 1977); Galal Amin, "External Factors in the Reorientation of Egypt's Economic Policy," in M. Kerr and E. S. Yassin, eds., *Rich and Poor States in the Middle East* (Boulder: Westview Press, 1982), 285–315; Raimo Vayrynen and Thomas Ohlson, "Egypt: Arms Production in a Transnational Context," in M. Brzoska and T. Ohlson, eds., *Arms Production in the Third World* (Philadelphia: Taylor and Francis, 1986), 105–24; and Ibrahim Karawan, "Egypt's Defense Policy," in S. Neuman, ed., *Defense Planning in Less Industrialized States* (Lexington: Lexington Books, 1984), 147–79.

30. See Stephan Walt, *The Origins of Alliances* (Ithaca: Cornell University Press, 1987); and Shibley Telhami, *Power and Leadership in International Bargaining: The Path to the Camp David Accords* (New York: Columbia University Press, 1990).

31. The domestic sources of Egypt's alliance behavior are more fully developed in Michael Barnett and Jack Levy, "Domestic Sources of Alliances and Alignments," *International Organization* 45 (Summer 1991): 369–95.

32. See Gehad Auda, "The State of Political Control: The Case of Nasser, 1960–1967," *The Arab Journal of the Social Sciences* 2 (April 1987): 95–111; Nazih Ayubi, *Bureaucracy and Politics in Contemporary Egypt* (London: Ithica Press, 1980); Raymond Baker, *Egypt's Uncertain Revolution Under Nasser and Sadat* (Cambridge: Harvard University Press, 1978); R. H. Dekmejian, *Egypt*

Under Nasir: A Study in Political Dynamics (Albany: State University of New York Press, 1971); Migdal, *Strong Societies and Weak States*; P. J. Vatikiotis, *Nasser and His Generation* (New York: St. Martin's Press, 1978); and Amos Perlmutter, *Egypt: The Praetorian State* (New Brunswick: Transaction Books, 1974) emphasize the power-seeking behavior of Nasir and Sadat. For those that emphasize the domestic political economy, see Trimberger, *Revolution from Above*; Anwar Abdel-Malek, *Egypt: Military Society* (New York: Random House, 1968); Mark Cooper, *The Transformation of Egypt* (Baltimore: Johns Hopkins University Press, 1982); and John Waterbury, *The Egypt of Nasser and Sadat* (Princeton: Princeton University Press, 1983), and Waterbury, "The 'Soft State' and the Open Door: Egypt's Experience with Economic Liberalization, 1974–84," *Comparative Politics* 18 (October 1985): 65–83; Raymond Hinnebusch, *Egyptian Politics Under Sadat: The Post-Populist Development of an Authoritarian State* (New York: Cambridge University Press, 1985); Robert Bianchi, *Unruly Corporatism: Associational Life in Twentieth-Century Egypt* (New York: Oxford University Press, 1989); and Hani Shukrallah, "Political Crisis/ Conflict in Post-1967 Egypt," in C. Tripp and R. Owen, eds., *Egypt Under Mubarak* (New York: Routledge, 1989), 53–102. Many are also quick to note the importance of Egypt's oriental despotic history and the historical centrality of the state owing to its control by the Nile River's rhythms. See Abdel Monem Said, "Nation State and Transnational Society: The Case of Egypt" (Paper presented at the Conference on Dynamics of States and Societies in the Middle East, Cairo, 1989), for a brief but good discussion of the oriental despotism tradition in Egyptian historiography. This characterization has been challenged by many scholars on the grounds that British colonialism was a more important factor in explaining the development of the contemporary Egyptian state. See Ellis Goldberg, *Tinker, Tailor, Textile Worker* (Berkeley: University of California Press, 1986), 58. Moreover, this approach cannot account for the tremendous changes that have occurred in Egyptian state power over the last four decades.

33. It is worth noting that the relative absence of conflict in explaining Egyptian state formation is duplicated in much of the literature on Arab state formation more generally. For instance, war is conspicuous only by virtue of its absence in an otherwise provocative collection of essays on the Arab state. Giacomo Luciani, ed., *The Arab State* (Berkeley: University of California Press, 1990).

34. For the state's authoritarian nature, see Perlmutter, *Egypt: Praetorian Society*; and Vatikiotis, *Nasser and His Generation*. For its autonomy from private economic elites, see Abdel-Malek, *Egypt: Military Society*. For economic-oriented analyses, see Waterbury, *The Egypt of Nasser and Sadat*, and "The 'Soft State.'" For a state-structural analysis, see Migdal, *Strong Societies and Weak States*.

35. In general, when Israel does reemerge into normality, it tends to be classified as a Western, semideveloped country, owing to its political culture, socialization patterns, educational system, the origins of the political elite, its democratic form of governance, and selected economic indicators. Attention, then, is directed toward many of those same indicators advanced by modernization theo-

rists to classify and typologize developed versus developing countries. The conclusion is that, if typologized at all, Israel is best classified with other advanced, Western capitalist democracies. Recognize, however, that the reliance on descriptive indicators for ascertaining Israel's "status" embodies a series of theoretical assumptions that have been heavily criticized in the modernization literature.

36. See S. N. Eisenstadt, *The Transformation of Israeli Society: An Essay in Interpretation* (London: Weidenfeld and Nicolson, 1985), 152.

37. Alex Rubner, *The Economy of Israel: A Critical Account of the First Ten Years* (London: Frank Cass, 1960), 230–34.

38. A growing number of scholars of Israel have attempted to situate its political and economic development within a broader theoretical context. See, for example, Eisenstadt, *The Transformation of Israeli Society*; Yoram Peri, *Between Ballots and Bullets: Israeli Military in Politics* (New York: Cambridge University Press, 1983), 3–6; Joel Migdal, *Strong Societies and Weak States*; Migdal, "The Crystallization of State and Struggles Over Rulemaking: Israel in Comparative Perspective," in B. Kimmering, ed., *The Israeli State and Society: Boundaries and Frontiers* (Albany: State University of New York, 1989), 1–27; and Michael Shalev, *Labour and the Political Economy in Israel* (New York: Oxford University Press, 1991).

39. Avner Yaniv, *Deterrence Without the Bomb: The Politics of Israeli Strategy* (Lexington: Lexington Books, 1987).

40. Michael Mandelbaum, *The Fate of Nations: The Search for National Security in the Nineteenth and Twentieth Centuries* (New York: Cambridge University Press, 1988), 272.

41. Walt, *The Origins of Alliances*.

42. Peter Medding, *Mapai In Israel: Political Organization and Government in a New Society* (New York: Cambridge University Press, 1972); Don Peretz, *Government and Politics in Israel* (Boulder: Westview Press, 1981); Eisenstadt, *The Transformation of Israeli Society*; Mitchell Cohen, *Zion and State: Nation, Class, and the Shaping of Modern Israel* (London: Basil Blackwell, 1987); Baruch Kimmerling, "Boundaries and Frontiers of the Israeli Control System: Analytical Conclusions," in B. Kimmerling, ed., *The Israeli State and Society* (Albany: New York University Press, 1989), 265–84; and Michael Shalev, *Labour and the Political Economy in Israel*.

43. Avishai Ehrlich, "Israel: Conflict, War, and Social Change," in M. Shaw and C. Creighton, eds., *The Sociology of War and Peace* (New York: Sheridan House, 1987), 121–42, provides an interesting discussion of why most Israeli scholars have failed to include war in their analyses. He argues that it is partly owing to the dominant sociological traditions in Israel, which have tended to adopt Parsonian/Eistenstadtian frameworks emphasizing the role of internal dynamics to the exclusion of international forces. Baruch Kimmerling, however, has written extensively on the subject of war and the Israeli state, but not directly on the relationship between war and state power. See "Determination of the Boundaries and Frameworks of Conscription: Two Dimensions of Civil-Military Relations in Israel," *Studies in Comparative International Development* 14 (Spring 1979): 22–41; *Zionism and Economy* (Cambridge, Mass.:

Schenkman, 1983); *Zionism and Territory* (Berkeley: Institute of International Studies, 1983); and "Making Conflict a Routine: Cumulative Effects of the Arab-Jewish Conflict Upon Israeli Society," in M. Lissak, ed., *Israeli Society and Its Defense Establishment* (London: Frank Cass, 1984).

Chapter Two
The Framework

1. A common empirical referent for such phenomenon is the "defense burden," which indicates the amount of societal resources channelled toward national security. Although there are numerous ways to operationalize this concept, they share a common attempt to capture the amount of available and potential resources diverted to national security expenditures and are therefore unavailable for other types of domestic spending. See Eitan Berglas, "Defense and Economy," in Y. Ben-Porath, ed., *The Israeli Economy* (Cambridge: Harvard University Press, 1986), 173–75. Consequently, the "defense burden" presupposes what I want to explain, for it aspires to evaluate the security burden shouldered by society and, therefore, either assumes that or limits its consideration to how governments have met their security requirements by imposing its costs on society. Governments, however, have a variety of means for meeting their national security needs, most notably the expansion of the governmental debt that must be settled by future generations and the construction of strategic alliances, neither of which are reflected by such indicators as the "defense burden."

2. A second, possible, way of determining the motivation for these security processes is by the examining the types of actions governments undertake in accord with their self-understandings. For instance, those governments that believe there is substantial urgency from an internal threat will emphasize those instruments most appropriate for counterinsurgency warfare, rather than the creation of self-sufficiency in such military hardware as planes that are more directly useful for interstate conflict. Without denying that the instruments of coercion can have both external and internal functions, qualitatively different military procedures exist for meeting the foreign threat as opposed to countering domestic opposition and civil strife.

3. See Jack Levy, "The Diversionary Theory of War," in M. Midlarsky, ed., *The Handbook of War Studies* (Boston: Unwin Hyman, 1989).

4. I have bracketed two sorts of concerns from my discussion of war preparation. The first is how the nature of the external threat translates into different kinds of war preparation strategies. Whether the government faces a war of attrition or a war of annihilation undoubtedly affects what sorts of strategies it pursues, as it lengthens or shortens the shadow of the future. The level of physical hostilities is indirectly incorporated by changes in defense expenditures, for it can be assumed that a state facing possible extinction channels more resources toward defense than a state that does not. I have also bracketed how geostrategic considerations particular to each country shape the government's war preparation strategies. For instance, Israeli military doctrine holds that because of Israel's limited geographical size and manpower pool it can ill afford to fight either

a prolonged war or one waged on its territory; therefore, Israel has emphasized air and technological superiority over its Arab enemies. Although these geostrategic factors shape the government's military preparations, they are not given any attention in this chapter and mentioned only where most relevant in the Israeli and Egyptian cases. This denigration of geostrategic concerns follows not only from the practical necessity of limiting the scope of the study but also from a belief that this aspect of the government's war preparation strategies has received considerable attention; moreover, the strategies are shaped by not only these narrow strategic considerations but also the socioeconomic constraints on its actions.

5. This assumption incorporates neo-Marxists, neo-liberals, and neo-Weberians. See Fred Block, "The Ruling Class Does Not Rule"; Charles Lindblom, *Politics and Markets* (New York: Basic Books, 1977); and Frank Parkin, *Marxism and Class Theory*, respectively.

6. See Lindblom, *Politics and Markets*, for the former; Bianchi, *Unruly Corporatism*, and Hinnebusch, *Egyptian Politics Under Sadat*, for the latter.

7. For good overviews of economic nationalism and its policy implications, see Gilpin, *Political Economy of International Relations*; Carr, *The Twenty Years Crisis*; Viner, "Power versus Plenty"; and R. B. J. Jones, *Conflict and Control in the World Economy* (New York: Humanities Press, 1986), chaps. 3 and 6.

8. Ernst Haas, *When Knowledge is Power* (Berkeley: University of California Press, 1990), 2–3, 29.

9. Skocpol, *States and Social Revolutions*, 29.

10. Kocka, *Facing Total War*, 143.

11. Shahrom Chubin and Charles Tripp, *Iran and Iraq at War* (London: I. B. Tauris and Co., 1988), 37.

12. Kocka, *Facing Total War*, 151.

13. I explore fully the nature of the state's relative autonomy later in this chapter.

14. Michael Mann, "The Autonomous Power of the State: Its Origins, Mechanisms, and Results," *European Journal of Sociology* 25 (1984): 189.

15. See, for instance, Isaac, *Power and Marxist Theory*, 178–84; and David Held and Joel Krieger, "Accumulation, Legitimation, and the State: The Ideas of Claus Offe and Jurgen Habermas," in David Held et al., eds., *States and Societies* (New York: New York University Press, 1983), 487–97.

16. Stein, *The Nation at War*, 12, argues that wartime extraction differs from peacetime extraction in two ways. First, the "process entails the extraction of resources not normally controlled by the government." Second, the purpose of extraction, and hence the benefit to individuals, is clearly specified. Thus, the tax is more visible. Margaret Levi, *Of Rule and Revenue*, chap. 3, adds that individuals might be more willing to give financially during times of war because this public good cannot easily be apportioned unevenly to different societal groups.

17. An additional factor in explaining the state's extraction policies is the degree of the economy's monetization. Most Third World finance ministers would readily agree that their jobs are made exceedingly difficult by the basic fact that

much of the economy does not pass through markets, and therefore, cannot be easily monitored. Direct taxes, for instance, became feasible only after the economy was heavily monetized. See Tilly, *Coercion, Capital, and European States*, 87–90, for a good discussion on the relationship between the monetization of the economy and the likely types of exctractive policies that would be used by the state.

18. Douglass North and Robert Thomas, *The Rise of the Western World* (New York: Norton, 1973), 99.

19. Phyllis Deane, "War and Industrialization," in J. M. Winter, ed., *War and Economic Development* (Cambridge: Cambridge University Press, 1975), 97.

20. Herbert Wulf, "Developing Countries," in N. Ball and M. Leitenberg, eds., *Structure of Defense Industries: An International Survey* (New York: St. Martin's Press, 1983), 310–43, and "Arms Production in the Third World: An Overview," in M. Brzoska and T. Ohlson, eds., *Arms Production in the Third World* (Philadelphia: Talyor and Francis, 1985), 7–33; and Stephanie Neuman, "International Stratification and Third World Military Industries," *International Organization* 38 (Winter 1984): 167–97. Although military factories in the Third World often represent a budgetary drain, this may be acceptable if these state-owned enterprises meet other state objectives, e.g. employment or national security. This reflects the politically motivated character of state intervention. See M. Brzoska and T. Ohlson, "Arms Production in the Third World," in M. Brzoska and T. Ohlson, *Arms Production in the Third World*, 21–22. This partially accounts for the tremendous rise in Third World arms exports over the past decade; many Third World states attempt to expand the export market to improve the economies of scale.

21. Wulf, "Developing Countries," 336.

22. Although major international conflicts have certainly been fought successfully without using the period's most advanced weaponry, most notably the North Vietnamese campaign against the United States and most recently Chad's conflict with Libya, such instances are rare. The possibility for low-technology warfare has led some scholars to argue for "self-reliant defense," which is premised on mass mobilization. See Herbert Wulf, "Dependent Militarism in the Periphery and Possible Alternative Concepts," in S. Neuman and R. Harkavy, eds., *Arms Transfers in the Modern World* (New York: Praeger Press, 1979), 259; and Hans Park and Kyung Park, "Ideology and Security: Self-Reliance in China and North Korea," in E. Azar and C. Moon, eds., *National Security in the Third World* (Hants, Eng.: Edward Elger Publishers, 1988), 102–35. This sort of military strategy was thrust upon Iranian military commanders as a result of Iran's strategic isolation in the interstate system.

23. See Neuman, "International Stratification," 185. Alan Milward's excellent *War, Economy, and Society*, a study of the Great Powers' economic policy during World War Two, is also representative of this problem. The tendency here is to take a state-centered approach to the neglect of the societal determinants of the state's production policy. Although some studies acknowledge that the state must negotiate with private actors to meet the state's production targets, these studies tend to be primarily historical, and rarely theoretical, in

nature. For instance, in *French Capitalism at War*, Godfrey provides a detailed analysis of the negotiations that occurred between French bureaucrats and French industrialists during World War One, but he makes little attempt to generalize from the French experience.

24. See Mandel, *The Meaning of the Second World War*, and Neuman, "International Stratification," respectively.

25. Throughout much of the Third World the country's arms industries are under the control of the state. This undoubtedly affects its need to negotiate with societal actors to produce in accordance with the state's military objectives. However, even those states that have placed arms production under the state's roof have typically allowed some room for private sector participation.

26. See Charles Tilly, "Reflections on the History of European Statemaking," in C. Tilly, *Formation of the National States in Western Europe* (Princeton: Princeton University Press, 1975), 3–83; Ron Ayres, "Arms Production as a Form of Import-Substituting Industrialization," *World Development* 11 (1983): 813–23; and Alex Mintz, "The Military Industrial Complex."

27. David Brinkley, *Washington Goes to War* (New York: Alfred A. Knopf, 1988), 56.

28. There are certainly a host of other variables that affect the government's conscription policy, among which are the societal attitude toward warfare. This is particularly evident with the Enlightenment, which both established that scholarship and intellectual pursuits were noble professions and challenged the privileged and "enlightened" status of warfare in society. See Andre Corvisier, *Armies and Societies in Europe, 1494–1789* (Bloomington: Indiana University Press, 1979), 15–16. In addition, many theorists have applied forms of exchange theory to the state's enlistment policy; they prefer to see it as trading protection and economic benefits for military service. This approach is evident in F. C. Lane, "The Economic Meaning of War and Protection," in F. C. Lane, ed., *Profits from Power* (Albany: State University of New York Press, 1979), and Tilly's, "War Making and State Making," "protection racket" perspective of Western European conscription, and Amii Omora-Otunnu's, *Politics and the Military in Uganda, 1890–1985* (New York: St. Martin's Press, 1987), description of African military service and its relationship to patron-client relations.

29. Anderson, *Lineages of the Absolutist State*, 31. See Tilly, *Coercion, Capital, and European State*, 76–84, and Janice Thomson, "State Practices, International Norms, and the Decline of Mercenarism," *International Studies Quarterly* 34 (March 1990): 23–48, for a good discussion of mercenarism and its decline.

30. Giddens, *The Nation-State and Violence*, 56.

31. See Michael Walzer, "Political Alienation and Military Service, in *Obligations: Essays on Disobedience* (Cambridge: Harvard University Press, 1970). Even before the development of the modern nation-state, those European principalities that had a strong basis in society were able to enlist their populations for defense. Herman Beukema, "The Social and Political Aspects of Conscription: Europe's Experience," in M. Anderson, ed., *The Military Draft* (Stanford: Hoover Press, 1982), 482, writes: "The thirteenth century furnishes a short-lived example of conscription in the north Italian communes, which for a brief

period approached democracy in their social and political organization. Internecine strife led to the substitution of the mercenary, the professional soldier for the less efficient citizen levy. With the collapse of democracy went its democratic counterpart, universal conscription."

32. Giddens, *The Nation-State and Violence*, 233–34.

33. There is a vast literature on the role of the military in developing countries. The bulk of these studies, however, are concerned with civil-military relations, military intervention, and the propensity for praetorian politics. It is significant that these studies direct little attention to the composition of the military, yet they seem a natural avenue of inquiry given the generally "politicized" nature of military rule and the tendency to see the military (and the state) as susceptible to problems of legitimation. These problems are largely due to the postcolonial character of these Third World states. Not only is the state's lack of legitimacy attributable to its colonial heritage, but also most colonial powers built local armies with a strong ethnic imbalance so that they would be responsive to their directives. Consequently, the colonial power generally balked at arming those elements of society that might use such knowledge and arms against them. See Morris Janowitz, *Military Institutions and Coercion in Developing Societies* (Chicago: University of Chicago Press, 1977), 127–30. For example, the British resisted conscripting and training members of the Yishuv in Palestine to fight Nazi Germany during World War Two, while the French used the minority Alawite population in Syria during the 1930s and 1940s to contain nationalist forces. In general, scholars of Third World militaries tend to overlook the relationship between colonialism, the Third World state's legitimacy, and conscription strategies. See Alexander Wendt and Michael Barnett, "Systemic Sources of Third World Militarization," 1991, manuscript.

34. For example, Saadam Hussein of Iraq attempted to instill a sense of nationality and increase the legitimacy of the state to add to his mobilization potential in the war against Iran. Chubin and Tripp, *Iran and Iraq at War*, 94. The importance of the state's legitimacy is not confined to the capitalist context but is also noted in socialist states. When discussing the possibility of mass mobilization in China and North Korea, Park and Park, "Ideology and Self-Reliance," 109, contend that "mass mobilization here is made possible by political indoctrination of the people with measures of ideological education."

35. Capitalism also effectively challenged the military's monopoly on prestige and status, when creating and expanding productive and material wealth emerged as the site of society's most coveted rewards: during "the great economic expansion of the late seventeenth and eighteenth centuries, money joined land as a force to turn young gentlemen away from military preoccupations." Corvisier, *Armies and Societies*, 15–16. Prestige and rewards were generated by these new capitalist enterprises. Alexis de Tocqueville wrote that "the military men [in capitalism] fall to the lowest rank of public servants; they are little esteemed and no longer understood. The reverse of what takes place in aristocratic ages then occurs: the men who enter the army are no longer those of the highest, but of the lowest rank. Military ambition is only indulged in when no other is possible." "On War, Society, and Military," in L. Bramson and G. Goethals, eds., *War: Studies from Psychology, Sociology, and Anthropology*

(New York: Basic Books, 1964), 323. For de Tocqueville, because the army has a lesser status in capitalist society, it is susceptible to restlessness and, therefore, inherently war-prone.

36. Howard, *War In European History*, 69. During English medieval history "the traditional inclination was to keep at home the richest and most skilled men for the defense of England and to send abroad the troops consisting of men whom the country wished to get rid of. On the other hand, many militiamen who were well off chose to avoid service by hiring substitutes from the very lowest levels of men." Corvisier, *Armies and Societies in Europe*, 35.

37. Soviet conscription policy resembles that of many capitalist societies in two respects. First, the linkage between military service and citizenship is quite explicit. Ellen Jones, *Red Army and Society* (Boston: Allen and Unwin, 1985), 52. Second, although military service is required of all male citizens, those whose fathers have a higher status in society have a greater likelihood of obtaining deferments or exemptions. These exclusions are often granted on the basis of educational criteria. William Zimmerman and Michael Bernbaum, "Regime Goals, Working the System, and Soviet Military Manpower Policy" (Paper presented at the 1988 meetings of the American Political Science Association), Atlanta, September.

38. Levi, *Of Rule and Revenue*, 16, uses similar language to discuss revenue-maximizing strategies of rulers; she argues that "within the limits of the constraints upon them, they will design revenue production policies that maximize revenues to the state."

39. G. John Ikenberry, "Conclusion: An Institutional Approach to American Foreign Economic Policy," *International Organization* 42 (Winter 1988): 226–28.

40. Levi argues that leaders with high discount rates, who are therefore uncertain about the future, "will encourage agents to extract all there is from constituents." *Of Rule and Revenue*, 33. This, she suggests, is particularly so during times of war. This impliies that as the threat of extinction increases, one should find increased predatory behavior among rulers (everything else being equal). The analysis offered here suggests that this may not be completely accurate for two reasons. First, rather than hasten their demise through predatory behavior, rulers are likely to attempt to maintain their rule through various coalition-building, coopting, and crushing practices. Only when they are most convinced that such strategies are ineffective are they likely to be as predatory as she suggests, and by then it might be too late. Yet it is also the case that a state facing extinction probably benefits from greater societal cohesion; therefore, the state finds that its bargaining power, and its ability to extract, would increase. Second, Levi fails to incorporate how international sources of aid represent an additional source of revenue that might lengthen the ruler's domestic shadow.

41. G. John Ikenberry, *Reasons of State* (Ithaca: Cornell University Press, 1988), 40.

42. With regard to the state's intervention in the economy, the general oft-made assumption is that such movements automatically elicit strong opposition from domestic capital. The degree to which state intervention directly chal-

lenges the dominant class (in this or any situation), however, needs to be examined and cannot be assumed a priori. There are a number of instances in which state intervention (and, indeed, nationalization) complements the domestic capital's interests, as the state's increased control over production may weaken foreign capital, or serve the objectives of the capitalist class. See Rueschemeyer and Evans, "The State and Economic Transformation."

43. Although it is theoretically conceivable, I know of no instance during wartime in which the state moved, for instance, from a draft to a volunteer army to increase the societal manpower contribution.

44. In "A Realist Theory of State Action," Mastanduno et al. argue that states can either engage in mobilization, by which they mean the investment in economic growth as a source of future revenue and material assets, or extraction, by which they equate with the immediate transfer of societal resources to government agents. Their discussion shares some common features, but does not duplicate, the distinction offered here. In addition to the underlying societal distribution of power, I suggest in the following discussion that an additional consideration involves the ideological orientations and beliefs of state managers concerning the proper organizing economic principles for increasing the societal contribution to the war effort.

45. Howard, *War in European History*, 22.

46. I focus on the role of alliances in an international strategy. Conceivably, however, an international strategy might involve policies such as territorial expansion, although this was probably more prevalent in the pre-"trading era" than before. See Richard Rosecrance, *The Rise of the Trading State: Commerce and Conqest in the Modern World* (New York: Basic Books, 1986). See also David Lake, "The State and Grand Strategy" (Paper presented at the 1990 American Political Science annual meetings), San Francisco, September.

47. Seth Carus, "Defense Planning in Iraq," in S. Neuman, ed., *Defense Planning in Less-Industrialized Countries: The Middle East and South Asia* (Lexington: Lexington Books, 1984), 30–31.

48. The state can also adopt a technological solution to capitalize on either a lack of manpower or a reluctance to mobilize more troops than is politically and economically desirable. See Wendt and Barnett, "The Systemic Sources of Third World Militarization"; and Barry Posen, *The Sources of Military Doctrine* (Ithaca: Cornell University Press, 1985).

49. Mastanduno et al., "A Realist Theory of State Action."

50. Even when foreign sources of manpower are available, an international strategy here represents a double-edged sword: it loosens the domestic noose, but it increases the state's reliance on foreign actors in one of its most symbolic areas of sovereignty—the monopoly of coercive force and the defense of its territorial domain. Be that as it may, such a solution may be preferred to one that either increases domestic opposition or conscripts unreliable elements.

51. Ed Azar and Chung-in Moon, "Legitimacy, Integration, and Policy Capacity: The 'Software' Side of Third World National Security," in E. Azar and C. Moon, eds., *National Security in the Third World* (Hants, Eng.: Edward Elger Publishers, 1988), 81.

52. See John Mueller, *Wars, Presidents, and Public Opinion* (New York: Wiley, 1973); and Jack Levy, "A Diversionary Theory of War."

53. See Chubin and Tripp, *Iran and Iraq at War*. The importance of propagating the state's legitimacy to mobilize greater amounts of resources is noted in both the Israeli, Avner Yaniv, "National Security and Nation-Building," *International Interactions* 11 (1984): 193–217, and the North Korean cases, Park and Park, "Ideology and Security."

54. See Charles Tilly, *As Sociology Meets History*, 112–15; Lamborn, "Power and the Politics of Extraction"; and Kocka, *Facing Total War*.

55. Tilly, *Coercion, Capital, and European States*, 28.

56. Tilly, *As Sociology Meets History*, 206.

57. Tilly, *Coercion, Capital, and European States*, 84.

58. Moreover, the methods developed for and used by the military for war, including logistics and administration, may subsequently carry over to "civilian" sectors and promote the state's control over society. This was particularly evident during the nineteenth century when the military introduced transportation and communication systems—for example, the telegraphs and railroads—that provided European armies with greater control over disperse populations and territories. See Howard, *War in European History*, 121. These newly implanted mechanisms of control then furthered the state's control over society during peacetime. Furthermore, a vast bureaucracy was established to coordinate logistics and supplies to these armies in the field. Ibid., 64. This became particularly important once citizens' rights during war were established and invading armies were no longer allowed to "live off" the land and the forced "hospitality" of the vanquished.

59. Although I treat the outcome of state-society interactions as a bargain, I do not mean to suggest that there are "open and frank" discussions between government officials and societal actors for the latter's permission for the former's actions. Similarly, Tilly, *Coercion, Capital, and European States*, 30, notes three ways in which rulers can extract societal resources: (1) coercion-intensive, where "rulers squeezed the means of war from their populations and others they conquered"; (2) capital-intensive, in which "rulers relied on compacts with capitalists—whose interests they served with care—to rent or purchase military force, and thereby warred without building vast permanent state structures"; (3) capitalized coercion, in which "rulers did some of each, but spent more of their effort than did their capital-intensive neighbors on incorporating capitalists and sources of capital directly into the structures of their states." The first two forms were more prevalent in premodern states, whereas the third variant is more common to most modern capitalist states.

60. In addition to the government's ideas about what policy might be most efficient, an additional, complementary, variable is the immediacy of the external threat. Simply put, where war is on-going, intense, and life-threatening, governments may be less likely to rely on market mechanisms and more willing to extract from their societies.

61. Tilly, "War Making and State Making," 183.

62. See Tilly, "Reflections on the History of European State-Making," and

Coercion, Capital, and European States, 30; North, *Structure and Change in Economic History*, chap. 11; and Shaw, "Introduction: War and Social Theory."

63. North, *Structure and Change in Economic History*, chap. 11. Also see Brewer, *Sinews of War*.

64. Linda Weiss, *Creating Capitalism: The State and Small Business Since 1945* (London: Basil Blackwell, 1988).

65. North, *Structure and Change in Economic History*, 205–7; P. Evans et al., "On the Road Toward a More Adequate Understanding of the State," in P. Evans et al., eds., *Bringing the State Back In* (New York: Cambridge University Press, 1985), 361–63; Ikenberry, "Conclusion: An Institutional Approach"; and Rasler and Thompson, *War and Statemaking*, 16–17.

66. North, *Structure and Change in Economic History*, chap. 11.

67. Mann, "The Autonomous Power of the State," 188.

68. This understanding of state power, then, goes beyond the decision-making abilities of institutional actors to overcome societal opposition—more than the ability of A to get B to do what B would not do otherwise. There is a problem with the behavioral perspective: power is acknowledged only through the actions of actors and "conflates the possession with the exercise of power. . . . An adequate formulation of the concept of power must recognize that power one agent exercises 'over' another agent in interaction is parasitic upon the relatively enduring powers to act that the agents possess." See Isaac, *Power and Marxist Theory*, 38.

69. Giddens, *The Nation-State and Violence*, 9. See Stephen Lukes, ed., *Power* (New York: New York University Press, 1986); and Isaac, *Power and Marxist Theory*, chap. 1, for good reviews of the concept of power.

70. This relates intimately to the state's capacity, which the editors of *Bringing the State Back In* argue "is the identification of specific organizational structures the presence (or absence) of which seems critical to the ability of the state authorities to undertake given tasks." P. Evans et al., "On the Road Toward a More Adequate Understanding of the State," 351. In this respects it parallels Weber's general understanding of the state: an organization that is responsible for governance of society, extracts resources, and retains a near monopoly of the means of coercion. See Max Weber, "Politics as a Vocation," in H. Gerth and C. W. Mills, eds., *For Max Weber* (New York: Oxford University Press, 1975), 77–80.

71. Levi, *Of Rule and Revenue*, 17.

72. Claus Offe, "Theses on the Theory of the State," *New German Critique* 6 (1975): 137–47; Lindblom, *Politics and Markets*; Parkin, *Marxism and Class Theory*; Isaac, *Power and Marxist Theory*; and Adam Przeworski and Michael Wallerstein, "The Structural Dependence of the State on Capital," *American Political Science Review* 82 (March 1988): 11–30.

73. Przeworski and Wallerstein, "Structural Dependence of the State on Capital," 11.

74. The literature on the relative autonomy of the state, and the societal and state properties that condition such autonomy, traces its heritage back to Karl Marx, *The Eighteenth Brumaire of Louis Bonaparte* (New York: International

Publishers, 1963), and has been carried forward by a number of distinctive neo-Marxist (and neo-Weberian) interpretations and applications. For various interpretations and employments of this term, see Ralph Miliband, *The State in Capitalist Society* (New York: Basic Books, 1970); Nicos Poulantzas, "The Problem of the Capitalist State," *New Left Review* 58 (1969): 67–78; Ernesto Laclau, "The Specificity of the Political: The Poulantzas-Miliband Debate," *Economy and Society* 4 (1975): 87–110; Therborn, *What Does the Ruling Class Do When It Rules?*; and Isaac, *Power and Marxist Theory*, 150–91. Although the concept of relative state autonomy has come under vigorous attack in recent years, it is beyond the purposes here either to vitiate or to defend such attacks. See Paul Hirst, "Economic Classes and Politics," in A. Hunt, ed., *Class and Class Structure* (London: Lawrence and Wisehart, 1978); Roger Benjamin and Raymond Duvall, "The Capitalist State in Context," in R. Benjamin and S. Elkin, eds., *The Democratic State* (Lawrence: University Press of Kansas, 1985); Jon Elster, *Making Sense of Marx* (New York: Cambridge University Press, 1985), chap. 7; and Nicos Mouzelis, *Politics in the Semi-Periphery* (New York: St. Martin's Press, 1986). Although these critiques present a number of convincing arguments concerning the problematic treatment and concept of relative autonomy, particularly as they revolved around Marxist aspirations to understand the function of the state in capitalist society and its relationship to the economic base, they do not undermine my attempt to isolate the societal constraints on state action.

75. Three distinct approaches to state autonomy attempt to isolate the societal constraints on the state's ability to move against dominant class interests. First, the class balance approach posits that when there is a balance of class forces, when no single class is dominant, the state may have a certain autonomy from societal forces. This approach, closely associated with Marx's writings on Bonapartist France, *The Eighteenth Brumaire*, examines how this societal balance enables the state's leaders to pursue class alliances with dominated classes, and thereby potentially construct policies that injure the long-term interests of the dominant class. Also see Leon Trotsky, *The Struggle Against Fascism in Germany* (London: Penguin Books, 1975), 263; and Nora Hamilton, *The Limits of State Autonomy* (Princeton: Princeton University Press, 1982).

The second approach examines how extraordinary environmental conditions, such as war or economic depressions, can weaken the dominant classes and provide the pretext for the state to move against the capitalist class. See Block, "The Ruling Class Does Not Rule," and "Beyond Relative Autonomy: State Managers as Historical Subjects," in R. Miliband and J. Saville, eds., *Socialist Register* (London: Merlin Press, 1980); Skocpol, *States and Social Revolutions*. As Block, "Beyond Relative Autonomy," 231, argues, "state managers are impelled to act to regulate the market both to protect society and to protect their own rule."

The third approach, by contrast, focuses on the composition and cohesion of the state apparatus and the degree to which these features facilitate the construction and implementation of policies that oppose the interests of the dominant class. See Trimberger, *Revolution From Above*, and Parkin, *Marxism and Class Theory*. Most important is that the state apparatus must consist of person-

nel not allied with the dominant societal classes, have a fairly independent resource base, and centralize its power. Therefore, autonomy is enhanced when
the different institutional actors share an orientation that opposes the interests
of the dominant classes, and their ability to oppose these interests is substantially increased when the state's political and economic fortunes are unencum-
bered by these dominant forces.

Important here is that scholars like Hamilton, Block, and Skocpol see relative
autonomy during those moments when the state opposes the *fundamental interests*, such as a change in property rights, of the dominant class. This contrasts
with neopluralist conceptions, which argue that such autonomy is unmistakable
whenever the state happens to step on the toes of the capitalist class. See
Stephen Krasner, *Defending the National Interest*; and Eric Nordlinger, *On the
Autonomy of the Democratic State* (Cambridge: Harvard University Press,
1981).

76. Rueschmeyer and Evans, "The State and Economic Transformation," 54.

77. Organski and Kugler, *The War Ledger*; Mann, "The Automous Power of
the State"; Stephen Krasner, "Approaches to the State: Alternative Conceptions
and Historical Dynamics," *Comparative Politics* 16 (1984): 223–46; Skocpol,
"Bringing the State Back In"; and Lewis Snider, "Identifying the Elements of
State Power: Where Do We Begin?" *Comparative Political Studies* 20 (October
1987): 314–56.

78. For shaping by multiple factors, see R. M. Bird, "Assessing Tax Performance in Developing Countries: A Critical Review of the Literature," in J. F. J.
Toye, ed., *Taxation and Economic Development* (London: Frank Cass, 1978),
33–61; Eprime Eshag, *Fiscal and Monetary Policies and Problems in Developing
Countries* (New York: Cambridge University Press, 1983); F. C. Afxentiou,
"Fiscal Structure, Tax Effort, and Economic Development," *Economia Internazionale* 38 (August/November 1984): 286–301; and John Due, *Indirect Taxation
in Developing Countries* (Baltimore: Johns Hopkins University Press, 1988), for
a survey of the determinants of the state's fiscal basis. For distribution of power,
see Michael Best, "Political Power and Tax Revenues in Central America," *Journal of Development Economics* 3 (1976): 49–82; Alex Radian, *Resource Mobilization in Poor Countries* (New Brunswick: Transaction Books, 1980); and Richard
Rose, "Maximizing Tax Revenue While Minimizing Political Costs," *Journal of
Public Policy* 5 (August 1985): 289–320.

For development and competence, see Tilly, "Reflections on the History of
European State-Making"; Organski and Kugler et al., *Birth, Death, and Taxes*;
Mann, "On the Autonomous Power of the State"; and Skocpol, "Bringing the
State Back In."

79. See also Organski and Kugler, *The War Ledger*; Lamborn, "Power and
the Politics of Extraction"; Snider, "Identifying the Elements of State Power";
Levi, *Of Rule and Revenue*; and, Migdal, *Strong Societies and Weak States*.

80. Organski et al., *Birth, Death, and Taxes*, 48.

81. Due, *Indirect Taxation in Developing Countries*, 19.

82. Ibid.

83. Ibid.; also see Tilly, *Coercion, Capital, and European States*, 87–9.

84. Eshag, *Fiscal and Monetary Policies*, 90–92; Mann, "On the Autonomous Power of the State"; and Snider, "Identifying the Elements of State Power."

85. Snider, "Identifying the Elements of State Power," 325–26.

86. For "openness," See Harley Hinrichs, *A General Theory of Tax Structure Change During Economic Development* (Cambridge: Harvard Law School, 1965). For feasibility, see Snider, "Identifying the Elements of State Power," 326. A general observation is that certain policy tools are more predominant given a specific structure of production and level of economic development. See Eshag, *Fiscal and Monetary Policies and Problems*, 103–18. For example, the greater the percentage of the population in agriculture, the more likely the state must rely on indirect forms of taxation. In general, as society becomes more industrialized and service-oriented, the state's direct extraction abilities are generally enhanced.

87. The state, of course, might rationally choose to rely more heavily on indirect techniques if its economy more heavily depends on international trade because these tools may be able to raise more revenue at decreased economic and political costs. This is certainly evident in most AOPEC states that have no or a very limited income tax.

88. "Identifying the Elements of State Power," 328. Also, those states with a wide selection of policy tools are better positioned to respond to crisis situations and external shocks. See Skocpol, "Bringing the State Back In," 16.

89. One oft-used measure that I will not use is the state's tax "effort," which refers to what a "normal" state should, under objective conditions, be able to extract. See Sadiq Ahmed, "Public Finance in Egypt: Its Structure and Trends," *World Bank Staff Working Papers*, no. 639 (Washington, D.C.: World Bank, 1984), 30–32; and W. T. Newlyn, "Measuring Tax Effort in Developing Countries," *Journal of Development Studies* 22 (April 1985): 390–405. The central problem with this concept is that economic variables are viewed as the primary determinants of the state's capacity and efforts, and all residuals and deviations are accounted for by political forces. The political, however, is not a residual explanatory variable.

90. Levi, *Of Rule and Revenue*, 52.

91. Frederico J. Herschel, "Tax Evasion and Its Measurements in Developing Countries," *Public Finance* 33 (1978): 234.

92. There is an important difference between tax evasion and tax avoidance. The former, an illegal act, implies paying less taxes than established by law or evading them altogether. Tax avoidance is produced by tax loopholes, either intentionally or unintentionally established, and individuals use these legally established loopholes to underreport and misrepresent their financial situation.

93. This relates to a primary feature of the Weber's definition of the state, its monopolization of the means of violence. In fact, Giddens argues that the "capability to back up taxation demands through the use of forces remained the single most essential element of state power." See *The Nation-State and Violence*, 58. Although the armed forces is traditionally analyzed with respect to its capability against foreign foes, the state's ability to control rival internal groups, maintain a police force, and establish the disciplinary mechanisms to pursue and punish those that evade or conflict with its policies is an important feature of the state's

capacity. See Weber, "Politics as a Vocation"; Barbara Stallings, "International Lending and the Relative Autonomy of the State: A Case Study of Twentieth-Century Peru," *Politics and Society* 14 (1985): 257–88; Alfred Stepan, *The State and Society: Peru in Comparative Perspective* (Princeton: Princeton University Press, 1978), preface; and Skocpol, "Bringing the State Back In." These argue that control over territory may be an important and basic feature of the state's ability to enforce its rule.

94. See Herschel, "Tax Evasion and Its Measurements," for a good overview of the tax evasion literature. Although many tax systems are constructed to eliminate or diminish the propensity of citizens to evade fiscal responsibility, this measure, in conjunction with the other indicators of state power, nonetheless captures an important aspect of the state's administrative capabilities.

95. Max Weber, *Theory of Social and Economic Organization* (New York: Oxford University Press, 1947), 339.

96. See Mouzelis, *Politics in the Semi-Periphery*, 204; Mann, "On the Autonomous Power of the State"; and Giddens, *The Nation-State and Violence*, 11.

97. Giddens, *The Nation-State and Violence*.

98. Herschel, "Tax Evasion and Its Measurements"; Eshag, *Fiscal and Monetary Policies and Problems*; and Levi, *Of Rule and Revenue*, chap. 3.

99. Levi, *Of Rule and Revenue*, 60.

100. There is a causal connection between the state's monitoring capacities and initial tax bargain. Specifically, Levi makes the point that repeat transactions provide the bureaucracy with monitoring capabilities to enforce the state's decrees. Ibid., 64.

101. Weber also spoke of charismatic and traditional forms of domination. See Reinhard Bendix, *Max Weber: An Intellectual Portrait* (Berkeley: University of California Press, 1977) 419–22; and David Beetham, *Max Weber and the Theory of Modern Politics*, 2d ed. (New York: Polity Press, 1985), 115, for a good discussion.

102. The development of these institutions also enabled certain societal actors greater control over the state's decision-making process. Although the state may increase its capacity to penetrate and more effectively intervene in society, it may not necessarily be more autonomous; these interventions may either require that the state grant greater control over its actions from those very forces it hopes to dominate, or it (un)intentionally increases its susceptibility to societal interests from these newly established channels. See Rueschemeyer and Evans, "The State and Economic Transformation," 69: Gourevitch, *The Politics of Hard Times* (Ithaca: Cornell University Press, 1986), 230. Institutional linkages can be understood metaphorically as a bridge constructed for transporting troops into enemy territory during wartime. Although the bridge allows for easier penetration of alien terrain, the same bridge can be easily transformed from a penetrating device into a point of vulnerability. Institutional linkages can be thought of in a similar manner.

103. "Fiscal Structure, Tax Effort, and Economic Development," 300–301.

104. See Held and Krieger, "Accumulation, Legitimation, and the State," 488; and Isaac, *Power and Marxist Theory*, 178.

105. See Block, "The Ruling Class Does Not Rule," and "Beyond Relative

Autonomy"; Hamilton, *The Limits of State Autonomy*, 7; and Callaghy, *The State-Society Struggle*.

106. "International Lending," 260.

107. For a similiar attempt, see Therborn, *What Does the Ruling Class Do When It Rules?*

108. Hamilton, *The Limits of State Autonomy*, 7. For analyses of the tax structure and the relative incidence and impact on certain social classes, see James Miller, "The Fiscal Crisis of the State Reconsidered: Two Views of the State and the Accumulation of Capital in the Post War Economy," *Review of Radical Political Economics* 18 (1986): 236–60.

109. See Barbara Stallings, "International Lending," and "External Finance and the Transition to Socialism in Small Peripheral Societies," in R. Fagen et al., eds., *Transition and Development* (New York: Monthly Review Press, 1986).

110. See Stallings, "External Finance," for a developed typology of foreign financing and its implications for the state's autonomy.

111. See Waterbury, *The Egypt of Nasser and Sadat*; and Rueschemeyer and Evans, "The State and Economic Transformation."

112. E. V. K. Fitzgerald, "The Fiscal Crisis of the Latin American State," in J. F. J. Toye, ed., *Taxation and Economic Development* (London: Frank Cass, 1978), 35, emphasis added.

113. Trimberger, *Revolution from Above*; Rueschemeyer and Evans, "The State and Economic Transformation," 65–66; and Stallings, "International Lending," 260.

114. Relative autonomy also may increase during periods of economic crisis. See Block, "The Ruling Class Does Not Rule" and "Beyond Relative Autonomy"; Poulantzas, *State, Power, Socialism*; Haldun Gulalp, "Capital Accumulation, Classes, and the Relative Autonomy of the State," *Science and Society* 51 (Fall 1987): 311; and Isaac, *Power and Marxist Theory*. A decline in economic growth can lead to one of two possible responses by the state. The first is when "business confidence" is wooed by the state to "invest at rates that will assure high levels of economic activity"; Block, "Beyond Relative Autonomy," 231. Therefore, the state not only abstains from those actions that might injure business's propensity to invest but, in fact, develops those policies that directly benefit the capitalist class. The second type of response is more likely to occur during periods of severe economic depression, wherein the state may be forced to intervene more forcefully to restructure sluggish patterns of capital accumulation. Under "normal" circumstances excessive state intervention represents a threat to capitalist sensitivities, but during economic crises state intervention may be necessary for capitalism's long-term prospects. As Isaac, *Power and Marxist Theory*, 182, argues, "state intervention thus becomes imperative particularly in times of economic crisis—when the problems of 'business confidence' is diminished by the manifest inability of the market to promote prosperity." Whether certain fractions of capital look favorably upon such state intrusions is historically contingent; however, the state's intervention in the economy is viewed as both enabled by the dire circumstances and the necessity for restructuring an outmoded capital accumulation pattern. This analysis, then, stands in contrast to Bonapartism, where the state emerges dominant because of a balance of class

forces. See Rueschemeyer and Evans, "The State and Economic Transformation," 63, on this point.

115. The term is Robert Bates's *Essays on the Political Economy of Rural Africa* (Berkeley: University of California Press, 1987), ix.

Chapter Three
Egypt and Israel in Historical Perspective

1. See P. J. Vatikiotis, *The History of Egypt* (Baltimore: Johns Hopkins University Press, 1980); Lufti al-sayyid Marsot, *Egypt in the Reign of Muhammad Ali* (New York: Cambridge University Press, 1984). Ali's drive toward modernization centered on substantial military reforms that would provide the foundation for both military industrialization and, he hoped, industrial development. To develop without the assistance of foreign financial or industrial capital, he pursued a policy of import-substitution industrialization. To generate the financial capital needed to finance a large-scale industrialization effort without the assistance of the European banking houses, he nationalized all state land and collectivized the peasantry, thereby fostering the transfer of resources from the agricultural to the industrial sectors. In fact, a most far-reaching change was his introduction of Jumal cotton, a new long-staple, high-quality variety raised nowhere else and ideally suited for Egyptian soils. This act, while not totally financing his modernization program, did make cotton king in Egypt.

2. Robert Mabro and Samir Radwan attribute industrial decline to both external and internal factors: "we prefer to stress the interaction between a variety of causes. Backwardness calls for a large measure of state intervention if industrialization and modernization are to be achieved; but the effectiveness of the state in controlling the economy and implementing policy is impaired by the very backwardness of the country." *The Industrialization of Egypt, 1933–76* (Oxford: Clarendon Press, 1976), 17.

3. Charles Issawi, *Egypt at Mid-Century: An Economic Survey* (New York: Oxford University Press, 1954), 7–8.

4. The sources of Egypt's financial straits are undoubtedly overdetermined. There were tributes to the Ottoman treasury and military contributions, a downturn in the world market price for cotton after the American Civil War, and loans at exorbitant interest rates taken out to finance such items as the restoration of the Khedive's palace, the Alexandria-Cairo railway, irrigation inputs, and the Suez Canal. In fact, as a result of fiscal crisis of 1876 Khedive Ismail was forced to sell all of Egypt's financial interest in the Suez Canal to British interests. On the supply side, the state's inability to raise revenue was severely circumscribed by the capitulations (I detail this aspect later). For a good discussion of Egypt's financial difficulties during the late 1800s, see Roger Owen, *The Middle East in the World Economy* (London: Menthuen, 1983), 122–52; A. E. Crouchley, *The Economic Development of Modern Egypt* (New York: Longman, Green, 1938), and Crouchley, *The Investment of Foreign Capital in Egyptian Companies and Public Debt* (New York: Arno Press, 1977); and Eric Davis, *Challenging Colonialism: Bank Misr and Egyptian Industrialization, 1920–1941* (Princeton: Princeton University Press, 1983), 12–27. For a particularly interesting account of the

state's relationship to international finance capital, see David Landes, *Bankers and Pashas: International Finance and Economic Imperialism in Egypt* (Cambridge: Harvard University Press, 1979).

5. Robert Tignor, *Modernization and British Rule in Egypt, 1881–1914* (Princeton: Princeton University Press, 1966), 22–23.

6. British economic objectives in Egypt are summarized in the following official statement: "The policy of the government may be summed up thus: 1) export of cotton to Europe subject to 1 percent export duty; 2) imports of textile products manufactured abroad subject to 8 percent import duty. . . . Since Egypt is by her nature an agricultural country, it follows logically that her industrial training could lead only to the neglect of agriculture while diverting the Egyptians from the land." Quoted from Abdel-Malek, *Egypt: Military Society*, 7–8. British policy was only too successful.

7. For instance, needing to raise revenue while being denied foreign loans by the Ottomans in 1871, Khedive Ismail implemented a land tax "whereby a landowner who paid the land tax six years in advance would acquire full ownership rights over his land. This law, which became compulsory in 1874 and was adhered to throughout most of Egypt, tended to benefit the larger landowners as only they were able to raise the payments required." Davis, *Challenging Colonialism*, 27. Although this measure did little to alleviate the treasury's plight, it did assist the creation of greater class inequities. Also see Owen, *Middle East in the World Economy*, 135–48.

8. See Gabriel Baer, *Studies in the Social History of Modern Egypt* (Chicago: University of Chicago Press, 1969); Robert Tignor, *State, Private Enterprise, and Economic Change, 1918–52* (Princeton: Princeton University Press, 1984), 9; Mabro and Radwan, *The Industrialization of Egypt*, 22–26; and Vatikiotis, *The History of Egypt*, 322.

9. Joel Beinin and Zachary Lockman, *Workers on the Nile: Nationalism, Communalism, Islam, and the Egyptian Working Class: 1882–1954* (Princeton: Princeton University Press, 1988), 9.

10. Owen, *Middle East in the World Economy*, 224–25.

11. Abdel-Malek, *Egypt: Military Society*, 2–15; Mabro and Radwan, *The Industrialization of Egypt*, 25.

12. For rise in capital, see Beinin and Lockman, *Workers on the Nile*, 48; also see Crouchley, *The Economic Development of Modern Egypt*, 179–80. For investment, see K. M. Barbour, *Growth, Structure, and Location of Industry in Egypt* (New York: Praeger Press, 1972), 57.

13. See Vatikiotis, *The History of Egypt*, 321–24. Moreover, most manufacturing profits were repatriated abroad, leaving little for domestic investment. See Mabro and Radwan, *The Industrialization of Egypt*, 19–23.

14. See Davis, *Challenging Colonialism*, for a detailed study of the Bank Misr group and its activities.

15. Beinin and Lockman, *Workers on the Nile*, 11.

16. Tignor, *State, Private Enterprise, and Economic Change*, 134.

17. See Mabro and Radwan, *The Industrialization of Egypt*, 82–84; Tignor, *State, Private Enterprise, and Economic Change*, 76–79, 106–7.

18. The 1930s also witnessed the beginning of some joint commercial ventures and the Egyptian parliament's enactment of a series of laws designed to Egyptianize domestic industry. The results of such legislation were nominal, as both the control and the laws themselves were not designed to ensure that local ownership would by necessity promote local interests.

19. Peter Mansfield, *The British in Egypt* (London: Weidenfeld and Nicolson, 1971), 248. For good overviews of this period, see Marius Deeb, *Party Politics in Egypt: The Wafd and Its Rivals* (London: Ithica Press, 1979); Vatikiotis, *The History of Modern Egypt*, 271–96, 317–72; and Tignor, *State, Private Enterprise, and Economic Change*.

20. Abdel-Malek paints a less heterogenous picture of the Wafd, as he argues that it essentially "brought together forces whose ties with the occupant [the British] were not organic, but resulted essentially from the entanglement of the whole of the Egyptian economy with the dominant Egyptian interests." *Egypt: Military Society*, 12.

21. For Wafd's interests, see Goldberg, *Tinker, Tailor, Textile Worker*, 66. For rank and file, see Beinin and Lockman, *Workers on the Nile*, 12. The emergence of some manufacturing and industrial activity during the interwar period stimulated a change in the economic elite and the Wafd's composition. This group, more tied to foreign capital, split from the Wafd in 1937 to form the Sa'dist party.

22. There is some disagreement concerning how exact were the divisions within the capitalist class. For instance, Patrick Clawson, "Egypt's Industrialization: A Critique of Dependency Theory," *MERIP Reports* 72 (1978): 17–23, and Tignor, *State, Private Enterprise, and Economic Change*, chap. 6, argue that no matter how prominent and well-represented foreign capital was among domestic societal elites, domestic capital was neither solely a comprador elite nor a progressive class; rather, it varied according to the interests generated by the origins of capital. Beinin and Lockman, however, reject the conventional characterization of a significant split between these fractions of capital and argue instead that "by the Second World War there was . . . no sharp division between a 'comprador' and a 'national' bourgeoisie in Egypt, for the leading indigenous industrialists found common group with foreigners and mutamassirun [people of foreign origin who had become permanent residents of Egypt] involved in industrial development. There was likewise no sharp distinction between the agrarian and industrial sections of the bourgeoisie." *Workers on the Nile*, 11.

23. Tignor, *State, Private Enterprise, and Economic Change*, chap. 6. The combined failure of the constitutional governments, the emergence of fascism in Europe, and economic decline contributed to a growing radicalization of Egyptian society. For instance, two extremist religio-political organizations, the Moslem Brotherhood and Young Egypt (which included the paramilitary group the Green Shirts), flourished during this period. Despite their different political programs, both derived membership from assorted classes, from the peasantry to professionals, and both shared a belief in the use of violence to attain their objectives. Vatikiotis, *The History of Egypt*, 317. For detailed studies of the

Egyptian working class and unionization, see Goldberg, *Tinker, Tailor, Textile Worker*, and Beinin and Lockman, *Workers on the Nile*.

24. Beinin and Lockman, *Workers on the Nile*, 12.

25. Tignor, *State, Private Enterprise, and Economic Change*, 235–38.

26. Also see Clawson, "Egypt's Industrialization."

27. Craig Clapham, *Third World Politics* (Madison: University of Wisconsin Press, 1984), 39–43.

28. See Tignor, *Modernization and British Rule*; and Goldberg, *Tinker, Tailor, Textile Worker*.

29. See Ayubi, *Bureaucracy and Politics in Modern Egypt*.

30. The lone exception in the modern era is with respect to the Sudan's territorial status.

31. Morroe Berger, *Bureaucracy and Society in Modern Egypt* (Princeton: Princeton University Press, 1957); Trimberger, *Revolution from Above*; and Ayubi, *Bureaucracy and Politics*, have convincingly argued that the state apparatus was permeated by representatives of the landed classes.

32. According to Goldberg "these courts saw themselves as the protectors not only of natural individuals but also of foreign companies (imbued with legal personality after all) even if only partly owned by foreigners." *Tinker, Tailor, Textile Worker*, 62.

33. Ibid., 58.

34. Perlmutter, *Egypt*, 23–24.

35. Ibid., 24.

36. Ibid.

37. Jacques Berque, *Egypt: Imperialism and Revolution* (London: Faber and Faber, 1972), 299.

38. J. C. Hurewitz, *Middle East Politics: The Military Dimension* (Boulder: Westview Press, 1982), 33.

39. Ibid., 34.

40. Ibid., 53.

41. Tignor, *Modernization and British Rule*, 126.

42. Perlmutter, *Egypt*, 57–58.

43. Landes, *Bankers and Pashas*, 91–92.

44. Quoted in Tignor, *Modernization and British Rule*, 108.

45. Ibid., 116; Central Bank of Egypt, "Development and Taxation in Egypt," *Central Bank of Egypt Economic Review* 22 (1982): 2.

46. Owen, *Middle East in the World Economy*, 220–26.

47. While the landed classes were the most powerful actors in Egyptian society, their development was sponsored by both the palace and British authorities in order to increase the tax revenue derived from the agricultural sector. This implied that the British, while aiding the landed classes' development, had an interest in taxing this source of revenue. Because the Palace could not change the tax code, British authorities were relatively impervious to the interest of the landed classes, though taking their interests into consideration, if it meant undermining their basis of revenue and decreasing the amount of debt redemption handed over to foreign creditors.

48. Tignor, *State, Private Enterprise, and Economic Change*, 152–54.

49. "Development of Taxation in Egypt," 3.

50. Nonetheless collection from agricultural taxes rose steadily throughout this period. See Tignor, *State, Private Enterprise*, 237.

51. Ibid.

52. Ibid., 154.

53. For an overview and summary of the state's fiscal policy before 1952, see Bent Hansen and Girgis Marzouk, *Development and Economic Policy in the UAR (Egypt)* (Amsterdam: North-Holland Publishing Company, 1965), 246–56; and Central Bank of Egypt, "Development of Taxation."

54. Central Bank of Egypt, "Development of Taxation," 4.

55. See Issawi, *Egypt at Mid-Century*, 233–34.

56. For good overviews of the Zionist movement, see Arthur Hertzberg, *The Zionist Idea: A Historical Analysis and Reader* (New York: Antheum Press, 1969); Shlomo Avineri, *The Making of Modern Zionism: The Intellectual Origins of the Jewish State* (New York: Basic Books, 1981); and David Vital, *Zionism: The Formative Years* (London: Oxford University Press, 1982).

57. See Yosef Gorny, *Zionism and the Arabs, 1882–1948: A Study of Ideology* (London: Oxford University Press, 1987), 14; Vital, *Zionism*, 54–56.

58. The Turks were right to mistrust Great Powers' motivations for facilitating Jewish immigration. Although many in the West saw a certain romanticism involved with the ancient peoples' attempt to return to their biblical homeland, there was also the hope that such immigration would increase their control over this strategic area in the fertile crescent. See Barbara Tuchman, *Bible and Sword: England and Palestine from the Bronze Age to Balfour* (New York: New York University Press, 1956).

59. Gorny, *Zionism and the Arabs*, 14.

60. See Roger Owen, "Introduction," and Alexander Scholch, "European Penetration and Economic Development of Palestine, 1856–1882," in R. Owen, ed., *Studies in the Economic and Social History of Palestine in the Nineteenth Century* (Carbondale: Southern Illinois University Press, 1982), for extended discussions of European economic penetration of Palestine.

61. There were five "waves" of Jewish immigration to Palestine, each of which was distinctive for its sociological contribution to the Yishuv. The first "wave" (1881–1905) of approximately 20,000 to 30,000 came after the 1881 Russian pogroms and anti-Semitic outbursts in Eastern Europe. The second wave (1905–1914) was small in number but provided the major stamp on the Yishuv. The third wave (1917–1924) brought an additional 35,000 Jews to Palestine who, like the second wave, were relatively young, unattached, and ideologically committed to developing socialism in Palestine. The fourth wave (1924–1933) saw nearly 85,000 arrive, most from Poland. The fifth wave (1933–1939) was a response to both the virulent anti-Semitism that swept through Europe and the immigration restrictions imposed on Jews throughout most of the world. Nearly 220,000 Jews arrived during this period, with nearly 40,000 from Germany. These last two waves, less ideologically committed to socialism, introduced an important private sector into the Jewish economy.

62. Daniel Shimshoni, *Israeli Democracy: The Middle of the Journey* (New York: Free Press, 1982), 19.

63. Shimshoni, *Israeli Democracy*, 19. Also see Yonatan Shapiro, *The Formative Years of the Israeli Labor Party: The Organization of Power, 1919–30* (Beverly Hills: Sage Press, 1976).

64. The kibbutz's spiritual, political, and economic status often resulted in material benefits such as tax breaks, subsidies, investment opportunities, or special legal protection by the state. S. N. Eisenstadt, *Israeli Society* (New York: Basic Books, 1967), 174–75. For good overviews of the kibbutz movement in Palestine and early Israel, see Medding, *Mapai in Israel*, and Shapiro, *The Formative Years of the Israeli Labor Party*.

65. This curious phenomenon occurred principally because of Jewish Palestine's strong socialist movement, its need to develop economically autonomous from the Arab sector, and the lack of funds from foreign sources. For a more detailed history, see Shalev, *Labour and the Political Economy in Israel*.

66. Migdal, *Strong Societies and Weak States*, 147.

67. Tuchman, *The Bible and the Sword*; David Fromkin, *A Peace to End All Peace: The Fall of the Ottoman Empire and the Rise of the Modern Middle East* (New York: Henry Holt, 1989), 25–31, 148.

68. Indeed, under these conditions it was difficult for the local Jewish community to persuade potential Jewish foreign investors to partake in foreign direct investment in Palestine.

69. As is well known, the task of reconciling two competing nationalisms would prove impossible. According to Arab leaders, British authorities had promised Arab independence in Palestine in the MacMahon-Husayn correspondence of 1915. Although Britain steadfastly denied that they made such a promise, they were determined to protect the rights of local Arabs if only to maintain local stability, Arab goodwill, and thus their security interests. The Zionists claimed, however, that the Balfour Declaration, which was explicitly incorporated into the Palestine Mandate, had pledged to facilitate the creation of a Jewish national home in Palestine. At the heart of the conflict was Jewish immigration. The Jews claimed that their ability to establish a national home was dependent on continued numbers, but the Arabs charged that the local character of Palestine was being distorted by the continued Jewish influx. Moreover, neither nationalist group was enamored with the introduction of democratic institutions. The Zionists were convinced that their fewer numbers would lead to closed immigration doors and thus truncate any possibility for obtaining a majority, while the Arabs refused to acknowledge that the Zionists had any kind of legitimate presence in Palestine. For contending perspectives of this period and the Arab-Zionist confrontation, see Connor Cruise O'Brien, *The Siege: The Saga of Israel and Zionism* (New York: Simon and Schuster, 1986); and Ibrahim Abu-Lughod, ed., *The Transformation of Palestine* (Evanston: Northwestern University Press, 1987).

70. Moreover, many members of the World Zionist Organization, including its leader Chaim Weizmann, were not disposed toward socialism but were rather staunch proponents of capitalism.

71. I follow Shalev, *Labour and the Political Economy in Israel*, in arguing that socialist successes must be understood in *relation* to other societal agents.

I extend his argument, however, by including the important (absent) role of the world economy and foreign capital.

72. Hurewitz, *The Struggle for Palestine* (New York: Norton Press, 1976), 41.

73. Migdal, *Strong Societies and Weak States*, 150. He further notes that during the late 1930s the British made an unsuccessful attempt to hamper Jewish activities, By this point, however, Jewish leaders had become so powerful that they were able to circumvent any British restriction (167).

74. Ibid., 169.

75. Shabtai Teveth, *Ben-Gurion: The Burning Ground, 1886–1948* (Boston: Houghton and Mifflin, 1987), 722. Akin to the Jewish community's willingness to learn important administrative skills from British mandatory authorities, local Jewish authorities actively petitioned to be included in the fight against Nazi and pro-Nazi forces in Europe and neighboring Arab countries, respectively. Military service was requested because of the strong desire not only to participate in and contribute to the battle against Nazism but also to learn military skills that could then be transferred to the battle for statehood in Palestine. Although it took from 1939 until September 1944 to persuade British authorities to allow Palestinian Jews to join the fight, the Jewish Brigade Group served the purposes of both the British and the Zionists. While the British were able to supplement their troop strength with a highly motivated fighting regiment, the Zionists were able to develop "their own combat-hardened army, which they believed would be put to effective use after the war, when they hoped to create their own independent state." Hurewitz, *Middle Eastern Politics*, 62.

76. Hurewitz, *The Struggle for Palestine*, esp. chap 3.

77. Three principal Jewish organizations had formal responsibilities for promoting a Jewish national home in Palestine. The first, the Zionist Executive of the Yishuv, was the main governing body of the Palestine Zionists. The organization was controlled by Labor in general and Ben-Gurion in particular. The other two organizations featuring institutionalized functions were the World Zionist Organization (WZO) and the Jewish Agency. Both were recognized by the League of Nations's mandate with the task of carrying out the establishment of a Jewish home. The WZO controlled both the Jewish Agency and the Jewish National Fund (the latter was in charge of all land purchases).

78. Midgal, *Strong Societies and Weak States*, 158.

79. Ibid. WZO leader Arthur Ruppin explained the abdication of responsibility in favor of the Histadrut in this way: "Experience had taught us that, the settlements of ours go to pieces as the result of inner division, where there does not exist at least a kernel of individuals with a more or less unified outlook to give the tone, and to assimilate to their unified outlook the other members of the group." Shapiro, *The Formative Years of the Israeli Labor Party*, 79; cited from Migdal, *Strong Societies and Weak States*, 158.

80. I am bracketing the role of the Arab economy in Palestine and its relationship to the Jewish economy because I am concerned with the genesis of Israeli state power and those features of the economy that contributed to its development. Although there was an intimate relationship between the Arab and Jewish economies, I am less concerned with how Jewish immigration, capital inflows,

and economic development, transformed Arab Palestine. Moreover, the Arab riots and strike between 1936 and 1939 effectively divorced the two economies into two relatively autonomous sectors. See Talal Asad, "Class Transformation Under the Mandate," *MERIP Reports* 53 (1976): 3–8, for a good overview of the transformation of the Arab community.

81. See Shapiro, *The Formative Years of the Israeli Labor Party*; E. Etzioni-Halevy, *Political Manipulation and Administrative Power: A Comparative Perspective* (Boston: Routledge and Kegan Paul, 1979).

82. See Appendix 1 for capital flow and investment into Jewish Palestine.

83. Before the 1920s most capitalist-oriented Jews immigrated from Eastern Europe to either Western Europe or, more likely, the United States. Only when the United States closed its immigration doors did these European Jewish bourgeoisie immigrate to Palestine during the "fourth wave" of Jewish immigration in the 1930s as a result of increasing anti-Semitism and Nazi persecution.

84. See Nadav Halevi and Ruth Klinov-Malul, *The Economic Development of Israel* (New York: Praeger Press, 1968); Glenn Yago, "Whatever Happened to the Promised Land? Capital Flows and the Israeli State," *Berkeley Journal of Sociology* 21 (1976): 117–46; Kimmerling, *Zionism and Economy*; and Shalev, *Labour and the Political Economy in Israel*. Immigration and capital inflow were highly correlated; they provided further evidence for the "exogenously" determined direction of the Yishuv's economic development. Halevi and Klinov-Malul, *The Economic Development of Israel*, 22.

85. This discussion borrows heavily from Shalev, *Labour in the Political Economy in Israel*.

86. See Kimmerling, *Zionism and Economy*, chap. 2.

87. Ibid., 34.

88. Histadrut leaders, although anticapitalist in spirit, recognized that capital could play an important role in the nation-building process and absorb surplus labor during the economically troubled interwar years. In fact, Histadrut encouraged their participation and undertook joint ventures with capital because of the functional role it could play in developing the economy.

89. Also Eisenstadt, *Israeli Society*, 95–97, and *The Transformation of Israeli Society*, 219; Shimshoni, *Israeli Democracy*, 234–35.

90. Halevi and Klinov-Malul, *The Economic Development of Israel*, 25, 26–27.

91. Michael Shalev, "The Political Economy of Labor Dominance and Decline in Israel," in T. J. Pempel, ed., *Uncommon Democracies* (Ithaca: Cornell University Press, 1990), 96.

92. Of course, one notable group did not recognize the Jewish state's authority or legitimacy, this being the local Arab inhabitants and neighboring states. See Benny Morris, *The Birth of the Palestinian Refugee Problem, 1947–1949* (New York: Cambridge University Press), for what is widely considered the most definitive and complete account of the origins of the Palestinian flight from Israel, and Tom Segev, *1949: The First Israelis* (New York: Free Press, 1986), for a revisionist analysis of the new state's treatment of its Arab citizens. In general, however, the nature of the first Arab-Israeli War and the Palestinian exodus is not of direct relevance here.

93. Both the WZO and the Jewish Agency retained jurisdiction over some minor policy areas, notably over future Jewish immigration.

94. Eisenstadt, *The Transformation of Israeli Society*, 174–77, and Peretz, *The Goverment and Politics of Israel*, chap. 3, provide an overview of the different political parties and their representative status over the history of the state.

95. Moreover, because the country's political parties and other interest groups find entry into the state apparatus relatively easy, "[n]o one party official can build a strong government that can say 'no' to claimants. There are strong incentives to share resources widely. It is difficult to defend the economy by denying the resource demands of one or another group." Ira Sharkansky, *The Political Economy of Israel* (New Brunswick: Transaction Books, 1987), 25.

96. In Israel's first election, Mapai formed a coalition with the Communist party, Mapaam. Only after the 1951 election did religious parties wield more influence, although the religious parties were included in every Israeli coalition government.

97. This feature became more pronounced in later years when their importance grew as the electoral division between Likud and Mapai diminished.

98. For overviews of the Israeli political system and its political parties, see Eisenstadt, *The Transformation of Israeli Society*, 174–77; and Peter Medding, *The Foundation of Israeli Democracy, 1948–1967* (New York: Oxford University Press, 1990).

99. Shalev, *Labour and the Political Economy in Israel*, places Mapai's status as a "dominant" party in both theoretical and comparative perspective.

100. Eisenstadt, *The Transformation of Israeli Society*, 187–89.

101. Etzioni-Halevy, *Political Manipulation*.

102. Eisenstadt, *The Transformation of Israeli Society*, 193.

103. See Efraim Torgovnik, "Israel: The Persistent Elite," in F. Tachau, ed., *Political Elites and Political Development in the Middle East* (Cambridge, Mass.: Schenkman Press, 1975), 45; Kimmerling, *Zionism and Territory*, esp. chap. 3.

104. There are numerous studies of the origins of the Israeli political elite, its background, and patterns of interaction. See R. H. Dekmejian and D. Koutsoukis, "Comparative Patterns of Elite Recruitment," *The Greek Review of Social Research* 38 (January/April 1980): 147–63; Torgovnik, "Israel."

105. Eisenstadt, *Israeli Society*, 149–50.

106. Nadav Halevi, "The Economy of Israel: Goals and Limitations," *Jerusalem Quarterly* (Fall 1976): 84. Also see Rubner, *The Economy of Israel*, 232; and Eisenstadt, *Israeli Society*, 301–6.

107. See Cohen, *Zion and State*, 201–60. The divisions between the state's interests and those of the particular classes became important to societal tensions during the 1960s. During this early period, however, the two were considered mutually compatible.

108. Eisenstadt, *The Transformation of Israeli Society*, 188–90.

109. See A. Granovsky (Grannot), *The Fiscal System of Palestine* (Jerusalem: Palestine and Near East Publications, 1935); and Harold Wilkenfeld, *Taxes and People in Israel* (Cambridge: Harvard University Press, 1973).

110. With the onset of World War Two Ben-Gurion successfully demanded from the Jewish Agency additional funds from both Yishuv taxes and Kofer ha-Yishuv (the Yishuv ransom) to enlarge the size of the Haganah. The Yishuv ransom established on July 24, 1939, was the Yishuv's "fundraiser for security. The principle behind the name was that those who could not physically fulfill their obligation to the Haganah would pay a 'ransom' to its treasury. The money was collected by means of a tax on luxuries, restaurant bills, cigarettes, and so on." Teveth, *Ben-Gurion*, 722. The ransom was abolished with statehood.

111. Halevi and Klinov-Malul, *The Economic Development of Israel*, 188.

112. See Eisenstadt, *Israeli Society*, 106; and Cohen, *Zion and State*, 249–59. Ben-Gurion brought an etatist vision to the state and used Histadrut for the state's purposes. Mapai's ability to deliver Histadrut to the state was later challenged, with tremendous consequences for state-society relations.

113. Shalev, "The Political Economy of Labor Party Dominance," 92–96.

114. Prime Minister's Office, *Israel Economic Development* (Jerusalem: Government Printing Office, 1970), 100–101.

Chapter Four
Explaining Egyptian War Preparation Strategies

1. Amin Huwaidi, Interview with author, Cairo, January 2, 1991.

2. For good overviews of the Free Officers movement, see Dekmejian, *Egypt Under Nasir*; Baker, *Egypt's Uncertain Revolution*, 17–44; and Hinnebusch, *Egyptian Politics Under Sadat*, chap. 2, 92–97.

3. Mohrse Mahmoud Hussini, *Soviet-Egyptian Relations, 1945–1985* (New York: St. Martin's Press, 1987), 56.

4. Ayubi, *Bureaucracy and Politics in Contemporary Egypt*, 161–62.

5. Ibid., 159–61. Vatikiotis's *Nasser and His Generation* portrays Nasser as a power-seeking, self-aggrandizing leader. Most of Nasser's actions are intelligible once one understands this primeval force.

6. From 1952 until 1974 the cabinet was dominated by military men. See Dekmejian, *Egypt Under Nasir*; and Mark Cooper, "Demilitarization of the Egyptian Cabinet," *International Journal of Middle Eastern Studies* 14 (May 1982): 203–25.

7. Hinnebusch, *Egyptian Politics Under Sadat*, 19; Baker, *Egypt's Uncertain Revolution*, 33, 34.

8. Baker, *Egypt's Uncertain Revolution*, 26.

9. In fact, one principal source of disagreement between Naguib and Nasser was over the former's attempt to reintroduce some form of parliamentary democracy. Hamied Ansari, *Egypt: The Stalled Society* (Albany: State University of New York Press, 1986), 84.

10. Hinnebusch, *Egyptian Politics Under Sadat*, chap. 2.

11. Ibid., 15–17. Also see Clement Henry Moore, "Authoritarian Politics in Unincorporated Society: The Case of Nasser's Egypt," *Comparative Politics* 6 (January 1974): 193–218.

12. Waterbury, *The Egypt of Nasser and Sadat*, 48.

13. Abdel-Malek, *Egypt: Military Society*, preface; Baker, *Egypt's Uncertain Revolution*, 42–43.

14. For instance, Baker writes: "Guided by no systematic ideology that might have provided a pattern or model for socio-economic change, they were left with a vague but widely shared dream of a purified, developed, and strong Egypt, purged of its colonial past"; *Egypt's Uncertain Revolution*, 43. Robert Stephens contends that "the movement from a basically free enterprise economy, through a phase of 'Guilded Capitalism' to an at least partially socialist society did not take place in accordance with a clear and pre-determined ideological doctrine, but pragmatically in response to economic and political pressures"; *Nasser: A Political Biography* (London: Allen, Lane, 1971), 324–25.

15. Khalid Ikram, *Egypt: Economic Management in a Period of Transition* (Baltimore: Johns Hopkins University Press, 1980), 17–19. Capital's influence was always limited to the economic, and never allowed to permeate the political, sphere. Baker, *Egypt's Uncertain Revolution*, 49.

16. Leonard Binder, *In a Moment of Enthusiasm* (Chicago: University of Chicago Press, 1978); Vatikiotis, *Nasser and His Generation*, 205.

17. Gamal Nasser, *Philosophy of the Revolution* (New York: Buffalo, Smith, Keyze, Marshall, 1959).

18. Vatikiotis, *Nasser and His Generation*, 249.

19. Karawan, "Egypt's Defense Policy," 154.

20. Berger, *Bureaucracy and Society*; Ayubi, *Bureaucracy and Politics*, 177.

21. Abdel-Malek, *Egypt: Military Society*, 101; Trimberger, *Revolution from Above*.

22. Vatikiotis, *Nasser and His Generation*, 158.

23. Ayubi, *Bureaucracy and Politics*, 344. Ayubi further argues that "the new elite is not basically different than the old one, either in social background or in professional experience. The new bureaucratic leaders come from similar homes, among which civil servants are strongly represented, and they move through similar careers that can be described as mainly bureaucratic. The only outstanding change in the characteristics of the bureaucratic leadership is that concerning education. Not only is the new leadership more formally educated, but its education is more specifically technical rather than legal or humanistic." Ibid., 370.

24. Trimberger, *Revolution from Above*; Hinnebusch, *Egyptian Politics Under Sadat*, 17–18.

25. Gabriel Ben-Dor, "Egypt," in E. Kolodziej and R. Harkavy, eds., *Security Policies of Developing Countries* (Lexington: Lexington Books, 1982), 180; Karawan, "Egypt's Defense Policy," 149. It is interesting that Nasser, *Philosophy of the Revolution*, 66, writes somewhat admiringly of Chaim Weizmann's attempt to use the Great Powers to further his goal of establishing a Zionist state in Palestine.

26. Baker, *Egypt's Uncertain Revolution*, 177; Hinnebusch, *Egyptian Politics Under Sadat*, 22.

27. Riad El-Sheikh, "The Egyptian Taxation System: An Evaluation from a Long-Term Development Point of View," *L' Egypte Contemporaine* 19 (April 1968): 83, writes that the two principal functions of Egypt's fiscal and budgetary system are the allocation of resources to defense and investment.

28. Central Bank of Egypt, "Development of Taxation in Egypt," 6.

29. Ibid. This was later amended by Law No. 266 of 1960 and 108 of 1962.

30. Saad el-Shazli, *The Crossing of the Suez* (San Francisco: American Middle East Research, 1980), 141–42; Rubenstein, *Red Star on the Nile*, 5. See Appendix 4 for an overview of Soviet assistance to Egypt.

31. Moshe Efrat, *The Defense Burden in Egypt During the Deepening of Soviet Involvement in 1962–72* (Ph.D. thesis, London University, May 1981), 6.

32. Waterbury, *The Egypt of Nasser and Sadat*, 395–99; Vayrynen and Ohlson, "Egypt," 108.

33. M. E. Selim, "Egypt," in J. Katz, ed. *Arms Production in Developing Countries* (Lexington: Lexington Books, 1984), 124; Vayrynen and Ohlson, "Egypt," 106–7. Also see Balbour, *Growth, Structure, and Location*; Marsot, *Egypt in the Reign of Muhammad Ali*, 164–67; and John Ralston, *Importing the European Army* (Chicago: University of Chicago Press, 1990), chap. 4.

34. Selim, "Egypt," 124.

35. Ibid., 125; Vayrynen and Ohlson, "Egypt," 107.

36. Under the terms of the 1936 Anglo-Egyptian Treaty Egypt was allowed to expand the size of the military.

37. Selim, "Egypt," 125.

38. Ibid., 126–29; Vayrynen and Ohlson, "Egypt," 107.

39. Vayrynen and Ohlson, "Egypt," 105. Also see Ali Dessouki and Adel al-Labban, "Arms Race, Defense Expenditures, and Development: The Egyptian Case, 1952–1973" *Journal of South Asian and Middle Eastern Studies* 4 (Spring 1981): 65.

40. Most of the initial projects failed to become established and productive owing to the Western boycott and their low level of productivity. See Selim, "Egypt," 131; Vayrynen and Ohlson, "Egypt," 107–8.

41. Joe Stork, "Arms Industries in the Middle East," *MERIP Report* 144 (January/February 1987): 13. For a description of Egypt's military production, plants, and types of weapons produced, see Vayrynen and Ohlson, "Egypt."

42. Amin Huwaidi interview with author, Cairo, January 2, 1991.

43. Hussini, *Soviet-Egyptian Relations*, 56.

44. See Mohamed Heikal, *The Sphinx and the Commissar* (New York: Harper & Row, 1978), 56–64, for a good overview of this initial arms deal between the Soviets and the Egyptians.

45. Only after the 1956 War, which was blamed on the West, did Nasser develop a more genuine pro-Soviet orientation. See Mohamed Heikal, *The Road to Ramadan* (London: Collins Press, 1975), 171–77.

46. See Rubenstein, *Red Star on the Nile*, chap. 10

47. Efrat, *The Defense Burden in Egypt*, 148.

48. Karawan, "Egypt's Defense Policy," 147–48.

49. See Mohamed Heikal, *Cutting the Lion's Tail: Suez Through Egyptian Eyes* (New York: Arbor House, 1987) for the Suez War from an Egyptian perspective.

50. Vatikiotis, *Nasser and His Generation*, 254.

51. Karawan, "Egypt's Defense Policy," 156.

52. See Malcom Kerr, *The Arab Cold War* (New York: Oxford University Press, 1971), for a good overview of the intra-Arab struggle.

53. The Suez War also clearly situated Egypt in the Soviet fold. This antagonized the Americans and frustrated Dulles's containment strategy; thus, Nasser became the main nemesis of U.S. policy in the Middle East. Although the Kennedy administration attempted a détente of sorts with Nasser, any possible reconciliation was shattered by Egypt's entrance into the Yemen War.

54. For reactions, see Ayubi, *Bureaucracy and Politics*, 163–65; Baker, *Egypt's Uncertain Revolution*, 63; Waterbury, *The Egypt of Nasser and Sadat*, 66–70. For political economy, see Roger Owen, "The Economic Consequences of the Suez Crisis for Egypt," in William Roger Louis and Roger Owen, eds., *Suez 1956: The Crisis and Its Consequences* (New York: Oxford University Press, 1989), 370, who argues that there was still an on-going cabinet debate concerning what role the state should have in the development process. Individuals like Aziz Sidqi, who became minister of planning in 1956, came to positions of authority during this period and argued for greater state involvement; these men did so not on ideological grounds per se but rather on the charge that the state was a better allocator of investment priorities.

55. For public sector, see Abdel-Malek, *Egypt: Military Society*, 132–33; for government's impatience, see also 129. Also see Eliyahu Kanovsky, *The Economic Impact of the Six-Day War: Israel, the Occupied Territories, Egypt, Jordan* (New York: Praeger, 1970), 215–49, for an overview of the 1960–1965 Five-Year Plan.

56. Abdel-Malek, *Egypt: Military Society*, 139–42; Baker, *Egypt's Uncertain Revolution*; and Nissim Rejwan, *Nasserist Ideology: Its Exponents and Critics* (New York: John Wiley and Sons, 1974), 99.

57. Ansari, *Egypt*, 88. See Rejwan, *Nasserist Ideology*, 195–265, for a translation of the Socialist Charter.

58. I must make two additional points. First, Nasser's lack of affection for the private sector and increased affection for the public sector did not translate into any great love for the Left; in fact, he demonstrated a simultaneous ability to argue that his was a variant of socialism, embrace the Soviets, and jail and repress the Left when he believed it to be too rambunctious and threatening. Abdel-Malek, *Egypt: Military Society*, 133–39. Second, Arab Socialism was never designed to rid the country of the private sector, for it both continued to exist in the government's economic program and to control a substantial amount of the economy, particularly in certain economic areas like the agricultural sector. Be that as it may, the private sector's status had certainly been diminished over this period and its hopes were now decidedly subordinate to the needs of the government.

59. Trimberger, *Revolution from Above*; Auda, "The State of Political Control."

60. Karawan, "Egypt's Defense Policy," 150.

61. Ayubi, *Bureaucracy and Politics*, 239–40.

62. Ibid., 439–51, for a general discussion of the ASU.

63. Cooper, *The Transformation of Egypt*, 38.

64. Vatikiotis, *Nasser and His Generation*, 183.

65. As industrialization proceeded over the decade, albeit not as fast as Nasser would have hoped, the percentage of the economy derived from industrial

and manufacturing activity increased. Specifically, agricultural production as a percentage of total output declined from 32.3 percent in 1955 to 27.5 percent in 1967, while industrial output increased from 17.6 percent to 28 percent over the same period.

66. Hansen and Marzouk, *Development and Economic Policy*, 272.

67. Baker, *Egypt's Uncertain Revolution*, 61, 63–64.

68. Central Bank of Egypt, "The Development of Taxation in Egypt," 12–13. In fact, while the income tax rates rose considerably between 1952 and 1967, the effect had been merely to ensure that the ratio of direct taxation as a percentage of GNP did not decline. See El-Sheikh, "The Egyptian Taxation System," 86. This may be owing in part to the fact that "in a scheme where taxation began at LE1,000 per annum net income, it was difficult to find many Egyptians who made that much money in a year." Vatikiotis, *Nasser and His Generation*, 217. The highest ratio of direct to indirect taxation came in 1964 and 1966 when the rates of defense tax and national security taxes were raised.

69. Vatikiotis, *Nasser and His Generation*, 217.

70. Richard Adams, *Development and Social Change in Rural Egypt* (Syracuse: Syracuse University Press, 1986), 63; El-Sheikh, "The Egyptian Taxation System," 94.

71. M. Abdel-Fadil, *The Political Economy of Nasserism* (Cambridge: Cambridge University Press, 1980), 88.

72. Adams, *Development and Social Change*, 50; Alan Richards and John Waterbury, *A Political Economy of the Middle East: State, Class, and Economic Development* (Boulder: Westview Press, 1990), 156. The peasantry often found ways to evade the heavy taxation, primarily by switching to less taxed products and not using the market as frequently; see Adams, *Development and Social Change*, 66. This would have disastrous consequences for Egypt's production of foodstuffs and its coming reliance on agricultural imports.

73. Jorgen Lotz, "Taxation in the U.A.R. (Egypt)," *IMF Staff Papers* 13 (March 1966): 136; El-Sheikh, "The Egyptian Taxation System," 88.

74. For favorable tax bias, see Mark Cooper, "Egyptian State Capitalism in Crisis: Economic Policy and Political Interests, 1967–71," *International Journal of Middle East Studies* 10 (November 1979): 481–83. The defense tax on land was raised from 3.5 percent to 7 percent of rental value in 1962, and then subsequently raised to 10.5 percent in 1965. For unfavorable tax bias, see Lotz, "Taxation in the U.A.R." The defense tax is the only part of the tax that is paid by the user of the land.

75. Lotz, "Taxation in the U.A.R.," 122.

76. Vatikiotis, *Nasser and His Generation*; Waterbury, *The Egypt of Nasser and Sadat*, 93, 97.

77. Heikal, *The Sphinx and the Commissar*, 148–49.

78. Ali Abdel Rahman Rahmy, *Egyptian Policy in the Arab World: Intervention in Yemen, 1962–67* (Washington, D.C.: University Press of America, 1983), 208–9. Vatikiotis, *Nasser and His Generation*, 162, cites the figure of LE4,000 million.

79. Cooper, *The Transformation of Egypt*, 38; Waterbury, *The Egypt of Nasser and Sadat*, 98.

80. Ansari, *Egypt: The Stalled Society*, 91. The Egyptian-Soviet entente had existed since 1955, but both sides were still wary of the other's motivations and the potential costs of any closer association or level of commitment. Although Egypt had been able to translate the rigid bipolar system of the 1950s into security assistance from the Soviets, Egypt's importance in superpower affairs had markedly declined over the next decade. Now Nasser was rightfully worried that the Soviets might attempt to use their leverage to control Egypt's domestic and foreign policy. In addition, after Khrushchev's ouster in 1964, partially caused by the premier's Egypt policy, the new Soviet leadership spent the next period evaluating its Middle East policy. In short, the pre-1967 period evidenced both tremendous friendship, as during Khrushchev's visit to Egypt in early 1964, and concealed suspicions, as during the early post-Khrushchev period; neither side, however, was enthusiastic of extending or deepening, and certainly not formalizing, the level of commitment. Nasser was generally wary of providing the Soviets any greater control over Egyptian foreign or domestic policy. See Heikal, *The Sphinx and the Commissar*, 148–71.

81. Anwar Sadat, *In Search of Identity* (New York: Harper & Row, 1978), 213; Waterbury, *The Egypt of Nasser and Sadat*, 93–100.

82. Rahmy, *Egyptian Policy in the Arab World*, 246–47.

83. Efrat, *The Defense Burden in Egypt*, 94–95.

84. *Quarterly Economic Review*, no. 1 (1966): 4. Part of the public debt was owing to Soviet arms deliveries. Egypt's annual payments were $18 million during this period, unless an arms deal was concluded during that year, whereby they paid $28 million. Although Egypt had paid in full its arms debt incurred before 1960, after this year it had paid just 35 percent of the estimated value of the equipment. See Heikal, *The Sphinx and the Commissar*.

85. According to Walt, *The Origins of Alliances*, 90, the Soviets moved quickly to assist "Egypt's intervention in Yemen, as military aid increased in both quality and quantity, and Soviet pilots reportedly flew the transport planes ferrying equipment from Egypt to Sanaa."

86. Hinnebusch, *Egyptian Politics Under Sadat*, 34.

87. Ansari, *Egypt: The Stalled Society*, 235.

88. Stewart Reiser, *The Israeli Arms Industry* (New York: Holmes and Meier, 1989), 47.

89. For a breakdown of the different military industries and their "civilian" production, see Barbour, *Growth, Structure and Location*, 132–35.

90. Selim, "Egypt," 132–34; Vayrynen and Ohlson, "Egypt," 108.

91. Vatikiotis, *Nasser and His Generation*, 160, 162. The number of Egyptian troops in Yemen rose from 20,000 in 1963, to 40,000 in 1964, to 70,000 in 1965. Anthony McDermott, *Egypt from Nasser to Mubarak: Flawed Revolution* (London: Croom Helm, 1988), 156. The state also granted those soldiers fighting in Yemen certain privileges not available to other military personnel, which extended from admission to the university, positions in the public sector, and the ability to accrue vast profits through black market activities by transporting luxury goods and household appliances into Egypt through the port of Aden. See Vatikiotis, *Nasser and His Generation*, 162; Rahmy, *Egyptian Policy in the Arab World*; and McDermott, *Egypt from Nasser to Mubarak*, 156.

92. General Ahmed Abdel-Halim interview with author, Cairo, January 2, 1991.

93. See Fouad Ajami, *The Arab Predicament* (New York: Cambridge University Press, 1981), 79.

94. Ansari, *Egypt: The Stalled Society*, 142.

95. Shukrullah, "Political Crisis/Conflict," 64, gives this episode a decidedly up-beat interpretation, as he argues that the Egyptian people "for the first time actively and of their own initiative chose their President. The message was not lost on those concerned; if the people can keep the great leader himself in power, so too they can have a say in how he exercises it."

96. Ajami, *The Arab Predicament*, 85.

97. Ansari, *Egypt: The Stalled Society*, 141–42. Over the course of the next few years he would be confronted with ideological assaults and charges of "middle-of-the-roadism." See Rejwan, *Nasserist Ideology*, 183–85.

98. Quoted in Vatikiotis, *Nasser and His Generation*, 185.

99. Ajami, *The Arab Predicament*, 90.

100. Rubenstein, *Red Star on the Nile*, 50. Societal dissatisfaction took the form of street demonstrations because the masses had two "official" institutional mechanisms for channeling its complaints, the Arab Socialist Union and the National Assembly, both of which were rightly perceived as the creation and creature of the government and thus not truly responsive or accountable to societal concerns. Consequently, societal grievances were filed in nonsanctioned arenas, and the political arena expanded dramatically as groups sought new outlets for their dissatisfaction.

101. Hinnebusch, *Egyptian Politics Under Sadat*, 36.

102. Ayubi, *Bureaucracy and Politics*, 399.

103. Ibid., 393–94; Hinnebusch, *Egyptian Politics Under Sadat*, 109.

104. Vatikiotis, *Nasser and His Generation*, 186. Nasser also granted greater autonomy to the state-owned enterprises and replaced the managers with younger and better-trained men. See Kanovsky, *The Economic Impact of the Six-Day War*, 293–94.

105. Hinnebusch, *Egyptian Politics Under Sadat*, 31–33.

106. Ismail Sabri Abdallah interview with author, December 26, 1990, Cairo.

107. Although the military's position was jeopardized by, and shouldered much of the blame for, the defeat, it still retained an important decision-making position and certainly influenced the policy choices over the following years. Thus, the decision-making process was typically a function of intra-elite and bureaucratic bargaining between the important factions and political alliances. This made elite patterns and personal ties even more important than they had been under Nasser.

Sadat continued the trend toward a personalization of the decision-making process. Those who enjoyed Sadat's trust and confidence, situated in an unmatched position of influence, were able to act as powerbrokers. See Hinnebusch, *Egyptian Politics Under Sadat*, 122–24. This process of centralization, which included the demilitarization of the cabinet, allowed Sadat both to surround himself with those accountable and loyal to him and to solidify support for his military strategy, including his dealings with the Soviets, the Saudis, and the Israelis. His final moves toward centralizing power came in December 1972, when he replaced the heads of the Arab Socialist Union with those more accountable to his economic and security policies and perceived more legitimate by the masses. See Rubenstein, *Red Star on the Nile*, 221; Hinnebusch, *Egyptian Politics Under Sadat*, 49–50. Since 1952 the decision-making process became steadily more centralized and personalized.

108. Hinnebusch, *Egyptian Politics Under Sadat*, 35, writes that "the 1967 defeat, coming at a time when the Egyptian political system was already weakening, threw the regime into a profound crisis. Its energies and resources diverted to coping with the consequences of defeat, the system proved incapable of self-reform; instead, the defeat accelerated the forces undermining it."

109. Vatikiotis, *Nasser and His Generation*, 257.

110. Janice Gross Stein, "Calculation, Miscalculation, and Conventional Deterrence, I: The View from Cairo," in Robert Jervis et al., *Psychology and Deterrence* (Baltimore: Johns Hopkins University Press, 1985), 34–59.

111. Egyptian war preparation extended beyond the mobilization of financial, productive, and human resources. Heikal tells the story of Vice-President Sadat arriving at an ASU meeting wearing a khaki outfit. When queried about the clothing's significance, he replied that it was necessary to be ready for war on a moment's notice. When Nasser heard of the exchange, he asked, "'Is that what our readiness for war amounts to?' he asked, laughing. 'Wearing khaki?'" Mohamed Heikal, *Autumn of Fury: The Assassination of Sadat* (London: Deutsch, 1983), 85.

112. See Table 5.1. Whereas before 1967 the defense budget included all Egyptian defense expenditures, after the June War it represented *only* the "normal development" of defense expenditures, which comprised defense expenditures before 1967. An Emergency Fund was created to absorb all post-1967 defense expenditures.

Defense Budget, 1961–1973 (in millions of Egyptian pounds)

	Supplemental Defense Expenditures	Emergency Fund
1961/62	87	—
1965/66	235	—
1967/68	198	60
1973	282	399

Source: Efrat, *The Defense Burden in Egypt*, 122.

It is highly likely, however, that there were substantial defense costs hidden in other parts of the budget.

113. Ismail Abdallah interview with author, Cairo, December 26, 1990; Ajami, *The Arab Predicament*, 91.

114. Also see Cooper, *The Transformation of Egypt*, 40–43. There also was increased intra-elite conflict, notably between Mohammad Heikal, who defended the military against the increasing attempt by the ASU to politicize it,

and Ali Sabri, the head of the ASU. These intracabinet political maneuverings, particularly evident during Sadat's consolidation of power in 1971, did not really impinge on or concern themselves with the government's war preparation strategies.

115. Ismail Abdallah interview with author, Cairo, May 14, 1987. For war preparation, see Heikal, *The Road to Ramadan*, 52.

116. One of the first causalties of the June War and the imperative of systemic and domestic survival was governmental investment; it declined dramatically after 1967. See Ibrahim Issawi and Muhammed Nassar, "An Attempt to Estimate the Economic Losses Inflicted by the 1967 Arab-Israeli War" (paper presented to the third annual Conference of Egyptian Economists, Cairo, March 23–25, 1978) (in Arabic). Also see Waterbury, *The Egypt of Nasser and Sadat*, 112.

117. Ajami, *The Arab Predicament*, 83.

118. Hinnebusch, *Egyptian Politics Under Sadat*; Waterbury, *The Egypt of Nasser and Sadat*; and Ansari, *Egypt: The Stalled Society*, also focus on structural, as opposed to personality, factors. This perception was evoked by many government officials of the period whom I interviewed.

119. *Speeches and Interviews of President Mohammed Anwar El-Sadat*, September 1970–December 1971, Ministry of Information, Arab Republic of Egypt.

120. See Ansari, *Egypt: The Stalled Society*, for a detailed study of the symbolic importance of this episode for marking the changed orientation of the Nasserite regime.

121. Ansari, *Egypt: The Stalled Society*, 142.

122. Ajami, *The Arab Predicament*, 90–91.

123. Both relied on the military and elements of the bureaucracy, but Nasser built up the working classes while Sadat cultivated the support of the upper classes. Hinnebusch, *Egyptian Politics Under Sadat*, 299. Accordingly, Nasser attempted to control the masses, occasionally by using them against the upper classes and personally dispensing and administering his view of their interests; Sadat, however, viewed the bourgeoisie as a positive force, both in the economy and the polity, and tended to view with some hostility the demands of the masses. However much Sadat attempted to portray himself as defender and protector of the common man, those institutional mechanisms that had connected Nasser to the masses rarely reached to the upper branches of decision making under Sadat. Hinnebusch, *Egyptian Politics Under Sadat*, 226–27.

124. Historical narratives, Ansari, *Egypt: The Stalled Society*; Rubenstein, *Red Star on the Nile*; and Ghali Shoukri, *Egypt: Portrait of a President* (London: Zed Press, 1981); and autobiographical accounts by Egyptian officials, Shazli, *The Crossing of the Suez*; Heikal, *The Road to Ramadan*, and *The Sphinx and the Commissar*, testify to the tremendous change that occurred in Egyptian society with Sadat's replacement of Nasser. In *In Search of Identity*, Sadat acknowledges the domestic discontent, but he attributes it to either Soviet-backed plots (234) or journalists who were attempting to "create a sense of instability . . . in the country" (245). Whatever the source, the lasting impression is that Egyptian officials felt themselves under greater societal constraints and pressures after 1971.

125. Shoukri, *Egypt: Portrait of a President*, 93–101.

126. Ansari, *Egypt: The Stalled Society*, 162–76. These societal objections were not peculiar to Sadat, for Nasser also confronted a similar set of complaints.

127. Rubenstein, *Red Star on the Nile*, 180.

128. Ahmed Abdalla, *The Student Movement and National Politics in Egypt* (London: Al-Saqi Books, 1985), 190; Heikal, *The Road to Ramadan*, 20.

129. Stein, "Calculation, Miscalculation, and Conventional Deterrence, I," 54.

130. Karen Dawisha, *Soviet Foreign Policy Towards Egypt* (London: Macmillan, 1979), 61.

131. Ibid.

132. See Hinnebusch, *Egyptian Politics Under Sadat*, 29.

133. *Monthly Survey of Arab Economies*, June (1969): 18.

134. Efrat, *The Defense Burden in Egypt*, 152.

135. Kanovsky, *The Economic Impact of the Six-Day War*, 279–87.

136. For a broad overview of Egypt's postwar fiscal and monetary policy, see ibid., 303–6.

137. *Quarterly Economic Review* 3 (1967): 2–9.

138. Abdel-Aziz Higazi, interview with author, Cairo, May 10, 1987; Waterbury, *The Egypt of Nasser and Sadat*, 224–27.

139. Reda al-Edel, "Impact of Taxation in Income Distribution: An Exploratory Attempt to Estimate Tax Incidence in Egypt," in G. Abd al-Khalek and R. Tignor, eds., *The Political Economy of Income Distribution in Egypt* (Boulder: Westview Press, 1982), 142.

140. Abdel-Aziz Higazi, interview with author, Cairo, May 10, 1987.

141. This is a duty "levelled on all deeds, documents, applications, registers, and contracts; gas, electricity and water suppliers; and electricity and gas consumption, etc." J. Lotz, "The Taxation System in the U.A.R.," 136–37.

142. Cooper, *The Transformation of Egypt*, 40; also see Waterbury, *The Egypt of Nasser and Sadat*, 225.

143. Ikram, *Egypt*, 315; Issawi and Nassar, "An Attempt to Estimate the Economic Losses."

144. Central Bank of Egypt, "The Development of Taxation in Egypt," 14.

145. Ansari, *The Stalled Society*, chap. 5.

146. Other signs of a changed attitude toward the private sector occurred soon after the 1967 War with the decision to rely on foreign capitalist firms to develop the local oil industry and to help spur tourism. Moreover, the public sector came under attack, and there occurred the first, but minor, denationalizations. Although these moves were countered by strong criticism from the Left, this was the first evidence that the government was willing to reconsider the role of the private sector in the country's development since the nationalizations of 1961. See Kanovsky, *The Economic Impact of the Six-Day War*, 291–92.

147. The "Exchange Control Regulations" laws may be found in Central Bank of Egypt, *Central Bank of Egypt Economic Review* 8 (1968): 49–50.

148. A. Higazi, interview with author, Cairo, May 10, 1987. Also see Cooper, "Egyptian State Capitalism in Crisis," 493. According to Ismail Sabri Abdallah, the deputy minister of planning, the attempt to lure private capital was fairly

minimal and isolated during this period. The only liberalization that did oc-cur was in the realm of foreign trade. Before 1968 there was a unified exchange rate. After 1968 the government had a parallel, or dual, system, whereby tour-ists and Egyptian workers sending remittance payments abroad were encour-aged to do so. This was done to attract foreign currency to pay for the defense-related imports. It was fairly minimal, however, for out of a total bill of $800 million, only $150 million was attracted by these laws. Higazi interview, Cairo, May 14, 1987.

149. Baker, *Egypt's Uncertain Revolution*, 116; Malak Zaalouk, *Power, Class, and Foreign Capital in Egypt* (London: Zed Press, 1988), 54.

150. A. Higazi, interviews with author, Cairo, May 10, 1987; January 7, 1991.

151. When Sadat took office in 1971, Egypt's foreign debt included the fol-lowing: $380 million and $1.7 billion in military debt to the Soviet Union; $205 million to the United States (mainly wheat shipments); $122 million to Italy; $106 million to Germany. The total nonmilitary debt was $1.3 billion. Heikal, *Autumn of Fury*, 86–87.

152. Ajami, *Arab Predicament*, 93–94. This new "realism" was evident in Nasser's acceptance of the Rogers Plan to end the War of Attrition and his back-ing of Hussein of Jordan against the PLO in September 1970. See Ansari, *Egypt: The Stalled Society*, 150.

153. Rubenstein, *Red Star on the Nile*, 38; Heikal, *The Road to Ramadan*, 52.

154. Efrat, *The Defense Burden in Egypt*, 152. Heikal, *The Road to Rama-dan*, 52, however, minimizes the Arab contribution: "The entire amount prom-ised by King Feisal and others at Khartoum was spent within less than one-half year on a single project."

155. Quoted in Rubenstein, *Red Star on the Nile*, 102.

156. For a good overview of this relationship see Shazli, *The Crossing of the Suez*; Rubenstein, *Red Star on the Nile*; and Heikal, *The Sphinx and the Commissar*.

157. Heikal, *The Sphinx and the Commissar*, 191. This attitude continued under Sadat, who proclaimed that Egypt must "keep and strengthen our rela-tions with the Soviet Union until we have built a modern and powerful country both economically and militarily." Shazli, *The Crossing of the Suez*, 105.

158. Dawisha, *Soviet Foreign Policy toward Egypt*, 43–49.

159. In *Red Star on the Nile*, Rubenstein claims that Nasser and Sadat were able to minimize any possible autonomy costs.

160. Efrat, *The Defense Burden in Egypt*, 101. The clear apex of Soviet-Egyptian relations during the Sadat years came on May 27, 1971, at the signing of the "Soviet-Egyptian Treaty of Friendship and Cooperation." Although the Soviets were most pleased by the economic and military guarantees of the treaty, particularly aiding the reconstruction of Egyptian society along socialist lines, the Egyptians were clearly more impressed with the military stipulations and pledges of Soviet defense for Egyptian territory. Rubenstein, *Red Star on the Nile*, 144–49.

161. *Quarterly Economic Review* 2 (1970): 6.

162. Shazli, *The Crossing of the Suez*.

163. Arms Control and Disarmament Agency, *World Military Expenditures and Arms Transfers* (Washington, D.C.: Government Printing Office, various years). Also see Appendix 4.

164. According to Nasser on July 23, 1968: "We have so far paid not one millieme for the arms we obtained from the Soviet Union. We have no money to buy arms." Quoted in Rubenstein, *Red Star on the Nile*, 29, also see 63–64, 81.

165. Efrat, *The Defense Burden in Egypt*, 34, 36, 95; Kanovsky, *The Economic Impact of the Six-Day War*, 288. After the Six-Day War Egypt's imports from the Soviet Union increased by 50 percent, but Egypt officially registered a favorable balance of payments with the Soviet Union. Obviously this was misleading, for it allowed for the "nonregistration of goods imported actually under the 'Temporary Admission Rules,' " and the Soviets paid higher than world market prices for Egyptian exports, anywhere from 8 to 45 percent between 1964 and 1972. Efrat, *The Defense Burden in Egypt*, 9, 11, 24.

166. Egypt's barter relationship had the effect of depleting its major source of hard currency. *Quarterly Economic Review* 2 (1970): 6.

167. Ibid., 216.

168. Heikal, *The Road to Ramadan*, 171–77; Vayrynen and Ohlson, "Egypt," 108.

169. Ansari, *Egypt: The Stalled Society*, 176.

170. Shazli, *The Crossing of the Suez*, 143.

171. Further student unrest in December 1972 contributed to the government's unease and belief that society would not tolerate much more of the current policies. Heikal, *The Road to Ramadan*, 20.

172. Rubenstein, *Red Star on the Nile*. In *Egypt: The Stalled Society*, 175, Ansari argues that Sadat began both to use religious claims and themes and to encourage the formation of Islamic groups in order to bolster his sagging support.

173. *In Search of Identity*, Sadat advances this interpretation, but he also conveys the impression that he had become impatient with never-ending series of unfulfilled Soviet promises. Ansari, *Egypt: The Stalled Society*, 176–77, notes that Egyptian military officials and society at large registered a fair number of complaints over the growing Egyptian dependence, and this may have caused Sadat to distance himself from the Soviets. Although undoubtedly this contributed to the chorus of complaints, if feared Egyptian dependence was the primary motivator of Sadat's decision, one might also expect to see a change in Egyptian dependence and internal balancing behavior. No such behavior was evidenced, however.

An additional systemic argument derives from the emergence of superpower détente and the type of war that might be waged against the Israelis. As it became clear that the Soviets were not going to supply the long-range bombers and other weapons systems needed to reach into Israel's interior, in early 1972 Sadat switched the military strategy from a comprehensive campaign designed to liberate the entire Sinai to a limited one intended to demonstrate to the Israelis that they could not hold indefinitely onto the Sinai. Moreover, by evicting the Soviets from Egypt Sadat was sending a signal to Kissinger and the Americans that he was looking to improve their chilly relations. Hafez Ismail, interview with author, Cairo, January 3, 1991.

174. The eviction of the Soviets initiated Sadat's use of a "surprise" or a dramatic foreign policy gesture to bolster his dwindling political fortunes. See A. Dawisha, "Arab Regimes: Legitimacy and Foreign Policy," in Giacomo Luciani, ed., *The Arab State* (Berkeley: University Of California Press, 1990), 291. The Soviets were the likely target because Egypt was widely perceived as its satellite.

175. After Sadat expelled the Soviet advisers, the Egyptian military coordinated their departure in such a way that it would minimize the possible damage to its national security. Soviet equipment for which Egypt had no substitute would be allowed to stay, provided that it remained under Egyptian command. Shazli, *The Crossing of the Suez*, 164–65.

176. ACDA, various years.

177. K. Dawisha, *Soviet Foreign Policy*, 64.

178. Heikal, *The Sphinx and the Commissar*, 253.

179. For the 1973 agreement, see Shazli, *The Crossing of the Suez*, 140–43, 157; Rubenstein, *Red Star on the Nile*, 235; Sadat, *In Search of Identity*, 238. For Russians, see K. Dawisha, *Soviet Foreign Policy*, 65. Indeed, Telhami, *Power and Leadership*, 68, and Rubenstein, *Red Star on the Nile*, 199, claim that Sadat's strategy was not all that risky because he correctly anticipated that there was little else that the Soviets could do under the situation.

180. Rubenstein, *Red Star on the Nile*, 196.

181. Ibid., 154.

182. Ibid., 241.

183. See Jake Wien, *Saudi-Egyptian Relations: The Political and Military Dimensions of Saudi Financial Flows to Egypt* (Santa Monica: Rand, 1980).

184. Efrat, *The Defense Burden in Egypt*, 143; Nadav Safran, *Saudi Arabia: The Ceaseless Quest for Security* (Cambridge: Harvard University Press, 1985), 148. Because Egypt was forced to bear a substantially disproportionate financial burden in the Arab-Israeli conflict, Shazli's goal was to even the burden and possibly unify the Arab countries' defense budgets: "A utopian dream. When I floated even the broad outline of the project unofficially around the Arab League, I found it so unacceptable that it would have been inadvisable to broach it officially." Shazli, *The Crossing of the Suez*, 109.

185. The government did take some additional domestic measures designed to forestall the fiscal crisis while readying the country for war; however, these actions excluded any substantial attempt to increase the revenue base. On February 11, 1973, the government announced a number of austerity measures that included suspending long-term projects, freezing salaries, raising taxes, cutting the budget in services not directly related to production of public utilities, and tightening the restrictions on luxury imports. Sadat also established the right to impose additional taxes and duties without prior consultation with the Parliament until, "the end of the current year or the removal of the traces of aggression, whichever is earlier." Quoted in Rubenstein, *Red Star on the Nile*, 223. Moreover, Sadat instructed Treasury Minister Higazi to prepare for even fur-

ther revenue-saving measures (while also instructing him to go forward on the creation of a Free Trade Zone and a Bank for Foreign Trade and Development designed to attract foreign capital). See Rubenstein, *Red Star on the Nile*, 223; Baker, *Egypt's Uncertain Revolution*, 130.

186. Quoted from Rubenstein, *Red Star on the Nile*, 282. Rubenstein further argues that "the situation must have been more severe than Sadat had admitted. Given the enormous allocations to the military—defense expenditures from 1967 to 1973 were five times those allotted for development—the decision to go to war could scarcely have had worse consequences than continued despairing acceptance of the status quo."

187. Shukrallah, "Political Crisis/Conflict," 70.

188. Heikal, *The Road to Ramadan*, 20. Indeed, Egypt received $500 million in aid immediately once war began. Rubenstein, *Red Star on the Nile*, 282.

189. If Sadat was able to go to war at this point it is because the objectives of the military campaign had changed significantly. Whereas before 1972 the military high command was planning on fighting a war to liberate totally the Sinai through force, after this year there was a shift in strategic thinking to a war whose goals would be limited to taking the East Bank of the Suez. Two principal factors contributed to this shift. First, the military campaign was intended as a political victory, one designed both to establish a new reality in the Arab-Israeli conflict and to prove to the Israelis that there was no such concept as "total security." Second, it became clear by this time that the resources with which to wage the campaign were limited, and Egyptian command was intent on bringing into correspondence their military strategy with the available resources. Hafez Ismail, interview with author, Cairo, January 3, 1991.

190. Waterbury, *The Egypt of Nasser and Sadat*, 113.

191. Also see Hinnebusch, *Egyptian Politics Under Sadat*, 36, 38.

192. As already mentioned, the decline of the arms industry was owing to the fact that the economy lacked the manufacturing and industrial base, scientific know-how, and financial capital to support military industrialization without foreign assistance, and the Soviets were not about to help on this score. Many military corporations that did exist ran into financial difficulties and subsequently closed by the late 1960s. The remaining fifteen military corporations were confined to repairing imported weapons. Efrat, *The Defense Burden in Egypt*, 16; Stork, "Arms Industries in the Middle East," 13. By 1972 total output was estimated at $93 million (compared to $70 million in 1966).

193. Moreover, many Egyptian officers blamed the 1967 defeat on inferior Soviet equipment. Heikal, *The Road to Ramadan*, 171–77.

194. Ibid.; Vayrynen and Ohlson, "Egypt," 108.

195. Shazli, *The Crossing of the Suez*, 196.

196. Ibid., 113–14; Rubenstein, *Red Star on the Nile*, 134. The Soviets had also agreed in February 1972 to help Egypt manufacture its own MIG-21s by 1979. Shazli, *The Crossing of the Suez*, 137. This, like the previous coproduction agreements, did not survive the downturn in Soviet-Egyptian relations. See Efrat, *The Defense Burden in Egypt*, 16.

197. Shazli, *The Crossing of the Suez*, 196; Vayrynen and Ohlson, "Egypt," 109.

198. I. Abdallah, interview with author, Cairo, May 14, 1987.

199. I. Abdallah, interview with author, Cairo, December 26, 1990.

200. A. Higazi, interview with author, Cairo, May 14, 1987.

201. Ayubi, *Bureaucracy and Politics*, 404.

202. And even in 1969 the private sector included 148,229 establishments employing 510,659 workers; this accounted for nearly 49 percent of labor in the industrial sector.

203. *Monthly Review of Arab Economies* (November 1970): 33.

204. Hinnebusch, *Egyptian Politics Under Sadat*, 38. The ten-year plan of 1972–1981 included more liberalization provisions, greater freedom and responsibility for public sector managers, and the establishment of an investment organization that would allow concessions and privileges, such as tax exemptions and insurance against nationalizations, for foreign investors. *Arab Economist* (October 1972): 33.

205. Waterbury, *The Egypt of Nasser and Sadat*, 167. See Aliboni et al., *Egypt's Economic Potential* (Dover: Croom Helm, 1984), 26–27, for an overview of these economic policies.

206. The Soviets also shared the perception that a key reason for Egypt's poor performance in the Six-Day War was owing to the Egyptian army's social composition. "Observing that the social base of the Israeli military was a well-trained army of educated men knowledgeable in the use of modern weapons, the program contrasted them with the fundamentally peasant composition of Arab armies." The Soviets viewed this as the critical difference between Arab defeats and Israeli victories. In general, their military weakness reflected the basic weakness of their societies. The Soviets also recommended purging the top military command of its bourgeois influences. Rubenstein, *Red Star on the Nile*, 22, 35.

207. Ajami, *The Arab Predicament*, 89.

208. *The Crossing of the Suez*, 50.

209. Rubenstein, *Red Star on the Nile*, 41; Efrat, *The Defense Burden in Egypt*, 148. Referring to the 1973 successes, Heikal, *The Road to Ramadan*, 43, writes: "what the Israelis did not appreciate was that of the 800,000 Egyptians under arms, no fewer than 100,000 were graduates of universities or institutes of higher education. . . . So Egypt had begun to match Israel in the quality of its troops, while having of course greater potential in quantity."

210. Rubenstein, *Red Star on the Nile*, 18, 30; Shazli, *The Crossing of the Suez*, 13–14, 164–65.

211. For 1967 Soviet rejection, see Rubenstein, *Red Star on the Nile*, 18. For 1969 rejection, see K. Dawisha, *Soviet Foreign Policy*, 46. She continues, "On this occasion, the Soviet leaders declined what they must have thought would be an entangling alliance." For Soviet agreement, see Rubenstein, *Red Star on the Nile*, 107–8; he argues that Nasser's decision to visit Moscow at this time is a good indication of his regime's increasing instability. Society was becoming more and more dissatisfied with the "no war/no peace" situation while being

burdened by war preparation, and the military, Nasser's main basis of support, was becoming increasingly disgruntled with the current situation. On July 23, 1970, Nasser announced to the Egyptian people the coming of Soviet military assistance:

> During those days [of Nasser's visit to Moscow] I sensed much interest in the safety of the Egyptian people, in their cities and villages, in saving the Egyptian people from exposure to the enemy's raids and in ensuring Egypt's ability to defend its territory with all means. The Soviet leaders subsequently issued a decision saying that the Soviet Union would help us with all its power to defend our homeland. . . . They told me during my January visit that the support we required would reach us in no more than 30 days.

212. The Soviets did not come cheap, for the Egyptians had to buy the equipment for the Soviets to use on Egyptian territory, provide food and field clothing for the Soviet forces, and pay Moscow the equivalent of L150 sterling for a soldier and L170 sterling for an officer in hard currency to cover their salaries. Shazli, *The Crossing of the Suez*, 138.

213. Quoted in Rubenstein, *Red Star on the Nile*, 72.

214. Shazli, *The Crossing of the Suez*, 192–95.

215. Heikal, *Autumn of Fury*, 56.

216. Shazli, *The Crossing of the Suez*, 73.

217. Ibid. These discharges directly affected Egypt's battle plans. The key to Egypt's planned surprise attack on Israel was the ability to mobilize its troops without detection by the Israelis. Egyptian Chief of Staff Shazli notes that this "became a problem for us only in June 1972. Up until then, we had no reserves" (71). In fact, rehearsing the mobilization and demobilization of soldiers, an institutionalized practice before the Yom Kippur War, served the purpose of both practicing reserve mobilization and getting the Israelis used to the practice and thus lulling them into a false sense of security (75, 207).

218. This strategy was especially evident immediately prior to the October War. Specifically, the military released some of those conscripts in nonessential elements as a way of lulling the Israelis into a false sense of security while maintaining their military capabilities. Hafez Ismail, interview with author, Cairo, January 3, 1991.

219. Shazli, *The Crossing of the Suez*, 106.

220. Hafez Ismail, interview with author, Cairo, January 3, 1991.

221. For an exact breakdown of each country's contribution, see Shazli, *The Crossing of the Suez*, 84, 277–79. The Egyptians also received a North Korean contingent, including twenty fighter pilots.

222. Ajami, *The Arab Predicament*, 96.

223. See Dawisha, *Soviet Foreign Policy*, and Heikal, *The Sphinx and the Commissar*, for good overviews of this period of Egyptian-Soviet relations.

224. The Emergency Budget, whose purpose was to account for military expenses after 1967, included another 9 percent of the defense budget. *Arab Economist* (January 1974): 16.

225. That Egypt was expending billions of dollars on defense without any overt hostility save a border skirmish with Libya in 1977 was not lost on Sadat's critics. See, for instance, Heikal, *Autumn of Fury*, 79.

226. Karawan, "Egypt's Defense Policy," 160.

227. Aliboni et al., *Egypt's Economic Potential*, 218.

228. Tahseen Bashir, interview with author, Cairo, December 28, 1990.

229. Ibid. Tahseen Bashir suggested that after 1973 Sadat was quite anxious to deliver military goods to the army as a way of immediately demonstrating to them that the switch from the Soviets to the Americans would not cause them hardship. Because of the rush, Sadat failed to negotiate as good a financial package as he might have. Nasser himself revealed the importance of placating the military, when he stated in 1959 that "the army is my Parliament. The army has not carried out the Revolution simply to make me a ruler and then to leave me and go." Quoted in K. Dawisha, *Soviet Foreign Policy*, 179.

230. Hinnebusch, *Egyptian Politics Under Sadat*, 56, writes that the economy and security "pulled in the same direction. Egypt's options were sharply constrained by her economic problems; . . . the war had opened up new sources of economic help, surplus petro-dollars, and Western aid and investment."

231. Sadat hoped to curtail the growth, if not trim the size, of the public sector, which was viewed as a weighty drag on economic growth. The lengths to which he went in this direction, however, were questionable. Although the technocratic elite momentarily feared that the opening of the economy meant an eroding public sector, the core of the public sector—the banking, finance, and major corporations—were left untouched, for they were viewed as providing an important source of support for foreign and domestic capital. See Baker, *Egypt's Uncertain Revolution*, 192–93. As a result, public sector elites had mixed feelings toward infitah. On the one hand, many generally favored the new opportunities and rewards that might emerge with Western investment. Ayubi, *Bureaucracy and Politics*, 477–80. On the other hand, infitah was an implicit attack on the public sector's poor performance over the past decade. Moreover, the state both targeted the private sector for certain privileges and enticements and had greater sympathy from the executive office. No matter Sadat's underlying attitude toward the public sector, he could not seriously consider moving against it. The public sector not only formed an important part of his political base, but trimming it also implied transferring its workers to the streets where nothing but unemployment awaited their arrival. Idle time is the revolutionary's playground. The only industrial area that remained the exclusive domain of the public sector were those connected to military industries and national security needs.

232. The government's intention more fully to incorporate the private sector was in motion soon after the Yom Kippur War. On December 8, 1973, Dr. Abdel-Qadir Hatem told the People's Assembly that the government would continue its path established last April of more fully including the private sector in the economy. *Quarterly Economic Review* 4 (1973): 9.

233. Delwin Roy, "Private Industry Sector Developments in Egypt: An Analysis of Trends, 1973–1977," *Journal of South Asian and Middle Eastern Studies* 1 (Spring 1978): 12.

234. Ismail Abdallah, interview with author, Cairo, May 14, 1987.

235. Quoted in Baker, *Egypt's Uncertain Revolution*, 136.

236. In his interview with the author, Cairo, January 7, 1991, former Finance Minister Higazi also traces part of the roots of al-infitah to the interwar period, though not necessarily to the demands of war preparation per se. He and other cabinet officials were quite impressed by the Soviet ability to seek out Western investment and technology, which was embodied in the 1972 Soviet-American Agreement of Understanding; they were especially struck by the fact that the Soviets had concluded an agreement for materials that the Egyptians themselves were negotiating for with the Soviets. This, according to Higazi, led him to argue that what was good for the Soviets was good for the Egyptians.

237. This concern over the Egypt's trade dependence on the Soviet Union was reinforced by Soviet-Egyptian arms negotiations. In 1973 Egypt attempted to renegotiate its debts to the Soviet Union into two packages—one military, the other economic. This proposal, initially refused in 1973, was later accepted. However, tensions over the debt provided a further stimulus to infitah and shifting the balance of Egypt's trade to the West. Ismail Abdallah, interview with author, Cairo, May 14, 1987.

238. A. Higazi, interview with author, Cairo, May 10, 1987.

239. Ismail Abdallah, interview with author, Cairo, May 14, 1987; Ayubi, *Bureaucracy and Politics*, 477–80.

240. Waterbury, *The Egypt of Nasser and Sadat*, 70, 128–33.

241. Ibid., 354–58; Ali Dessouki, "Policymaking in Egypt: A Case of the Open Door Economic Policy," *Journal of South Asian and Middle Eastern Studies* 28 (April 1981): 410–16.

242. Hinnebusch, *Egyptian Politics Under Sadat*, 174–80.

243. Bianchi, *Unruly Corporatism*, 46.

244. *Egyptian Politics Under Sadat*, 254–55.

245. Heikal, *Autumn of Fury*, 94–95, argues that during al-infitah the private sector "never had it so good." Capitalizing on their family names and association with the old ruling class, they had access to many in the state apparatus and used such connections to realize huge profits. For a summary of the various layers of the Egyptian political elite under Sadat, see Hinnebusch, *Egyptian Politics Under Sadat*, 91–109.

246. Bianchi, *Unruly Corporatism*, 46.

247. Ibid., 47.

248. Ansari, *Egypt: The Stalled Society*, 185.

249. Ibid.

250. Hinnebusch, *Egyptian Politics Under Sadat*, 156, 58, 114, for the tax benefits granted investors and the financial burden of al-infitah.

251. Central Bank of Egypt, "Development of Taxation in Egypt," 15.

252. Hinnebusch, *Egyptian Politics Under Sadat*, 145.

253. For general concession, see ibid., 265. For elite evasion, see Waterbury, *The Egypt of Nasser and Sadat*, 225–27; Jihan Kamel Tawfik Diab, *The Hidden Economy in Egypt: A Social Accounting Matrix Approach*, M.A. thesis (Department of Economics and Political Science, American University of Cairo, 1983), 41–62.

254. Hinnebusch, *Egyptian Politics Under Sadat*, 267; Aliboni et al., *Egypt's Economic Potential*, 40–45.

255. Hinnebusch, *Egyptian Politics Under Sadat*, 267.

256. *Quarterly Economic Review* 1 (1975): 8–9.

257. The government also began printing money to cover part of the resource gap, and because nearly 40 percent of the deficit was financed from domestic banks inflationary pressures began to rise. Ikram, *Egypt*, 317.

258. Quoted from Baker, *Egypt's Uncertain Revolution*, 135. Waterbury provides an examination of the type of loans and financial external sources of funding. *Egyptian Politics Under Nasser and Sadat*, 414–22.

259. Ajami, *The Arab Predicament*, 99.

260. *Arab Economist* (January 1974): 17; *Quarterly Economic Review* 4 (1973): 8.

261. Efrat, *The Defense Burden in Egypt*, 96. Libya, who was rumored to have pledged approximately a quarter of the Arab contribution, made their assistance conditional on Egypt's postwar posture. *Arab Economist* 5 (November 1973): 57.

262. *Quarterly Economic Review* 2 (1975): 8–9. The Saudis also helped finance Egypt's commodity imports to the tune of $100 million. Most Arab funds came through such agencies as the Kuwaiti Fund and the Abu Dhabi Fund, which were used primarily for development assistance. Kuwait also agreed to help finance $1.3 billion of Egypt's development projects, while other Gulf States chipped in another $100 million. See also Heikal, *Autumn of Fury*, 87.

263. Ansari, *Egypt: The Stalled Society*, 188. See Appendix 5. How much aid Egypt received from the Arab states cannot be determined with any precision because a fair percentage of the Arab transfers never went through the Central Bank of Egypt. For example, at the Rabat Summit in 1975 the Arab countries agreed that Syria and Egypt should split an additional $1 billion to cover their expenses from the Yom Kippur War. Sadat stipulated that the $500 million should not go into the Central Bank, but rather be transferred to a separate account under his control, on the grounds that the money should not be viewed as ordinary revenue but used for emergency purposes. The Kuwaitis refused and channeled the money into the Central Bank. Heikal, *Autumn of Fury*, 88. Wein, *Saudi-Egyptian Relations*, 4, notes that "the majority of funds . . . probably changed hands in an obscure way, discretely allocated from treasury to treasury. Such are military transfers, whether of equipment, or of financial assistance; the largest capital transfers from Saudi Arabia to Egypt may in fact have been for military ends." For instance, Kuwaiti Finance Minister Abdel Latif El-Hamad reported that Egypt had received $2.2 billion between 1971 and 1980, most of which came before Sadat's trip to Jerusalem in 1977, while Egypt's former Finance Minister Abdel Munim Kaisouny placed the figure at $1.4 billion. Heikal, *Autumn of Fury*, 87.

264. Ansari, *Egypt: The Stalled Society*, 187–88.

265. Quoted from ibid., 187–88.

266. Ibid., 189.

267. In a speech to the Parliament in January 1976, Prime Minister Salem claimed that Egypt "had settled all of its military debts to the Soviet Union for

the 1955–60 period; 35 per cent for the 1960–67 period and 25 per cent for the 1967–73 period." K. Dawisha, *Soviet Foreign Policy*, 181.

268. Ibid., 76–77.

269. Ansari, *Egypt: The Stalled Society*, 188.

270. Heikal, *Autumn of Fury*, 78.

271. Quoted in Rubenstein, *Red Star on the Nile*, 302. Also see K. Dawisha, *Soviet Foreign Policy*, 179.

272. Heikal, *The Sphinx and the Commissar*, 14.

273. Efrat, *The Defense Burden in Egypt*, 96.

274. Rubenstein, *Red Star on the Nile*, 297, 300.

275. *Quarterly Economic Review* 1 (1975): 8–9.

276. Rubenstein, *Red Star on the Nile*, 326; Vayrynen and Ohlson, "Egypt," 109.

277. Rubenstein, *Red Star on the Nile*, 302, claims that Egypt also had access to the mounting arms exports to the oil-rich Gulf states, including some of the most sophisticated U.S.-made military equipment. It was inconceivable that in a future Arab-Israeli conflict these weapons would not be shared with Egypt.

278. Selim, "Egypt," 136–38. The only exception to this was Egypt's desire to remain independent in the production of spare parts.

279. Quoted in ibid., 136.

280. Selim, "Egypt," 140. The exception to this was a limited joint venture with the Yugoslavs and the Chinese.

281. By the early 1980s Egyptian military production was estimated at $100 million. Although most output is consumed domestically, recently Egypt has increased its exports. See Stork, "Arms Industries in the Middle East," 13.

282. See Wein, *Saudi-Egyptian Relations*, for a good discussion of the AMIO and its financial and political dimensions.

283. Selim, "Egypt," 142–46; Vayrynen and Ohlson, "Egypt," 110–11.

284. Ben-Dor, "Egypt," 195.

285. General Abdel-Halim, interview with author, Cairo, January 2, 1991.

Chapter Five
Explaining Israeli War Preparation Strategies

1. David Ben-Gurion, *Rebirth and Destiny* (New York: Philosophical Library, 1954), 210.

2. Asher Arian, Ilan Talmud, and Tamar Hermann, *National Security and Public Opinion in Israel* (Boulder: Westview Press, 1988), 23–24.

3. While almost all Israeli leaders believed that Israel must remain as free from foreign influence as possible, there was some debate concerning the Israel's posture toward the international system. For instance, Moshe Dayan argued the defiant and self-reliant stance, particularly when it came to portraying an aggressive posture vis-à-vis the Arab states, while Moshe Sharrett believed that because Israel was weak and vulnerable it must remain dependent on the goodwill of the Great Powers and therefore must avoid those actions that might jeopardize it. Ben-Gurion seemed to combine both, as he embraced Dayan's military strategy but also recognized that Israel could benefit from a Great

Power ally. Yaniv, *Deterrence Without the Bomb*, 64–70. I discuss Israel's relationship to the international system more fully later.

4. Segev, *1949*, 97.

5. Halevi, "The Economy of Israel," 83.

6. Zvi Dinstein, interview with author, Ramat Aviv, June 16, 1987.

7. Moshe Zambar, interview with author, Tel-Aviv, June 12, 1987.

8. Moreover, Nadav Safran, *Israel: The Embattled Ally* (Cambridge: Harvard University Press, 1978), 165–71, argues that the security imperative had the general effect of sliding both the Left (Mapaam) and the Right (Herut) toward Mapai's lead on security issues.

9. Yaniv, *Deterrence Without the Bomb*, 21, 63.

10. Safran, *Israel: The Embattled Ally*, 112; Haim Barkai, *Theory and Praxis of the Histadrut Industrial Sector* (Jerusalem: Maurice Falk Institute for Research, 1962).

11. Some argue that the significant presence of the Israeli state was a product of Zionist ideology, which held the future Jewish state in a quasi-Hegelian, quasi-communitarian formulation, for the state was never an end in itself but rather intended to alter the status and condition of the modern Jew. See Avineri, *The Making of Modern Zionism*, esp. 3–14. This required a rather large state apparatus that would be able to control, albeit in a democratic and consensual manner, the citizenry's condition in all aspects of civil affairs.

12. Ben-Gurion, *Ben-Gurion Looks Back* (New York: Schocken Books, 1970), 144–46.

13. See Uri Bialer, *Between East and West: Israel's Foreign Policy Orientation, 1948–56* (New York: Cambridge University Press, 1990), for a good overview of this critical period in Israeli foreign policy.

14. Yaniv, *Deterrence Without the Bomb*, 50.

15. Michael Michaely, *Foreign Trade Regimes and Economic Development: Israel, Vol. III* (New York: Columbia University Press, 1975), 22, contends that Israel was not the recipient of large amounts of foreign investment and thus had no such motivation. This might mean, however, that Israel was attempting to attract foreign capital, but that its attempts were unsuccessful.

16. Radian, "The Dynamics of Policy Formation: Income Tax Rates in Israel, 1948–75," *Environment and Planning C: Government and Policy* 2 (1984): 275.

17. Kimmerling, *Zionism and Economy*, 163–69.

18. Radian, "Dynamics of Policy Formation," 274.

19. Ibid., 274.

20. Michaely, *Foreign Trade Regimes*, 22–23.

21. Zeev Schiff, *A History of the Israeli Army* (New York: Macmillan, 1985), 56.

22. *Israel Economist* (October 1951), 233. Moreover, there was a change in the budgetary process as the regular budget now included a greater part of the defense budget. Previously a significant part of the defense budget was hidden under other budgets and expenditures. See Peri, *Between Ballots and Bullets*, chap. 10; and Yehezkal Dror, "The Politics of Defense Budgeting: A Comparison Between Western Europe and Israel," in Zvi Lanir, ed., *Israeli Security Plan-*

ning in the 1980s (New York: Praeger Press, 1985), 200–38, for good overviews of the Israeli defense budgeting process.

23. *Israel Economist* (October 1951), 235. In fact, one study concluded that the self-assessed had a ratio of income tax paid to national income as low as 5 percent. *Israel Economist* (November 1955), 196.

24. In fact, tax rates were reduced in 1955 for middle-income groups, primarily government and Histadrut employees. To get this legislation approved, the government provided a tax concession to the self-employed, a demand of the General Zionist party, which was both more representative of this group and part of the cabinet coalition. In general, the administration hoped that decreased tax rates would be offset by improved collection and compliance. Because the government did (or could) not raise either direct or indirect taxes, any increase in tax revenue depended primarily on enhanced collection abilities.

25. Moshe Zambar, interview with author, Tel-Aviv, June 19, 1987.

26. Oded Liviatan, "Israel's External Debt," *Bank of Israel Economic Review* 48/49 (May 1980): 1–45.

27. See Appendix 5 for listing of unilateral transfers. See Leopold Laufer, "U.S. Aid to Israel: Problems and Perspectives," in Gabriel Sheffer, ed., *Dynamics of Dependence: U.S.-Israeli Relations* (Boulder: Westview Press, 1987), 125–64, for a good overview of U.S. financial assistance to Israel since 1948.

28. Howard Sachar, *A History of Israel* (New York: Alfred A. Knopf, 1979), 426.

29. See Appendix 7.

30. Although unilateral transfers were legally restricted to nonmilitary expenditures, they essentially freed more resources for defense. Zambar made the point that "legally all this money . . . was used for social development . . . while our domestic resources were used for defense. In reality it made little difference. If we got more money for development, we could just channel that much more for defense. . . . Money has no taste and no smell." Moshe Zambar, interview with author, Tel–Aviv, June 19, 1987.

31. The origins and stimuli for the development and growth of the Israeli arms industry has almost always corresponded to periods of external violence and hostile forces. The first push came immediately following the Arab riots of 1929, whereby the Yishuv established home production (known as "ta'as") of small arms and ammunition. Subsequent spurts occurred in 1949, 1967, and 1973.

32. According to Ben-Gurion, "They [the Soviet-supplied weapons] saved the state. There is no doubt of this. Without these weapons, its doubtful whether we could have won. The arms deal with the Czechs was the greatest assistance we received." Quoted in Schiff, *A History of the Israeli Army*, 37.

33. Ibid., 52.

34. In *The Israeli Arms Industry*, 21, Reiser claims that this loosely applied guide allowed Israel and the Arab states to acquire some modern weapons.

35. Peres, *David's Sling*, 118.

36. Ibid., 110–11.

37. Reiser, *The Israeli Arms Industry*, 18, 26.

38. Ibid., 19, 34.

39. For Bedek, see Gerald Steinberg, "Israel," in N. Ball and M. Leitenberg, eds., *Structure of Defense Industries: An International Survey* (New York: St. Martin's Press, 1983), 278–309. For Tadiran, see Reiser, *The Israeli Arms Industry*, 22.

40. The government was attracted to an import-substitution industrialization policy for a number of reasons. First, there was a wariness of export-led growth. Israel's industries were sufficiently small and its wage structure abnormally high that its exports would have found few foreign markets. Second, the state's policy instruments were more conducive to the control of imports than to the promotion of exports. Third, Israel relied heavily on capital imports and manufactured goods, which drained its foreign exchange reserves. The government hoped a successful ISI policy would curb Israel's appetite for foreign products and thus save its foreign exchange. Finally, state-led industrialization fit comfortably with Ben-Gurion's etatist view of the Zionist state as society's economic, political, and ideological beacon. See Avineri, *The Making of Modern Zionism*, chap. 17; and Cohen, *Zion and State*, 201–59.

41. Richard Pomfret, *Trade Policies and Industrialization in a Small Country: The Case of Israel* (Tubingen, West Germany: University Kiel, 1975), estimates that 49.2 percent of all tariffs were used for increasing revenues, 7.2 percent for reducing imports (because these tariffs did not increase demand for domestic products), and 49.9 percent for protecting infant industries.

42. Howard Pack, *Structural Change and Economic Policy in Israel* (New Haven: Yale University Press, 1971), 79. For a breakdown of the amount of growth in each industry, see Michaely, *Foreign Trade Regimes*, 196. See Appendix 8.

43. Reiser, *The Israeli Arms Industry*, 30.

44. Ibid.

45. Michaely, *Foreign Trade Regimes*, 5.

46. Moreover, there was no relationship between the absolute import substitution and the absorptive capacity of the industry; this provides further evidence of the state's bias toward defense-related sectors. See Pack, *Structural Change and Economic Policy*, 78–79.

47. Reiser, *The Israeli Arms Industry*, 30.

48. The state's willingness to use the economy for its security needs is also evident in the agricultural sector. The government's investment policy during these early years clearly favored the agricultural sector and reflected the composition and ideological disposition of the cabinet officials and the role of agriculture in development. See Pack, *Structural Change and Economic Policy*, 135. The role of the agricultural sector is more fully explored in the next section under the government's conscription policy.

49. See Mordechai Gazit, "Israeli Military Procurement from the U.S.," in Gabriel Sheffer, ed., *Dynamics of Dependence* (Boulder: Westview Press, 1987), 83–124, for an overview of U.S. military shipments to and strategic relationship with Israel.

50. Peres, *David's Sling*, 38.

51. For a detailed account of the emergence of French-Israeli strategic cooperation, see Peres, *David's Sling*, 42–65; Sylvia Kowitt Crosbie, *A Tacit Alliance: France and Israel From the Suez to the Six-Day War* (Princeton: Princeton University Press, 1974).

52. Steinberg, "Israel," 280–81.

53. This chapter of Israeli history, though quite important for future civil-military relations, is beyond the scope of this study. Briefly, Ben-Gurion absorbed Palmach into the IDF but purged the top IDF post of most Palmach officers because their allegiance leaned toward Mapaam, Mapai's closest political rival on the Left. Ben-Gurion also moved to establish civilian control over the armed forces by replacing most officers who had not demonstrated their loyalty and sympathy to Mapai in general and Ben-Gurion in specific. See Shimshoni, *Israeli Democracy*, 180, 187; Peri, *Between Ballots and Bullets*, chap. 3; and, Schiff, *A History of the Israeli Army*, 46–57.

54. Eisenstadt, *Israeli Society*, 321.

55. Edward Luttwak and Dan Horowitz, *The Israeli Army* (New York: Harper & Row, 1975), 44, 70. As evidence of the legitimacy of the state was the fact that the Palmach, which was Mapai closest rival on the Left, quickly and effortlessly subsumed its command under that of Ben-Gurion's and that of the new Israeli army's.

56. Luttwak and Horowitz, *The Israeli Army*, 65–67; Schiff, *A History of the Israeli Army*, 33.

57. Israel has continued to benefit from foreign, principally Jewish, volunteers in each of its wars. The only instance in which it received official government manpower support was before the commencement of the 1956 war when three French interceptors were stationed over Israel to forestall any possible Jordanian intervention. Schiff, *A History of the Israeli Army*, 149.

58. Luttwak and Horowitz, *The Israeli Army*, 76. The army's responsibility extended from defending Israel's sovereignty to assisting the establishment of the state's control over society. One of the army's early social functions was to integrate the disparate national and ethnic groups and to instill a unifying national ideology and identity, one that was both Israeli and Zionist. See Moshe Lissak, "The Israeli Defense Forces as an Agent of Socialization and Education: A Research in Role Expansion in Democratic Society," in M. R. Van Gils, ed., *The Perceived Role of the Military* (Rotterdam: Rotterdam University Press, 1971). For instance, the army was responsible for cultivating a single national language, Hebrew, from a literal "tower of Babel."

59. *Ben-Gurion Looks Back*, 141.

60. Schiff, *A History of the Israeli Army*, 50; Yaniv, *Deterrence Without the Bomb*, 30–31.

61. Luttwak and Horowitz, *The Israeli Army*, 79. The government's impulse behind the conscription of women stemmed from its desire to promote full gender equality and a recognition of the state's severe manpower shortage. To avoid conflict with the "traditional concept of womanhood" Orthodox women were exempt. Moreover, women were rarely required to serve in the reserves. Release for reasons of conscience are permitted for women only, but

others may be exempted for religious conviction (but very rarely on pacifist beliefs). In general, approximately 40 percent of all women are exempt from military service for one reason or another. See Schiff, *A History of the Israeli Army*, 109–13.

62. Yaniv, *Deterrence Without the Bomb*, 31–32. He makes further claims: "it seems that one important reason that the transition from full mobilization to a reserve-based army proved so relatively smooth was that the IDF was, in terms of its weapons, an infantry army." It proved difficult to maintain the same conscription patterns once the IDF became more mechanized.

63. See Horowitz, "Strategic Limitations," 281.

64. Quoted in Schiff, *A History of the Israeli Army*, 59.

65. That the kibbutz community was able to successfully pressure the government to alter the conscription formula reflects its political power at this time.

66. Peres, *David's Sling*, 24.

67. Schiff, *A History of the Israeli Army*, 52.

68. Ibid., 58.

69. Ibid., 66.

70. Peres, *David's Sling*, 23.

71. Yaniv, *Deterrence Without the Bomb*, 36. The agricultural settlements, however, were "achieved by settling civilians, including a great number of bewildered new immigrants who had almost no inkling of the overall strategic purpose their presence was supposed to serve." Ibid., 34. This policy later caused a great deal of resentment on the part of the immigrants.

72. Schiff, *A History of the Israeli Army*, 64.

73. Ibid., 118. Since then, many on the Israeli Right have evoked this argument in support of settlement expansion in the occupied territories.

74. Dan Horowitz and Baruch Kimmerling, "Some Social Implications of Military Service and the Reserve System in Israel," *Archives Europeens de Sociologie* 15 (1974): 267.

75. Ibid., 268.

76. Ibid. Also see Bernard Reich, "Israel," in E. Kolodziej and R. Harvaky, eds., *Security Policies in Developing Countries* (Lexington: Lexington Books, 1982), 219–21.

77. There is the highly uncommon situation whereby status in society does not affect an individual's status in the army. This can potentially diffuse class and ethnic tensions. See Horowitz and Kimmerling, "Some Social Implications of Military Service," 272–74.

78. This affects approximately six thousand students a year. Schiff, *A History of the Israeli Army*, 105.

79. Also see Eisenstadt, *The Transformation of Israeli Society*, 182–84. There were other exemptions, notably for the mentally and physically handicapped and married women and those with children.

80. Kimmerling, "Determination of the Boundaries," 22.

81. Horowitz and Kimmerling, "Some Social Implications of Military Service," 265–66.

82. Yaniv, *Deterrence Without the Bomb*, 48.

83. Indeed, in 1954 Israel made an unsuccessful attempt to join NATO. Safran, *Israel: The Embattled Ally*, 167.

84. Yaniv, *Deterrence Without the Bomb*, 51–53.

85. Ibid., 53.

86. Reiser, *The Israeli Arms Industry*, 21.

87. Ibid., 50–52.

88. Safran, *Israel: The Embatted Ally*, 380.

89. Eisenstadt, *The Transformation of Israeli Society*, 214–16.

90. Ibid., 428.

91. Eisenstadt, *Israeli Society*, 303–4.

92. Ibid., 304. Also see Benjamin Azkin and Yehezkal Dror, *Israel: High Pressure Planning* (Syracuse: Syracuse University Press, 1966).

93. Eisenstadt, *Israeli Society*, 165–66.

94. I rely on Shalev, *Labour and the Political Economy in Israel*, for much of this discussion. Although the Histadrut might have been under the guidance of the same party that cared for the state apparatus, this does not imply that the Histadrut is part of the state per se. Rather, the view offered here is that the Histradrut is part of the private sector. The public sector, which is juridically an arm of the state apparatus and owned by various ministerial authorities, is part of the state.

95. Eisenstadt, *The Transformation of Israeli Society*, 425.

96. Moshe Zambar, interview with author, Tel-Aviv, June 29, 1987.

97. Yaniv, *Deterrence Without the Bomb*, 114, argues that the real change was effected by Eshkol's assumption of the prime minister's office. Ben-Gurion, who kept relatively strict control over the country's defense expenditures, argued that the country must live within its means to avoid the perils of dependence. Eshkol's deviation from Ben-Gurion's rule led to an inflammation of the defense budget. Although certainly individual differences are important, it is significant that Israel's defense budget during this period was relatively constant, but would consume a greater proportion of the government's budget with the 1965–1967 recession.

98. Liviatan, "Israel's External Debt," 19–20.

99. Pack, *Structural Change and Economic Policy*, 188–91.

100. Moreover, there is evidence that Israel's largest export, diamonds, escaped the proper taxes due to its own system of assessment. *Israel Economist* (July 1961), 130.

101. Pack, *Structural Change and Economic Policy*, 188–91.

102. In fact, the government reduced business taxes during this period to encourage greater investment.

103. *Israel Economist* (March 1961), 44.

104. Eisenstadt, *The Transformation of Israeli Society*, 227.

105. Yaniv, *Deterrence Without the Bomb*, 80.

106. Liviatan, "Israel's External Debt," 17.

107. The Israelis were not the only ones to profit from the deepening relationship. The French also benefited by having an ally in the region, after they had been effectively excluded by Algeria and other Western defense alliances,

such as the Baghdad Pact. Moreover, Israel contributed to the development of the French arms industry. See Gerald Steinberg, "Indigenous Arms Industries and Dependence: The Case of Israel," *Defense Analysis* 2 (December 1986): 291–305.

108. See Steinberg, "Israel," 280–81. Moreover, it reached other licensing agreements with FN Herstal of Belgium for the production of guns and rifles, Turbomenca of France for aircraft engines, and Tampella of Finland for the manufacture of mortars. See Steinberg, "Indigenous Arms Industries and Dependence."

109. Peres, *David's Sling*, 66–86; Safran, *Israel: The Embattled Ally*, 375–76; Reiser, *The Israeli Arms Industry*, 42–43.

110. Safran, *Israel: The Embattled Ally*, 581.

111. Although the state had embarked on loosening the protective barriers around its industries in 1962, this liberalization was controlled and uneven. The state continued to protect, favor, and develop those industries considered integral to defense, particularly metals, machinery, electronics, and chemicals. These industries all had higher nominal tariff rates, nearly double those of other economic sectors. See Michaely, *Foreign Trade Regimes*, 71.

112. The Defense Ministry's desire to expand production, however, often brought it into conflict with the IDF. Specifically, there had been a running debate between the two over whether Israel's security needs were better served by developing a domestic arms industry or relying on already produced, sophisticated, weapons imports. The Arava, the first of IAI's locally produced jet aircraft, illustrates the contentious relationship. Although the IDF protested that the Arava had no military applications and that it would not be a prospective buyer, the government overrode its objection to domestic production and authorized the use of state funds, which ostensibly might have gone for arms imports. See Reiser, *The Israeli Arms Industry*, 54–55. The issues over the Arava would be repeated in the future, most notably with the Lavi.

113. Illustrative is the Defense Ministry's efforts with respect to the electronics industry and the firm of Tadiram, owned jointly by the Defense Ministry and the private sector. See Peres, *David's Sling*, 132–35.

114. Reiser, *The Israeli Arms Industry*, 39.

115. Yaniv, *Deterrence Without the Bomb*, 75.

116. Ibid., 88–89, 91; Peres, *David's Sling*, 146–47. Israel also began exploring a variety of regional security alliances, tying together the non-Muslim/Arab countries in the region, namely Iran, Ethiopia, Turkey, and Lebanon's Maronite and Druze communities.

117. Amos Elon, *The Israelis*, 29.

118. Ibid., 25.

119. See Stephen Spiegel, *The Other Arab-Israeli Conflict* (Chicago: University of Chicago Press, 1985), 158–65, for an analysis of the U.S. decision to commit to a strategic alliance with the Israelis following the 1967 War.

120. Safran, *Israel: The Embattled Ally*, 583.

121. Yaniv, *Deterrence Without the Bomb*, 154–56.

122. In 1969 Mapai and Rafi formed the Labor party.

123. Eisenstadt, *The Transformation of Israeli Society*, 356–63.

124. Kimmerling, *Zionism and Territory*, 147–81; Yaniv, *Deterrence Without the Bomb*, 180.

125. See Gad Wolfsfeld, *Politics of Provocation: Participation and Protest in Israel* (Albany: State University of New York Press, 1988), 11–15.

126. Howard Sachar, *A History of Israel: Volume II, From the Aftermath of the Yom Kippur War* (New York: Oxford University Press, 1987), 18.

127. Safran, *Israel: The Embattled Ally*, 190.

128. Yamiv, *Deterrence Without the Bomb*, 130.

129. The government's objective of independence became of lesser importance and, in fact, signified a major change in attitude among Israeli decision makers. As Moshe Zambar, former governor of the Bank of Israel, related, Israel's history has witnessed a changing scenario of friends and enemies, reinforcing an aversion to depending on outside help for Israel's survival; see his interview with author, Tel-Aviv, June 29, 1987. According to Ya'acov Arnon, former director general of the Treasury Ministry, the government viewed independence from foreign influence as essential and considered that this could be monitored through the balance of payments; see his interview with author, Jerusalem, June 10, 1987.

130. Although technically these unilateral transfers were restricted to financing development, they essentially freed more resources for defense. Zambar said, "Legally all this money . . . was used for social development . . . while our domestic resources were used for defense. In reality it made little difference. If we got more money for development, we could just channel that much more for defense. . . . Money has no taste and no smell"; see his interview with author, Tel-Aviv, June 29, 1987. Be that as it may, the government was cognizant of its "freedom" from foreign financial entanglements; it still did not consider the current situation of excessive dependence and reliance on foreign infusions healthy. In fact, one the government's stated objectives was to reduce its dependence on capital imports. Prime Minister's Office, *Israel's Economic Development* (Jerusalem: Government Printing Office, 1968), 3.

131. In fact, a rather startling development occurred: the actual collection from the Defense Loan, which was approximately IL 275 million by April 1970, exceeded the projected IL 200 million. This can be attributed to the tremendous societal cohesion following the 1967 War. Also see Kanovsky, *The Economic Impact of the Six-Day War*, 45.

132. Yaacov Arnon, interview with author, Jerusalem, June 10, 1987. Also see Pack, *Structural Change and Economic Policy*, 188–91.

133. See Halevi, "The Economy of Israel"; Berglas, "Defense and Economy"; Appendix 10.

134. Halevi, "The Economy of Israel," 90.

135. Moshe Zambar, interview with author, Tel-Aviv, June 29, 1987.

136. Israel also was now a good credit risk. During its early years Israel inspired little confidence in its prospects for economic viability or survival. The period of rapid economic development during the 1950s and 1960s and the U.S. as a guarantor for any loans, however, provided additional confidence in Israel's credit-worthiness.

137. Israel's occupation of the captured territories provided it with additional

fiscal burdens and opportunities. While generally maintaining the pre-1967 fiscal arrangement, Israeli officials did introduce three changes: (1) West Bank and Gaza workers were now subject to payroll deductions; (2) West Bank and Gaza residents had to bear the burden of Israeli duties on goods imported through Israel; and (3) residents of Jerusalem after the 1967 annexation were subject to higher Israeli taxes. Despite such measures, from 1967 until 1972 "revenues directly accruing to the public sector in the territories have been consistently lower than expenditures, the balance being met from military government sources." After this date the picture becomes more ambiguous, and it is likely that the territories were no longer a financial drain but rather a net contributor to the Israeli budget. See Brian Van Arkadie, *Benefits and Burdens: A Report on the West Bank and the Gaza Strip Since 1967* (New York: Carnegie Endowment for International Peace, 1977), 98–101.

138. Ofira Seliktor, "The Cost of Vigilance: Linking the Economic and Social Costs of Defense," *Journal of Peace Research* 17 (4 1980): 342–43.

139. Ibid. An indication of the defense ministry's lessening autonomy came in April 1968, when the minister of Finance revealed the relative size of the budget, although only for supplementary authorization: 60 percent was to be derived from defense bonds; the other 40 percent from the Development Budget. The Defense Ministry's lessening autonomy took another dive in the early 1970s, when the vast resources that were being channeled to defense and perceived at the neglect of other welfare issues led to the first public confrontations. See Shimshoni, *Israeli Democracy*, 204.

140. Eitan Berglas, interview with author, Tel-Aviv, June 6, 1987. Amnon Noibach, former Finance Ministry official, explained that it was a matter of a "change in the government's priorities. After 1967 there was a dramatic change in the government's economic outlook, and one can witness a real change in the government's fiscal attitude. The attempt at fiscal independence ends completely at this point"; see his interview with author, Herzelyia, June 13, 1987.

141. Berglas, "Defense and Economy," 187.

142. Inflation is an indirect tax because it artificially pushes taxpayers into higher tax brackets; yet it is indirect because the government's actions are not directly observed or attributed to the increased extraction. During this period, and especially in the latter part of the 1970s, inflation hit hardest the middle- and low-income groups.

143. Arnon Gafni, interview with author, Tel-Aviv, June 24, 1987.

144. Amnon Sella and Yael Yishai, *Israel: The Peaceful Belligerent, 1967–79* (New York: St. Martin's Press, 1986), 116.

145. Arnon Gafni, interview with author, Tel-Aviv, June 24, 1987.

146. Ibid. According to a public opinion poll soon after the war, "65.1 percent of the public are unreservedly prepared to tighten their belts and pay higher taxes and another 15.2 percent are prepared to pay a little more. Only 14.9 percent are absolutely opposed to paying any more taxes and 4.9 percent have no views one way or another. The higher one goes up the economic-social scale, the more readiness there is to pay higher taxes." *Israel Economist* (December 1973), 20.

147. During this period of increased burden, however, there were lavish tax

concessions for the large investment firms. This was included under the "Encouragement of Capital Investments (Capital Intensive Companies) 1973." *Israel Economist* (October 1973), 287.

148. To offset the impact on lower-income groups, the government instituted a 4 percent cost-of-living raise for its employees.

149. *Israel Economist* (January 1974), 22.

150. Israel has traditionally been able to finance the import surplus through unilateral transfers, "thus increasing the resources available for allocation between private consumption, investment, and public consumption (which includes defense expenditures)." Halevi, "The Economy of Israel," 89. This ability ceased after 1973.

151. Sachar, *A History of Israel, II*, 18. In 1975 the government also moved to overhaul the tax structure, which, because of years of incrementalism, had contributed to high rates of evasion, lack of capital investment, and generally negative societal consequences. See Yoram Ben-Porath and Michael Bruno, "The Political Economy of a Tax Reform: The Case of Israel, *Journal of Public Economics* 7 (June 1977): 17–29. This tax reform, however, did not introduce any significant change in either the distribution of the burden or the percentage of revenue that derived from domestic sources.

152. Safran, *Israel: The Embattled Ally*, 194–95.

153. See also Appendix 11.

154. Originally U.S. military assistance came in the form of grants. Only later was it a mixture of grants and loans. These grants did not necessarily directly affect Israel's economy or growing military-industrial complex because most grants had to be spent on U.S. products.

155. Moshe Zambar, interview with author, Tel-Aviv, June 29, 1987.

156. Liviatan, "Israel's External Debt," 1; Appendix 12.

157. Reiser, *The Israeli Arms Industry*, 136.

158. Alex Mintz, "The Military-Industrial Complex: The Israeli Case," in Moshe Lissak, ed., *Israeli Society and Its Defense Establishment* (London: Frank Cass, 1984); Steinberg, "Israel: High-Technology Roulette," 164.

159. Reiser, *The Israeli Arms Industry*, 130.

160. Ibid., 80.

161. Mintz, "The Military-Industrial Complex: The Israeli Case," 116–19; Berglas, "Defense and Economy," 185–86. Moreover, the IDF, a key actor that had traditionally stood opposed to domestic production and preferred purchasing weapons from abroad because of the more reliable delivery time, finally acceded to indigenous production. This is probably owing to the fact that an expanding defense budget meant that increasing domestic production would not decrease weapons imports, and possibly because of the fact that a number of military officers retired from military service and took positions in the military industries. See Reiser, *The Israeli Arms Industry*, 81. There are other important considerations for promoting arms production, including the usefulness of using arms exports for cementing friendships with other countries, gaining employment/scientific benefits, and reducing foreign leverage. See Robert Harkavy and Stephanie Neuman, "Israel," in James Katz, ed., *Arms Production in Developing Countries* (Lexington: Lexington Books, 1984), 202; and Steinberg, "Indigenous Arms Industries," 164–70.

162. Eisenstadt, *The Transformation of Israeli Society*, 209.

163. Zvi Dinstien, interview with author, Ramat Aviv, June 16, 1987.

164. Steinberg, "Indigenous Arms Industries," 167.

165. Reiser, *The Israeli Arms Industry*, 131.

166. Ibid., 120.

167. See Prime Minster's Office, *Israel Economic Development*. The government dramatically increased the amount of investment toward defense industries (see Appendix 13). This, in turn, affected other defense-related industries, primarily metals, machinery, and electronics. See Kanovsky, *The Economic Impact of the Six-Day War*, 117. Some inefficient industries were government subsidized owing to the demands of national security. For example, the iron and steel industry is inefficient in comparison to international standards, yet so long as "the security situation remains as at present, the argument that less than total dependence on iron and steel imports is worth paying a price for cannot be dismissed outright . . . because the danger that our military industries might go short of their basic materials must be averted at all costs." *Israel Economist* (September 1968), 305.

168. Rieser, *The Israeli Arms Industry*, 82.

169. Since the late 1970s defense sector investment has outstripped investment in nondefense activities. Steinberg, "Israel," 289.

170. Ibid.

171. Berglas, "Defense and Economy," 184.

172. This contributed to increased industrial concentration. See Jerusalem Institute of Management, *Export-Led Growth Strategy for Israel: A Final Report* (Tel-Aviv: Jerusalem Institute of Management, 1987).

173. Pinchas Zusman, interview with author, Rehovot, June 24, 1987.

174. This is noted in the Development Plan of 1968, which states that "a considerable portion of the production and investment programmes included in the plan will be undertaken by the private sector. . . . Hence the Government measures indicated in the plan are designed to bring about such responses from private entrepreneurs as will assume the fulfillment of the plan." Prime Minister's Office, *Israel's Economic Development*, 7.

175. Tzvi Tropp, interview with author, Tel-Aviv, May 30, 1987. The actual investment figures are classified, and therefore it is impossible to verify the percentage of defense funds that went to the private and public sectors.

176. Also see Alex Mintz, "Arms Production in Israel," *Jerusalem Quarterly* 42 (Spring 1987): 89–99. There also was increased interest in the benefits from increased foreign capitalist activity, although foreign capital had been courted in some fashion since before 1967. See Sheila Ryan, "U.S. Military Contractors in Israel," *MERIP Reports* 144 (January/Febuary 1987): 17–22.

177. Because military industrialization became more sophisticated and expensive and domestic demand was not enough to lower production costs, there was a turn to export promotion. This market became both more central to the industry's success and an increasing source of the state's revenue. For overviews of Israel's arms export market, see Steinberg, "Israel: High Technology Roulette," 181–88; and Aaron Klieman, *Israel's Global Reach: Arms Sales as Diplomacy* (New York: Pergamon Press, 1985).

178. Eisenstadt, *The Transformation of Israel*, 403–31.

179. Zvi Dinstien, interview with author, Ramat Aviv, June 16, 1987.

180. Pinchas Zusman, interview with author, Rehovot, June 24, 1987.

181. Ibid.

182. Zvi Dinstien, interview with author, Ramat Aviv, June 16, 1987; Ya'acov Arnon, interview with author, Jerusalem, June 10, 1987.

183. Reiser, *The Israeli Arms Industry*, 82.

184. T. Tropp, interview with author, Tel-Aviv, May 30, 1987; T. Dinstein, interview with author, Ramat Aviv, June 16, 1987. The Defense Ministry's efforts to fund the private sector are noted in the following excerpt from the comptroller's report on the Defense establishment:

> The efforts of the Defense establishment to produce certain kinds of equipment locally sometimes induced the Ministry [of Defense] to by-pass normal business procedures. Thus for the manufacture of a certain component it was agreed with a private investor that a plant be established in a developing area, and that the Army would buy IL 20m. worth of the article annually for five years. Negotiations began in May, 1969, and the plant began operating in October of the following year. The contract with the firm was, however, signed only in December, 1971, by which time the State had paid the company IL 1.7m. on account for future deliveries. The Comptroller quotes the opinion of a manager of a Defence establishment plant that his factory could have done the job with a much smaller initial outlay. The comptroller also criticizes the fact that the private enterprises were allotted $240,000 as a "commission" on equipment purchased abroad directly by the Ministry of Defense, on the understanding that the money would be invested in the factory. This, says the Comptroller, was no way to camouflage a grant to the company.

Other sorts of transgressions are noted in the comptroller's report, all of which testify to the "unorthodox" procurement practices of the Defense Ministry. *Israel Economist* (May 1972), 122.

185. Pinchas Zusman, interview with author, Rehovot, June 24, 1987.

186. Given the previous history of hostility toward domestic capital, it is noteworthy that there was relatively little opposition to capital's new-found importance in the state's development and security plans. The old-guard Socialists did present some limited opposition, but by this time their influence had waned considerably. Second, because the defense pie was expanding, most interested investors were the recipients of defense contracts. There is also evidence that these firms were not necessarily competing for resources, but that there was an interlinking network of ownership between the various defense firms. See Shimshon Bichler, *The Political Economy of National Security in Israel* (M.A. thesis, Department of Political Science, Hebrew University of Jerusalem, 1984); and Mintz, "The Military-Industrial Complex: The Israeli Case" and "Arms Production in Israel."

187. Reiser, *The Israeli Arms Industry*, 112, 149.

188. Mintz, "The Military-Industrial Complex: The Israeli Case," 123.

189. Horowitz and Kimmerling, "Some Social Implications of Military Service," 264.

190. Kimmerling, "Determination of the Boundaries," 34–38.

191. Luttwak and Horowitz, *The Israeli Army*, 327; Yaniv, *Deterrence Without the Bomb*, 136.

192. Luttwak and Horowitz, *The Israeli Army*, 359.

193. Yaniv, *Deterrence Without the Bomb*, 191–93, 235. It also added to the already present and ever growing level of societal dissatisfaction. After the Yom Kippur War the government kept the front-line reserve forces, those who suffered the heaviest casualties, on active duty longer than others. "The result was a gradual buildup of discontent even in some of the IDF's best reserve units." This resulted in greater caution from the Meir government on the possibility of the conflict's escalation.

194. Yaniv, *Deterrence Without the Bomb*, 192.

195. Ibid.

196. Eisenstadt, *The Transformation of Israeli Society*, 160–61.

197. Yaniv, *Deterrence Without the Bomb*, 192–93.

198. Ibid., 206.

199. The other major move made to alleviate manpower pressures, financial constraints, and uncertain ally support during times of need, was technological. Not only has Israel emphasized the importance of air superiority as a method for overcoming its manpower disadvantage, but the development of nuclear capability is also viewed as a logical outcome of these various pressures.

Chapter Six
War and the Transformation of State Power

1. Waterbury, *The Egypt of Nasser and Sadat*, 62.

2. Patrick O'Brien, *The Revolution in Egypt's Economic System: From Private Enterprise to Socialism, 1952–65* (New York: Oxford University Press, 1966).

3. Waterbury, *The Egypt of Nasser and Sadat*, 233–34.

4. Ibid., 67.

5. One could present a counterfactual argument and note that even had the state not engaged in seven years of war preparation the public sector was already revealing signs of economic decline before 1967, which is partially attributed to the Yemen intervention, and it was a matter of when, not if, Nasser would be forced to liberalize the economy and create a greater role for the private sector. I simply rely on the fact that those governmental officials I talked to referred specifically to how war, not the economy, stimulated this changed reorientation. Moreover, scholars such as Waterbury, *The Egypt of Nasser and Sadat*, and Hinnebusch, *Egyptian Politics Under Sadat*, appear rather agnostic concerning whether Nasser would have leaned in this privatist direction if not for the inter-war period.

6. Robert Bianchi writes that "the infitah has not entirely abandoned the Nasserist commitment to social equity, but it has clearly sought to subordinate equity to growth while reducing the mechanisms of state intervention that were designed to encourage social mobility." *Unruly Corporatism*, 46. It certainly meant to strip privileges from certain groups, notably the military and the bureaucrats, of their privileges, and confer them on new ones, notably the private

sector elites, contractors, and financiers. Although in hindsight both sides gave infitah "more credit than it deserved," each side recognized that they "were witnessing a painful but decisive shift in the balance of power between two mutually incompatible systems [socialism and capitalism] for organizing the economy as a whole" (48).

7. Tilly, *Coercion, Capital, and European States*, 206; emphasis mine.

8. I argue in Chapter 2 that the extent of tax evasion partially captures the state's ability to monitor society. Waterbury argues that approximately 17 percent of the GNP is unaccounted for because of the "black economy," of which nearly 25 percent of this figure is attributed to tax evasion. "The 'Soft State' and the Open Door," 76. I have no evidence with which to place these figures in historical perspective, however. I queried former Minister of Finance Higazi about this aspect, who responded that not only did they not have this type of information, but that only in 1975 were the first studies dedicated to surveying the problem undertaken. In part this was because, as I was told by one bureaucrat in the Ministry of Taxation, that there was no evasion, because, if there were, that would imply that individuals like himself were negligent in their duties; hence, because they were competent there was no evasion.

9. Heikal, *Autumn of Fury*, 90, 219–20; Waterbury, *The Egypt of Nasser and Sadat*, 408.

10. Moreover, Egypt's three major sources of revenue—the Suez Canal receipts, tourism, and worker remittances—are not from productive activity. The implication is that the government's fiscal basis is more susceptible to instability and shocks. This problem emerged in dramatic fashion after the 1990 Iraqi invasion of Kuwait, when Egyptian revenue declined precipitously because of the drop in Suez Canal tolls and the approximately 300,000 Egyptian workers that were forced to flee Kuwait and Iraq. For instance, one estimate places the drop in revenue totaling $4.5 billion. "Gulf Crisis Produces Surge of Egyptian Confidence," *New York Times*, November 11, 1990.

11. Ikram, *Egypt*, 361.

12. David Butter, "Debt and Egypt's Financial Policies," in C. Tripp and R. eds., *Egypt Under Mubarak* (New York: Routledge and Kegan Paul, 1989), 127.

13. Ibid., 129–31.

14. Yet this annual savings does not approximate the estimated $4.5 billion in lost revenue from the Iraqi invasion of Kuwait.

15. Waterbury, *The Egypt of Nasser and Sadat*, 406–14; Paul Rivlin, *The Dynamics of Economic Policy Making in Egypt* (New York: Praeger Press, 1985), 177–83.

16. See Aliboni et al., *Egypt's Economic Potential*, 46, for an overview of the government's growing expenditure on subsidies.

17. Eli Sagi, "An Economic Study of Some Issues in the Economic Development of Egypt: Agricultural Supply, Industrial Growth, and the Burden of Defense Expenditure" (Ph.D. diss., University of Pennsylvania, 1980).

18. Roy, "Private Industry Sector Developments in Egypt"; and Waterbury, "The 'Soft State' and the Open Door," 68–69.

19. Ibrahim Helmy Abdel-Rahman and Mohammed Sultan Abu Ali, "Role of the Public and Private Sectors with Special Reference to Privatization: The Case

of Egypt," in Said el-Nagger, ed., *Privatization and Structural Adjustment in the Arab Countries* (Washington, D.C.: International Monetary Fund, 1989), 152–55.

20. Bianchi, *Unruly Corporatism*, 50–51.

21. Roy, "Private Industry Sector Developments in Egypt," 14.

22. Bianchi, *Unruly Corporatism*, 48.

23. Hinnebusch, *Egyptian Politics Under Sadat*, 148, 261; Shukrullah, "Political Crisis/Conflict," 83.

24. Hena Ahmed Handoussa, "Time For Reform: Egypt's Public Sector Industry," in H. M. Thompson, ed., *Studies in Egyptian Political Economy*, Cairo Papers in Social Science, vol. 2, 2d ed. (Cairo: American University in Cairo Press, 1983), 102.

25. Ibid., 103. Moreover, Aliboni et al., *Egypt's Economic Potential*, 146, write that "Law 43, which it was originally hoped would stimulate foreign investment, has in fact had the dual effect of promoting private domestic investment and 'privatising' public enterprises."

26. Abdel-Rahman and Abu Ali, "Role of Public and Private Sectors."

27. Bianchi, *Unruly Corporatism*, 51; emphasis mine.

28. Pack, *Structural Change and Economic Policy*, 182–83.

29. Although the recession of 1965–1967 exposed economic inefficiencies and caused some governmental members and Histadrut officials to question openly the dominant statist ideology, these liberalization measures were relatively nominal when compared to the post-1967 developments.

30. Arnon Gafni, interview with author, Tel-Aviv, June 24, 1987.

31. In fact, the government's tax reform of 1975 was designed to increase its efficiency, decrease the amount of tax evasion, and provide the proper incentives for capital investment. Ben-Porath and Bruno, "The Political Economy of a Tax Reform."

32. Shimshoni, *Israeli Democracy*, 248; emphasis mine.

33. Michael Shalev, Israel's Domestic Policy Regime: Zionism, Dualism, and the Rise of Capital," in F. G. Castles, ed., *The Comparative History of Public Policy* (London: Polity Press, 1989), 131.

34. Ibid., 132.

35. Ibid., 132.

36. Ibid., 131.

37. Liviatan, "Israel's External Debt," 2–3.

38. See Sella and Yishai, *Israel: The Peaceful Belligerent*, 54–66; Laufer, "U.S. Aid to Israel," 157–60; and Liviatan, "Israel's External Debt."

39. Liviatan, "Israel's External Debt," 1. Reiser, *Israeli Arms Industry*, 144, too, notes the dramatic change: "In the mid-1950s half of the debt was owed to Jewish bondholders; in the 1980s only one-quarter of the foreign debt is accountable to bondholders, with most of the remainder owed to the United States."

40. A full appraisal of the state's weakening control over the economy depends on how one conceptualizes the state's relationship to the Histadrut. The interlocking relationship between the public sector, domestic capital, and the Histadrut makes the analysis of the state's control over the economy and its relationship to societal interests somewhat difficult to define precisely. Al-

though some have recently attempted to analyze the intertwined interests of domestic capital, the public sector, and the Histadrut, I am unable to go beyond this level of imprecision. See Shmuel Hadar, *Blurring the Boundaries Between Public and Private Relations Between State and Industry* (Ph.D. diss., Hebrew University of Jerusalem, 1988) for an in-depth analysis of this relationship.

41. Shalev, "Israel's Domestic Policy Regime."

42. The recession was shaken, however, not by greater efficiency but rather by the tremendous military procurement after the 1967 War and the capture of the occupied territories, which gave Israel access to an underdeveloped Arab market and a cheap source of labor.

43. Alex Mintz and Daniel Maman, "Center vs. Periphery in Israel's Military Industrial Sector: Implications for Civil-Military Relations" (manuscript). Cited in Mintz, "Arms Production in Israel," 91.

44. Shalev, "Israel's Domestic Policy Regime," 132.

45. Neuman, "International Stratification." See Steinberg, "Indigenous Arms Industries and Dependence," for a review of the various items produced by Israel's defense industries. See Mintz, "Military-Industrial Linkages in Israel," *Armed Forces and Society* 12 (Fall 1985): 9–27; and Klieman, "Israel's Global Reach," for a breakdown of the Israeli defense industries.

46. Harkavy and Neuman, "Israel," 194; Mintz, "Arms Production in Israel"; Steinberg, "Israel: High Technology Roulette"; and Reiser, *Israel's Arms Industry*. Moreover, Naftali Blumenthal, "The Influences of Defense Industry Investment on Israel's Economy," in Z. Lanir, ed., *Israeli Security Planning in the 1980s* (New York: Praeger Press, 1984), argues that the development of the arms industry has had a significant impact on industrial growth between the years 1968 and 1972. Steinberg, "Israel: High-Technology Roulette," 290–91, also refers to how a significant proportion of the labor force is directly employed by the military-industrial complex, which has created a large voting bloc with an interest in maintaining a large defense industry machine and high levels of defense expenditures.

47. Zvi Zusman, interview with author, Rehovot, June 24, 1987.

48. See Mintz, "The Military-Industrial Linkages in Israel," 12–15.

49. Mintz, "Arms Production in Israel," 96–97. In "The Military-Industrial Complex: The Israeli Case," 112, Mintz also notes other dangers from the Israeli military-industrial complex: "This increase in concentration may intensify industrial dependence upon an economy of war—a situation which has significant security-related, national, and social ramifications: economic dependence upon weapons manufactures may lead to a dangerous situation wherein defense industries will be accorded extensive allocations for development of systems not necessarily because of demands of national security interests alone but rather defense industries." Baruch Kimmerling, "Making Conflict a Routine: Cumulative Effects of the Arab-Jewish Conflict Upon Israeli Society," in M. Lissak, ed., *Israeli Society and Its Defense Establishment* (London: Frank Cass, 1984), 169–71, also notes that the creation of the military-industrial complex has influenced the decision-making process and the state's goals and objectives. After years of warfare "the economic system loses its autonomy and is to a large extent controlled by extra-economic considerations." Also see Reiser, *Israel's Arms Industry*, 229.

50. An important theoretical and practical issue emerges here: how is the relationship between the state and the state-owned arms industries to be conceptualized? Because, as I have indicated, many of Israel's largest defense industries are state-owned, this should indicate that the state's control has not been significantly weakened. These are, then, state-owned and -operated revenue-generating enterprises. Although this is true, there are a number of reasons to question whether the state's autonomy has remained the same as its pre-1967 status, given the presence of these companies. First, although government officials can hire and fire public sector managers, they are now less prone to punishment should they go against the desires of governmental officials because they now generate a larger percentage of their own source of revenue through arms exports. Second, these state-owned arms industries are not autonomous from the private sector, for as already noted there are growing linkages between the private and public sectors such that it has become more difficult to alter the state's production decisions as a result.

51. See, for example, Mintz, "Arms Production in Israel," and Shalev, "Israel's Domestic Policy Regime."

52. Shalev, "Israel's Domestic Policy Regime," 124.

53. See Jerusalem Institute of Management, *Export-Led Growth Strategy*; and Mintz and Maman, "Center versus Periphery in Israel's Military Industrial Sector."

54. R. Rowley, S. Bichler, and J. Nitzan, "Some Aspects of Aggregate Concentration in the Israeli Economy, 1964–1986," Department of Economics Working Papers (Montreal: McGill University, 1988), 15. Quoted from Shalev, "Israel's Domestic Policy Regime," 128.

55. Shalev, "Israel's Domestic Policy Regime," 124–27, 131.

56. See Horowitz and Kimmerling, "Some Social Implications of Military Service and the Reserve System in Israel," and Kimmerling, "Determination of the Boundaries and Frameworks of Conscription," on the benefits to be derived from military service.

57. Kimmerling, "Determination of the Boundaries and Frameworks of Conscription," 34.

58. Ibid., 34.

59. Ibid., 39, n. 23; emphasis added.

60. This discussion is based on a series of discussions with academics, current Israeli officers, and soldiers.

61. Sella and Yishai, *Israel: The Peaceful Belligerent*, chap. 3, provide some further evidence concerning the state's lack of legitimacy and inability to mobilize societal resources. They use such indicators as anomie, as measured through suicides, immigration and emigration figures, and strikes as reflections of the state's weakening authority in society.

62. Peri, *Between Ballots and Bullets*, esp. chap. 4.

63. This interpretation derives from Kimmerling's interesting account of the Left and the Right's visions of Israel. "Between Primordial and Civil Definitions of the Collective Identity: Eretz Israel or the State of Israel," in E. Cohen, et al., eds., *Comparative Social Dynamics* (Boulder: Westview Press, 1985), 262–83. Also see Ian Lustick "Israeli State Building in the West Bank and Gaza: Theory and Practice," *International Organization* 41 (1988): 151–71.

64. Quoted from Amos Elon, "Letter from Jerusalem," *New Yorker*, April 23, 1990, 94; emphasis mine.

65. Ibid., 98.

Chapter Seven
Egypt and Israel in Comparative and Theoretical Perspective

1. Fred Halliday, "The Middle East in International Perspective: Problem of Analysis," in R. Bush et al., eds., *The World Order: Socialist Perspectives* (London: Polity Press, 1987), 217. Also see Fred Halliday and Hamza Alavi, "Introduction," in F. Halliday and H. Alavi, eds., *State and Ideology in the Middle East and Pakistan* (New York: Monthly Review Press, 1988).

2. Halliday, "The Middle East in International Perspective," 217.

3. Ibid.

4. Levi, *Of Rule and Revenue*, 33.

5. Although soon after the international crisis government leaders capitalized on the societal cohesion to extract more resources from society, over time this window closed and society became less compliant. Levi argues that to extract revenue the ruler must convince its population that it will deliver the promised goods and that its failure to do so will create difficulties for future revenue extraction; *Of Rule and Revenue*, 60. For instance, once Sadat's 1971 "year of decision" passed with no decision further extractive efforts became that much more politically unwise.

6. See Robert Jackson and Carl Rosberg, "Why Africa's Weak States Persist: The Empirical and Juridical in Statehood," *World Politics* 35 (October, 1982): 1–24; David Strong, "Anomaly and Commonplace in European Expansion," *International Organization* 45 (Spring 1991): 143–62; and Joseph Nye, *Bound to Lead* (New York: Basic Books, 1990), 179–82.

7. For the German case, see Kocka, *Facing Total War*; for the Iranian and Iraqi cases, see Chubin and Tripp, *Iran and Iraq at War*.

8. This argument does not imply that there were not problems associated with being a client-like partner, as there certainly were; however, given the domestic limitations it did represent a rational security strategy. Moreover, I am not arguing that Middle Eastern conflict has been caused by development concerns gone awry, but rather that these sorts of domestic variables reinforced already established fears and conflicts.

9. See Barnett and Levy, "Domestic Sources of Alliances and Alignments," and David, "Explaining Third World Alignments."

10. The only instance of foreign manpower support came in January 1991 when the United States sent U.S.-operated Patriot antiballistic missiles in response to Iraqi missile attacks on Tel-Aviv. Although this is the lone instance of state-to-state assistance, Israel has benefited from Jewish volunteers since 1948. However, because they were primarily Jewish volunteers, not troops in the enlistment of foreign states, they were not viewed as lessening Israeli sovereignty.

11. When the Soviets did become involved in Egyptian defenses it led to a military clash, in which it was reported that Israel successfully shot down a number of Soviet-piloted aircraft with no loss to themselves. Nixon, quite worried that this could escalate into major international episode and superpower con-

frontation, told the Israelis to halt their dramatics. The other instance in which the Soviets said that they would directly enter the hostilities was during the Yom Kippur War, when it appeared that if the Israelis continued their intrusions into the Egyptian interior Sadat was in danger of being toppled. That a Soviet client would fall because of the military successes of an American-backed country was more than Brezhnev could allow.

12. Judith Goldstein, "The Impact of Ideas on Trade Policy," *International Organization* 43 (1989): 67.

13. See Gordon White, "Revolutionary Socialist Development in the Third World: An Overview," in G. White et al., eds., *Revolutionary Socialist Development in the Third World* (London: Wheatsheaf, 1987), 19, for a similar argument concerning the transformation of state socialist societies from planning to market mechanisms.

14. Michael Taylor, "Rationality and Revolutionary Collective Action," in M. Taylor, ed., *Rationality and Revolution* (New York: Cambridge University Press, 1988), 85.

15. There is a growing literature on learning and application to both foreign policy and international relations theory. See Lloyd Etheredge, *Can Governments Learn?* (New York: Pergamon Press, 1985); Joseph Nye, "Nuclear Learning and U.S.-Soviet Security Regimes," *International Organization* 41 (Summer 1987): 371–402; and Ernst Haas, *Knowledge as Power*.

16. Nye, "Nuclear Learning," 380. Also see Robert Axelrod, *The Evolution of Cooperation* (New York: Basic Books, 1984).

17. Ibid., 381. Moreover, Ikenberry argues, "simplifying assumptions about states as unitary and rational agents are useful for clarifying some types of political phenomenea, but they can obscure others. To understand particular policy outcomes or sequences of strategies, it is useful to adopt a more differentiated, historically grounded, institutional conception of the state." "Conclusion," 194.

18. *The Transformation of Israeli Society*, 403–18. Moreover, a new generation of Israeli economists, many of whom were trained in orthodox economics, now occupied key economic positions in the state apparatus. See Peter Hall, ed., *The Political Power of Economic Ideas* (Princeton: Princeton University Press, 1986), for interesting discussions of the transmission of economic ideas.

19. Rather than see this as a case of complex learning, this analysis also suggests that it may not have been that the *same* government leaders viewed the world differently, but rather there was a changed composition of the state apparatus because of an infusion of new bureaucratic actors. This is an important aspect of some state autonomy approaches. See, for example, Trimberger, *Revolution from Above*.

20. Goldstein, "The Impact of Ideas on Trade Policy," 71, referring to the similar case of the United States in the 1930s, argues that "liberalization occurred not because of its inherent logic, but because Hull was appointed Secretary of State."

21. See Michael Taylor, "Structure, Culture, and Action in the Explanation of Social Change," *Politics and Society* 17 (June 1989): 115–62, for an interesting reading of cultural explanations and their relationship to rational choice approaches.

22. Peter Manicas, "Explanation, Generalisation, and Marxist Theory Vis-à-Vis Third World Development," in D. Banarjee, ed., *Marxian Theory and the Third World* (Beverly Hills: Sage Press, 1985), 313.

23. Ikenberry, "Conclusion," 233. Arthur Stinchcombe's "liability of newness" provides one venue for explaining why during moments of crises such as wars institutional change emerged. "Social Structure and Organizations," in James March, ed., *Handbook of Organizations* (Chicago: Rand McNally, 1965), 148–49. He argues that these institutions tend to endure and remain rather impervious to radical alteration because the newer institution and organization must be appraised as far superior and beneficial to the well-established institutions, "which compensates for the relative weakness of the newer social structure." For this reason institutional change tends to succeed "only when the alternatives are stark (generally in wartime)." Quoted from Ikenberry, "Conclusion," 194. In *War and Statemaking*, 16–17, Rasler and Thompson offer a similar conception by way of their "oyster shell" analogy. State-society relations resemble an oyster shell, for it is rather impervious to leakage and change most of the time. However, during domestic and international crises the oyster (society) becomes more receptive to new arrangements, more fluid and open to realignments, and more susceptible to new coalition arrangements. After the crisis the oyster (society) once again becomes protected and invulnerable to change.

24. This stands in contrast to the common characterization of some neo-Marxist and neo-Weberian readings of the impact of war on the relative autonomy of the state. For instance, both Block, "The Ruling Class Does Not Rule," and Skocpol, *States and Social Revolutions*, point to an increase in the state's relative autonomy as a consequence of international conflict. In both the Israeli and Egyptian cases, however, the opposite trend developed, wherein there was a general decline in the state's autonomy from the dominant classes. Interestingly, in this respect the development of Israel's political economy resembles that of many West European countries. While mercantilism was the order of the day during early capitalism, once the bourgeoisie gained greater political and economic power the ideology of free trade capitalism soon supplanted the ideology of mercantilism.

25. Howard, *War in European History*, 38; Karen Rasler and William Thompson, "Warmaking and Statemaking: Governmental Expenditures, Tax Revenues, and Global Wars," *American Political Science Review* 79 (June 1985): 491–507.

26. See Gabriel Kolko, *Anatomy of a War: Vietnam, the United States, and the Modern Historical Experience* (New York: Pantheon Press, 1985), 283–93; and Aaron Friedberg, "The Political Economy of American Strategy," *World Politics* 41 (April 1989): 381–406.

Bibliography

Books and Articles

Abdalla, Ahmed. 1985. *The Student Movement and National Politics in Egypt.* London: Al-Saqi Books.

Abdel-Fadil, M. 1980. *The Political Economy of Nasserism.* Cambridge Department of Applied Economics. Cambridge: Cambridge University Press.

Abdel-Khalek, Gouda. 1981. "Looking Outside or Turning Northwest? On the Meaning and External Dimension of Egypt's Infitah, 1971–80." *Social Problems* 28 (4) (April):394–409.

Abdel-Malek, Anwar. 1968. *Egypt: Military Society.* New York: Random House.

Abdel-Rahman, A. M. 1978. "The Egyptian Income Tax Reform: Toward a Unitary Income Tax." *L' Egyptiane Contemporaine* 69 (2) (October):5–36.

Abdel-Rahman, Ibrahim Helmy, and Mohammed Abu Ali. 1989. "Role of the Public and Private Sectors with Special Reference to Privatization: The Case of Egypt." In *Privatization and Structural Adjustment in the Arab Countries*, edited by Said el-Naggar. Washington, D.C.: International Monetary Fund.

Abrams, Philip. 1982. *Historical Sociology.* Ithaca: Cornell University Press.

Abu-Lughod, Ibrahim, ed. 1987. *The Transformation of Palestine.* Evanston: Northwestern University Press.

Adams, Gordon. 1981. *The Iron Triangle: The Politics of Defense Contracting.* New York: Council on Economic Priorities.

Adams, Richard. 1986. *Development and Social Change in Rural Egypt.* Syracuse: Syracuse University Press.

Afxentiou, F. C. 1984. "Fiscal Structure, Tax Effort, and Economic Development." *Economia Internazionale* 38 (3/4) (August/November):286–301.

Ahmed, Sadiq. 1984. "Public Finance in Egypt: Its Structure and Trends." *World Bank Staff Working Papers*, no. 639. Washington, D.C.: World Bank.

Akhavi, Shahrough. 1975. "Egypt: Neo-Patrimonial Elite." In *Political Elites and Political Development in the Middle East*, edited by Frank Tachau. Cambridge, Mass.: Schenkman Press.

Ajami, Fouad. 1981. *The Arab Predicament.* New York: Cambridge University Press.

Alavi, Hamza. 1972. "The State in Post-Colonial Societies." *New Left Review* 74:59–82.

Aliboni, Roberto, et al. 1984. *Egypt's Economic Potential.* Dover: Croom Helm.

Allon, Yigal. 1970. *The Making of Israel's Army.* London: George Weidenfeld and Nicolson.

Ames, E., and R. T. Rapp. 1977. "The Birth and Death of Taxes: A Hypothesis." *Journal of Economic History* 37:161–78.

Amin, Galal. 1982. "External Factors in the Reorientation of Egypt's Economic Policy." In *Rich and Poor States in the Middle East*, edited by M. Kerr and E. S. Yassin. Boulder: Westview Press.

Anderson, Martin, ed. 1982. *The Military Draft*. Palo Alto: Hoover Press.

Anderson, Perry. 1974. *Lineages of the Absolutist State*. New York: New Left Books.

Andreski, Stanislav. 1954. *Military Organization and Society*. New York: Routledge and Kegan Paul.

Ansari, Hamied. 1986. *Egypt: The Stalled Society*. Albany: State University of New York Press.

Ardant, Gabriel. 1975. "Financial Policy and Economic Infrastructure of Modern States and Nations." In *The Formation of the National States in Western Europe*, edited by Charles Tilly. Princeton: Princeton University Press.

Arian, Asher, ed. 1975. *Israel: A Developing Society*. Amsterdam: Van Gorcum Press.

Arian, Asher, Ilan Talmud, and Tamar Hermann. 1988. *National Security and Public Opinion in Israel*. Boulder: Westview Press.

Arms Control and Disarmament Agency. Various years. *World Military Expenditures and Arms Transfers*. Washington, D.C.: Government Printing Office.

Asad, Talal. 1976. "Class Transformation Under the Mandate." *MERIP Reports* 53:3–8.

Ashley, Richard. 1981. "Political Realism and Human Interests." *International Studies Quarterly* 25:204–36.

———. 1984. "The Poverty of Neo-Realism." *International Organization* 38 (Spring):225–86.

Axelrod, Robert. 1984. *The Evolution of Cooperation*. New York: Basic Books.

Axelrod, Robert, and M. Cohen. 1984. "Coping with Complexity: The Adaptive Value of Changing Utility." *American Economic Review* 74 (1):30–42.

Auda, Gehad. 1987. "The State of Political Control: The Case of Nasser, 1960–1967." *Arab Journal of the Social Sciences* 2 (1) (April):95–111.

Aveniri, Shlomo. 1981. *The Making of Modern Zionism: The Intellectual Origins of the Jewish State*. New York: Basic Books.

Ayres, Ron. 1983. "Arms Production as a Form of Import-Substituting Industrialization: The Turkish Case." *World Development* 11 (9):813–23.

Ayubi, Nazih. 1980. *Bureaucracy and Politics in Contemporary Egypt*. London: Ithica Press.

Azar, Edward, and Chung-in Moon. 1988. "Legitimacy, Integration, and Policy Capacity: The 'Software' Side of Third World National Security." In *National Security in the Third World*, edited by E. Azar and C. Moon. Hants, Eng.: Edward Elger Publishers.

Azkin, Benjamin, and Yehezkel Dror. 1966. *Israel: High Pressure Planning*. Syracuse: Syracuse University Press.

Baer, Gabriel. 1962. *A History of Land Ownership in Modern Egypt, 1800–1950*. London: Oxford University Press.

———. 1969. *Studies in the Social History of Modern Egypt*. Chicago: University of Chicago Press.

Bahl, Roy. 1971. "A Regression Approach to Tax Effort and Tax Ratio Analysis." *IMF Staff Papers* 18 (3):570–612.

Baker, Raymond. 1978. *Egypt's Uncertain Revolution Under Nasser and Sadat.* Cambridge: Harvard University Press.

Ball, Nicole. 1988. *Security and Economy in the Third World.* Princeton: Princeton University Press.

Bank of Israel. Various years. *Annual Report.* Jerusalem.

Baran, Paul, and Paul Sweezy. 1966. *Monopoly Capitalism.* New York: Monthly Review Press.

Barbour, K. M. 1972. *Growth, Structure, and Location of Industry in Egypt.* New York: Praeger.

Barkai, Haim. 1962. *Theory and Praxis of the Histadrut Industrial Sector.* Jerusalem.

Barkay, R. M. 1957. *The Public Sector Accounts of Israel, 1948/9–1954/5.* Jerusalem: Maurice Falk Project for Economic Research.

Barnett, Michael. 1990. "High Politics is Low Politics: The Domestic and Systemic Sources of Israeli Security Policy, 1967–1977." *World Politics* 42 (4) (July):529–62.

Barnett, Michael, and Jack Levy. 1991. "The Domestic Sources of Alliances and Alignments: The Case of Egypt, 1962–73." *International Organization* 45 (3):369–95.

Bates, Robert. 1987. *Essays on the Political Economy of Rural Africa.* Berkeley: University of California Press.

Bates, Robert, and Da-Hsiang Donald Lien. 1985. "A Note on Taxation, Development, and Representative Government." *Politics and Society* 14 (1): 53–70.

Bean, Richard. 1973. "War and the Birth of the Nation State." *Journal of Economic History* 33 (March):203–21.

Beetham, David. 1985. *Max Weber and the Theory of Modern Politics.* 2d ed. New York: Polity Press.

Beinin, Joel, and Zachary Lockman. 1988. *Workers on the Nile: Nationalism, Communalism, Islam, and the Egyptian Working Class, 1882–1954.* Princeton: Princeton University Press.

Bendix, Reinhard. 1977. *Max Weber: An Intellectual Portrait.* Berkeley: University of California Press.

Ben-Dor, Gabriel. 1982. "Egypt." In *Security Policies of Developing Countries,* edited by E. Kolodziej and R. Harkavy. Lexington: Lexington Books.

———. 1983. *The Post-Colonial State and the Middle East Conflict.* New York: Praeger Press.

Ben-Gurion, David. 1954. *Rebirth and Destiny of Israel.* New York: Philosophical Library.

———. 1970. *Ben-Gurion Looks Back.* New York: Schocken Books.

Benjamin, Roger, and Raymond Duvall. 1985. "The Capitalist State in Context." In *The Democratic State,* edited by R. Benjamin and S. Elkin. Lawrence: University Press of Kansas.

Benoit, E. 1973. *Growth and Defense in Developing Countries.* Lexington: Lexington Books.

Ben-Porath, Yoram, ed. 1986. *The Israeli Economy*. Cambridge: Harvard University Press.

Ben-Porath, Yoram, and Michael Bruno. 1977. "The Political Economy of a Tax Reform: The Case of Israel." *Journal of Public Economics* 7 (June):285–307.

Berger, Morroe. 1957. *Bureaucracy and Society in Modern Egypt*. Princeton: Princeton University Press.

Berglas, Eitan. 1970. "An Empirical Evaluation of Israel's Income Tax, 1953–1965." In *Israel and the Common Market*, edited by P. Uri. Jerusalem: George Weidenfeld and Nicolson.

———. 1986. "Defense and Economy." *The Israeli Economy*, edited by Y. Ben-Porath. Cambridge: Harvard University Press.

———. 1986. "Taxes and Transfers in an Inflationary Decade." In *The Israeli Economy*, edited by Y. Ben-Porath. Cambridge: Harvard University Press.

Berque, Jacques. 1972. *Egypt: Imperialism and Revolution*. London: Faber and Faber.

Best, Michael. 1976. "Political Power and Tax Revenues in Central America." *Journal of Development Economics* 3 (1):49–82.

Beukema, Herman. 1982. "The Social and Political Aspects of Conscription: Europe's Experience." In *The Military Draft*, edited by M. Anderson. Stanford: Hoover Press.

Bialer, Uri. 1990. *Between East and West: Israel's Foreign Policy Orientation, 1948–56*. New York: Cambridge University Press.

Bianchi, Robert. 1989. *Unruly Corporatism: Associational Life in Twentieth-Century Egypt*. New York: Oxford University Press.

Bichler, Shimshon. 1985. *The Political Economy of National Security in Israel*. M.A. thesis, Hebrew University of Jerusalem (in Hebrew).

Binder, Leonard. 1978. *In a Moment of Enthusiasm: Political Power and Second Stratum*. Chicago: University of Chicago Press.

Bird, R. M. 1978. "Assessing Tax Performance in Developing Countries: A Critical Review of the Literature." In *Taxation and Economic Development*, edited by J. F. J. Toye. London: Frank Cass.

Block, Fred. 1977. "The Ruling Class Does Not Rule: Notes on the Marxist Theory of the State." *Socialist Revolution* 33:6–28.

———. 1980. "Beyond Relative Autonomy: State Managers as Historical Subjects." In *Socialist Register*, edited by R. Miliband and J. Saville, London: Merlin Press.

Blumenthal, Naftali. 1984. "The Influences of Defense Industry Investment on Israel's Economy." In *Israeli Security Planning in the 1980s*, edited by Zvi Lanir. New York: Praeger Press.

Bonnell, Victoria. 1980. "The Uses of Theory, Concepts, and Comparisons in Historical Sociology." *Comparative Studies in Society and History* 22 (2):156–73.

Brinkley, David. 1988. *Washington Goes to War*. New York: Alfred A. Knopf.

Brzoska, Michael, and Thomas Ohlson. 1986. "Arms Production in the Third World: An Overview." In *Arms Production in the Third World*, edited by M. Brzoska and T. Ohlson. Philadelphia: Taylor and Francis.

Bukharin, Nikolai. 1972. *Imperialism and the World Economy*. New York: Monthly Review Press.

Butter, David. 1989. "Debt and Egypt's Financial Policies." In *Egypt Under Mubarak*, edited by Charles Tripp and Roger Owen. New York: Routledge and Kegan Paul.

Caiden, Gerald. 1970. *Israel's Administrative Culture*. Berkeley: University of California Press.

Callaghy, Thomas. 1984. *The State-Society Struggle: Zaire in Comparative Perspective*. New York: Columbia University Press.

Callinicos, Alex. 1987. *Making History*. Ithaca: Cornell University Press.

Cardoso, Enrique, and Enzo Faletto. 1979. *Dependency and Development in Latin America*. Berkeley: University of California Press.

Carnoy, Martin. 1984. *The State and Political Theory*. Princeton: Princeton University Press.

Carr, David. 1979. *Foreign Investment and Development in Egypt*. New York: Praeger Press.

Carr, E. H. 1964. *The Twenty Years Crisis, 1919–1939*. New York: Harper & Row.

Carus, Seth. 1984. "Defense Planning in Iraq." In *Defense Planning in Less-Industrialized Countries: The Middle East and South Asia*, edited by Stephanie Neuman. Lexington: Lexington Books.

Central Bank of Egypt. 1982. "Development of Taxation in Egypt." *Central Bank of Egypt Economic Review* 22 (1):1–31.

Chambers, John. 1987. *To Raise an Army: The Draft Comes to Modern America*. New York: Free Press.

Chirot, Daniel. 1976. "Introduction: Thematic Controversies and New Developments in the Uses of Historical Material by Sociologists." *Social Forces* 55 (2):232–41.

Chubin, Shahrom, and Charles Tripp. 1988. *Iran and Iraq at War*. London: I. B. Tauris and Co.

Clapham, Craig. 1984. *Third World Politics*. Madison: University of Wisconsin Press.

Clawson, Patrick. 1978. "Egypt's Industrialization: A Critique of Dependency Theory." *MERIP Reports*, no. 72:17–23.

Cohen, Mitchell. 1987. *Zion and State: Nation, Class, and the Shaping of Modern Israel*. London: Basil Blackwell.

Cooper, Mark. 1979. "Egyptian State Capitalism in Crisis: Economic Policy and Political Interests, 1967–71." *International Journal of Middle East Studies* 10 (4) (November):481–516.

———. 1982. "Demilitarization of the Egyptian Cabinet." *International Journal of Middle East Studies* 14 (2) (May):203–25.

———. 1982. *The Transformation of Egypt*. Baltimore: Johns Hopkins University Press.

Corrigan, Philip, ed. 1980. *Capitalism, State Formation, and Marxist Theory*. London: Quartet Books.

Corvisier, Andre. 1979. *Armies and Societies in Europe, 1494–1789*. Bloomington: Indiana University Press.

Crosbie, Sylvia Kowitt. 1974. *A Tacit Alliance: France and Israel from the Suez to the Six-Day War.* Princeton: Princeton University Press.

Crouchley, A. E. 1938. *The Economic Development of Modern Egypt.* New York: Longman, Green.

————. 1977. *The Investment of Foreign Capital in Egyptian Companies and Public Debt.* New York: Arno Press.

Crowley, Ronald. 1971. "Long Swings in the Role of Government: An Analysis of Wars and Government Expenditures in Western Europe Since the Eleventh Century." *Public Finance* 26:27–43.

Dahl, Robert. 1957. "The Concept of Power." *Behavioral Science* 12 (July): 203–4.

Dandeker, Chris. 1983. "Warfare, Planning, and Economic Relations." *Economy and Society* 12 (1) (February):109–28.

David, Stephen. 1991. "Explaining Third World Alignments." *World Politics* 43 (January):233–56.

Davis, Eric. 1983. *Challenging Colonialism: Bank Misr and Egyptian Industrialization, 1920–1941.* Princeton: Princeton University Press.

Dawisha, Adeed. 1990. "Arab Regimes: Legitimacy and Foreign Policy." In *The Arab State*, edited by Giacomo Luciani. Berkeley: University of California Press.

Dawisha, Karen. 1979. *Soviet Foreign Policy Towards Egypt.* London: Macmillan.

Deane, Phyllis. 1975. "War and Industrialization." In *War and Economic Development*, edited by J. M. Winter. New York: Cambridge University Press.

Deeb, Marius. 1979. *Party Politics in Egypt: The Wafd and Its Rivals.* London: Ithica Press.

Dekmejian, R. H. 1971. *Egypt Under Nasir: A Study in Political Dynamics.* Albany: State University of New York Press.

Dekmejian, R. H., and D. Koutsoukis. 1980. "Comparative Patterns of Elite Recruitment." *The Greek Review of Social Research* 38 (January/April):147–63.

Dessouki, Ali. 1981. "Policymaking in Egypt: A Case of the Open Door Economic Policy." *Social Problems* 28 (4) (April):410–16.

Dessouki, Ali, and Adel al-Labban. 1981. "Arms Race, Defense Expenditures, and Development: The Egyptian Case, 1952–1973." *Journal of South Asian and Middle Eastern Studies* 4 (3) (Spring):65–77.

de Tocqueville, Alexis. 1964. "On War, Society, and Military." In *War: Studies from Psychology, Sociology, and Anthropology*, edited by L. Bramson and G. Goethals. New York: Basic Books.

Diab, Jihan Kamel Tawfik. 1983. *The Hidden Economy in Egypt: A Social Accounting Matrix Approach.* M. A. thesis. Department of Economics and Political Science, American University of Cairo.

al-Din Hadidi, Salah. 1983. "Military Dependency: The Egyptian Case." In *Sociology of the "Developing Societies": The Middle East*, edited by Talal Asad and Roger Owen. New York: Monthly Review Press.

Domke, William. 1988. *War and the Changing Global System.* New Haven: Yale University Press.

Dror, Yehezkal. 1984. "The Politics of Defense Budgeting: A Comparison Between Western Europe and Israel." In *Israeli Security Planning in the 1980s*, edited by Zvi Lanir. New York: Praeger Press.

Due, John. 1988. *Indirect Taxation in Developing Economies*. Baltimore: Johns Hopkins University Press.

al-Edel, Reda 1982. "Impact of Taxation in Income Distribution: An Exploratory Attempt to Estimate Tax Incidence in Egypt." *The Political Economy of Income Distribution in Egypt*, edited by G. Abd al-Khalek and R. Tignor. Boulder: Westview Press.

Efrat, Moshe. 1981. *The Defence Burden in Egypt During the Deepening of Soviet Involvement in 1962–72*. Ph.D. diss., London University.

Ehrlich, Avishai. 1987. "Israel: Conflict, War, and Social Change." In *The Sociology of War and Peace*, edited by M. Shaw and C. Creighton. New York: Sheridan House.

Eisenstadt, S. N. 1967. *Israeli Society*. New York: Basic Books.

———. 1985. *The Transformation of Israeli Society: An Essay in Interpretation*. London: Weidenfeld and Nicolson.

El-Barawi, Rashed. 1951. "The Taxation System in Egypt." *Middle Eastern Affairs* 2(12) (December):401–9.

Elon, Amos. 1971. *The Israelis: Fathers and Sons*. New York: Holt, Rinehart, and Winston.

———. 1990. "Letter from Jerusalem." *New Yorker*, April 23.

Elster, Jon. 1985. *Making Sense of Marx*. New York: Cambridge University Press.

Eshag, Eprime. 1983. *Fiscal and Monetary Policies and Problems in Developing Countries*. New York: Cambridge University Press.

Etheredge, Lloyd. 1985. *Can Governments Learn?* New York: Pergamon Press.

Etzioni-Halevy, E. 1975. "Protest Politics in Israeli Democracy." *Political Science Quarterly* 90 (Fall): 497–520.

———. 1979. *Political Manipulation and Administrative Power: A Comparative Study*. Boston: Routledge and Kegan Paul.

Evans, Peter. 1979. *Dependent Development*. Princeton: Princeton University Press.

———. 1989. "Predatory, Developmental, and Other Apparatuses: A Comparative Political Economy Perspective on the Third World State." *Sociological Forum* 4 (4):561–87.

Evans, Peter, D. Rueschemeyer, and T. Skocpol, eds. 1985. *Bringing the State Back In*. New York: Cambridge University Press.

———. 1985. "On the Road Toward a More Adequate Understanding of the State." In *Bringing the State Back In*.

Finer, S. E. 1975. "State-and Nation-Building in Europe: The Role of the Military." In *The Formation of the National States in Western Europe*, edited by Charles Tilly. Princeton: Princeton University Press.

Fitzgerald, E. V. K. 1978. "The Fiscal Crisis of the Latin American State." In *Taxation and Economic Development*, edited by J. F. J. Toye. London: Frank Cass.

Frankel, Boris. 1979. "On the State of the State: Marxist Theories of the State after Leninism." *Theory and Society* 7:199–242.

Freedman, Lawrence. 1986. *The Price of Peace: Living With the Nuclear Dilemma*. New York: Harry Holt and Company.

Friedberg, Aaron. 1989. "The Political Economy of American Strategy." *World Politics* 41 (April):381–406.

Fromkin, David. 1989. *A Peace to End All Peace: The Fall of the Ottoman Empire and the Rise of the Modern Middle East*. New York: Harry Holt.

Frost, Roger, et al. 1985. "Cairo Emphasizes Local Production." *International Defense Review* 18 (2):213–22.

Gabby, Joseph. 1975. "Israel's Fiscal Policy, 1948–75." In *Israel: A Developing Society*, edited by Asher Arian. Amsterdam: Van Gorcum.

Gaddis, John Lewis. 1982. *Strategies of Containment*. New York: Oxford University Press.

Gazit, Mordechai. 1987. "Israeli Military Procurement from the U.S." In *Dynamics of Dependence: U.S.-Israeli Relations*, edited by Gabriel Sheffer. Boulder: Westview Press.

George, Alexander, and Timothy McKeown. 1985. "Case Studies and Theories of Organizational Decision Making." In *Advances in Information Processing in Organizations, Research on Public Organizations*, vol. 2, edited by R. Coulam and R. Smith. Greenwich: JAI Press.

Giddens, Anthony. 1984. *The Constitution of Society*. Berkeley: University of California Press.

———. 1985. *The Nation State and Violence*. Berkeley: University of California Press.

Gilpin, Robert. 1987. *The Political Economy of International Relations*. Princeton: Princeton University Press.

Girgis, Maurice. 1977. *Industrialization and Trade Patterns in Egypt*. Tubingen, Germany: J. C. B. Mohr.

Godfrey, John. 1987. *French Capitalism at War: Industrial Policy and Bureaucracy in France, 1914–1918*. New York: St. Martin's Press.

Goldberg, Ellis. 1986. *Tinker, Tailor, Textile Worker*. Berkeley: University of California Press.

Goldstein, Judith. 1989. "The Impact of Ideas on Trade Policy." *International Organization* 43 (1):31–71.

Gorny, Yosef. 1987. *Zionism and the Arabs, 1882–1948: A Study of Ideology*. London: Oxford University Press.

Gourevitch, Peter. 1978. "The Second Image Reversed: The International Sources of Domestic Politics." *International Organization* 32 (4) (Autumn): 881–912.

———. 1986. *The Politics of Hard Times*. Ithaca: Cornell University Press.

Granovsky. [Grannot], A. 1935. *The Fiscal System of Palestine*. Jerusalem: Palestine and Near East Publications.

Gulalp, Haldun. 1987. "Capital Accumulation, Classes, and the Relative Autonomy of the State." *Science and Society* 51 (3) (Fall):287–313.

Gurr, Ted Robert. 1988. "War, Revolution, and the Growth of the Coercive State." *Comparative Political Studies* 21 (1) (April): 46–65.

Haas, Ernst. 1990. *When Knowledge is Power*. Berkeley: University of California Press.

Hadar, Shmuel. 1988. *Blurring the Boundaries Between Public and Private Relations Between State and Industry*. Ph.D. diss., Hebrew University of Jerusalem (in Hebrew).

Hadidi, Salal al-Din. 1983. "Military Dependency: The Egyptian Case." In *Sociology of the "Developing Societies," Middle East*, edited by Talal Asad and Roger Owen. New York: Monthly Review Press.

Halevi, Nadav. 1970. "Exchange Rate Control in Israel." In *Israel and the Common Market*, edited by Pierre Uri. Jerusalem: George Weidenfeld and Nicolson.

———. 1976. "The Economy of Israel: Goals and Limitations." *Jerusalem Quarterly* 1 (Fall):83–92.

Halevi, Nadav, and R. Klinov-Malul, eds. 1968. *The Economic Development of Israel*. Praeger Special Studies in International Economics and Development. Jerusalem: Bank of Israel and Praeger.

Halevi, Nadav, and Y. Kops, eds. 1975. *Issues in the Economy of Israel*. Jerusalem: Maurice Falk Institute for Economic Research.

Hall, John. 1987. "Introduction." In *States in History*, edited by John Hall. London: Basil Blackwell.

Hall, Peter, ed. 1986. *The Political Power of Economic Ideas*. Princeton: Princeton University Press.

———. 1987. *Governing the Economy*. New York: Oxford University Press.

Halliday, Fred. 1987. "The Middle East in International Perspective: Problem of Analysis." In *The World Order: Socialist Perspectives*, edited by R. Bush et al. London: Polity Press.

———. 1987. "State and Society in International Relations: A Second Agenda." *Millennium* 16 (2):215–29.

Halliday, Fred, and Hamza Alavi. 1988. "Introduction." In *State and Ideology in the Middle East and Pakistan*, edited by F. Halliday and H. Alavi. New York: Monthly Review Press.

Hamilton, Nora. 1982. *The Limits of State Autonomy*. Princeton: Princeton University Press.

Handoussa, Hena Ahmed. 1983. "Time For Reform: Egypt's Public Sector Industry." In *Studies in Egyptian Political Economy*, edited by H. M. Thompson. Cairo Papers in Social Science, vol. 2. 2d ed. Cairo: American University in Cairo Press.

Hansen, Bent, and Girgis Marzouk. 1965. *Development and Economic Policy in the UAR (Egypt)*. Amsterdam: North-Holland Publishing Company.

Hansen, Bent, and Karim Nashashibi. 1975. *Foreign Trade Regimes and Economic Development: Egypt*. New York: Columbia University Press.

Haries-Jenkins, Gwyn, and Jacques van Doorn, eds. 1976. *The Military and the Problem of Legitimacy*. Beverly Hills: Sage Press.

Harkavy, Robert, and Stephanie Neuman. 1984. "Israel." In *Arms Production in Developing Countries*, edited by J. Katz. Lexington: Lexington Books.

Haskel, Barbara. 1980. "Access to Society: A Neglected Dimension of State Power." *International Organization* 34 (1) (Winter):89–120.

Hechter, Michael, and William Brustein. 1980. "Regional Modes of Production and Patterns of State Formation in Western Europe." *American Journal of Sociology* 85:1061–94.

Heikal, Mohammed. 1973. *The Cairo Documents*. New York: Doubleday.

———. 1975. *The Road to Ramadan*. London: Collins Press.

———. 1978. *The Sphinx and the Commissar*. New York: Harper & Row.

———. 1983. *Autumn of Fury: The Assassination of Sadat*. London: Deutsch Press.

———. 1987. *Cutting the Lion's Tail: Suez Through Egyptian Eyes*. New York: Arbor House.

Held, David, and Joel Krieger. 1983. "Accumulation, Legitimation and the State: The Ideas of Claus Offe and Jürgen Habermas." In *States and Societies*, edited by D. Held et al. New York: New York University Press.

Herschel, Frederico J. 1978. "Tax Evasion and Its Measurements in Developing Countries." *Public Finance* 33 (3):232–68.

Hertzberg, Arthur. 1969. *The Zionist Idea: A Historical Analysis and Reader*. New York: Antheum Press.

Hinnebusch, Raymond. 1985. *Egyptian Politics Under Sadat: The Post-Populist Development of an Authoritarian State*. New York: Cambridge University Press.

Hinrichs, Harley. 1966. *A General Theory of Tax Structure Change During Economic Development*. Cambridge: Harvard Law School.

Hintze, Otto. 1975. "Economics and Politics in the Age of Modern Capitalism." In *The Historical Essays of Otto Hintze*, edited by F. Gilbert. New York: Oxford University Press.

———. 1975. "Military Organization and the Organization of the State." In *The Historical Essays of Otto Hintze*, edited by Felix Gilbert. New York: Oxford University Press.

Hirst, Paul. 1978. "Economic Classes and Politics." In *Class and Class Structure*, edited by A. Hunt. London: Lawrence and Wishart.

Horowitz, Dan. 1987. "Strategic Limitations of 'A Nation in Arms.'" *Armed Forces and Society* 13 (2) (Winter):272–94.

Horowitz, Dan, and Baruch Kimmerling. 1974. "Some Social Implications of Military Service and the Reserve System in Israel." *Archives Européens de Sociologie* 15:265–88.

Horowitz, Dan, and Moshe Lissak. 1978. *Origins of the Israeli Polity*. Chicago: University of Chicago Press.

Howard, Michael. 1976. *War in European History*. New York: Oxford University Press.

Huntington, Samuel. 1961. *The Common Defense*. New York: Columbia University Press.

———. 1968. *Political Order in Changing Societies*. New Haven: Yale University Press.

Hurewitz, J. C. 1976. *The Struggle For Palestine*. New York: Norton Press.

———. 1982. *Middle East Politics: The Military Dimension*. Boulder: Westview Press.

Hussini, Mohrse Mahmoud. 1987. *Soviet-Egyptian Relations, 1945–1985*. New York: St. Martin's Press.

Ikenberry, G. John. 1988. "Conclusion: An Institutional Approach to American Foreign Economic Policy." *International Organization* 42 (Winter):219–43.

————. 1988. *Reasons of State*. Ithaca: Cornell University Press.

Ikram, Khalid. 1980. *Egypt: Economic Management in a Period of Transition*. Baltimore: Johns Hopkins University Press.

Isaac, Jeffrey. 1987. *Power and Marxist Theory: A Realist View*. Ithaca: Cornell University Press.

Issawi, Charles. 1954. *Egypt at Mid-Century: An Economic Survey*. New York: Oxford University Press.

————. 1963. *Egypt in Revolution: An Economic Analysis*. New York: Oxford University Press.

Issawi, Ibrahim, and Muhammed Ali Nassar. 1978. "An Attempt to Estimate the Economic Losses Inflicted by the 1967 Arab-Israeli War." Paper presented to the third annual conference of Egyptian Economists, Cairo, March 23–25 (in Arabic).

Jackson, Robert, and Carl Rosberg. 1982. "Why Africa's Weak States Persist: The Empirical and Juridical in Statehood." *World Politics* 35 (October):1–24.

Janowitz, Morris. 1976. "Military Institutions and Citizenship in Western Societies." In *The Military and the Problem of Legitimacy*, edited by Gwyn Haries-Jenkins and Jacques van Doorn. Beverly Hills: Sage Press.

————. 1977. *Military Institutions and Coercion in the Developing Nations*. Chicago: University of Chicago Press.

Jerusalem Institute of Management. 1987. *Export-Led Growth Strategy for Israel: A Final Report*. Tel-Aviv: Jerusalem Institute of Management.

Jessop, Bob. 1982. *The Capitalist State*. New York: New York University Press.

————. 1985. *Nicos Poulantzas*. New York: St. Martin's Press.

Jones, Ellen. 1985. *Red Army and Society*. Boston: Allen and Unwin.

Jones, R. B. J. 1986. *Conflict and Control in the World Economy*. New York: Humanities Press.

Kaldor, Mary. 1983. "Warfare and Capitalism." In *Exterminism and the Cold War*, edited by E. P. Thompson et al. London: New Left Books.

Kanovsky, Eliyahu. 1970. *The Economic Impact of the Six-Day War: Israel, the Occupied Territories, Egypt, Jordan*. New York: Praeger.

Karawan, Ibrahim. 1984. "Egypt's Defense Policy." In *Defense Planning in Less Industrialized States*, edited by Stephanie Neuman. Lexington: Lexington Books.

Kardouche, G. K. 1967. *The U.A.R. in Development: A Study in Expansionary Finance*. New York: Praeger Press.

Katz, James, ed. 1984. *The Implications of Third World Military Industrialization*. Lexington: Lexington Books.

Katzenstein, Peter, ed. 1978. *Between Power and Plenty*. Madison: University of Wisconsin Press.

Kennedy, Paul. 1987. *The Rise and Decline of the Great Powers*. New York: Random House.

Kerr, Malcom. 1971. *The Arab Cold War*. New York: Oxford University Press.

Kidron, Michael. 1968. *Western Capitalism Since the War*. London: Weidenfeld and Nicolson.

Kiernan, V. G. 1973. "Conscription and Society in Europe Before the War of 1914–18." In *War and Society*, edited by M. R. D. Foot. London: Paul Elek.

Kimmerling, Baruch. 1974. "Anomie and Integration in Israeli Society and the Salience of the Arab-Israeli Conflict." *Studies in Comparative International Development* 9 (3) (Fall):64–89.

———. 1979. "Determination of the Boundaries and Frameworks of Conscription: Two Dimensions of Civil-Military Relations in Israel." *Studies in Comparative International Development* 14 (1) (Spring):22–41.

———. 1983. *Zionism and Economy*. Cambridge: Schenkman.

———. 1983. *Zionism and Territory*. Berkeley: Institute of International Studies.

———. 1984. "Making Conflict a Routine: Cumulative Effects of the Arab-Jewish Conflict Upon Israeli Society." In *Israeli Society and Its Defense Establishment*, edited by Moshe Lissak. London: Frank Cass.

———. 1985. "Between Primordial and Civil Definitions of the Collective Identity: Eretz Israel or the State of Israel?" In *Comparative Social Dynamics*, edited by E. Cohen et al. Boulder: Westview Press.

———. 1989. "Boundaries and Frontiers of the Israeli Control System: Analytical Conclusions." In *The Israeli State and Society: Boundaries and Frontiers*, edited by B. Kimmerling. Albany: State University of New York Press.

Kindleberger, Charles. 1984. *A Financial History of Western Europe*. New York: George Allen and Unwin.

Klieman, Aaron. 1985. *Israel's Global Reach: Arms Sales as Diplomacy*. New York: Pergamon Press.

———. 1987. "Current Crisis in the Israeli Defense Industry." *Israel Economist* (September):46–49.

Knorr, Klaus. 1956. *The War Potential of Nations*. Princeton: Princeton University Press.

———. 1973. *Power and Wealth: The Political Economy of International Power*. New York: Basic Books.

Knorr, Klaus, and Frank Trager, eds. 1977. *Economic Issues and National Security*. Lawrence: University of Kansas Press.

Kocka, Jürgen. 1984. *Facing Total War*. Cambridge: Harvard University Press.

Kolko, Gabriel. 1984. *Anatomy of a War: Vietnam, the United States, and the Modern Historical Experience*. New York: Pantheon Press.

Krasner, Stephen. 1978. *Defending the National Interest*. Princeton: Princeton University Press.

———. 1984. "Approaches to the State: Alternative Conceptions and Historical Dynamics." *Comparative Politics* 16 (2) (January):223–46.

Kugler, Jacek, and William Domke. 1986. "Comparing the Strength of Nations." *Comparative Political Studies* 19 (April):36–39.

Laclau, Ernesto. 1975. "The Specifity of the Political: The Poulantzas-Miliband Debate." *Economy and Society* 4 (1):87–110.

Lake, David. 1990. "The State and Grand Strategy." Paper presented at the American Political Science Association annual meetings, San Francisco.

Lamborn, Alan. 1983. "Power and the Politics of Extraction." *International Studies Quarterly* 27 (2):125–46.

Landes, David. 1979. *Bankers and Pashas: International Finance and Economic Imperialism in Egypt.* Cambridge: Harvard University Press.

Lane, F. C. 1979. "The Economic Meaning of War and Protection." In *Profits From Power*, edited by F. C. Lane. Albany: State University of New York Press.

Laufer, Leopold. 1987. "U.S. Aid to Israel: Problems and Perspectives." In *Dynamics of Dependence: U.S.-Israeli Relations*, edited by Gabriel Sheffer. Boulder: Westview Press.

Lee, Su-Hoon. 1988. *State-Building in the Contemporary Third World.* Boulder: Westview Press.

Lenin, V. I. 1968. *Imperialism: The Highest Stage of Capitalism.* Moscow: Progress Press.

Levi, Margaret. 1981. "A Predatory Theory of Rule." *Politics and Society* 10 (4):431–65.

———. 1988. *Of Rule and Revenue.* Berkeley: University of California Press.

Levy, Jack. 1988. "The Domestic Politics and War." *Journal of Interdisciplinary History* 18 (4) (Spring):653–73.

———. 1989. "The Diversionary Theory of War." In *Handbook of War Studies*, edited by Manus Midlarsky. Boston: Unwin Hyman.

Leys, Colin. 1976. "The 'Overdeveloped' Post-colonial State: A Re-evaluation." *Review of African Political Economy* 5 (January–April):39–48.

Lifshitz, Y. 1975. "Defense Expenditure and the Allocation of Resources." In *Issues in the Economy of Israel*, edited by N. Halevi and Y. Kop. Jerusalem: Maurice Falk Institute for Economic Research in Israel.

Lindblom, Charles. 1977. *Politics and Markets.* New York: Basic Books.

Lissak, Moshe. 1971. "The Israeli Defense Forces as an Agent of Socialization and Education: A Research in Role Expansion in Democratic Society." In *The Perceived Role of the Military*, edited by M. R. Van Gils. Rotterdam: Rotterdam University Press.

Liviatan, Oded. 1980. "Israel's External Debt." *Bank of Israel Economic Review*, no. 48–49 (May):1–45.

Lotz, Jorgen. 1966. "Taxation in the U.A.R. (Egypt)." *IMF Staff Papers* 13 (1) (March):121–53.

Lotz, Jorgen, and Elliot Morss. 1967. "Measuring 'Tax Effort' in Developing Countries." *IMF Staff Papers* 14 (3) (November):478–99.

———. 1970. "A Theory of Tax Level Determinants for Developing Countries." *Economic Development and Cultural Change* 18 (3):328–41.

Luciani, Giacomo, ed. 1990. *The Arab State.* Berkeley: University of California Press.

Lukes, Steven, ed. 1986. *Power.* New York: New York University Press.

Lustick, Ian. 1988. "Israeli State-Building in the West Bank and Gaza: Theory and Practice." *International Organization* 41 (1):151–171.

Luttwak, Edward, and Dan Horowitz. 1975. *The Israeli Army*. New York: Harper & Row.

Luxemburg, Rosa. 1963. *The Accumulation of Capital*. New York: Routledge and Kegan Paul.

Mabro, Robert. 1974. *The Egyptian Economy, 1952–72*. London: Oxford University Press.

Mabro, Robert, and Samir Radwan. 1976. *The Industrialization of Egypt, 1933–76*. Oxford: Claredon Press.

MacKenzie, Donald. 1983. "Militarism and Socialist Theory." *Capital and Class* 19:33–73.

Maital, Shlomo. 1970. "Some Aspects of a Value-Added Tax for Israel." In *Israel and the Common Market*, edited by Pierre Uri. Jerusalem: George Weidenfeld and Nicolson.

Mandel, Ernest. 1986. *The Meaning of the Second World War*. London: New Left Books.

Mandelbaum, Michael. 1988. *The Fate of Nations: The Search for National Security in the Nineteenth and Twentieth Centuries*. New York: Cambridge University Press.

Manicas, Peter. 1985. "Explanation, Generalisation and Marxist Theory Vis-à-Vis Third World Development." *Marxian Theory and the Third World*, edited by D. Banarjee. Beverly Hills: Sage Press.

Mann, Michael. 1984. "The Autonomous Power of the State: Its Origins, Mechanisms, and Results." *European Journal of Sociology* 25:185–213.

———. 1987. "Capitalism and Militarism." In *The Sociology of War and Peace*, edited by Martin Shaw and Colin Creighton. New York: Sheridan House.

———. 1989. *States, War, and Capitalism*. London: Basil Blackwell.

Mansfied, Peter. 1971. *The British in Egypt*. London: Weidenfeld and Nicolson.

Marsot, Lufti al-sayyid. 1984. *Egypt in the Reign of Muhammad Ali*. New York: Cambridge University Press.

Marwick, Arthur. 1974. *War and Social Change in the Twentieth Century: A Comparative Study of Britain, France, Germany, Russia, and the United States*. New York: St. Martin's Press.

Marx, Karl. 1963. *The Eighteenth Brumaire of Louis Bonaparte*. New York: International Publishers.

Mastanduno, Michael, David Lake, and G. John Ikenberry. 1989. "Towards a Realist Theory of State Action," *International Studies Quarterly* 33 (4) (December):457–74.

McDermott, Anthony. 1988. *Egypt from Nasser to Mubarak: A Flawed Revolution*. London: Croom Helm.

McNeill, William. 1982. *The Pursuit of Power: Technology, Armed Forces, and Society Since A.D. 1000*. Chicago: University of Chicago Press.

Mead, Donald. 1967. *Growth and Structural Change in the Egyptian Economy*. Homewood: Richard D. Irwin.

Medding, Peter. 1972. *Mapai in Israel: Political Organization and Government in a New Society*. Cambridge: Cambridge University Press.

————. 1990. *The Foundation of Israeli Democracy, 1948–1967.* New York: Oxford University Press.

Melman, Seymor. 1974. *The Permanent War Economy: American Capitalism in Decline.* New York: Simon and Schuster.

Michaely, Michael. 1975. *Foreign Trade Regimes and Economic Development: Israel, Vol. III.* New York: Columbia University Press.

Migdal, Joel. 1988. *Strong Societies and Weak States.* Princeton: Princeton University Press.

————. 1989. "The Crystallization of the State and Struggles Over Rulemaking: Israel in Comparative Perspective." In *The Israeli State and Society: Boundaries and Frontiers*, edited by Barcuh Kimmerling. Albany: State University of New York Press.

Miliband, Ralph. 1969. *The State in Capitalist Society.* New York: Basic Books.

Miller, James. 1986. "The Fiscal Crisis of the State Reconsidered: Two Views of the State and the Accumulation of Capital in the Post War Economy." *Review of Radical Political Economics* 18 (1/2):236–60.

Milward, Alan. 1979. *War, Economy, and Society, 1939–1945.* Berkeley: University of California Press.

Mintz, Alex. 1984. "The Military-Industrial Complex: The Israeli Case." In *Israeli Society and Its Defense Establishment*, edited by Moshe Lissak. London: Frank Cass.

————. 1985. "The Military-Industrial Complex: American Concepts and Israeli Realities." *Journal of Conflict Resolution* 29 (4):623–39.

————. 1985. "Military-Industrial Linkages in Israel." *Armed Forces and Society* 12 (1) (Fall):9–27.

————. 1987. "Arms Production in Israel." *Jerusalem Quarterly*, no. 42 (Spring):89–99.

Mintz, Alex, and Daniel Maman. 1985. "Center vs. Periphery in Israel's Military-Industrial Sector: Implications for Civil-Military Relations." Manuscript.

Monem Monem Said, Abdel. 1989. "Nation State and Transnational Society: The Case of Egypt." Paper presented at the Conference on Dynamics of States and Societies in the Middle East, Cairo.

Moore, Clement Henry. 1974. "Authoritarian Politics in Unincorporated Society: The Case of Nasser's Egypt." *Comparative Politics* 6 (2) (January):193–218.

Morgenthau, Hans. 1978. *Politics Among Nations.* 5th ed. New York: Alfred A. Knopf.

Morsey, Laila. 1984. "The Military Clauses of the Anglo-Egyptian Treaty of Friendship and Alliance, 1936." *International Journal of Middle Eastern Studies* 6 (1):67–97.

Morris, Benny. 1987. *The Birth of the Palestinian Refugee Problem, 1947–1949.* New York: Cambridge University Press.

Mouzelis, Nicos. 1986. *Politics in the Semi-Periphery.* New York: St. Martin's Press.

Mueller, John. 1973. *Wars, Presidents, and Public Opinion.* New York: Wiley and Sons.

Nachmain, David, and David Rosenbloom. 1978. *Bureaucratic Culture and Administrators in Israel*. New York: St. Martin's Press.

Nasser, Gamal. 1959. *Philosophy of the Revolution*. New York: Buffalo, Smith, Keyze, Marshall.

National Bank of Egypt. *Economic Bulletin*. Various years.

Neuman, Stephanie. 1984. "Third World Arms Production and the Global Arms Transfer System." In *The Implications of Third World Military Industrialization*, edited by James Katz. Lexington, Mass.: Lexington Press.

———. 1984. "International Stratification and Third World Military Industries." *International Organization* 38 (1) (Winter):167–97.

Neumann, Sigmund, and Mark von Hagen. 1986. "Engels and Marx on Revolution, War, and Army in Society." In *The Makers of Modern Strategy*, edited by Peter Paret. Princeton: Princeton University Press.

Newlyn, W. T. 1985. "Measuring Tax Effort in Developing Countries," *Journal of Development Studies* 22 (3) (April):390–405.

Nordlinger, Eric. 1981. *On the Autonomy of the Democratic State*. Cambridge: Harvard University Press.

North, Douglass. 1981. *Structure and Change in Economic History*. New York: W. W. Norton.

North, Douglass, and Robert Thomas. 1973. *The Rise of the Western World*. New York: W. W. Norton.

Nye, Joseph. 1987. "Nuclear Learning and U.S.-Soviet Security Regimes." *International Organization* 41 (3) (Summer):371–402.

———. 1990. *Bound to Lead*. New York: Basic Books.

Nye, Joseph, and Sean Lynn-Jones. 1988. "International Security Studies: A Report of a Conference on the State of the Field." *International Security* 12 (4) (Spring):5–27.

O'Brien, Connor Cruise. 1986. *The Siege: The Saga of Israel and Zionism*. New York: Simon and Schuster.

O'Brien, Patrick. 1966. *The Revolution in Egypt's Economic System: From Private Enterprise to Socialism, 1952–65*. New York: Oxford University Press.

O'Connor, James. 1973. *The Fiscal Crisis of the State*. New York: St. Martin's Press.

Offe, Claus. 1975. "Theses on the Theory of the State," *New German Critique* 6:137–47.

Omar-Otunnu, Amii. 1987. *Politics and the Military in Uganda, 1890–1985*. New York: St. Martin's Press.

Organski, A. F. K., and Jacek Kugler. 1980. *The War Ledger*. Chicago: University of Chicago Press.

Organski, A. F. K., Jacek Kugler et al. 1984. *Births, Deaths, and Taxes: The Demographic and Political Transitions*. Chicago: University of Chicago Press.

Owen, Roger. 1982. "Introduction." In *Studies in the Economic and Social History of Palestine in the Nineteenth Century*, edited by Roger Owen. Carbondale: Southern Illinois University Press.

———. 1983. *The Middle East in the World Economy*. London: Methuen.

———. 1989. "The Economic Consequences of the Suez Crisis for Egypt." In

Suez 1956: The Crisis and Its Consequences, edited by Wm. Roger Louis and Roger Owen. New York: Oxford University Press.

Pack, Howard. 1971. *Structural Change and Economic Policy in Israel*. New Haven: Yale University Press.

Park, Hans, and Kyung Park. 1988. "Ideology and Security: Self-Reliance in China and North Korea." In *National Security in the Third World*, edited by Edward Azar and Chung-in Moon. Hants, Eng.: Edward Elger Publishers.

Parkin, Frank. 1979. *Marxism and Class Theory: A Bourgeois Critique*. New York: New York University Press.

Patinkin, Donald. 1960. *The Israeli Economy: The First Decade*. Jerusalem: Falk Project for Economic Development in Israel.

Paul, Jim. 1983. "The Egyptian Arms Industry." *MERIP Reports* 112 (February):26–28.

Peres, Shimon. 1970. *David's Sling*. London: George Weidenfeld and Nicolson.

Peretz, Don. 1981. *Government and Politics of Israel*. Boulder: Westview Press.

Peri, Yoram. 1983. *Between Ballots and Bullets*. New York: Cambridge University Press.

Perlmutter, Amos. 1974. *Egypt: The Praetorian State*. New Brunswick: Transaction Books.

———. 1977. *Military and Politics in Israel: Nation-Building and Role Expansion*. London: Frank Cass.

———. 1978. *Politics and the Military in Israel, 1967–77*. London: Frank Cass.

Pigou, A. C. 1942. *The Political Economy of War*. New York: Macmillan.

Poggi, Giafranco. 1978. *The Development of the Modern State*. London: Hutchinson Press.

Pollard, Robert. 1985. *Economic Security and the Origins of the Cold War, 1945–1950*. New York: Columbia University Press.

Pomfret, Richard. 1976. *Trade Policies and Industrialization in a Small Country: The Case of Israel*. Tubingen, West Germany: University Kiel.

Posen, Barry. 1985. *The Sources of Military Doctrine*. Ithaca: Cornell University Press.

Poulantzas, Nicos. 1969. "The Problem of the Capitalist State." *New Left Review*, no. 58:67–78.

———. 1978. *State, Power, Socialism*. London: Verso Press.

Praedicta. 1987. "Analyzing U.S. Aid and Trade." *Israel Economist* (October): 24–26.

Przeworski, Adam, and Michael Wallerstein. 1988. "The Structural Dependence of the State on Capital." *American Political Science Review* 82 (1) (March):11–30.

Putnam, Robert. 1988. "Diplomacy and Domestic Politics." *International Organization* 42 (Summer):422–60.

Radian, Alex. 1979. "On the Difference Between the Political Economy of Introducing and Implementing Tax Reform—Israel, 1975–78." *Journal of Public Economics* 11:261–71.

———. 1980. *Resource Mobilization in Poor Countries*. New Brunswick: Transaction Books.

———. 1984. "The Dynamics of Policy Formation: Income Tax Rates in Israel, 1948–75." *Environment and Planning C: Government and Policy* 2:271–84.

Radian, Alex, and Ira Sharkansky. 1979. "Tax Reform in Israel: Partial Implementation and Ambitious Goals." *Policy Analysis* 5 (3):351–66.

Radwan, Samir. 1974. *Capital Formation in Egyptian Industry and Agriculture, 1882–1967*. London: Ithica Press.

Ragin, Charles. 1985. *The Comparative Method*. Berkeley: University of California Press.

Rahmy, Ali Abdel Rahman. 1983. *Egyptian Policy in the Arab World: Intervention in Yemen, 1962–67*. Washington, D.C.: University Press of America.

Ralston, John. 1990. *Importing the European Army*. Chicago: University of Chicago Press.

Rasler, Karen, and William Thompson. 1983. "Global Wars, Public Debt, and the Long Cycle." *World Politics* 35:489–516.

———. 1985. "Warmaking and Statemaking: Governmental Expenditures, Tax Revenues, and Global Wars." *American Political Science Review* 79 (2) (June): 491–507.

———. 1989. *War and Statemaking*. Boston: Unwin Hyman.

Reich, Bernard. 1982. "Israel." In *Security Policies in Developing Countries*, edited by E. Kolodziej and R. Harkavy. Lexington: Lexington Books.

Reiser, Stewart. 1989. *The Israeli Arms Industry*. New York: Holmes and Meier.

Rejwan, Nissim. 1974. *Nasserist Ideology: Its Exponents and Critics*. New York: John Wiley and Sons.

Richards, Alan, and John Waterbury. 1990. *A Political Economy of the Middle East*. Boulder: Westview Press.

Rivlin, Paul. 1985. *The Dynamics of Economic Policy Making in Egypt*. New York: Praeger Press.

Rose, Richard. 1985. "Maximizing Tax Revenue While Minimizing Political Costs." *Journal of Public Policy* 5 (3) (August):289–320.

Rosecrance, Richard. 1986. *The Rise of the Trading State*. New York: Basic Books.

Rowley, Robin, S. Bichler, and J. Nitzan. 1988. "Some Aspects of Aggregate Concentration in the Israeli Economy, 1964–1986." *Department of Economics Working Papers*. Montreal: McGill University.

Roy, Delwin. 1978. "Private Industry Sector Developments in Egypt: An Analysis of Trends, 1973–1977." *Journal of South Asian and Middle Eastern Studies* 1 (Spring): 11–33

Rubenstein, Alvin. 1977. *Red Star on the Nile*. Princeton: Princeton University Press.

Rubner, Alex. 1960. *The Economy of Israel: A Critical Account of the First Ten Years*. London: Frank Cass.

Rueschemeyer, D., and P. Evans. 1985. "The State and Economic Transformation: Toward an Analysis of the Conditions Underlying Effective Intervention." In *Bringing the State Back In*, edited by P. Evans et al. New York: Cambridge University Press.

Ryan, Sheila. 1987. "U.S. Military Contractors in Israel." *MERIP Reports* 144 (January–February):17–22.

Sachar, Howard. 1979. *A History of Israel: From the Rise of Zionism to Our Time*. New York: Alfred A. Knopf.

———. 1987. *A History of Israel, Volume II: From the Aftermath of the Yom Kippur War*. New York: Oxford University Press.

Sadat, Anwar. 1977. *In Search of Identity*. New York: Harper & Row.

Safran, Nadav. 1978. *Israel: The Embattled Ally*. Cambridge: Harvard University Press.

———. 1985. *Saudi Arabia: The Ceaseless Quest for Security*. Cambridge: Harvard University Press.

Sagi, Eli. 1980. *An Econometric Study of Some Issues in the Economic Development of Egypt: Agricultural Supply, Industrial Growth, and the Burden of Defense Expenditures*. Ph.D. diss., University of Pennsylvania.

Sayer, Andrew. 1984. *Method in Social Science: A Realist Approach*. London: Hutchinson.

Schiff, Zeev. 1985. *A History of the Israeli Army*. New York: Macmillan.

Scholch, Alexander. 1982. "European Penetration and Economic Development of Palestine, 1856–1882." In *Studies in the Economic and Social History of Palestine in the Nineteenth Century*, edited by Roger Owen. Carbondale: Southern Illinois University Press.

Segev, Tom. 1986. *1949: The First Israelis*. New York: Free Press.

Seliktor, Ofira. 1980. "The Cost of Vigilance: Linking the Economic and Social Costs of Defense." *Journal of Peace Research* 17 (4):339–55.

Selim, Mohammed el-Sayed. 1984. "Egypt." In *Arms Production in Developing Countries*, edited by James Katz. Lexington: Lexington Books.

Sella, Amnon, and Yael Yishai. 1986. *Israel: The Peaceful Belligerent, 1967–79*. New York: St. Martin's Press.

Semmel, Bernard. 1981. *Marxism and the Science of War*. New York: Oxford University Press.

Sen, Guatem. 1984. *The Military Origins of Industrialization and International Trade*. New York: St. Martin's Press.

Shafir, Gershon. 1976–1977. "Response to Yago's 'Whatever Happened to the Promised Land?' Some Reflections on Labor, Capital, and Zionism." *Berkeley Journal of Sociology* 21:147–55.

Shalev, Michael. 1983. "The Mitun: The Political Economy of Unemployment in Israel." Manuscript.

———. 1989. "Israel's Domestic Policy Regime: Zionism, Dualism, and the Rise of Capital." In *The Comparative History of Public Policy*, edited by F. G. Castles. London: Polity Press.

———. 1990. "The Political Economy of Labor Party Dominance and Decline in Israel." In *Uncommon Democracies: The One-Party Dominant Regimes*, edited by T. J. Pempel. Ithaca: Cornell University Press.

———. 1992. *Labour and the Political Economy in Israel*. New York: Oxford University Press.

Shapiro, Yonatan. 1976. *The Formative Years of the Israeli Labor Party: The Organization of Power, 1919–30*. Beverly Hills: Sage Press.

Sharkansky, Ira. 1987. *The Political Economy of Israel*. New Brunswick: Transaction Books.

Shaw, Martin. 1985. "Introduction: War and Social Theory." In *War, State, and Society*, edited by Martin Shaw. New York: St. Martin's Press.

————. 1987. *The Dialectics of Total War: An Essay on Social Theory of War and Peace*. London: Pluto Press.

Shaw, Martin, and Colin Creighton. 1987. "Introduction." In *The Sociology of War and Peace*, edited by M. Shaw and C. Creighton. New York: Sheridan House.

Shazli, Lt. General Saad el-. 1980. *The Crossing of the Suez*. San Francisco: American Middle East Research.

Sheikh, Riad el-. 1968. "The Egyptian Taxation System: An Evaluation from a Long-Term Development Point of View." *L'Egypte Contemporaine* 19 (April):83–99.

Shimshoni, Daniel. 1982. *Israeli Democracy: The Middle of the Journey*. New York: Free Press.

Shoukri, Ghali. 1981. *Egypt: Portrait of a President*. London: Zed Press.

Shukrullah, Hani. 1989. "Political Crisis/Conflict in Post-1967 Egypt." In *Egypt Under Mubarak*, edited by Charles Tripp and Roger Owen. New York: Routledge.

Singer, J. David, Stuart Bremer, and John Stuckey. 1979. "Capability Distribution, Uncertainty, and Major Power War, 1820–1965." In *Explaining War*, edited by J. David Singer et al. Beverly Hills: Sage Press.

Skocpol, Theda. 1979. *States and Social Revolutions: A Comparative Analysis of France, Russia, and China*. New York: Cambridge University Press.

————. 1985. "Bringing the State Back In: Strategies of Analysis in Current Research." In *Bringing the State Back In*, edited by P. Evans et al. New York: Cambridge University Press.

————, ed. 1985. *Vision and Method in Historical Sociology*. New York: Cambridge University Press.

Skowronek, Steven. 1982. *Building the New American State*. New York: Cambridge University Press.

Snider, Lewis. 1987. "Identifying the Elements of State Power: Where Do We Begin?" *Comparative Political Studies* 20 (3) (October):314–56.

Spiegel, Stephen. 1985. *The Other Arab-Israeli Conflict*. Chicago: University of Chicago Press.

Springborg, Robert. 1982. *Family, Power, and Politics in Egypt*. Philadelphia: University of Pennsylvania Press.

Stallings, Barbara. 1985. "International Lending and the Relative Autonomy of the State: A Case Study of Twentieth-Century Peru." *Politics and Society* 14 (4):257–88.

————. 1986. "External Finance and the Transition to Socialism in Small Peripheral Societies." In *Transition and Development*, edited by R. Fagen et al. New York: Monthly Review Press.

Stein, Arthur. 1976. "Conflict and Cohesion: A Review of the Literature." *Journal of Conflict Resolution* 20 (1) (March):143–72.

————. 1979. *The Nation at War*. Baltimore: Johns Hopkins University Press.

————. 1987. "Strategy as Politics, Politics as Strategy: Domestic Debates, Statecraft, and Star Wars." In *The Logic of Nuclear Terror*, edited by R. Kolkowicz. Boston: Unwin and Hyman.

Stein, Arthur, and Bruce Russett. 1980. "Evaluating War: Outcomes and Consequences." In *The Handbook of Political Conflict*, edited by Ted Robert Gurr. New York: Free Press.

Stein, Janice Gross. 1985. "Calculation, Miscalculation, and Conventional Deterrence, I: The View from Cairo." *Psychology and Deterrence*, by R. Jervis, N. Lebow, and J. Stein. Baltimore: Johns Hopkins University Press.

Steinberg, Gerald. 1983. "Israel." In *Structure of Defense Industries: An International Survey*, edited by Nicole Ball and Milton Leitenberg. New York: St. Martin's Press.

———. 1985. "Technology, Weapons, and Industrial Development: The Case of Israel." *Technology in Society* 7:387–98.

———. 1985. "Israel: High-Technology Roulette." In *Arms Production in the Third World*, edited by Michael Brzoska and Thomas Ohlson. Philadelphia: Taylor and Francis.

———. 1986. "Indigenous Arms Industries and Dependence: The Case of Israel." *Defense Analysis* 2 (4) (December):291–305.

Stepan, Alfred. 1978. *The State and Society: Peru in Comparative Perspective*. Princeton: Princeton University Press.

Stephens, Robert. 1971. *Nasser: A Political Biography*. London: Allen, Lane.

Stinchcombe, Arthur. 1965. "Social Structure and Organizations." In *Handbook of Organizations*, edited by James March. Chicago: Rand McNally.

Stork, Joe. 1987. "Arms Industries in the Middle East." *MERIP* 144 (January/February):12–16.

Strong, David. 1991. "Anomaly and Commonplace in European Political Expansion." *International Organization* 45 (Spring):143–62.

Tal, Eliezer, and Yoram Ezrach. 1970. "Science Policy and Development: The Case of Israel." In *Science, Development, and Defense*, edited by E. D. Bergmann. New York: Gordon and Breach Science Publishers.

Taylor, Michael. 1988. "Rationality and Revolutionary Collective Action." In *Rationality and Revolution*, edited by Michael Taylor. New York: Cambridge University Press.

———. 1989. "Structure, Culture, and Action in the Explanation of Social Change," *Politics and Society* 17 (2) (June):115–62.

Telhami, Shibley. 1990. *Power and Leadership in International Bargaining: The Path to the Camp David Accords*. New York: Columbia University Press.

Teveth, Shabtai. 1987. *Ben-Gurion: The Burning Ground, 1886–1948*. Boston: Houghton and Mifflin.

Therborn, G. 1978. *What Does the Ruling Class Do When It Rules?* London: New Left Books.

Thompson, E. P. 1982. "Introduction." In *Exterminism and the Cold War*, edited by E. P. Thompson et al. London: New Left Books.

Thomson, Janice. 1990. "State Practices, International Norms, and the Decline of Mercenarism." *International Studies Quarterly* 34 (1) (March):23–48.

Tignor, Robert. 1966. *Modernization and British Rule in Egypt, 1881–1914*. Princeton: Princeton University Press.

———. 1984. *State, Private Enterprise, and Economic Change, 1918–52*. Princeton: Princeton University Press.

Tilly, Charles. 1975. "Reflections on the History of European State-Making." In

The Formation of the National States in Western Europe, edited by Charles Tilly. Princeton: Princeton University Press.

————. 1981. *As Sociology Meets History*. New York: Academic Press.

————. 1982. "Sinews of War." In *Mobilization, Center-Periphery Structures, and Nation Building*, edited by P. Torsvik. Bergen, Norway: Universitetsforlaget.

————. 1985. "War Making and State Making as Organized Crime." In *Bringing the State Back In*, edited by P. Evans et al. New York: Cambridge University Press.

————. 1987. "Shrugging Off the Nineteenth-Century Incubus." In *Beyond Progress and Development*, edited by J. Berting and W. Blockmans. Aldershot: Avedury.

————. 1990. *Coercion, Capital, and European States*. London: Basil Blackwell.

Torgovnik, Efraim. 1975. "Israel: The Persistent Elite." In *Political Elites and Political Development in the Middle East*, edited by Frank Tachau. Cambridge: Schenkman Press.

Trimberger, Ellen Kay. 1978. *Revolution From Above: Military Bureaucrats and Development in Japan, Turkey, Egypt, and Peru*. New Brunswick: Transaction Books.

Trotsky, Leon. 1975. *The Struggle Against Fascism in Germany*. London: Penguin Books.

Tuchman, Barbara. 1956. *Bible and Sword: England and Palestine from the Bronze Age to Balfour*. New York: New York University Press.

van Arkadie, Brian. 1977. *Benefits and Burdens: A Report on the West Bank and the Gaza Strip Since 1967*. New York: Carnegie Endowment for International Peace.

van Creveld, Martin. 1984. "The Making of Israel's Security." In *Defense Planning in Less Industrialized States*, edited by Stephanie Neuman. Lexington: Lexington Books.

Vatikiotis, P. J. 1961. *The Egyptian Army in Politics*. Bloomington: Indiana University Press.

————. 1978. *Nasser and His Generation*. New York: St. Martin's Press.

————. 1980. *The History of Egypt*. Baltimore: Johns Hopkins University Press.

Vayrynen, R., and T. Ohlson. 1986. "Egypt: Arms Production in a Transnational Context." In *Arms Production in the Third World*, edited by Michael Brzoska and Thomas Ohlson. Philadelphia: Taylor and Francis.

Viner, Jacob. 1948. "Power vs. Plenty as Objectives of Foreign Policy in the Seventeenth and Eighteenth Centuries." *World Politics* 1 (October):1–29.

Vital, David. 1982. *Zionism: The Formative Years*. London: Oxford University Press.

Wallerstein, Immanuel. 1983. *Historical Capitalism*. London: Verso Press.

Walt, Stephen. 1987. *The Origins of Alliances*. Princeton: Princeton University Press.

Waltz, Ken. 1979. *A Theory of International Politics*. New York: Addison-Wesley.

Walzer, Michael. 1970. "Political Alienation and Military Service." In his *Obligations: Essays on Disobedience*. Cambridge: Harvard University Press.

Waterbury, John. 1983. *The Egypt of Nasser and Sadat: The Political Economy of Two Regimes*. Princeton: Princeton University Press.

———. 1985. "The 'Soft State' and the Open Door: Egypt's Experience with Economic Liberalization, 1974–84." *Comparative Politics* 18 (1) (October): 65–83.

Weber, Max. 1947. *Theory of Social and Economic Organization*. New York: Oxford University Press.

———. 1975. "Politics as a Vocation." In *For Max Weber*, edited by H. Gerth and C. W. Mills. New York: Oxford University Press.

Wein, Jake. 1980. *Saudi-Egyptian Relations: The Political and Military Dimensions of Saudi Financial Flows to Egypt*. Santa Monica: Rand.

Weiss, Linda. 1988. *Creating Capitalism: The State and Small Business Since 1945*. London: Basil Blackwell.

Wendt, Alexander, and Michael Barnett. 1991. "Systemic Sources of Third Militarization." Manuscript.

White, Gordon. 1987. "Revolutionary Socialist Development in the Third World: An Overview." In *Revolutionary Socialist Development in the Third World*, edited by Gordon White et al. London: Wheatsheaf Publishers.

Wilkenfeld, Harold. 1973. *Taxes and People in Israel*. Cambridge: Harvard University Press.

Wolsfeld, Gad. 1988. *Politics of Provocation: Participation and Protest in Israel*. Albany: State University of New York Press.

Wulf, Herbert. 1979. "Dependent Militarism in the Periphery and Possible Alternative Concepts." In *Arms Transfers in the Modern World*, edited by Stephanie Neuman and Robert Harkavy. New York: Praeger Press.

———. 1983. "Developing Countries." In *Structure of Defense Industries: An International Survey*, edited by Nicole Ball and Milton Leitenberg. New York: St. Martin's Press.

———. 1985. "Arms Production in the Third World." In *Arms Production in the Third World*, edited by M. Brzoska and T. Ohlson. Philadelphia: Taylor and Francis.

Yago, Glenn. 1976. "Whatever Happened to the Promised Land? Capital Flows and the Israeli State." *Berkeley Journal of Sociology* 21:117–46.

Yaniv, Avner. 1983. "National Security and Nation-Building." *International Interactions* 11:193–217.

———. 1987. *Deterrence Without the Bomb: The Politics of Israeli Strategy*. Lexington: Lexington Books.

Zaalouk, Malak. 1988. *Power, Class, and Foreign Capital in Egypt*. London: Zed Press.

Zaret, David. 1978. "Sociological Theory and Historical Scholarship." *American Sociologist* 13 (2):114–21.

Zimmerman, William, and Michael Bernbaum. 1988. "Regime Goals, Working the System, and Soviet Military Manpower Policy." Paper Presented at the American Political Science Association annual meetings, Washington, D.C.

Zolberg, Aristide. 1980. "Strategic Interactions and the Formation of Modern States: France and England." *International Social Science Journal* 32:687–716.

Interviews Conducted by Author in Israel

Agmon, Avraham. Director General, Finance Ministry, 1972–1975. June 25, 1987. Tel-Aviv.

Arnon, Yaacov. Director General, Treasury Ministry, 1956–1970. June 10, 1987. Jerusalem.

Berglas, Eitan. Director of Budget, 1977–1979. June 6, 1987. Tel-Aviv.

Dinstien, Zvi. Deputy Minister, Defense Ministry, 1964–1967; Deputy Minister, Treasury Ministry, 1967–1971; Chair, Industrial Development Bank, 1971–1977. June 16, 1987. Ramat Aviv.

Gafni, Arnon. Director of Budget, Finance Ministry, 1970–1975; Director General, Finance Ministry, 1975–1976; Governor, Bank of Israel, 1976–1981. June 24, 1987. Tel-Aviv.

Soroker, Simchas. Director of Budget, Finance Ministry, 1950–1959. June 12, 1987. Tel-Aviv.

Tropp, Tzvi. Chief Economic Adviser, Defense Ministry, 1984–present. May 30, 1987. Tel-Aviv.

Zambar, Moshe. Director of Budget, 1963–1968; Economic Adviser, Finance Ministry, 1969–1971; Governor, Bank of Israel, 1971–1976. June 29, 1987. Tel-Aviv.

Zusman, Pinchas. Economic Adviser, Defense Ministry, 1968–1972; Director General, Defense Ministry, 1975–1978. June 24, 1987. Rehovot.

Interviews Conducted by Author in Egypt

Abdallah, Ismail Sabri. Deputy Minister of Planning, 1969–1975. May 14, 1987, December 26, 1990. Cairo.

Abdel-Halim, General Ahmed. January 2, 1991. Cairo.

Bashir, Tahseen. Nasir and Sadat Adviser and Press Spokesperson, 1969–1978. December 28, 1990; January 7, 1991. Cairo

Higazi, Abdel-Aziz. Finance Minister, 1968–1975. May 10, 1987, January 7, 1991. Cairo.

Huwaidi, Amin. Minister of War, 1967–1971. January 2, 1991. Cairo.

Ismael, Hafez. National Security Adviser Under Sadat. January 3, 1991. Cairo.

Sidqi, Aziz. Minster of Industry, Vice-President, 1968–1970, Minister of Defense Mobilization. May 10, 1987. Cairo.